The Epistemic

Steven B. Katz

Southern Illinois University Press

Carbondale and Edwardsville

Music of Rhetoric ——

Toward the Temporal Dimension of
Affect in Reader Response and Writing

99   98   97   96   4   3   2   1

Library of Congress Cataloging-in-Publication Data

Katz, Steven B., date.
    The epistemic music of rhetoric : toward the temporal dimension
of affect in reader response and writing / Steven B. Katz.
        p.   cm.
    Includes bibliographical references and index.
        1. Rhetoric—Philosophy.   2. Reader-response criticism.
    3. Knowledge, Theory of.   4. Metaphysics.   5. Music and language.
    I. Title.
    P301.K37   1996
    808'.001—dc20   94-31584
    ISBN 0-8093-1903-9   CIP

For my wife, Alison, who had to endure my absent presence, and our son, Jason, who in his eleven years has never known a time when I wasn't working on this book.

There are more things in heaven and earth, Horatio, than are dreamt of in your philosophy.

—*Hamlet*, Act I, Scene V

Contents

Preface

I began this book many years ago with some research on the parallel philosophical shift that occurred in literary and scientific theory in the twentieth century; I was interested then in how that shift is revealed in similar metaphors of knowledge in these disciplines. The underlying assumption of this book is still that our modes and methods of knowing are grounded in epistemic metaphors that constitute cultural ways of knowing. But here I am particularly concerned with how in our highly visual, logocentric, scientific society, those modes, methods, and metaphors, in philosophy, in rhetoric, in literary criticism, in composition, in speech communication, as in the sciences, are predominantly visual. In fact, almost all our knowledge—or what counts as valid knowledge in our culture—is visual. Our knowledge is visual, of course, because it is based on an empiricism that is defined exclusively in terms of the sense of sight; if the definition of empiricism were expanded—and perhaps it needs to be—it would include all the senses, not just sight, as the foundation of epistemology. But our knowledge is also visual insofar as logic itself seems to be conceived in spatial categories, is conceptualized as well as affirmed according to the sense of sight.

The question this book explores and attempts to answer is, how can we study, describe, and explain that which is beyond empirical or rational investigation or confirmation, such as indeterminate or affective experience? This is a problem not only in New Physics but in some composition and literary criticism as well, especially in Reader Response Criticism, which makes subjective response the focus of research and pedagogy. Like subatomic phenomena, affective experience seems to lie in another realm of logic and experience, one that extends beyond the rational categories or spatial schema we use to describe and interpret them. Indeed, affective experience, like subatomic phenomena, may be a different kind of reality altogether, one which somehow involves the nature of time that not even the New Physics understands very well. Our inability to comprehend and describe the nature of time except in terms of space may represent the limits not only of our understanding of indeterminate experience but of human consciousness itself. And yet, that is precisely what this book attempts to do: comprehend and "describe" the temporal dimension of affective response to style in reading and writing as a form of indeterminate knowledge, first by turning to the sophists and Cicero, and then to some contemporary philosophy of language and of music, where the sensuous and temporal nature of sound as knowledge is paramount.

It is hard for us to imagine a philosophy of language and knowledge based primarily on the sense of hearing rather than sight: a temporal philosophy based on immersion in sound rather than detachment by sight; a temporal philosophy based on musical categories of experience such as tone and rhythm rather than visual categories such as spatial form and mechanical force; a temporal philosophy based on a harmonic association and holistic synthesis of thought and feeling rather than the sequential extraction and hierarchical differentiation of meaning. Living in a more oral culture, the first sophists instinctively, and the later Isocrates and Cicero more consciously, perhaps knew the temporal realm of style a little better than we do, although some philosophy of language and music also may get us "closer" to the nature of this indeterminate experience. The epistemic music of rhetoric may help our attempt to understand affective response in reading and writing, which has been stymied both by the spatial nature of our methods and by the uncertain nature of affective experience itself. Aural metaphors and modes of thought and expression based on time rather than space might even alter, at least momentarily, our ways of experiencing, understanding, and knowing both language and world.

I am indebted to S. Michael Halloran, Lee Odell, David Porush, and Lou Hammer, who read the earliest prototypes of this book. It was Michael who encouraged me to revise and publish it, and I am only too happy to publicly express my appreciation to him here. I also would like to extend my gratitude to Peter Elbow and Richard Leo Enos for their thorough, generous, and insightful readings of the manuscript; their extensive comments and suggestions were invaluable in the later revisions of this work, for which I nevertheless must now take full responsibility. To my current and former colleagues at North Carolina State University, Carolyn Miller, Michael Carter, Tony Harrison, John Bassett, and Carl Herndl, who read and discussed various pieces of this book and harbored and encouraged me while I labored, I give belated thanks. My friend Edward Tick continues to guide and give me emotional support on this journey; I owe him more than I can say. I would also like to recognize Kelly Roeder, Veronica Norris, Jill Mooring, Robert Davis, and in particular Bonnie Nichols, who at various stages and in different ways assisted me in the technical preparation of the manuscript. Finally, I'd like to acknowledge the inspiration and advice of my student colleagues, especially Shawn Walsh and Patricia Watson, without whom none of this would have much meaning.

A Note on the Appendixes and Endnotes

In "Elegy for Excursus: The Descent of the Footnote" (*College English* 51 1989, 400–04), Betsy Hilbert laments the death of the long, discursive footnote that used to grace (or blot?) the pages of printed scholarship.

> The footnote was a writer's direct address to the reader, a message slipped under the door, a whispered aside in counterpoint to the formal discourse of the text. Footnotes could elucidate, castigate, praise, blame, or crow. Notes might wander off on scenic side-trips, discourse eloquently on stuff and nomenclature, and run happily on for pages and pages until the reader quite forgot she was supposed to be back at the text by dinnertime. (400)

The death of the footnote is perhaps another sign of hyperliteracy, the passing of another vestige of an earlier, more oral mode of thought in favor of streamlined efficiency. I offer a compromise here: longer, substantive appendixes and endnotes. Although they will force the amorously engaged reader to go "downstairs to answer the doorbell" (401), I encourage the reader to go there, for discussions, definitions, background, explanations, relations, asides, examples, and any other interest these notes might hold. In fact, this note is placed here to alert the reader to the fact that the appendixes and endnotes contain more than "op. cit." (402) and constitute a kind of subtext. To me, the appendixes and endnotes contain some of the most interesting material in the book.

The Epistemic Music of Rhetoric

One

Introduction: Epistemic Theories, Spatial Metaphors, and the Problem of Describing Emotion

New Theories, Old Methods

In *Small World: An Academic Romance*, a novel by David Lodge that bristles with the English profession's political infighting and proliferation of literary theories, Persse McGarrigle, a poet, travels from conference to conference all over the world searching for a mysterious scholar who is the elusive object of his love. Toward the end of the novel McGarrigle finds himself ensconced at an MLA session entitled "The Function of Criticism." McGarrigle listens with only partial interest and attention to the various theories being espoused—to what seems a hopeless tangle of opposing positions and bickering. At the end of the session, half beside himself, McGarrigle suddenly realizes he is standing at a microphone and asking a question that no one on the panel can answer: "What follows if everybody agrees with you?" (319).

This book will attempt to demonstrate that something can follow from Reader Response Criticism, something that even a poet could love: a theory of affective response in reading and writing based on the sensuous nature of language as sound. A central issue in the study of language, literature, and rhetoric, one about which there is growing debate, is the relationship between oral and literate modes of reasoning, between phonocentric and logocentric discourse. The consequences are important, for our theories of reading and writing, such as Reader Response Criticism, are predicated on assumptions or interpretations about such issues and the metaphors and methods we use to investigate and talk about emotion and language (see Lakoff and Johnson; Reddy). The central thesis of this book is that affect in reading and writing could perhaps be better (though not completely) described and understood by a phonocentric rather than logocentric theory of response—one based on aural, temporal modes of experiencing and reasoning that we perhaps find in the theory of the ancient sophists and Cicero rather than the visual, spatial ones that currently dominate our scientific culture.

To many contemporary scholars and critics on the cutting edge of literary theory, Reader Response Criticism, like the New Criticism that it sought to displace, seems deeply passé if not moribund compared, say, to deconstruction. Some may even ask, why resurrect and construct an oral theory of reading and writing on Reader Response Criticism? There are several reasons for doing so: the continued relevance and popularity of Reader Response Criticism, among both teachers of literature and teachers of writing, and the often noted connection between Reader Response Criticism and contemporary composition theory; the real and concerted attempt in Reader Response Criticism to deal with emotional response to literature and language generally; the relationship between Reader Response Criticism and contemporary philosophies of science, particularly those generated by the "metaphysical discoveries" of the New Physics; the similarities between Reader Response Criticism and sophistic and Ciceronian rhetoric in which the oral tradition of rhetoric is philosophically and pedagogically central; the possibilities for an aural theory of response already inherent in Reader Response Criticism.

A leisurely browse through the ERIC database will reveal that if its basic tenets are no longer hotly debated, Reader Response Criticism still continues to be the rage in the teaching of literature and writing in high school and university classrooms all across the country (see, for example, Beach and Hynds; Beach, *Teacher's Introduction*; Scriven; Shermis; Tierney et. al.; Van DeWeghe; Vine and Faust). Because of the similarity between Reader Response Criticism and contemporary composition theory in which both reading and writing are perceived as complementary processes of composing and revising texts—as making meaning—Reader Response Criticism was hailed in the 1970s and '80s by theorists and teachers on both sides of the aisle as a rhetorical method able to integrate reading and writing and so unite the increasingly disparate fields of literature and freshman composition (e.g., Bleich, "Discerning Motives; Petersen, "Writing About Responses"; Petrosky, "From Story to Essay; also see Baer; Fenstermaker; Memering; Moran; Odell and Cooper; Salvatori). If Reader Response Criticism is no longer touted as the answer to all our pedagogical problems, attempts continue to develop response heuristics to investigate and teach writing using literature, and literature using writing (e.g., Anderson and Rubano; Anson; Biddle and Fulwiler; Blake; Dobler; Dougherty; Farnan; Goetz et al., "Structure of Emotional Response," "Getting a Reading"; Schatzberg-Smith).

Perhaps one reason why Reader Response Criticism is considered passé is precisely because, like the New Criticism, it has been absorbed into the mainstream of pedagogical culture (even if Reader Response Criticism is still only a philosophical undercurrent in that culture). But another reason Reader Response Criticism is considered passé might have something to do with the epistemological dead end it seems to have reached in regard to the investigation of affective response as a form of knowledge.

Both New Criticism and Reader Response Criticism attempt to address the problem of subjectivity in literary knowledge, ostensibly in opposite ways. While New Criticism generally eschews subjectivity, Reader Response Criticism makes it the focus of pedagogy and study. New Criticism locates feeling in the factuality of the objective text itself and thus disposes of it; Reader Response Criticism locates feeling in the interaction of reader and text as a subjective "transaction" and thus renders it a form of knowledge. We return to Reader Response Criticism again because it tries to deal with the problem of studying subjective emotions in a way that no other literary criticism has attempted before or since.

In fact, Reader Response Criticism is one manifestation of an emergent sophistic in our culture that has implications well beyond the study of literature or criticism. Although a school of literary theory that actually began in the heyday of New Criticism and is therefore perhaps one of the oldest "poststructuralist" theories, Reader Response Criticism has been part of the so-called social-epistemic movement in rhetorical theory, in which knowledge is understood to be a subjective and social construct, a movement that may have its roots in the sophistic tradition of the classical era (see Katz, "Epistemic Trend"). Indeed, like enharmonic notes in music, Reader Response Criticism, New Physics, revisionist history of sophistic rhetoric, and expressive and social theories of writing are all different notations of the same philosophical tone in our culture, expressions of a movement away from the formalistic, rationalistic epistemology embodied in Newtonian science.

Briefly stated for now, the formalistic, rationalistic epistemology, which Gerald Holton argues underlies empirical method in science, consists of a combination of inductive and deductive ways of knowing. In this epistemology, a tentative, logical hypothesis is formed based on observation; that hypothesis is then confirmed or refuted empirically (Holton 47–48). Because the knowledge thus obtained is thought to be discovered and known objectively, by empirical (and rational) methods alone, "facts" are considered autonomous, independent of language and the mind, rather than something constituted by them—by the interests and experience that frame all our knowing, breathe life into facts, invest them with meaning. But for Holton, the empirical-analytical and the mathematical-logical dimensions of science, what he calls the x-y axes, cannot completely account for the discovery of facts or an understanding of knowledge, scientific or otherwise. Rather, Holton argues that there is another, z-axis at work, one that entails affect, intuition, and social, political, cultural, religious, and aesthetic factors that are suppressed in the formalistic, rationalistic plane of "public science."

Despite differences between them, it is well known that the founders of Reader Response Criticism, such as I. A. Richards, Louise Rosenblatt, Norman Holland, Stanley Fish, Wolfgang Iser, and David Bleich, all hold that meaning is not autonomous, contained in completed structure of the text and obtained by objective analysis and rationalistic interpretation alone. Rather, the reader actively makes or composes meaning and structures in relation to the text based on affective as well as conventional responses. In Reader Response Criticism, it is the reader's response, not only the text, that is the object of study. Another reason to return to Reader Response Criticism, then, is the relationship between it and contemporary trends in science that suggests the larger cultural issue of the unity of knowledge and our desire for a relationship between humanistic and scientific disciplines that have traditionally been opposed to one another.

As David Bleich makes clear in *Subjective Criticism* (esp. 10–26), Reader Response Criticism parallels trends in the philosophy of science that have their roots in the discovery by the Copenhagen school of New Physics of what we might call "methodological subjectivity," which runs counter to the formalistic, rationalistic epistemology of Newtonian science. Because of the limitations of empirical observation and the interactive nature of instrumentation at the subatomic or cosmic levels of reality, first pointed out by Heisenberg, Bohr, and Einstein, New Physics has given birth to a philosophy of science that holds scientific knowledge to be not an objective description of autonomous facts, but a subjective process of interpretation and a social construction of models and, hence, somewhat like literary interpretation, relative, probable, and uncertain.

Diverse contemporary scientists and philosophers of science such as Thomas Kuhn, Gerald Holton, and Paul Feyerabend also recognize the subjective and social nature of our knowledge and methods of investigation and the role language plays in them. This is not a soft reading of science, in which the existence of reality is denied (a mistake often made by students reading Kuhn, for instance), but rather a recognition that the perception of reality is at least partially influenced by "subjective" factors and thus that knowledge of reality must be socially validated and constituted. However, there are many schools in philosophy of science as well as literary theory, and many differences between them; neither the subjective-social philosophies of science nor Reader Response Criticism is universally accepted. In fact, Kuhn's position, though popular among humanists, is hotly disputed by scientists and philosophers alike.

More important for us, despite the epistemological advances represented by Reader Response Criticism and philosophy of science engendered by the New Physics, the *methods* of Reader Response Criticism and attempts to apply it to composition, like the methods of New Physics itself, remain to varying degrees grounded in the formalistic, rationalistic epistemology of Newtonian science—in the metaphorical imperatives of analysis and interpretation to describe accurately, completely, and logically processes and phenomena that are hard to observe and understand—a fact often overlooked by humanists, including this author, enthralled with the possibility of the unification of the humanities and science under the auspices of a subjectivist philosophy of knowledge. Just as New physicists reinterpret "description" but remain steadfastly committed to this metaphor of knowledge in attempting to account for the indeterminate subatomic processes of nature only in terms of empirical and rational methods, Reader Response critics and composition teachers reinterpret "interpretation" but remain committed to description in their attempts to account for the indeterminate affective processes of reading and writing only in terms of analysis and interpretation.

Old Methods, New Problems

Of course, one problem we will explore is that while analysis and interpretation as complementary inductive and deductive methods are necessary for and inherent in human reasoning, hardwired, so to speak, in the human brain, epistemologically they are somewhat reductive, indirect, and circular, and cannot give an "accurate" or "complete" picture of natural or mental processes that are not directly observable, but only a rational one. The problem of the dependence of induction on deduction is well known in the philosophy of science but is particularly troubling when trying to understand affective experience. The attempt to describe emotions exclusively in formalistic, rationalistic terms reduces them to logical categories, as in Aristotle's *Rhetoric* (Bk II), or to spatial schemata, as in cognitive approaches to writing (Flower, "Decision Points"; cf. Brand, *Psychology of Writing*). We will find the same problem in Reader Response Criticism and writing instruction that use analysis and interpretation as *the* method for understanding affective experience—even when those methods are based on a subjective and/or social philosophy of language and knowledge. Affective response may be more nonformalistic, nonrationalistic (or better understood that way) than our current methods allow us to realize.

But another related problem we will explore is the epistemological commitment to the logocentric metaphor that seems to underlie formalistic, rationalistic method itself: the commitment to arrive at an accurate or complete "picture," the imperative to *describe* affective experience at all. In making analysis and interpretation the goal of pedagogy and practice, Reader Response Criticism can be understood to more or less affirm the assumption that the "meaning" of emotional response can and must be understood spatially, as "contained in" and "extracted from" language or experience—even if the nature of response is subjective and uncertain (cf. Sontag). Chapter 2 will demonstrate that analysis and interpretation, as we currently understand them, are not only natural modes of thought but highly logocentric methods created by the exigencies of written texts and grounded in visual, spatial dimensions of experiencing and thinking that dominate our culture. In its attempt to *analyze and interpret* affective experience, Reader Response Criticism, like New Physics, can be understood to be chained by spatial assumptions to the fundamental epistemology it theoretically seeks to break away from.

What else is there besides analysis and interpretation? What else can we do with texts? These are questions that this book will need to explore. For analysis and interpretation, embedded in the practice and pedagogy of the New Criticism where they were wrought to a scientific art, have become the assumed goal of English studies—of all study, even of affective experience. As William Cain argues, New Critical method has come to seem the natural, inevitable method of literary study (*Crisis in Criticism* 104; cf. Culler 6, 10–11). Yet, in recent debates about literary theory, composition, even literacy, few have questioned the formalistic, rationalistic epistemology and logocentric metaphors that underlie and inform all our methods of investigating, describing, and teaching the affective dimension of reading and writing, or knowledge generally.

In this book, then, we will not talk about the feared anarchy of subjectivity that Reader Response Criticism, like the philosophy of science engendered by New Physics, was supposed to let loose in our classrooms and culture. Rather, we will talk of our seeming inability to comprehend language or affective response other than by methods of analysis and interpretation, which lead to formalistic, rationalistic descriptions of the emotional experience of language. While the "focus" in Reader Response Criticism has shifted from the text to the reader, methods for understanding, describing, and teaching feeling as an indeterminate form of knowledge have not: analysis and interpretation remain the goals of Reader Response Criticism and writing instruction using it. (In this book we also will not talk about the ideological assumptions in Reader Response concerning the existence of an individual "self" in relation to a socially constructed one [cf. Berlin, "Rhetoric and Ideology"; Bleich, *Double Perspective*]. Almost all literary and composition theory supposes some kind of self as a locus, if not a source, of knowledge and feeling. Despite the problems entailed in the study of emotion, insofar as we have feelings—even if they too are socially or ideologically constructed, and not wholly our own—and insofar as they seem to be fundamental to our experience of language and central to our knowing, they are worth investigating.)

So that this book won't be *mis*interpreted, let me state emphatically that it is not an attack on logocentrism, analysis, interpretation, empiricism, rationality, science, or technology. Nor is it an attack on Newtonian science, New Criticism, New Physics, Reader Response Criticism, or poststructuralist theory generally. We all use various methods of analysis and interpretation in writing and literature classes. We live in a logocentric world. And as such different critics as Cain (*Crisis* 2) and Eagleton (31) have indicated, analysis and interpretation—and thus formalism and rationalism—in many ways have been good for literature, just as they have been good for science (Holton 22–23). Indeed, analysis and interpretation, like logocentrism itself, provide the intellectual foundation for our knowledge; literary criticism like science (at least as we know them) would be impossible otherwise. So would this book. Our unavoidable reliance on formalistic, rationalistic methods as ways of investigating and knowing is not wrong, just limited.

But it is important that we *recognize* the limitations of the methods we have tacitly accepted as universal and true, particularly in regard to investigating affective experience as indeterminate knowledge and that we admit there may be other metaphors of knowledge besides spatial ones, other modes of knowing besides empirical and rational ones that could be important in reading and writing. Insofar as analysis and interpretation constitute the only method of Reader Response Criticism (and they constitute *all* our methods), those methods may undermine the very theory they are meant to support. And insofar as Reader Response critics and those who employ it remain committed to describing affective experience spatially, in terms of the formalistic, rationalistic imperatives of analysis and interpretation, they, like New physicists, run up against the limits of indeterminacy imposed by our metaphors, which block a fuller investigation of the nature of knowledge and the realization of an emergent sophistic in our scientific culture.

Old Problems, New Theories

Understood as an epistemological conflict, the contradiction between the theory of Reader Response Criticism and its implementation as a method of teaching reading and writing is the persistence of formalistic, rationalistic assumptions that seem to make description the only epistemological standard for ascertaining knowledge, and analysis and interpretation the only method of achieving it. But the insistence on empirical and rational description in the humanities as well as the sciences itself may be rooted in what Walter Ong might call the spatial ontology of literacy, created in consciousness and culture by the written and printed word. Analysis and interpretation, modes of thought wrought into scientific techniques, may be more rooted in spatial reasoning enhanced, if not engendered, by the technology of literacy itself.

There has been a spate of criticism concerning the orality/-literacy dichotomy (e.g., cf. Bizzell, "Arguing About Literacy," and Ong's "Comment"; Bleich, *Double Perspective*, and Middleton's Rev.; also see Jarratt [xxi–xxiii, 31–61]; Enos, *Oral and Written Communication*). While Middleton challenges the view that Ong is extolling the virtues of modern academic literacy, to me, and more poignantly, Ong, Havelock, and others working with orality are lamenting what we have lost. Whether one accepts the dichotomy or not, Ong's understanding of the relationship and effect of writing and print technology on epistemology perhaps can help us begin to make sense of the very real limitation of method that Reader Response Criticism seems to share with New Physics—a limitation that may at least partly result from the predominantly visual culture that writing and print helped foster.

Of course, Reader Response Criticism, like all "literary" theories and methods (but not all rhetorical ones [cf. Enos, *Greek Rhetoric*]), is "literate." Because literary criticism (and writing instruction) is predicated on the technology of literacy, it seems to share with science a kind of hypervisualism. Just as Wylie Sypher argues that the technological obsession with method in literature that rose in the Renaissance was related to the heightened visual awareness in arts and sciences made possible by the development of method, Ong argues that literary criticism, like modern science, is rooted in the increasing spatialization of consciousness and culture facilitated by the invention of the printing press, in which language as text becomes a visual, autonomous object (*Orality* 133, 156–71).

Ong levels the same criticism at Reader Response Criticism and deconstruction (*Orality* 171), the latter of which perhaps represents the extremities of hyperliterate modes of thought. For as Ong points out in *Orality and Literacy*, contemporary literary criticism—including Reader Response Criticism—is very much rooted in abstract, spatial, linear modes of understanding and reasoning engendered by the technology of writing and print—by literacy itself (133)—a fact hard to deny since the raison d'être of literary criticism is to somehow deal with the phenomena of literary *texts*. It should be no surprise, then, that a literate epistemology, a spatial ontology, should be manifest in and the basis of Reader Response Criticism as well.

The fundamental problem of describing affective response as indeterminate knowledge in Reader Response Criticism, then, may be the heightened textual mentality of our consciousness and culture, the ideology of literacy, if you will, that makes analysis and interpretation the epistemological method of choice. While Reader Response Criticism is an advance over

Formalism and New Criticism insofar as it is more *contextual* than New Criticism and thus more rhetorical in its supposition that the reader's interpretation and knowledge are subjective and validated by social communities, Reader Response Criticism remains text-bound precisely in its assumption that the primary use of literature (and writing) is to teach interpretation. While we have been very interested in the epistemic and social nature of knowledge as a theoretical construct subject to analysis and interpretation, we have been less interested in knowledge as a physical, affective response to language as the intuition of sound, subject only to the experience of performance.

While we don't have to believe in "the Great Divide," Ong's understanding of orality may be able to help us move beyond the "spatial limitations" of our current methods by allowing us to better understand the nature and relationship of affective response to language as sound. And the ontological basis for understanding the nature and relationship of affective response to language as sound may be time, not space. As we will "see" in subsequent chapters, neither Reader Response Criticism nor New Physics has been particularly good at describing the nature and effect of time, which is simply (and visually) regarded as another dimension of space. But the temporal dimension of linguistic experience may constitute the foundation for a new understanding of affective experience in reading and writing.

An orally based, as opposed to a visually based, mode of thought, one set adrift on a temporal rather than spatial ontology, may be fundamental in moving us beyond the assumptions about knowledge that Reader Response shares with science, and in researching, describing, and teaching affective experience in reading and writing as indeterminate knowledge. The affective experience of language as an aural, physical, temporal form of knowledge will be the primary concern in this book. And the dominant assumption of this book will be that the aural, physical, temporal dimension of the affective response to language can perhaps best be approached from an epistemology situated in what Ong calls "secondary orality"—

or to appropriate Linda Flower's phrases, in "writer-based" and "reader-based" *speech*. For as Ong writes: "Little has thus far been done . . . to understand reader response in terms of what is now known of the evolution of noetic processes from primary orality through residual orality to high literacy. . . . Opportunities for further work here are open and inviting, and they have practical implications for the teaching of both reading skills and writing skills—as well as implications for heady theorizing" (*Orality* 171).

Old Theories, New Alternatives

In attempting to "describe" the principles of affective experience of language as an aural, temporal phenomenon, this book in a sense responds to Ong's challenge. Against the spatial limitations of epistemology and of method, we will explore some alternate ways of thinking about affective response in reading and writing by examining the revisionist understanding of the theories and methods of the original sophists, such as Gorgias and Isocrates, and of Cicero, whose later treatises perhaps represent the mature culmination of the sophistic tradition. Their "oral philosophy" of musical style as a way of knowing may be able to help us understand and implement Reader Response Criticism in the literature and writing classroom in a way that is more nonformalistic, nonrationalistic—a theory of response rooted in the performance of language as sound rather than in the interpretation of language as meaning.

Chapter 3 will argue that Reader Response Criticism (and in some respects, New Physics) parallels many of the tenets of the sophistic and Ciceronian philosophy of style, which recent scholarship in the history of rhetoric has resurrected. (The sophistic movement in our culture is "emergent" precisely because it has a long history in Western culture but has been suppressed by dominant rational and empirical modes of thought and expression.) In a real sense, Reader Response critics are modern day sophists. But although Reader Response Criticism seems to share philosophical assumptions of the sophists, the latter also possessed an oral and, therefore, as Ong points out, a less formalistic, rationalistic conception of language and knowledge, one rooted in speech rather than writing.

However, it is more than the fact that theirs was an oral culture; the sophists (and Cicero) celebrated oral modes of thought and expression and built their epistemology of uncertainty around it. There is perhaps a direct connection between the oral culture of the ancient Greeks and Romans and the nonformalistic, nonrationalistic epistemology of the sophists and Cicero in which relativity, contingency, and uncertainty are primary. Taking into account the slow, uneven, and problematical transition between orality and literacy (Enos, "Composing Process"; Lentz), and recognizing that there are philosophical differences not only between the sophists and Cicero but also between the sophists themselves (Schiappa), the process of oral conceptualization and expression they did share may suggest a possible way out of the current paradox of knowledge and method in the study of affective response.

In the rhetorical philosophy of the sophists, Isocrates, and Cicero, we may find the development of an early, aural theory of reader response and a hint at how to implement it in a way that is not epistemologically retrograde or methodologically reductive. In fact, Cicero's philosophy of language and knowledge, contained in his later rhetorical treatises, seems to be at least partly based on a belief in an aural aesthetic faculty, on an intuitive response to the rhythm and sound of words that constitutes a kind of affective, indeterminate knowledge. Analysis and interpretation were not the primary focus of ancient "literary" pedagogy; recitation and delivery were. Given the parallels between the epistemology of the sophists and Reader Response Criticism, the sophists' belief in a nonformalistic, nonrationalistic response to the rhythm and sounds of words, rooted in a sensuality heightened by the physical performance of language, may be understood to constitute an ancient theory of reception that can inform our own attempt to understand, describe, and teach response to reading and writing as subjective knowledge.

And if sensuality is inherent in all discourse, this oral theory of reception may extend to all written prose styles (cf. Lanham), even scientific ones. As Morris Croll, Halloran and Whitburn, and Halloran and Bradford point out in different ways, the oratorical prose style has been neglected in the study of rhetoric and denigrated in the study of writing since the anti-Ciceronian movement in the Renaissance and the rise of the scientific plain style in the seventeenth century. But the "different music" created in different kinds of discourse by the sensuous experience of language as sound may be the basis of affective response as a nonreferential, temporal form of knowledge across the curriculum.

Having examined the sensuous dimension of language as affective, indeterminate knowledge in sophistic and Ciceronian rhetoric, in chapters 4 and 5 we will take the plunge into the nonreferential, temporal dimension of rhetoric itself by turning to some twentieth-century philosophies of language and of music that explore the epistemic nature of sound as sensuous form (e.g., Zuckerkandl, Meyer, Cassirer, Langer, *Feeling and Form*, *Philosophy*). The epistemic nature of language as a sensuous form may allow us to move toward a nonreferential, temporal theory of response for "describing," researching, and teaching affective response, a theory based not only on the spatial dimension of language as empirical, rational meaning but also on the temporal dimension of language as nonempirical, nonrational knowledge. As a temporal, nonreferential sequence of aesthetic shapes and sensuous patterns of physical sound, the epistemic music of rhetoric may be a slighted but important part of affective response in reading and writing. An aural theory of affective response in reading and writing in which the performance of the epistemic music of rhetoric is an experiential, indeterminate form of knowledge may at least supplement (but not replace) the analysis and interpretation of subjective and social meaning in Reader Response Criticism.

The epistemic music of rhetoric as an indeterminate form of knowledge may have been central in sophistic rhetorical "theory" and pedagogical practice. Indeed, a nonreferential, temporal theory of language may get us closer to the way the ancient sophists experienced and understood style as knowledge. It also may challenge some of our fundamental notions of literacy. It may even help us transcend what Roger Penrose, a mathematical physicist, admits in a recent book on the relation between New Physics and the mind is our purely spatial conception of time, which he believes may represent the limits of our current understanding of indeterminacy and of consciousness itself. Our metaphors, our methods, our literate minds limit our knowledge of affect, of indeterminacy, even of orality (Ong, *Orality* 2); this will be the concern of chapter 6. But the observations of those working with the oral, sensuous form of language and the philosophy of music, joined to recent interpretations of the classical rhetorical tradition of the sophists, Isocrates, and Cicero, may allow us to shift—if only temporarily— the ontological and metaphorical keys of our knowledge, to explore the temporal abyss of indeterminacy and understand (for brief moments anyway) another, more participatory, aurally based, holistic way of knowing.

Two

Reader Response Criticism, Writing, and the New Physics: The Spatial Limits of Affective Indeterminacy

Literature, Science, and Affective Experience

Since the Scientific Revolution in the seventeenth century, the antithetical relationship between the sciences and the humanities has been an object of lamentation, celebration, speculation, debate. In the earlier part of this century, C. P. Snow questioned the necessity of this division of culture, but much of the focus of study, especially in recent years, has been on the similarities between the humanities, science, and technology, on their convergence rather than their divergence. Indeed, Jacques Ellul goes so far as to make a persuasive, albeit somewhat paranoid, argument that technology—defined as the application (and embodiment in machines) of rational, systematic, and ever more efficient methods or procedures for accomplishing a task with predictable and uniform results—is a cultural phenomenon that has increasingly come to dominate and determine all aspects of contemporary life. For Ellul, technology does not merely consist of machines, as we commonly think;

rather, it also consists of techniques—those formalistic, rationalistic, repeatable procedures that are employed in all disciplines and professions throughout modern life. And William Barrett defines machines as "embodied decision procedures" (23). Thus, scientific methodologies are "machine-like," just as machines embody scientific method: "*Technology is embodied technique*" (Ellul 22). In this sense, science and technology appear to be related.[1]

Many important books have appeared in this century that in one way or another also investigate the conceptual relationship between literature and science, or literary work as technological systems (e.g., Buchanan; Serres; Porush). The Society for Literature and Science has been formed to help facilitate and disseminate such investigation. However, except for some Reader Response Criticism, no work investigates in any sustained way the epistemological relationship between scientific and literary method as the latter has traditionally been received, perceived, and taught in English departments, or the limits that relationship entails for researching, describing, and teaching the role of emotional experience in reading, writing, and epistemic knowledge generally. This is also true, perhaps, in the field of composition, where the relationship between the humanities and the sciences sometimes has been misunderstood.[2]

As part of a movement away from a formalistic, rationalistic conception of language and knowledge toward a subjective and social one, Reader Response Criticism parallels or shares many epistemological tenets with the philosophy of science engendered by the New Physics. "Formalism" entails the belief in the possibility and efficacy of detached and hence (to some degree) objective analysis of autonomous form (as opposed to subjective interaction of form with human experience or measuring instruments and the belief in the inseparability of form and context). "Rationalism" in our culture often entails a belief in the primacy of "technical reasoning" derived from technique, measuring instruments, or from the supposed rational structure or functioning of the form under study. The opposition implied here between formalistic/rationalistic epistemologies and subjective/social ones resembles Habermas's distinction between technological procedure and symbolic interaction.[3]

However, the parameters of the shift in both literary and scientific theory, and their relationship, while generally well known, are not defined enough to be revealing or useful. There are certainly many points of divergence between, say, New Criticism and Newtonian physics, and Reader Response Criticism and New Physics. But the convergences, when clearly defined, will reveal not only the philosophical undercurrents of Reader Response Criticism but also the limits of its method for investigating, describing, and teaching affective experience in reading and writing as indeterminate knowledge—limits imposed on us by logocentric conceptions of the spatial nature and referential function of language that result in a heightened emphasis on formalistic, rationalistic ways of knowing.

For now, we can define indeterminacy as the inability to calculate or predict the behavior of one event or region of space based on another except in terms of statistical probabilities. Because indeterminacy represents the limits of our "factual" knowledge, we can also understand it to be the ontological basis of the epistemic trend in our culture (Katz, "Epistemic Trends" 355–59). Indeterminacy in reading, writing, and epistemic knowledge generally can be considered the region of intuition, affect, creativity, emotion that cannot be wholly predicted from rational and/or empirical bases but rather must be based on statistical probability, intuition, or the tacit knowledge of the researcher.

While New Criticism and Reader Response Criticism seem to deal in completely antithetical ways with the problem of subjectivity and feeling as indeterminate knowledge in literary interpretation, we will see that both schools of criticism are limited by formalistic, rationalistic assumptions they seem to share with Newtonian physics and New Physics, respectively. This is not to say that there is a direct causal connection between science and literature—that developments in science produce changes in literary texts or theory, though they undoubtedly do, or that developments in literature affect science, though this may be true as well.[4] Nor is it to say that literary criticism should become more like science. On the contrary, in this chapter we will explore how literary criticism—even Reader Response Criticism as it is presently conceived and understood— is in some ways still too much like science in its methodological imperative to describe and explain affective response empirically and rationally. (The term *methodological imperatives* is meant to imply that it is the underlying epistemological assumptions and goals of research that are similar in science and literature rather than their actual procedures and instrumentation, which obviously differ given their different methods and objects of study. Somewhat like Foucault's *epistemes*, these methodological imperatives, often revealed in metaphors used to denote understanding, etc., may underlie the nature and pursuit of knowledge across disciplines and constitute cultural ways of knowing.)

The concern here is that logocentric metaphors and methods that drive research in both the sciences and the humanities (see Boyd; Kuhn, "Metaphor in Science;" Pylyshyn; Reddy; Turbayne) perhaps preclude understanding the nonempirical, nonrational nature of affective experience as a form of indeterminate, experiential knowledge. If there is a multicausal and hence somewhat indeterminate relationship between scientific and literary theory, it is one dominated by the formalistic, rationalistic epistemology of Newtonian science that underlies the methodological imperatives of both. To use an electrical metaphor, the "two cultures" are polarized in one direction. Given the fact that our society is a predominantly scientific and technological one, it is reasonable to suppose that the assumptions and goals of science and technology influence somewhat the perception and teaching of the language arts in ways that affect our understanding of the affective processes involved; but it is not even necessary to hold this assumption. In this chapter we will be content to point out the similarities between Newtonian mechanics, New Physics, New Criticism, and Reader Response Criticism without falling into the trap of trying to posit and prove causal relationships.

According to William Barrett, language *has* come to be understood and metaphorically described in terms of visualistic scientific technique (see Reddy). The attempt by the logical positivists to eliminate imprecision in science by constructing a symbolic logic in which a one-to-one correspondence would obtain between word and thing was, for Barrett, an attempt to turn language into an efficient instrument for communicating scientific knowledge accurately and with predictable results. By eliminating the problems of ambiguity, imprecision, emotion, and value inherent in language, the logical positivists hoped to construct a system of symbols that would be capable of representing, in mirror-like fashion, the facts. One can even see this tendency to view language as a mechanism in the seventeenth century with the rise of the scientific plain style in writing that accompanied the Newtonian revolution (Halloran and Whitburn 66). And it is certainly the popular view of language today (all visual and spatial metaphors for language, knowledge, and experience in this chapter are intentional).

This mechanistic, visual understanding of the relationship between language and knowledge can be understood to underlie literary criticism as well. In *Literature and Technology: The Alien Vision*, Wylie Sypher argues that from the seventeenth to the twentieth century, the study and creation of literature and art in general increasingly became dominated by a scientific concern for methodology through an extreme consciousness of and obsession with technique, an obsession rooted in a new emphasis on visual space. Sypher argues that both art and science came to be seen as "highly specialized executions or procedures" and traces the "the heavy investment in method" in both science and literature "back to Renaissance notions of exactness, detached observation, and accurate imitation" (xvi). Sypher's visual attitudes of exactness, detached observation, and accurate imitation, then, are perhaps methodological imperatives, shared disciplinary "ethics" and goals that govern study and research not only in science but in literature as well.

Indeed, Ong believes it was print technology, with its capability of and insistence on the exact visual replication of carefully worded observations, that also made exact description in modern science, and thus modern science itself, both possible and necessary (*Orality* 127)—an element in the development and procedures of modern science too often overlooked (cf. Bazerman). More controversially, Ong also believes that writing and print not only provided the technological means for the exact dissemination of information but also fostered in culture a relatively new set of scientific values and a new way of looking at the world, one lodged in an emphasis on visual space. If we accept at least one of these positions, the scientific development of civilization itself can be seen to be based on and culminate in what we might call an epistemology of the eye.

> By removing words from the world of sound where they had their origin in active human interchange and relegating them definitively to visual surface, and by otherwise exploiting visual space for the management of knowledge, print encouraged human beings to think of their own interior conscious and unconscious resources as more and more thing-like, impersonal and religiously neutral. Print encouraged the mind to sense that its possessions were held in some sort of inert mental space. (*Orality* 131–32)

In short, writing, and especially print technology, may help foster in literature and science the values associated with naive empiricism, with its view of the mind as a tabula rasa, an "inert mental space," and its view of language and knowledge as separate and "thing-like." Thus, Ong connects textuality, ontology, and epistemology in a way that may help us begin to understand the relationship between literary and scientific theory, and the limits of our methods for studying affective response. Ong draws attention to the fact that logocentrism, which is the basis of a " 'corpuscular epistemology', a one-to-one gross correspondence between concept, word and referent which . . . took the printed text, not oral utterance, as the point of departure and the model of thought" (*Orality* 168). This corpuscular epistemology, with its belief in the reality of discrete mass points in empty space, underlies not only Newtonian science and logical positivism but some reading and writing instruction as well (see Moffett 7). Perhaps we also recognize in the extended quote above the origins of the values associated with rationality, with its insistent belief in autonomous systems, and hence formalistic procedures: "writing presents utterance and thought as uninvolved with all else, somehow self-contained and complete" (Ong, *Orality* 132).

"Textual mentality," then, perhaps can be regarded as an ontological nexus of science and literature, the spatial point at which their methodological imperatives meet—and in more recent theory the theatre where the conflict between these imperatives and the epistemological assumptions they are meant to support emerge. Can methods based on a textual mentality comprehend and describe affective experience? The obsession with the application of technique, in which objective analysis and logical description of autonomous structure are regarded not only as the best but also as the only methods of ascertaining knowledge, is based on a formalistic, rationalistic philosophy. Like an epistemological plant, this philosophy has its roots deep in the fertile logocentric soil of Plato and Aristotle, of course, but grew Writ large in the inky intellectual waters of the Renaissance, and finally blossomed in the stark mechanistic sunshine of Newtonian science.

You will recall that, based on Euclidean geometry, classical Newtonian physics assumes among its absolutes that matter exists as discrete, solid, material mass points in empty space; that this space is static and uniform; and thus that space can serve as a reference for accurately determining the mathematical relations of these discrete material objects according to the Galilean system of coordinates, in which space is mapped three dimensionally. (The present tense is appropriate here, in regard both to Newtonian physics and to New Criticism, for it soon will become obvious that neither Newtonian physics nor New Criticism has been replaced by New Physics or Reader Response Criticism but rather has merely been supplemented by them.) Planted on this spatial ontology, classical Newtonian physics thus entails at least three epistemologically logocentric premises. First, in the Newtonian "worldview," it is assumed that from the discrete material objects we can infer the laws of nature governing their relations in space. Second, these laws are assumed to be autonomous, rational, uniform, and universal in their operation. Third, because it is assumed that the laws of nature are inherent in reality and mechanical in their operation, it is also assumed that the observer does not affect what is observed in any way; the material objects and the laws that govern them can and should be observed objectively, determined accurately, described precisely.

The goal of Newtonian science, then, is an accurate *description* of the laws that structure reality leading to a complete *picture* of nature. According to this view, promulgated by such traditional historians of science as Charles Coulston Gillispie in *The Edge of Objectivity*, science as a body of knowledge is an accumulation of discrete, autonomous facts objectively observed and described over time; in this linear view of science, in which objectivity like a knife cuts deeper into formally sacred realms of life,[5] each new fact merely adds to or slightly modifies what has already been accurately observed and described, eventually leading to a complete description of the laws of nature. In this worldview, then, the scientific enterprise can be seen to rest on a metaphorical model of knowledge as description, a model whose methodological imperatives include the precision, detached observation, and accurate imitation that Sypher mentions, a model that we will *see* has serious ramifications in any attempt to study feelings.

However, the Newtonian epistemology is both formalistic *and rationalistic*. While formalism and rationalism appear to be contradictory, and have in fact been opposed in the history of philosophy, Newtonian science actually rests on the twin philosophical pillars of empiricism and rationalism, on Baconian induction and Cartesian deduction—what Holton calls the "hypothetico-deductive, or inductive method."[6] While the formalistic detachment and objectivity of visual observation in Newtonian science implies an ideal (or naive) empiricism, the primacy of reason and order in Newtonian science implies an ideal rationality (both in the mind and in nature). As Turbayne demonstrates, the objective-rational model, in the guise of empirical method, is itself a function of the conceptual metaphor we hold; thus, what we regard as objective analysis is the result of "sort-crossing"—the confusion of metaphor, model, or procedure with reality (Turbayne 11–13, 17–18, 46–50)—and is impossible. Despite Newton's claim to the contrary ("hypotheses non fingo"—I make no hypotheses), Newtonian science rests as much on hypotheses and interpretation as it does on observation and description.[7]

Some implications for the study of reading and writing of this model of knowledge as formalistic, rationalistic description can easily be seen in the methods and metaphors of New Criticism, which in part can be understood to parallel, if not actually share, the epistemology of Newtonian physics. First, implicit (when not explicit) in New Criticism and those who follow in its deepest, most formalistic footsteps, is the belief that texts, like objects in space, consist of "facts"—discrete elements existing in a "psychological vacuum"—that can and should be known without reference to the reader's personal reactions or the biographical, historical, or moral considerations that marked earlier criticism.

Take, for example, the early critical theory of T. S. Eliot (whose poetry I admire, and even of whose essays I am a "closet fan"). In his later work Eliot talks about enjoyment, about feeling, about multiple and equally valid interpretations of the text in contradistinction to mere explanation of the text ("Music of Poetry" 23, "Frontiers of Criticism" 126–28) in a way that takes into consideration the subjectivity of experience that forms the basis of human understanding and informs all our judgments. But in his earlier, highly influential work, such as "The Function of Criticism," Eliot, one of the first to lay out the philosophy of New Criticism, avows that "a critic must have a highly developed sense of fact" (19). Eliot believes that although they may seem "arid, technical, and limited," the facts should be the basis of both the comprehension and the pleasure of the text. It is the function of literary criticism to discover the facts by returning again and again to the text (20), and to *describe* the text to the reader objectively for "the elucidation of the work of art and the correction of taste" (13). Although Eliot admits he does not define what "truth, or fact, or reality" are (22), he assumes, as we do, that if they exist his "scheme" will capture them.

Second is the belief that texts operate by and exhibit fixed principles, "laws" that organize the facts of the text and determine its structure (i.e., meaning) independent of the reader (Wellek and Warren 147; Ransom 343). Despite his later expressed belief that poets learn structure by subjective imitation, by the absorption of the musical structure into self ("Music of Poetry," esp. 19, 21), in "The Function of Criticism," Eliot also attempts "to find any common principles for the pursuit of criticism" (17), "a formula" (19). Eliot attempts this because he believes that the literary critic should proceed according to principles that circumvent his preferences and biases (19)— principles to be found in the structure of the text itself.

Thus, thirdly, the literary critic can and should proceed inductively by objective analysis and comparison to what is known (21): the facts and principles of the text alone. Indeed, in "The Perfect Critic," Eliot (metaphorically?) conceives of literary criticism as a kind of scientific description. For Eliot, it is the mark of a scientific mind to be able to inquire freely without drawing judgments or conclusions: "[I]n matters of great importance, the critic must not make judgments of worse or better. He must simply *elucidate*: the reader will form the correct judgment for himself" (11; emphasis mine). Despite his own sensitivity to language and emotion, Eliot believes that literary criticism should not involve emotional reactions to the text, but a sensibility that he compares to "scientific intelligence." For Eliot, the literary intelligence suffers to the degree that it is not of this kind: "A literary critic should have no emotions except those immediately provoked by a work of art—and these (as I have already hinted) are, when valid, perhaps not to be called emotions at all" (12–13). The connection between this scientific intelligence and teaching literature was pushed further by New critics in America who, staying home, located the establishment of literary science in academia.[8]

In New Criticism, emotion in interpretation is something to be gotten around if not entirely dispensed with. While Eliot in his later criticism recognized that "[w]e are in danger even of pursuing criticism as if it were a science, which it never can be," he also believes that if "we over-emphasize enjoyment, we will tend to fall into the subjective and impressionistic" ("Frontiers" 131). " 'Interpretation,' " says Eliot, "is only legitimate when it is not interpretation at all, but merely putting the reader in possession of facts which he would otherwise have missed" ("Function" 20). Here, then, Eliot can be understood to be somewhat suppressing the role of hypotheses and interpretation in describing a text, preferring instead to believe in empirical induction, just as Newton did: in taking "leave of the data of criticism," the critic "does not always appear to return to the work of art with improved perception and intensified, because more conscious, enjoyment; his centre of interest changes, his feelings are impure" ("Function" 13). For Eliot, this "is one more instance of the pernicious effect of emotion" (13).

As in Newtonian science, the ultimate goal of New Criticism is therefore the analysis (and interpretation) of texts as a spatially cumulative body of knowledge that leads to a complete description of Literature (with a capital L). For Eliot, literature as a body of knowledge, like science for Gillispie in the *Edge of Objectivity*, is an ideal progression in which each discrete, autonomous literary work "of significance" adds to or modifies the work that has come before. As in the traditional view of science, this body of work is

> already correct and complete in itself as well. The existing monuments form an ideal order among themselves, which is modified by the introduction of the new (the really new) work of art among them. The existing order is complete before the new work arrives; for order to persist after the supervention of novelty, the whole order must be, if ever so

slightly, altered; and so the relations, proportions, values of each work of art are readjusted; and this is conformity between the old and the new. ("Tradition" 5)

This view of knowledge as an "ideal order" that can be obtained by objective means has perhaps influenced and informed our philosophy and teaching of reading and writing in countless ways. Indeed, in "The Perfect Critic" Eliot restates this ideal order in terms of a theory of reading and writing, of criticism and creation, that can be seen to be similar to the Lockean psychology of perception (although as Eliot reveals in his never-submitted doctoral dissertation, it is actually quite different from it[9])—the epistemological/visual metaphor of the mind as a tabula rasa upon which sensations of reality are inscribed directly through the senses that also underlies Newtonian science as well as eighteenth- and nineteenth-century rhetorics (cf. Berlin, "Rhetoric and Poetics," "Richard Whately"; Harned):

We assume the gift of superior sensibility. And for sensibility wide and profound reading does not mean merely a more extended pasture. There is not merely an increase of understanding, leaving the original acute impression unchanged. The new impressions modify the impressions received from the objects already known. An impression needs to be constantly refreshed by new impressions in order to persist at all; it needs to take its place in a system of impressions. And this system tends to become articulate in a generalized statement of literary beauty. (14)

Thus, if one is to read (or do science) well, one needs a "superior sensibility" so that impressions take their place in an ideal "system of impressions," which then becomes the basis of objective statements and constitutes knowledge. In fact, "depersonalization" in reading and writing is made possible by the immersion into tradition, in which case "art may be said to approach to condition of science" ("Tradition" 7). It is the condition of tradition that allows the writer or reader to be objective, in which the process of criticism or creation can be understood as a scientific event. Thus, Eliot manages to retain the privileging of literary text and author at the same time that he argues for the scientific nature of the literary enterprise: "Poetry is not a turning loose of emotion, but an escape from emotion; it is not the expression of personality, but an escape from personality. Of course, only those who have personality or emotion know what it means to want to escape from these things" (10–11; cf. Eliot's "Hamlet" on the "objective correlative"—"a set of objects, a situation, a chain of events which shall be the formula of that *particular* emotion; such that when external facts, which must terminate in sensory experience, are given, the emotion is immediately evoked" [124–25]).

Obviously, there is not too much room for "personal feelings" here. The writer, like the reader, only needs a superior blank slate of mind upon which to receive the data of experience and to reflect on these in a system of impressions that form a higher, rational order. (This handling of emotions in literary knowledge also can be seen in the work of Allen Tate, whose arguments against logical positivism are remarkably similar to Eliot's critical theory in their epistemological moves [see appendix A]). In some nontrivial ways, the theory of the role of sensibility in reading (and writing) is certainly useful and "true." As a method of textual criticism, New Criticism is very visual in its empiricism and very spatial in its logic. Given its visual impetus and emphasis, New Criticism has helped us focus on the text in a way perhaps never done before, has helped us *see* more, know more in and about texts themselves. But as everyone knows, New Criticism presents us with the dilemma of how to account for the subjective knowledge that the reader brings to bear on the interpretation of a text, and the affective experience of reading and writing itself, which was so important to Eliot the poet.

While some New critics, like Blackmur, Brooks, Wimsatt and Brooks, openly discuss the aesthetic, religious, sometimes almost mystical dimension of analysis and interpretation that is also implicit in Eliot's treatment (cf. "Literature and Religion", *Knowledge and Experience*), this does not make their methods any less Newtonian (see Eagleton 46–49). In fact, just as Holton

(49–53) discusses how the aesthetic, "religious" dimension of scientific discovery, which cannot be proven empirically or rationally but is nevertheless essential, is suppressed in public science in favor of the empiric and analytic modes of investigation, so too New critics seem to suppress (or transmute) the aesthetic, "religious" dimension of literary experience—and the role of affect and belief—in favor of formalistic, rationalistic methods. In a real sense, objectivity is a state of reverence, an emotion.

In effect, in New Criticism, the affective experience of the reader is externalized, projected onto the assumed facts of the text based on rational hypotheses about its structure, and so "objectified" or "rationalized" without needing to understand the nature of that experience itself. Stanley Fish makes a similar point when he distinguishes between reading and interpretation, the latter of which entails group norms as strict as those of scientific communities ("Demonstration vs. Persuasion" 365–66). As he says elsewhere, "the proper practice of literary criticism demanded the suppressing of what is subjective and idiosyncratic in favor of the level of response everyone shares" (Introduction 5). While New Criticism contains within itself the epistemological problem of inductive knowing based on hypotheses, some of which are not empirically provable, it presents an even greater problem in regard to the unobservable feelings and knowledge a reader brings to a text, which introduces a higher degree of indeterminacy into the critical equation.

This is the problem in New Criticism, of course, that Reader Response Criticism tries to solve. But before we discuss Reader Response Criticism, let's look at the shift in epistemology that occurred in the New Physics, a shift that can inform our understanding of the philosophical problems of method encountered by Reader Response critics in their attempt to study the subjective experience of the reader. For in many ways the problem of studying the subjective experience of the reader is like the problem of studying subatomic phenomena. (In fact, later we will explore how affective experience and subatomic phenomena may be more closely related than we think.) While Sypher argues that with the advent of quantum mechanics and the new science in the twentieth century the obsession with efficiency, with order itself, is lessening, allowing "the recognition of the actuality of the contingent, the accidental" (241), Reader Response Criticism, and its application to writing, like New Physics, is ultimately and by practical necessity grounded by logocentric metaphor and method in the epistemology it seeks to redress.

Methodological Subjectivity in the New Physics and the Limits of Indeterminacy

With the advent of New Physics, in particular relativity and quantum mechanics, the Newtonian worldview is radically altered. Because Newtonian physics proves inadequate for describing cosmic or atomic reality, which can only be observed indirectly by experimental procedures, some early New physicists redefined the relation between the technique used to "observe" reality and that reality itself, and thus some of the epistemological assumptions of traditional science (Heisenberg 29), in a way that can help us understand the problems of investigating affective experience in reading and writing, and perhaps the nature of that experience itself.

Whereas Newtonian physics assumes that matter exists as material objects in empty space and that this space is constant and can serve as a reference for accurately determining the mathematical relations of these objects relative to one another, in *Relativity: The Special and the General Theory* Einstein postulates that at the cosmic level matter is not discrete or autonomous, that space is not uniform or static, and that objects and cosmic events are relative to and change with the position and speed of the observer (25–27). Thus, in the Special Theory of Relativity, the laws derived from observation of objects in space must take into account the position and speed of the observer as well as the phenomenon described (53–54). Furthermore, time in each coordinate system becomes another coordinate, a fourth dimension. For Einstein, space and time, as well as observer and event, appear to be interdependent (55–57).

Thus, in the Special Theory of Relativity, a degree of subjectivity *in the technique* of observation, in the interaction of the method of observation and the phenomena being observed, appears to be unavoidable. However, in the General Theory of Relativity, Einstein goes even further, pointing out that the Special Theory of Relativity, like Newtonian physics and the three-dimensional Galilean system of coordinates on which it is based, assumes that space is a vacuum and that gravity is absent. The Special Theory of Relativity also assumes that matter is rigid and that measuring devices are themselves unchanging (98–99). But in the General Theory of Relativity Einstein postulates that matter is equal to energy at the speed of light, that matter and energy are interchangeable and in fact one and the same (31–34). Einstein concludes that the measuring instruments themselves are not rigid and unchanging but are also affected by the space-time continuum in which they exist (98–99). Matter is not discrete, material mass points in empty space; rather, matter and energy and space constitute an electromagnetic field in which all elements of reality interact in a constant state of flux (44–48). "There is no such thing as empty space, i.e., a space without field. Space-time does not claim existence on its own, but only as a structural quality of the field" (155).

Moreover, the electromagnetic field itself is interactive and varies with the force of gravity. Under the influence of gravity, space can bend, curve, or become so dense that it forms a black hole out of which nothing, not even light, can escape (64–70). Thus, the highly visual geometry of the Galilean coordinate system on which both Newtonian mechanics and the Special Theory of Relativity are based is no longer adequate in the description and measurement of motion, since space, time, and even matter, change over short distances (71–73). In the General Theory of Relativity, Einstein substitutes the Gaussian system of coordinates (used to measure the rapid motion of molecules of gases) to measure each point in the space-time continuum as a multidimensional coordinate according to statistical probability (88–96). With this non-Euclidean geometry where light (the constant) does not travel in a straight line to infinity as Newton assumed, but rather curves due to the force of gravity (74), Einstein arrives at a paradoxical picture of the spatial universe as quasi-spherical, finite, and yet unbounded (114).

The same sorts of observational problems emerge in quantum mechanics with the study of subatomic reality. There are several important ways in which quantum mechanics, particularly the Copenhagen school of quantum mechanics, differs from Newtonian science. First, as Heisenberg claimed, matter consists not of discrete particles, but of "quanta," or energy packets, that can be seen as a particle or wave, but never both simultaneously. At the quantum level, physicists can only measure fairly accurately the position or velocity of an atomic particle. Thus, the relationship of the phenomena observed cannot be precisely determined according to fixed and mechanical laws but can only be measured according to the statistical laws of probability. This problem is the well-known "principle of uncertainty, or indeterminacy" (Heisenberg 43) and will have a direct bearing on our understanding of affective experience and the problem of investigating and describing it.

A second philosophical problem Heisenberg discusses is that in quantum physics, subatomic reality cannot exist independently of the observer and the measuring instruments used to perceive it. The observation of "objects" on the subatomic level as well as the macrocosmic level is in part determined by the expectations of the observer and the design of the experimental apparatus that makes observation possible at all. Because the phenomenon is affected by the measuring instrument, the result is again statistical indeterminacy. According to Schrodinger, what is being studied is a *gestalt*: not the "shape" of subatomic particles, but a "model"; the physicist can only ask whether phenomena conform to our models of them, "whether the expectations were reasonable, and thus whether the pictures or models we use are adequate" (22). Thus, the classical assumptions of a purely empirical, visual autonomy and objectivity are called into question, for the experiment itself is a condition of perception, an "arrangement" of reality rather than a mere "description" of it. In New Physics, knowing is a construction and confirmation of models rather than an exact description of an empirically verifiable reality, a "subjective" analysis and interpretation rather than an objective one; the arrangement must be taken into account in any understanding of the phenomena observed. And the result is probable rather than certain knowledge.

A third philosophical problem that Niels Bohr talks about in *Atomic Physics and Human Reality* is that because it is impossible to separate "the behavior of atomic objects and the interaction with the measuring instruments which serve to define the conditions under which the phenomena appear" (40), an experiment cannot encompass or explain the totality of a phenomenon. Any description of a phenomenon is incomplete. At best, experiments exhibit what Bohr, discussing this observational problem in quantum physics, calls "complementarity" (39–40); that is, the experiments only complement one another. Thus, the results of experiments are relative to one another and ultimately indeterminate since (as in the uncertainty principle where particles can only be measured according to position or velocity but not both at once) different frames of reference cannot be brought together into one whole, unified picture. [10]

The discovery of methodological subjectivity in physics, traditionally considered the "hardest" of the hard sciences in that it dealt with the visible, material world, has had a profound and relatively well-known impact on the philosophy of science. It also brings us one step closer to understanding the problem of studying emotional response based on logocentric values and assumptions. The realization that what we observe and know is in part determined by what Heisenberg demonstrates are a priori conditions of the experiment that must be taken into account in any description of the experiment (57–58) seems, as Heisenberg admits, to let subjectivity into scientific space; although the mind of the scientist does not enter the atomic event, experiments are selected and designed by the scientist

(59). As Heisenberg discusses in *Physics and Philosophy*, the a priori condition of the experiment "emphasizes a subjective element in the description of atomic events, since the measuring device has been constructed by the observer, and we have to remember that what we observe is not nature itself but nature exposed to our method of questioning. . . . It is understandable that in our scientific relation to nature our own activity becomes very important when we have to deal with parts of nature into which we can penetrate only by using the most elaborate tools" (58).

Heisenberg clearly does not subscribe to Kant's a priori forms of intuition—those innate, universal, and thus objective categories of knowledge not derived from sense experience, such as the concepts of space, time, causality, and substance—as " 'the basis of any future metaphysics that can be called science' " (88; cf. Kant, *Prolegomena*).[11] In fact, he argues that these forms have been "annihilated" by the discoveries of the New Physics: "[T]he theory of relativity has changed our views of space and time, it has in fact revealed entirely new features of space and time, of which nothing is seen in Kant's a priori forms of pure intuition. The law of causality is no longer applied in quantum theory and the law of the conservation of matter is no longer true for the elementary particles" (Heisenberg 88). However, Heisenberg does not completely throw out the Kantian a priori categories of pure reason either. In fact, he prefers Kant's categories to what he calls the "dogmatic realism" of Newtonian science and positivism based (ostensibly) on empiricism. Heisenberg points out that the use of these commonsense concepts by which we understand the world, "including space, time and causality, is in fact the condition for observing atomic events and is, in this sense of the word, 'a priori' " (90). As Farrell also suggests, Kant's categories of pure intuition are highly logocentric, spatial (cf. Whorf 153, who argues that they are linguistic).

Although modified, these a priori categories appear to be necessary to describe and explain the activity of the New Physics and are a condition of knowing any kind of phenomena:

"When we make an experiment we have to assume a causal chain of events that leads from the atomic event through the apparatus finally to the eye of the observer; if this causal chain was not assumed, nothing could be known about the atomic event" (90). But "classical physics and causality have only a limited range of applicability" (90). In New Physics, then, the categories of pure intuition, regarded by Kant as constituting a metaphysical basis of a universal objectivity, are "reduced to the method of scientific research; it is the condition which makes science possible" (Heisenberg 89). These categories also may be the condition that makes the study of affective experience difficult if not impossible.

Developments in New Physics such as these have led to speculation by philosophers and historians of science about the supposed "objectivity" of science. Although Heisenberg claims that "quantum theory does not contain genuine subjective features" in that "it does not introduce the mind of the physicist as part of the atomic event," he also states that it is not objective either (55–56). Indeed, for Schrodinger (22) in the quote cited above, the metaphors "picture" and "model" are interchangeable, and "adequacy" replaces "truth" as the criterion, for knowledge of subatomic reality is conceived of as a "subjective interpretation," a construction and testing of expectations, rather than as an objective description of autonomous events. For it is the experimental apparatus we construct that gives "shape" to the phenomena observed—that makes observation possible. And thus instead of objectivity, imitation, accuracy, knowing as an interpretive model entails contingency, chance, probability, uncertainty.

Other scientist-philosophers of science have noted that experiments are designed and selected by scientists not only on scientific bases but also according to social, cultural, religious, and aesthetic criteria that are generally suppressed in favor of the public ethos of objectivity and rationality (Holton). Metaphors can form a priori linguistic bases for conceptual models and research in science (Boyd; Kuhn, "Metaphor in Science;" Pylyshyn; Reddy; Turbayne). The structure of the senses and the brain can be regarded as the architectural foundation of all human knowledge (Bronowski). All of this would seem to let a high degree of subjectivity into science. In fact, Paul Feyerabend argues that scientific discovery is much more irrational in practice than "rationally reconstructed" methods, based on "the context of justification" rather than "the context of discovery," lead us to believe.[12] For Feyerabend, scientific practice consists of ad hoc approximations, ad hoc hypotheses, counterinductions, the use of adjustor words, the ignoring of whole domains of observation and data, propaganda, "prejudice, passion, conceit, error, sheer pigheadedness, in short . . . all the elements that characterize the context of discovery" (*Against Method* 55–68; 78–98; 145–61).

One way of handling the philosophical problem posed by this methodological subjectivity in science, of course, is to render "truth" a function of community by positing a "sociology of knowledge" as its basis. The notion of social models structuring not only observation and knowledge in New Physics but also the development of scientific ideas throughout history has perhaps been most fully developed by Thomas S. Kuhn in his well-known study *The Structure of Scientific Revolutions*. In fact, Kuhn's work was at least partially inspired by the Copenhagen school of quantum mechanics (Lakatos 92). Contrary to the traditional view of science expressed by Gillispie, who in *The Edge of Objectivity* portrays science (and thus perception) as a linear accumulation of facts leading to a complete description of nature, Kuhn understands science as an articulation and overthrow of *paradigms*, incomplete models that, like Bohr's complementary experiments, are a condition of observation but do not and cannot embrace the totality of the phenomenon under study (*Scientific Revolution* 7; 92; 96; 160–73; 206). As "social-epistemic" models, paradigms shape both perception and knowledge (113).

Here, then, in philosophically and historically simplified terms, objectivity has moved from the metaphysical realm of Plato's Ideal Forms to the observable realm of empirical reality, to the psychological realm of Kant's a priori categories, and finally to the practical realm of sociology. Subjective knowledge in science is thus externalized, projected outward onto the social plane, made visible, "objective." If the a priori categories of intuition and sense experience no longer hold at all levels of reality, one can account for the validity and stability of knowledge by its acceptance as a social construct. It is the social nature of knowledge that makes objectivity in this new, limited sense of consensus possible.

However, Kuhn's is not the undisputed paradigm in the history and/or philosophy of science (Kuhn himself admits that [*Scientific Revolutions* 121]), and his work has been vehemently attacked from both the right and the left.[13] Not all physicists agree with the early Copenhagen interpretation of quantum mechanics either. For Bohr, indeterminacy appeared to be not only an epistemological problem of method, of the current state of our experimental apparatus and our knowledge, as it is for most physicists, but also a problem of ontology, inherent in the nature of the interaction of the experimental apparatus with atomic reality itself—what we might call the strong principle of indeterminacy. For Heisenberg as well, the paradox in New Physics was in the commonsense concepts by which we understand the world—in the sensory and mental "apparatus" of human beings—and thus a paradox that increased knowledge or improved instrumentation could never overcome (56). But Roger Penrose, a contemporary mathematical physicist, disputes the Copenhagen interpretation of quantum mechanics, particularly that of Bohr, whose theory is "too pessimistic" and implies that "there is *no* objective picture at all. Nothing is actually 'out there', at the quantum level. Somehow reality only emerges in relation to the results of 'measurements'. Quantum theory, according to this view, provides merely a calculated procedure, and does not attempt to describe the world as it actually 'is' " (226; also see 255–56, 280).

Indeed, in that famous dispute with Bohr and the Copenhagen school of quantum theory, even Einstein was unable to abide the notion that uncertainty and random chance were ontologically inherent in nature (*Relativity* 157)—that God played dice with the universe. Despite the fact that Einstein believed in the role of intuition, creativity, and theory in scientific discovery and relied on "thought experiments" to formulate relativity theory, he also held the Newtonian position that empirical confirmation was the only basis of science—even New Physics; Einstein believed that the laws governing both subatomic and cosmic reality would, in time, be found, leading to a complete and unified description of nature (*Relativity* 123–24; but see Feyerabend, *Against Method* 18; 57–58n., for another interpretation of Einstein's position). Thus, for Einstein (148–57), but not for Thomas Kuhn (*Scientific Revolutions* 98–102), Newtonian mechanics is merely a special case of Special Relativity that holds for descriptions of events not approaching the speed of light; Special Relativity is in turn a special case of General Relativity.

In fact, despite the "metaphysical" findings of the New Physics concerning the subjectivity of our methods and thus the probability, relativity, and uncertainty of our knowledge, New physicists *must* fall back on the formalistic, rationalistic assumptions of classical Newtonian science (the metaphorical model of knowledge as description), and the a priori, spatial categories of experience it is based on, in order to make investigation into cosmic and subatomic reality, and communication of the results obtained, possible at all. And those assumptions, those categories, that metaphor, are logocentric. Earlier we touched on the fact that Schrodinger's use of the metaphors "picture" and "model" interchangeably is significant insofar as the experimental arrangement is considered a model of phenomena under study. Schrodinger's use of the metaphors "picture" and "model" interchangeably is also significant in that the goal of New Physics is still an *accurate description*, now of the interpretive arrangement (i.e., of the shape or model) rather than of an objective reality alone. Even Bohr states:

> [I]t is decisive to recognize that, *however far the phenomena transcend the scope of classical physical explanation, the account of all evidence must be expressed in classical terms.* The argument is simply that by the word "experiment" we refer to a situation where we can tell others what we have done and what we have learned and that, therefore, the account of the

experimental arrangement and of the results of the observations must be expressed in unambiguous language with suitable terminology of classical physics. (39)

Although New physicists *reinterpret description* to account for the subjective and indeterminate elements in their work, they remain just as committed to describing subatomic and cosmic reality empirically and rationally as Newtonian science does the reality of our senses. New Physics is not committed to an epistemology of subjective uncertainty. This was not a short-lived philosophical goal; it never was a goal at all. Despite the recognition of the role of probability and contingency in the New Physics and the belief that our current (and commonsense) knowledge is incomplete and uncertain, in their commitment to arrive at the fundamental laws governing the universe New physicists *must* actually proceed "methodologically" on the assumption that the further development of instrumentation and knowledge will lead to a complete description of Nature—still proceed on what we might call the weak principle of indeterminacy.

In fact, Penrose goes so far as to assert that indeterminacy exists only at the classical, Newtonian level of observation and that determinacy actually holds in both relativity theory and at the quantum level as a kind of "quantum formalism." Thus, descriptions of quantum states are objective if we dispense with determinism on the classical level at which such descriptions must take place (225–98); the question then becomes one of noncomputability, not indeterminacy. In contemporary New Physics, then, scientists continue Einstein's work, seeking the Grand Unification Theory (or, appropriately, GUT) that will bring together all the subatomic and macroscopic forces in nature and their interaction—gravity, magnetism, strong nuclear, and weak nuclear—into one comprehensive, rational law that will describe the origin and nature of the entire universe and that can be proven empirically.[14]

Thus, there may be a direct connection between a visual ontology rooted in empiricism and the epistemology that underlies our methods of research, even in regard to indeterminate knowledge. In any case, the conflict between an epistemology of uncertainty and the methodological necessity to *describe* formalistically and rationally represents the limits of indeterminacy in New Physics and science generally. This last point has often been overlooked by enthusiastic humanists (this author included [e.g., "Epistemic Trend"]) who, based on the discoveries of the New Physics, are excited by a possible "cultural unification" of the sciences and the humanities at the level of ontological as well as epistemological indeterminacy.

It has also been overlooked by a number of philosophers of science, including Lakatos and even Kuhn (cf. Lakatos 92). The fact is that most, if not all, physicists must and do proceed *in practice* on the basis of highly logocentric Newtonian metaphors and methods, with their imperatives to describe even indeterminate knowledge objectively, accurately, and completely (with the concomitant values of detached visuality, imitation, and linearity, respectively). This may have profound implications not only for our understanding of New Physics but also for investigating and describing affective experience in reading and writing, on which problem it may shed at least a few photons of light.

The Reinterpretation of Subjective Interpretation in Reader Response Criticism

There are important differences between New Physics and Reader Response Criticism: the latter does not strive to be a science (at least not ostensibly), does not require elaborate experimental apparatus (at least not yet), and contra Heisenberg does admit a high degree of subjectivity into the "experiment." But the models of knowledge in New Physics and Reader Response Criticism are similar. The selection and design of the experiment are a priori conditions for perception in New Physics; in Reader Response Criticism, the cognitive and "emotional apparatus" of the reader, and even the setting (Bleich, "Identity"), are conditions for creation of meaning and knowledge. For Schrodinger, the experimental model determines the "shape" (*gestalt*) of subatomic events and thereby confirms or changes what we already know; for Wolfgang Iser ("Reading Process" 57), interpretation involves the confirmation or reorganization of affective and cognitive schemata or *gestalten* as the reader interacts with the schematic structures of the text itself. Just as any description of an atomic event must take into account the experiment and instrumentation used, any description of the literary event "must both begin, and end with them [the readers]" (Fish, "Introduction" 2–3).

For Louise M. Rosenblatt (*Reader*) too, reading is a process of shaping, of giving form, of composing meaning in conjunction with the verbal and visual cues offered by the text, just as experiments in quantum mechanics are for Schrodinger, Heisenberg, and Bohr. For Rosenblatt, reading (like science) is an "evocation," an interpretive creation of perceived text. The relationship between the reader and the poem is "transactional," much as it is between the experiment and the reality observed in the New Physics: if in New Physics the "observer" is an "active participant" who with his or her models interacts with "the text" of the observed phenomenon and evokes "a poem" of subatomic reality containing such metaphoric quarks as "beauty," "color," and "charm," in Reader Response Criticism the reader is an active participant who evokes "the poem" of the text. (See Harding's "Role of the Onlooker" and "Psychological Processes in the Reading of Fiction" for an early but still invaluable discussion of the way all "observers," whether "active participant" or "passive onlooker," can be considered to "respond.")

Nature, then, appears to be even more like a book than we realized in the Newtonian worldview, for in New Physics and Reader Response Criticism the subjective process of reading nature and reading text seems to be similar indeed. And in more ways than one. For to varying degrees both New physicists and Reader Response critics metaphorically conceive of the process of responding as a process of visualization. As we will see, Reader Response Criticism is naturally committed to a logocentric paradigm of reading; although *description* of response is reinterpreted as an interpretive one, it is still predominately based on visual modes of perception and reference. In the simplest terms for now, if the experimental *gestalten* "shape" perception, experience, and meaning, those *gestalten*, that shape, and perception, experience, and meaning themselves, are conceptualized in terms of highly spatial categories, values, and assumptions only. What is evoked by scientist or reader is a hypothetico-visual "poem," a spatial model of the "text." We will explore the extent to which the *gestalt* psychology of reading itself is conceptualized visually—is committed to spatial metaphors and models—in chapter 4.

The problem that we will study in the rest of this chapter is that affective experiences, like subatomic phenomena, do not lend themselves well to visual study, to referential description, to spatial modes of reasoning. The first Reader Response critic to attempt to formally investigate the subjective processes involved in literary analysis and interpretation, I. A. Richards (*Practical Criticism*) studied how his university students read poetry in an attempt to understand what feelings, presuppositions, theories, beliefs, or ideologies they brought to their reading. In his attempt to develop a critical technique for teaching literature based on the affective experience of readers, Richards arrived at categories that bear some resemblance to the nonrational categories of scientific discovery reported by Feyerabend in *Against Method* (55–68; 78–98; 145–61): making sense of the poem, sensuous apprehension, imagery, mnemonic irrelevances, stock responses, sentimentality, inhibition, doctrinal adhesions, technical presuppositions, and general critical preconceptions (Richards, *Practical Criticism* 13–17).

But in an ironic twist, Allen Tate, who attacks the logical positivists' dictate of empirically verifying all meaning (appendix A), accuses Richards of reducing all literary statements to unverifiable (i.e., visually untestable) propositions about emotions. As Ludwig Wittgenstein understood, the meaning of statements that describe feeling, like statements that describe memory or cognition, are not empirically verifiable and are therefore uncertain at best. (Even statements like "I have a headache" are ultimately insupportable from data of general observation, such as verbal statements and physical behavior, all of which can be faked [see *Philosophical Investigations*, esp. 97e., 283–126e., 423; cf. De Rivera, "Emotional Experience and Qualitative Method" 677–88]). In attempting to construct a self-contained science of literary meaning and value based on emotional response, Tate states that Richards commits the positivist's mistake of distinguishing between emotion and meaning. More recently, Stanley Fish also attacks Richards on somewhat similar grounds: by studying affect as distinct from reason, Richards, Fish believes, unnecessarily limited the range of possible cognitive responses in interpreting literature to emotional ones ("Literature in the Reader" 53–55; also see Eagleton 45–46).

In fact, Fish argues that there is not really such a clearcut distinction between emotion and meaning and that much of what we take as emotional experience is really rational cognition. We will explore this problem later in this chapter. But if, in addition to empiricism and rationalism, affect, aesthetics, intuition, tacit knowledge, and metaphors are major factors in scientific discovery insofar as they at least influence the choice of the experiment and at most determine what a scientist sees and understands (Holton; Bronowski; Polanyi; Boyd; Turbayne; Kuhn "Metaphor In Science"), in Reader Response Criticism these nonempirical, nonrational "themata" can be considered a form of knowledge in themselves. Emotions as organized impulses tell us our feelings about, reactions to, and attitudes toward things or events in the world (Richards, *Principles* 98–102). And so we are left with the problem of how to study and describe them.

As in the philosophy of science, one way to do this is to try to deal with indeterminate experience socially—in the classroom as a community. In Reader Response Criticism too, the sociology of knowledge has become the basis of adjudicating subjective responses to arrive at valid interpretation, "objective" knowledge. In his well-known earlier work, represented in *Is There a Text in This Class: The Authority of Interpretive Communities*, Stanley Fish employs the notion of "interpretive communities" to account for how readers arrive at "the facts" of a text in a way that is similar to Schrodinger's account of how New physicists arrive at knowledge of subatomic phenomena: "Interpretive communities are made up of those who share interpretive strategies not for reading (in the conventional sense) but for writing texts, for constituting their properties and assigning their intentions. In other words the strategies exist prior to the act of reading and therefore determine the *shape* of what is read rather than, as is usually assumed, the other way around" (171; emphasis mine). In fact, Fish's notion of interpretive communities in many ways parallels Kuhn's notion of paradigmatic communities.[15] If we cannot verify subjective experience wholly, empirically, we can project it onto a social screen to render it "visible" and thus amenable to validation.

David Bleich also partially bases his Reader Response theory on the epistemological discoveries of the Copenhagen school of New Physics and Kuhn's philosophy of science. Indeed, Bleich sees his theory as a response to the need to explain interpretation in light of the discoveries of the New Physics. In *Subjective Criticism*, Bleich argues that *all* knowledge, including what is regarded as objective knowledge, is subjective. Bleich calls his model of knowledge "The Subjective Paradigm" (10). Both Reader Response Criticism and the New Physics are manifestations of the subjective paradigm "because in each case the role of the observer is paramount. An observer is a subject, and his means of perception define the essence of the object and even its existence to begin with. An object is circumscribed and delimited by a subject's motives, his curiosities, and above all, his language" (*Subjective Criticism* 18).

Bleich supports his position by drawing on the work of Piaget, Cassirer, and Langer to discuss the role of language acquisition and intellectual development, which are embodied for

Bleich in the process of "symbolization" and "resymbolization." Symbolization is the process, according to Langer (*Philosophy*), whereby the raw data of reality is organized by the language of the senses (and is perhaps prior to rational cognition or linguistic expression [cf. Gendlin, *Experiencing*; Weiskrantz]); resymbolization is the process whereby the language of the senses is interpreted by, presented in, and made intelligible to verbal consciousness as personal and social knowledge—or to use a culinary metaphor, when the smorgasbord of reality, already cooked by the senses and placed on the table of the mind, becomes food for thought. For Bleich, symbolization is perceiving, naming, identifying; resymbolization is the motivational demand to interpret perception based on subjective drives and the social need to adapt to the environment (*Subjective Criticism* 39, 65–67, 213).

Citing the work of Piaget in developmental psychology, Bleich argues that "representational intelligence" is an increasing consciousness and control through language of emotional drives and motivations—a symbolization of basic sensorimotor experience, instincts, and needs (*Subjective Criticism* 28). For Bleich, as for Piaget, language acquisition and intellectual development are simultaneous, if not synonymous, processes leading to self-awareness, social adaptation, intellectual growth, and survival (64). To account for how awareness of sensory input, drives, and inhibitions is articulated in language and conscious thought, Bleich turns to the work of Ernst Cassirer and Susanne Langer.

In *The Philosophy of Symbolic Forms* i, Cassirer argues that language, both historically and individually, originates with unconscious drives that result in mimesis, gesture, and finally sensuous sound (158–60, 181–90). Through this dialectic between "sensuous form" and "intellectual content," language, like other symbolic forms in our culture (science, religion, myth), progresses from the embodiment and expression of substance toward the articulation of purer logical relationships that correlate with the increasing abstraction of thought (178–79). In Cassirer's philosophy, then, Kant's innate categories of pure experience are understood as *symbolic forms of language* that allow the formation of concepts and classes of concepts through which we both synthesize and analyze the world of experience, and which thus constitute higher consciousness.

As for Bleich, the sensuous and the intellectual do not constitute subjective and objective, but rather an affective dialectic in all phases of cognitive development (Cassirer 285–302). Even at its logical purest, however, language for Cassirer retains its sensuous origins (its affective basis), expressing not only intellectual form but also the emotions and drives that first motivated its formation (158–59). In other words, the subjective instincts and emotions that motivate the articulation of language are embedded and bodied forth in its sensuous physical structure. The emotions that drive language imprint themselves on it. Later, the neglected dimension of language as a sensuous form will be essential in understanding affective response as nonspatial, nonreferential knowledge that can be understood experientially, described temporally, and taught orally.

In *Philosophy in a New Key*, Susanne Langer views the process of symbolization as both fundamental and necessary to the act of perception itself. The act of sensing the world does not simply involve the reception of raw data—humans need their reality cooked. Instead, the sense organs impose form on the world in order to begin to "make sense," to "know" it. These forms, then, are primordial symbols that for Langer underlie all knowledge of the world and thus all human activity. All human activities are constituted by the symbol-making function of the senses and the mind. All "facts" undergo symbolic transformation: "facts" are already interpreted. Not only language, but myth, ritual, music, art, mathematics, and science partake in the symbol-making function of the mind. For Langer, there is no essential difference between science and art *as symbolic activities*.[16]

What is most important here is that Bleich, like Piaget, Langer, and Cassirer, tries to take into account the affective nature of cognition. In fact, Bleich notes that for Langer, the primary need and distinguishing characteristic of human beings is the *desire* to symbolize; language, (and the interpretation of it) is only one manifestation of this need and is only secondarily communication (*Subjective Criticism* 43). Bleich thus goes further than any other Reader Response critic in maintaining that interpretation is *wholly* subjective, a resymbolization of experience in language "motivated by the demand that the knowledge thus symbolized be explained or converted into a more subjectively satisfying form" (213)—just as Bohr seems to maintain that quantum descriptions are only a description of the experiment rather than subatomic reality itself (Penrose 226, 280). "In this way all explanations are interpretive and may be understood as the construction of new knowledge" (Bleich, *Subjective Criticism* 213).

In addition, for Bleich, resymbolization is not merely personal but communal. In fact, more than any other critic, Bleich understands interpretation as a social activity that is necessary for adaptation, survival, and growth (*Subjective Criticism* 68). Thus, for Bleich, the literary text is not the object of interpretation at all. Rather, for Bleich, the text only serves as a social object through which to produce or symbolize the affective drives and motivations that underlie and inform all knowledge and to resymbolize and socialize these through interpretation. Because knowledge is wholly subjective, it is not the text but the drives and motivations that constitute knowledge. The goal of interpretation, therefore, is the production of knowledge about drives and motivations that are themselves the objects of further interpretation and validation (65).

Investigating and Describing Affective
Experience: The Indeterminacy Principle
of Reader Response Criticism

Just as Kuhn's epistemological paradigm is not the universal or even the predominant paradigm in science, Reader Response Criticism is not the paradigm of literary theory; it too is disputed.[17] However, many teachers and scholars in Reader Response Criticism and in composition, particularly those committed to "process" models in the expressive and social schools of writing theory, have perceived a relationship between reading and writing as parallel processes of creating and revising texts: reading entails the "writing" of subjective experience onto the text; writing entails "reading" in both the traditional and revisionist meaning of that term—as another form of arriving at and revising subjective knowledge.[18] (While other process models of writing, such as that derived from cognitive psychology and social-epistemic rhetoric, can be understood to parallel Reader Response Criticism,[19] the cognitive process model of writing does not deal explicitly with the issue of the use of Reader Response Criticism in composition; and, significantly, the social-epistemic model does not deal with the role of affect much at all [see Katz, "Aristotle's Rhetoric, 42–48].)

Like Reader Response Criticism, the expressive writing theory in particular takes affect as the starting point of knowledge. This is not to curse it but to praise it, for as in the Piaget-Cassirer-Langer-Bleich theory of language and knowledge, there are no naive senses, no childlike blanket of empiricism, no blackboard of the mind on which the chalky substance of world is written. Symbolization, through which reality speaks to us (whispers to us really) in the language of our senses—and resymbolization, in which the mind amplifies (and distorts) the message so we can hear and understand it—occurs in all cases, whether we read as participant or spectator (Harding, "Role of the Onlooker"), whether we write transactionally, expressively, or poetically (Britton), whether our purpose is efferent or aesthetic (Rosenblatt, *Reader*). For these reading and writing scholars and teachers, there is no knowledge that is not symbolized, no facts independent of our perception of them. In this regard, reading and writing are interrelated activities. Indeed, Anthony Petrosky goes so far as to warn of the danger of separating the interactive processes of reading and writing for the sake of constructing a reductive model ("From Story to Essay" 20).

Given the connections between reading and writing, between reception and production as similar processes of making meaning, there have been many attempts to develop heuristics to investigate and teach the process of writing using reading and to integrate literature and composition on more epistemologically and pedagogically palatable grounds—as subjective (and social) processes of response and interpretation.[20] It is in our attempts to develop heuristics to investigate and teach these processes that the problem of indeterminacy in New Physics begins to inform our understanding of the problem of capturing and describing subjective response in reading and writing; for it is in the attempts to develop heuristics that the formalistic, rationalistic parameters of the logocentric model of language and knowledge we use to spatially comprehend affective experience begin to emerge.

The first issue, of course, was the recognition and acceptance by researchers of the role of personal involvement in interpretation. As early as the 1960s, in the heyday of New Criticism, James Squire and James Wilson sought to describe the response processes of students by categorizing and statistically measuring them and to embody these categories in heuristics designed to teach students how to respond to and write about literature. Unlike Squire before him, Wilson found idiosyncratic evaluation in which students often distorted the text was not subordinate to "standards of interpretive accuracy," but relevant to response (see Bleich *Subjective Criticism* 103). However, Wilson could not specify how self-involvement correlated with literary interpretation. According to Bleich, despite Wilson's awareness of the difference between interpretive accuracy and self-involvement, Wilson, like Squire, was epistemologically inhibited insofar as they both took as primary the articulation of guidelines for teachers based on the belief in objective standards for accurately analyzing and interpreting texts (*Subjective Criticism* 104)—standards ultimately based on the formalistic, rationalistic imperatives of detached observation and precise description found in the logocentric, Newtonian model of knowledge.

If interpreting is not merely objective and accurate description but a central, symbolizing activity, as Reader Response critics believe, it has been argued that a problem with these early studies is that they only classify and measure types of responses rather than the subjective processes involved in interpreting and writing about a text. While acknowledging the difficulty of doing so, in "Describing Responses to Works of Fiction," Lee Odell and Charles R. Cooper set about to actually describe and measure "the reactions, perceptions, interpretations, and value judgments students make in response to a piece of literature" (203), using not only Alan Purves's categories of response (*Elements*) but also the tagmemic theory of Young, Becker, and Pike.[21] But despite the fact that Cooper and Odell go beyond Purves's attempt to classify only types of responses by looking at the intellectual processes that might be involved in response (cf. Bleich, *Subjective Criticism* 105–07), their sensitive study on teaching reading and writing, like all studies of subjective and hence essentially unobservable processes, seems to suffer at the rough hands of indeterminacy.

The purpose of Odell and Cooper's study is to provide teachers with a possible heuristic to help students interpret "more accurately, more sensitively, more fully" (204). Certainly tagmemic analysis can measure intellectual processes—even as a particle, wave, or field (see the "tagmemic heuristic," Young et al., *Rhetoric*)—insofar as these are reflected in student responses. Standards are not erected on the supposed stability and completeness of the text as a fixed reference point, complete, autonomous, and determinate—on an analysis of the text itself (cf. Holland's *The Dynamics of Literary Response*, an earlier psychological study of literary experience that Bleich says proceeds "from the close analysis of particular literary texts" in order to avoid "psychological generalizations" [*Subjective Criticism* xi]). However, a priori—and spatial—standards of accuracy and completeness in interpretation are still invoked and applied so that student reactions can be measured and problems of "accuracy" or "fullness" corrected. These standards are visual in origin and spatial in nature.

But when faced with the phenomena of affective experience (or subatomic reality), what does accuracy and fullness mean?

The standards are created by the very method we use to try to see phenomena—a problem of tautology we will touch on several times in this book. As Bleich says of Purves's classification of types of responses, "The fullness of response is defined objectively from the categories rather than subjectively from the personality orientation of the reader at that time" (*Subjective Criticism* 107). (In this regard, Bleich also criticizes Holland's *Five Readers Reading* on the grounds that it tries to study student responses from "traditional assumptions about knowledge. . . . [he] devised an experiment in which he would try to predict readers' responses from his own psychological analyses of short stories and his understanding of the readers' personalities as obtained in psychological tests such as the Rorschach and Thematic Apperception Test" [*Subjective Criticism* 115]).

Further, while the categories of response in studies such as Odell and Cooper's are (ostensibly anyway) derived inductively and confirmed empirically—from an analysis of what students do when they think about or respond to a text—the categories are in the end meant to be applied a priori to all students in every situation. In classifying responses so that categories may be applicable to the interpretation of other texts, we must hope, if not assume (as in Special Relativity Theory), that (1) the categories (the instruments) we use to evoke, define, analyze, classify, measure, and describe interpretation are themselves "stable" (i.e., valid); (2) readers' reactions (the phenomena under study) are universal (applicable to all students in every situation) and uniform (within an individual); or (3) complementary studies can capture enough of the processes of interpretation, which, if not completely observable, are still codifiable into logical (spatial) categories (cf. Bleich, "Identity" 352–53). As Odell and Cooper admit, "we can deal only with expressed responses. We cannot claim to know everything that goes on when a student responds to a text. It seems likely that some responses and some stages of the responding process will remain private and mysterious" (221).

But emotional reactions may not be stable, universal, or uniform (but cf. De Rivera). In "Putting Readers in Their Places,"

Purves warns against constructing an "ideal reader." Anthony Petrosky ("Reality Perception") suggests that not only are readers' reactions affective, highly personal, and sometimes idiosyncratic but that readers may not even perceive the same text. In fact, *an individual reader* may not even perceive the same text *at any given moment* (a phenomenon of consciousness recently noted in a New Physical study of the mind by Roger Penrose; cf. Bleich, "Cognitive Stereoscopy"). Perception may not be entirely visual; emotional reactions may not be entirely spatial. In "the universe of discourse," subjective responses to texts, which we essentially try to describe and measure with one- or two-dimensional heuristics, may not be so much like static points in three-dimensional space as multidimensional points in Einsteinian space-time. Thus, even within the space of one individual, a "*single quantum state* could in principle consist of a large number of activities, all occurring simultaneously" (Penrose 399; see 398–99 for a discussion of the role of "quantum parallelism" in consciousness, in which "different alternatives at the quantum level are allowed to coexist in linear superposition").

In "Cognitive Stereoscopy and the Study of Language and Literature," Bleich asserts that intellectual "growth and change are not arbitrary, even though they are unpredictable":

> For all practical purposes, knowledge of the stereoscopic shape of any one person's thoughts [dual perspectives or schemata revealed by "double essay assignments" and socially integrated in the classroom (105)] comes *only* retrospectively and collectively, which means that even when this knowledge is accepted and agreed upon by author and group, it is of only limited use—and perhaps none at all—in predicting either language initiatives or language responses by a particular person. (111; cf. Purves, "Putting Readers," 234)

In the indeterminate space-time of our experience, emotions can be understood as particle, wave (or field), but perhaps not simultaneously, for in measuring "position" (type or location of emotion) we lose velocity (force); in measuring for accuracy we lose completeness (cf. Brand, "Defining Our Emotional Life"). As Heisenberg points out in regard to quantum mechanics, the "[Kantian] categories of intuition and experience" that we use to "construct the experiment" and understand the phenomena are themselves a priori and limited insofar as "the old concepts fit nature only inaccurately" (43).

To account for possible error and variation in our *classical description* of affective response in subjective interpretation, perhaps a "probability function" representing the measurement of uncertainty in complementary experiments would help. Based on the mathematical laws of quantum physics, which I do not pretend to understand, a probability function in Reader Response Criticism would not be the statistical average of responses to a passage in a text but a number representing the likelihood or tendency of these (or other) multidimensional responses to occur at different times as determined by complementary experiments.[22] For a little like electrons under the electron microscope, texts interact and change with a reader's *image* of the world (Iser, *Reading*; cf. Boulding 3–18); and a reader's image of the world is continually changed by the text. (This may be more than mere analogy, for as Penrose points out, the seeming plasticity of the brain, where dendritic spines are believed to break and form new connections between neurons, may account for how long-term memories are laid down, which means that the physical brain is constantly changing [396–98]! As Penrose argues, this is not incidental but "is an *essential* feature of the activity of the brain" [397].) It may be that neither text *nor reader* is "invariable," a stable "field" of investigation.

But as with "black box" models in New Physics, it could be argued that in Reader Response Criticism even these multidimensional categories of response and subsequent measurements would not actually derive from an empirical analysis of what happens at all, what people feel/think when they respond to a text. Rather, these categories too would be derived "after the fact" from an analysis of the student's oral or written statements, from the "observational model" itself. The problem of

THE EPISTEMIC MUSIC OF RHETORIC

the validity, reliability, and accuracy of the reconstruction of mental processes is well known and has been a major criticism of protocol analysis (e.g., Cooper and Holzman; cf. Steinberg for a review and rebuttal of the criticism). The problem of rationally reconstructing phenomena is augmented, perhaps exponentially, in regard to affective processes. Again, as in New Physics, the problem seems to be one of *observing* the phenomena independent of our measuring devices. The expectations of the observer and the experimental model we use to perceive and measure phenomena at least partially determine the outcome. And those expectations, those models, and the outcome we obtain, are formalistic, rationalistic, spatial. At present, the best we can hope is complementarity at this visual level of experience.

To complicate matters even more, even at the superficial level of observation, different models or instruments, like different space-time coordinates between observer and phenomena, reveal different results. In an earlier study, Richard Beach concluded that there was a difference between written and oral responses to literature ("Literary Response"). In "The Identity of Pedagogy and Research in the Study of Response to Literature" Bleich also states that oral and written statements "each requires its own contextual justification" ("Identity" 147) and so will yield different results. Different methods of investigating response seem to tap different "dimensions" of understanding and feeling, and result in *different* responses.

All this, then, seems to represent an Indeterminacy Principle in Reader Response Criticism. And it may be more than a mere analogy. In a real sense, the problem of observing affective response in Reader Response Criticism may be directly related to the problem of observing particle or wave in New Physics. As Penrose argues (374–449), the laws governing the brain and consciousness itself may be quantum in nature (or lie between quantum and classical physics in some realm not yet formulated); in this case the uncertainty principle inherent in New Physics (and according to Penrose the result of the jump from the quantum to the classical level [225–301, 348–73]) would apply to the brain as a unique, remote, and relatively inaccessible region of space-time. Indeed, Penrose states that consciousness itself may be only an algorithmic (rational) reconstruction of as yet unknown physical processes (226, 400–13; cf. Cytowic, who suggests that consciousness is an emotion). Thus, as Penrose points out, parallel classical computation (the use of two or more computers—or in our case, complementary procedures) to simulate consciousness "is very unlikely to hold the key to what is going on with our *conscious* thinking" (398, see 226 as well).

The philosophical questions raised by the relationship between New Physics and Reader Response Criticism obviously have implications for all empirical and quantitative research into the processes involved in reading, writing, and knowing generally, research that has had a "decidedly cognitive bent" and has centered "on the process and structures of a writer's plans or on the study of written texts as records of cognitive activity" (Brandt 115). Our penchant for describing emotions in terms of logical categories and spatial schemata, while necessary and valuable, seems to rely heavily on logocentric assumptions about knowledge also found in Newtonian science. The problem in Reader Response Criticism could be one of observing the activity of the brain independent of our measuring devices—one of "noncomputability" (Penrose 216–17, 429–48); it also could be one of an "indeterminacy" inherent in the brain itself.[23] In either case, like nature (Heisenberg 57–58), students only seem to answer the questions they are asked.

The Spatiality of Method and
the Experience of Emotion

Despite the problem of indeterminacy in Reader Response Criticism, other attempts have been and still are being made in Reader Response Criticism to construct heuristics to describe or measure and teach composing strategies of student readers/writers (e.g., see Anderson and Rubano; Beach and Hynds; Biddle and Fulwiler; Blake; Dobler; Dougherty; Goetz "Structure of Emotional Response," "Getting a Reading"; Schatzberg-Smith; Tierney et al.). This work, like Reader Response Criticism itself, is important in helping us appreciate and explore the role of affect in reading and writing. But the attempt to describe and measure and teach composing strategies has been predominately spatial (cf. Flower et al., *Making Thinking Visible*). It seems that Reader Response critics and writing teachers, like New physicists, *must* rely on or construct spatial, empirical models of indeterminate processes based at least in part on a priori Kantian assumptions in order to measure, describe, and understand what are essentially unobservable phenomena. Perhaps it is more our formalistic, rationalistic methods than the subjective experience of the students that are verified by our analyses of their responses (just as in New Physics, experimental models as *gestalten* to some degree determine as well as verify what we find in them).

Whether we adopt the strong position of indeterminacy or not, the problem of researching and teaching affective processes of interpretation that may be involved in reading and writing perhaps derives from the spatial nature of heuristics as methods that assume or impose an empirical or rational structure on knowledge and experience, and the "nonspatial" dimension of subjective knowledge and experience. Let's summarize the problem of method first. It is common knowledge that in the natural sciences investigating some phenomena and then empirically verifying the results require that as many variables as possible in an experimental model be accounted for and/or controlled. In the natural sciences, this is normally done by constructing an "ideal type," that is, an experimental situation in which the primary elements of a phenomenon are isolated and examined independently so that the fundamental laws underlying appearances can be discovered and described. Variables that cannot be delimited and controlled must be carefully excluded from the experimental model (which is the same thing) or, as in New Physics, accounted for by a probability function.

And as everyone knows, the empirical experimental model thus represents a reduction of the total processes under study. (In quantum mechanics, for example, the measurement of the velocity of a subatomic particle precludes accurate measurement of its position, and vice versa.) Without reduction, prediction becomes very difficult. At the same time, the reductive nature of the experiment changes the very nature of the thing observed. This seems to be an epistemological dilemma that Reader Response critics and composition researchers share with scientists. For as empirical and rational models of human behavior, heuristics, no matter how unsystematic, reduce complex processes to visually verifiable behavior, to simpler (rational) terms—to an "ideal type" according to their own parameters— in order to account, describe and in some cases measure them. For Herbert A. Simon, an ardent proponent of the application of heuristics to mental phenomena, the value of heuristics lies precisely in their power to reduce phenomena to visually verifiable terms and to predict the behavior of "the outer environment" based only on the assumption of rationality concerning the "inner environment" (9–11).[24] We can predict behavior, says Simon, simply by asking, "How would a rationally designed system behave under these circumstances?" (15) and by constructing models that simulate that behavior. (Thus, rationality itself becomes an ideal type.)

The heuristics in Reader Response Criticism are not of the same order or magnitude as those Simon describes in *Sciences of the Artificial*. But the description, prediction, and control (or in the case of Bleich, the "predication" [see "Stereoscopy" 111]) of the visible outer environment—student performance—with a minimum of facts concerning the inner environment—the mind, about which we "make no hypotheses" (except, significantly, its rationality)—are more or less the goals of heuristics that seek to describe (and teach) the cognitive and affective processes of interpretation in reading and writing. In most Reader Response Criticism, the outer environment is not constituted by the text, as in New Criticism, but the students' oral or written statements. However, in using heuristics to investigate, describe, and teach the subjective processes of interpretation based on an analysis of the outer environment (the students' written or oral responses), the inner environment must be considered stable, determinate, and rational, even though the actual psychological processes involved—affective, social, cultural, psychological—are indeterminate and not empirically verifiable. (Hence, the reliance on the assumptions of a rational model.)

Of course, this is the general problem with seeking to describe empirically what is unobservable; a priori knowledge, and thus rational hypotheses and logical deduction, must be used to fill in "the gap" between observations and interpretive conclusion—the abyss of all empirical knowledge first noted perhaps by the sophists (cf. Kerferd, ch. 9, esp. 92–101; Enos, "Epistemology"). Since Hume, the circularity of induction and the problem of causal reasoning—of attributing effect to cause—has been a troubling one in the philosophy of science. If ideas are merely the sensations of objects, and no ideas are possible that have not been experienced, as the empiricists claimed, such concepts as causality, one of the cornerstones of science, become impossible to prove. Since we never actually experience cause directly by the senses, but only effect in a sequence in which one event follows another, causality is reduced for Hume to a mere mental habit, a way of seeing that may have no basis in reality. At best, the laws of nature could be a human invention that like a safety net seems to hold true for most of our experience; at worst, these laws could be an illusion that will eventually give way.

We have already touched on the highly deductive, self-contained, and in this sense solipsistic nature of human reasoning noted by Heisenberg (*Physics and Philosophy*, esp. 89). Even more recently, Alan Gross has discussed the myth of induction that is instantiated in the structure of the scientific paper. This is the abyss of human knowledge that Kant tried to account for with innate, a priori categories of pure reason and that contemporary philosophers of science such as Stephen Toulmin bridge with the notion of warrants. But it is an empirical gap that New Physics has opened wide. And the "filler," like this concept of knowledge itself, is highly spatial. The visual nature of the metaphors "accuracy" and "completeness" that act as warrants in science and underlie and reveal assumptions concerning the empirical nature of all our knowledge lead to and necessitate description and measurement as the only valid basis for hypotheses.

If one problem is the visual (and rational) nature of heuristics, the second problem is the little understood nature of affect—and the limitations of logocentric method in investigating and describing this area of human experience. Scholars in literature, philosophy, and rhetoric by and large no longer accept the mind/body duality; indeed, there may be little difference and much spillover between affect and rationality. If emotions are rational insofar as they involve cognition (Fish "Literature in the Reader" 53–55), rationality is affective insofar as cognition is a physical activity (see Cytowic 183–230). Rationality is located in the bodily brain; we experience ourselves thinking, can feel thinking, especially when we think long and hard and are conscious of it—even when it doesn't lead to an undemonstrable headache. However, rationality and affect, or thinking and experiencing, to use Gendlin's terms (*Experiencing*), are somewhat different processes, perhaps localized in different parts of the body and/or brain (though simultaneous), and so may represent different kinds of experience or, perhaps more precisely, be experienced somewhat differently. (For Gendlin, experiencing, or "felt sense," is prelogical, physical; it can be consciously focused on and differentiated by thought and symbols, but it is continual, prior to, and necessary for logic and meaning [cf. Weiskrantz, *Thought Without Language*].)

Put another way, thinking is a different kind of feeling, much as different emotions are. Thus, thinking and feeling (if not different feelings themselves) may need to be understood, studied, and described differently as well (see Brand, *Psychology of Writing*; "Defining Our Emotional Life"). And while rational thought seems to occur in the cerebral cortex, affective processes seem to be more physical, somewhat diffuse "in the body," indeterminate, and so harder to capture by logical categories or spatial schemata alone. Despite Fish's criticism of Richards concerning the separation of affect and rational cognition discussed previously, perhaps not all emotions can (or even should be) understood or explained in terms of rationality. Affect and intuition may not be so much an extension of rational, spatially oriented logic as another, physical kind of knowing altogether—one much more essential than our current heuristics allow us to admit. (The problems of heuristics as techniques to capture, describe, and teach affective experience are not unlike the problems associated with programming artificial intelligence discussed by Dreyfus in *What Computers Can't Do*.[25]) Another kind of logic, another kind of knowing, and how they are embodied in language, is the topic of chapters 3, 4, and 5.

In addition, if affect, like tacit knowledge, like human knowledge itself, is in a real sense physical—located in the body—as Polanyi and others have argued, interpretive heuristics may miss not only affective or intuitive factors but also perhaps a host of as yet unknown factors at the physical level of experience that influence the way a student responds to a text at any particular moment. Physiological "mechanisms," for instance, biological connections, events, or changes in the brain and/or body itself, may influence interpretation (for a related discussion of tacit and sensory knowledge in writing involving the neurological connections between eye, ear, and hand, see Ochsner's *Physical Eloquence and the Biology of Writing*). One could multiply physiological causes and sources of reactions almost indefinitely, even to the point of including such seemingly exotic influences as gravitational fluctuations, electromagnetic radiation, and other atomic and subatomic events, which New Physics has shown underlie the makeup of all matter and may therefore also influence the mind [Penrose 374–449].)

While the latter may seem a bit far-fetched, it makes some sense if we take into account Penrose's speculation concerning the possible role of a single photon on the retina in activating a nerve signal and bringing perception to conscious awareness, and whether the "one-graviton criteria" might apply to other brain cells as well (400–01). One subatomic particle may be enough to raise indeterminate perception into the threshold of conscious sensory experience. In technical terms, the asymmetric curvature of one graviton can bring about the classically observable collapse of simultaneous alternatives of linearity on the quantum level. But how many other subatomic events could affect the stability or course of the graviton? We may recognize here the increasing importance of New Physics (or its successor) in understanding and investigating both rational and affective experience. While some of these events can be measured and may be minimal, even theorists and researchers in neural nets, which rival workers in Artificial Intelligence, recognize that there are levels of physical structure that underlie all our experience of which we are not consciously aware [see Hofstadter]).

The idea of investigating the quantum level of sensory experience that underlies the subjective response in reading and writing is mind-boggling. But the complexity and physical structure of affective experience have implications for understanding the problems of studying the "Newtonian level of experience" as well. How do we describe sensory activity (which can be measured by electronic sensors) in relation not only to text but to thought, memory, and emotion? How research it? How predict it? How teach it? With current methods, we simply can't. Indeed, the nature and role of the senses are not even questions in the current Reader Response/composition paradigm[26] (though they seem to have been essential in sophistic rhetoric [Enos, "Epistemology," "Rhetorical Theory," "Composing Process"]).

The neglected role of the senses in reading and writing theory and pedagogy serves to point up the understandably limited, superficial, and narrowly *abstract*, visual nature of our heuristics for investigating affective response. Even with electronic equipment we could only measure this experience reductively, in terms of end-effects, could only describe it in terms of metaphoric models that, given the formalistic, rationalistic episte-mology upon which such studies are based, would be inher-ently spatial. In looking at the sensory level of experience, we will once again be confronted with the problem of investigation that confronts New physicists: the problem of *describing* inde-terminate substance, unobservable cause rationally and empiri-cally.

And what if the one-graviton criteria apply to affective ex-perience in reading and writing as well? How do we describe and measure the exact moment in space-time when a particle of nerve sensation pushes multidimensional experience into singular consciousness? How define and measure the "quality" of this in relation to thought? How improve it? Our "abstract" heuristics for research and teaching don't even begin to ask these questions. In this sense, all our methods of getting at the affective level of physical experience fail. The black box syn-drome is at work here again, of course, but the events in the box are too complex, too multidimensional, too indeterminate to describe spatially, rationally, reductively. (And if the Co-penhagen school of New Physics is correct, we may never be able to.)

Finally, even if we could measure these, we still could not conclude with any certainty that the physical structure or events described and measured are *the cause* of the experience per-ceived. As in research into the physical structure of memory, the problem is not only the empirical gap between cause and effect but also the gap between the biological mechanism that we think accounts for a physiological process and the nature of the phenomenon *as experienced*. For example, while the struc-ture of memory (which seems to be closely associated in the brain with smell and with emotions) may be identified as chemical traces in the spaces between synapses [Johnson], ques-tions remain: How is one memory differentiated from another? How are details of particular experiences and thoughts, images and ideas, physically encoded? And perhaps most important, how are these memories *experienced* physically? Science must perforce examine structural relations, rather than essences, while the actual experience of the phenomenon goes unexplained.

No one in Reader Response Criticism or composition research claims to describe and measure—or even want to describe and measure—all the cognitive and affective processes in reading and writing and their relationship (just as no one in New Physics claims to be able to fully describe and measure the interaction of subatomic particles). But the need and desire to do so as accurately and completely as possible in order to understand and teach is as much the underlying goal of research in literature and composition as it is in science. And this goal is logocentric, the result of an ideological ontology of literacy. Although the description of subjective processes in interpretation is admittedly incomplete, just as the description of the laws of nature is incomplete in New Physics, the belief that our model will work in limited circumstances, that enough of the subjective processes of interpretation in reading and writing can be captured and taught by empirical heuristics to justify our methods for research and pedagogy, underlies—must underlie—our efforts.

The fact that we can not know the total affective experience does not mean we can't know anything. It does not mean that we can't continue research and teaching. It does not even mean that we can't describe and predict with apparent accuracy and reasonable consistency some parts of subjective response. What it does mean is that we do not know how much of what we do not know would change what we do know. It means we can only find the answers to questions that our methods ask. Heuristics in Reader Response Criticism, like experimental models in New Physics, to some indeterminate extent, represent a spatial reduction of the phenomena set in motion or frozen in stasis by the axioms and "apparatus" of our heuristics for purposes of examination; by necessity these a priori models are grounded by empirical limitations and are reductive in their rationalistic bias, all of which they tend to impose on the more holistic nature of human experience.

In this philosophical critique of Reader Response Criticism, then, we *see* the epistemological limits of method and the paradox and problem of all human knowledge. In a sense, any classification, and therefore all knowledge, is formalistic, rationalistic, and reductive; language itself is a priori and to some degree deterministic in that it conceals as much as it reveals (Whorf; Lakoff and Johnson). Each method has its virtues and its limitations; each reveals and conceals different things. Yet without method, we would know little indeed. For as New Physics seems to show, in the subatomic realm, we really know with certainty neither essence nor cause but only method. We have only hypotheses and assumptions about what's going on below the threshold of our perception. We have only metaphors and models through which to examine and understand.

Reader Response critics such as Bleich, Petrosky, and Petersen do offer other less a priori and systematic, more social and "ethnographic" heuristics of interpretation than even the semiformalistic, rationalistic ones we have been discussing, and these heuristics have been applied to composition.[27] In fact, because of their lack of "methodological rigor," these heuristics, and others like them, have been characterized as "touchy-feely" (McCormick 837) and so have been dismissed, too hastily perhaps, based on a *formalistic, rationalistic desire* for logical systematicity and logocentric rigor commensurate with our cultural predisposition to view "true" knowledge as distant and abstract. To overcome the problem of capturing emotions in interpretation, we opt for more (or less) systematicity, rigor—but always seem to be constrained by formalist, rationalist assumptions concerning the nature of knowledge.

Bleich's response statements, being general and relatively undefined, are even less formalistic, rationalistic than the heuristics I discussed previously and therefore should allow (at least theoretically) more affective, personal, idiosyncratic responses to emerge that can then be "authorized" by the classroom as community. In fact, in "The Identity of Pedagogy and Research in the Study of Response to Literature," Bleich argues that with the classroom as a research site, the subjective, personal nature of a reader's development of a particular interpretive response, as well as the social process of authorizing that response as interpretation in the classroom, could be studied as social knowledge in the context of the community in which it is produced. Petersen's use of freewriting as a response heuristic is even more general than Bleich's three-pronged question designed to elicit motivations and therefore might be able to capture still more of the nonformalistic, nonrationalistic processes that occur in interpretation. For as Britton discusses in *The Development of Writing Abilities* (11–18), it is the spectrum from expressive to poetic that

> is closer to the way the individual thinks when he thinks by himself. . . . [E]xpressive writing . . . may also be used to follow the ebb and flow of the writer's consciousness, to articulate the concerns and interests of the writer, free of external demands. . . . Expressive writing, whether in the participant or spectator role, may be at any stage the kind of writing best adapted to exploration and discovery. It is language that externalizes our first stages in tackling a problem or coming to grips with an experience. (141, 197)

But it is questionable whether even these heuristics, despite their epistemically slight nature—or because of it, can as research and teaching tools ever capture or describe the most important physical, tacit, affective, intuitive processes involved in making sense of a text at any particular, multidimensional moment of space-time and whether these processes are generalizable at the level of interpretive heuristics at all. In addition, the social nature of knowledge, which, understandably in many ways has been the primary (because more "visible"?) focus of Reader Response Criticism, does not attempt to get at the nature of subjective knowledge as much as validate it. If Fish states that New Criticism "demanded the suppressing of what is subjective and idiosyncratic in favor of the level of response everyone shares" ("Introduction" 5), Reader Response Criticism, while acknowledging the centrality and importance of subjective response, can be understood to ultimately do the same. For Fish, social constraints act to stabilize (at least temporarily) subjective interpretation and provide an "objective," that is, a rational social standard, for determining its validity as knowledge (*"Variorum"* 171–72).

In *The Limits of Interpretation*, Umberto Eco, who seems to have thrown one of his many hats into the ring of decidability, argues that semiotic indeterminacy is constrained by the social context of meaning. But social context doesn't resolve the problem of indeterminacy; it just limits it. This is a point I think Eco would agree with as well. As we have discussed, in Reader Response Criticism, as in philosophy of science, the sociology of knowledge can be understood as a way of objectifying subjective experience by projecting it on an empirically social plane. Social reinterpretation constitutes another, equally powerful basis for arriving at valid standards of knowing, developing, and in effect replacing personal experience (or the Form of the text) with communally authorized knowledge.

If the sociology of knowledge doesn't obviate the need for method, it doesn't solve the problem of understanding, describing, investigating, and teaching affective experience either. Just as subjective experience in interpretation may in some profound ways already be an abstraction, a rational reconstruction of experience, as Eliot also understood (*Knowledge and Experience*), the social nature of knowledge is a rational reconstruction of subjective processes. In this sense, even the subjective-social model of knowledge in Reader Response Criticism becomes a crutch, much as Penrose (esp. 280–81, 296–97) thinks the indeterminacy principle is a crutch in New Physics. As Gerald Holton admits in regard to the subjective elements in science, "[t]he thematic hypothesis is often an impotency proposition in the sense that the search for alternatives has proved to be vain. . . . [T]he thematic hypothesis is precisely built as a bridge over the gap of ignorance" (52–53). The subjective-social model of interpretive knowledge, then, no matter what else it is or does, can be considered an "impotency proposition," a bridge over the gap of our ignorance of affective indeterminacy, a bridge in space that is supported by the pillars of induction and deduction and runs from empirical observation/verification to rational explanation/reconstruction and back again, without ever touching the dark water below.

Why do we try to describe, understand, and measure emotions in terms of formalistic, rationalistic methods? Why are we bound to the logocentric insistence that all knowledge be understood in terms of spatial concepts? Why can't we leave subjective experience in the phenomenological realm? If Reader Response theory and pedagogy are truly to be launched on an subjective philosophy of language and knowledge, floated on the methodological imperatives of contingency, relativity, and uncertainty, why do we feel the need to objectify and validate, to reinterpret and reconstruct affective experience at all? Why not plunge into the deep and open waters of indeterminate experience without the philosophical life preserver of rational empiricism? We will partially answer this question by discussing what may be not only the imperative that Reader Response Criticism shares with New Physics but the methodological limits of human knowledge itself.

Methodological Limits of Indeterminacy in Reader Response Criticism

There is a logocentric assumption that persists in Reader Response Criticism (indeed, in all criticism) and in attempts to apply Reader Response Criticism to the teaching of writing. It is an assumption that is so fundamental that it is hardly noticed and so pervasive that it blocks the further understanding of affective experience as a form of indeterminate knowledge on grounds other than formalistic and rationalistic ones, and so prevents the realization of Reader Response Criticism as a "new sophistic" for reading and writing. What impels us to describe, analyze, and measure subjective responses is the imperative and desire to *interpret* them. In Reader Response Criticism and its application to composition, as in other postmodern theories,[28] interpretation is still the primary function and goal of study, just as it is in New Criticism.

Interpretation is the fundamental methodology that underlies all classroom activity, whether it be an interpretation of a literary text, other kinds of texts, student responses to a text, or the motivations underlying student responses to a text. (In many ways, analytical method has been retained in Reader Response Criticism as well. Though not as formalistic as in New Criticism, analysis in Reader Response Criticism ranges from a return to a close examination of text based on subjective response, as in early Reader Response Criticism, to a "looser" discussion of the motives underlying response itself, designed to produce further interpretive knowledge, as in later theory such as Bleich's.) We construct heuristics to facilitate interpretation (of texts or response statements or subjective motivations). The classroom as a community is still an interpretive community.

Even Bleich, the most epistemologically extreme of Reader Response critics, makes interpretation the focus of his pedagogy, justifies it—that is, "reinterprets" it, as he admits—into a more satisfying form in order to provide a "rationale" for its retention in literary theory (much as Kuhn discusses how elements of the old paradigm are incorporated into the new paradigm in order to provide a persuasive rationale for the new paradigm and insure its acceptance and stability [*Scientific Revolutions* 7, 84–85, 103, 149, and 169]): "[U]nless I adduce a subjective logic of interpretation that resymbolizes the traditional notion of it in a more adaptive way, I will have no strong claim for any new interpretive authority. That is, unless we understand interpretation as a new systematic means of producing helpful knowledge, and unless there is a communal motive for believing in this means, there would be no point in setting any greater stock in interpretation now than we have in the past" (*Subjective Criticism* 69). But as Kuhn points out, although "interpretation of data is central to the enterprise that explores it. . . . [t]hat interpretive enterprise . . . can only articulate a paradigm, not correct it" (*Scientific Revolutions* 122). Kuhn goes on to say: "Paradigms are not corrigible by normal science at all. Instead . . . normal science ultimately leads only to the recognition of anomalies and to crises. And these are terminated, not by deliberation and interpretation, but by a relatively sudden and unstructured event like a gestalt switch" (122).

Despite the advances of Reader Response Criticism and other literary theories, interpretation, like New Criticism itself, remains the basis of teaching in English and of the institution of English studies itself (cf. Cain, *Crisis* 104; Culler 6, 10–11). Perhaps rightly so: interpretation not only helps us see more and know more about texts (at least within the parameters of the theory that employs it) but is also the foundation of all our knowledge. Exegesis is as old as myth and scripture, as old as the human race itself. As Bleich argues, "Whatever its degree of success, interpretation has consistently been the first and fundamental means of coping with the unsettling disharmonies of experience" (*Subjective Criticism* 68). But never has interpretation had the empirical and rational thrust it has had since Newtonian science; never in history has interpretation as a formalistic, rationalistic method been so much the focal point and sole purpose of study as it has since New Criticism.[29]

Interpretation as the method of teaching and criticism has become so embedded in our theory and practice that we regard it as a normal, natural, and inevitable (as well as a neutral) intellectual activity—as the only way of arriving at knowledge, as the only kind of knowing. This is a major consideration in our understanding of the limits of Reader Response Criticism for describing and teaching affective experience as a form of indeterminate knowledge. Reader Response critics recognize the importance of affect in reading and writing and attempt to explore it in a way that New Criticism could never allow (see Tompkins, *Reader Response Criticism* 21). But Reader Response Criticism and those who use it remain committed to comprehending affect—and comprehension itself—in terms of interpretation (in addition to the work discussed here, see, e.g., Blake; Farnan; Purves, *Porcupines*; Roskelly; Scriven; VanDe-

Weghe). In Reader Response Criticism, affective experience is conceived of and taught as a form of interpretive knowledge, rather than as a different kind of experience, another kind of knowledge as well.

The parallel between Reader Response Criticism and New Physics here is significant. Just as New physicists reinterpret interpretation (i.e., description) around the indeterminate elements introduced by methodological subjectivity but have to fall back on the formalistic, rationalistic imperatives of Newtonian science in order to describe subatomic phenomena, so too it seems that Reader Response critics reinterpret interpretation around the indeterminate elements of response but have to fall back on the formalistic, rationalistic imperatives of New Criticism in order to describe affective experience. If the need and desire to interpret propel description into the realms of subatomic phenomena and affective response, the exigencies of formalistic, rationalistic description to some extent drive interpretation.

The first problem with interpretation relates to the problem of method. We have already explored how inductive method is misleading, if not actually a fallacy, insofar as it is really highly deductive (Gross 22–23, Holton 48). Empirical observation, already doubtful given the nature of the senses and the role of symbolization of raw data into the structure of experience, is that much more problematic when investigating unobservable subatomic or affective processes even more dependent upon hypotheses and rational deduction. Given the difficulty of observation, Reader Response critics, like New critics, Newtonian scientists, and New physicists, *must* rely on rationality as the basis of interpretation (Fish, "Literature in the Reader" 55; Bleich, *Subjective Criticism* 66). Like Eliot and Tate (see appendix A), Fish and Bleich are concerned with preserving rationality as the basis of interpretation, though rationality is now "interpreted" differently. As Bleich explains it, "By consciously aiming for communal validation, the explainer is seeking relative truth value, as opposed to absolute truth. Ultimately, the only criterion of validation is the explanation's viability for the present, where viability refers to communal negotiation under existing standards of rationality" (66). While interpretation is necessary and not inappropriate to the study of subjective (and social) knowledge insofar as that knowledge is manifested in behavior amenable to empirical observation and rational explanation, what interpretation really gives us is a rational reconstruction (what Bleich calls resymbolization) of indeterminate phenomena (subatomic or affective) explicated in terms of theory or method itself. This is a problem that in some respects is like that found in the most extreme of scientific methods: logical positivism.[30]

In this sense, we can understand the reinterpretation of interpretation in both Reader Response Criticism and New Physics to be somewhat tautological insofar as it is based on the assumption of the necessity interpretation (just as arguments for technological procedures based on technological values are tautological [e.g., Skolimowski]). Edward Said makes a similar point concerning the prevailing "functionalist" view in literary criticism,[31] and faults Reader Response Criticism on these grounds as well. In considering the text "in itself a sufficient cause for certain precise effects it has on an ideal reader," Said says, "the text does not remain but is metamorphosed into what Stanley Fish has called a self-consuming artifact." Thus Said concludes that "[a] perhaps unforeseen consequence is that the text becomes idealized, essentialized, instead of remaining as the special kind of cultural object it is, with a causation, persistence, durability, and social presence quite its own" (48). In Reader Response Criticism and elsewhere, the *processes* of analysis and interpretation become the object of analysis and interpretation—the obscure object of desire.

Indeed, interpretation as a logocentric activity is perhaps not unrelated to the ideology of science and technology. The need and desire to interpret everything are perhaps at least partially driven by the "ideology of technique" itself—what Langdon Winner in *Autonomous Technology* calls a "technological imperative" (100–06)—the logical and ethical argument for the necessity and use of a technology based on technological values (cf.

Ellul, who actually indites interpretation *as a technology* [8]). As Patricia Bizzell observes in "Foundationalism and Anti-Foundationalism in Composition Studies," "anti-foundationalism is setting up its method in place of absolute standards of judgment it debunks. That is, it is promising that employment of method will confer objective mental powers similar to those that were supposed to be conferred by the absolute standard. This is what Fish calls the "theory-hope" of anti-foundationalism" (40). In fact, as Habermas demonstrates, the goals of logical explanation and systematic completeness may be the ideology of method itself, which drives research and so may actually work against or otherwise constrain the study of subjective (and social) knowledge. Subjective and social experience is transformed by the introduction of rational methods that "technologize" it (cf. Buber). Just as analysis commits us to describe even what we cannot see in empirical, referential terms, interpretation commits us to describe everything in its own, rational terms.

The second problem with interpretation is that formalistic, rationalistic description, endemic in a scientific culture, is highly spatial. Even a cursory examination may reveal that interpretation as a logocentric method is highly spatial not only in its commitment to induction, empiricism, and thus referentiality but also in its commitment to rationality and thus deductive logic. As Ong (*Orality* esp. 36–57, *Ramus* 51–130) and others have shown, the deductive method is predominantly "visual" insofar as it "places" abstract thought in spatially sequential, causal, and/or hierarchical relations. Although Ong's position, like Havelock's, has been characterized as bipolar, Ong states, "All thought, including that in primary oral cultures, is to some degree analytic: it breaks its materials into various components. But abstractly sequential, classificatory, explanatory examination of phenomena or of stated truths is impossible without writing and reading" (*Orality* 8–9).

The commitment to interpret, which leads to rational descriptions of affective experience, then, is also or at least in part a result of the epistemological visuality of our methods, grounded as they are in a spatial ontology of literacy itself. While certainly not as extreme as scientific analysis, literary interpretation as currently understood and practiced (even based on a subjective and social philosophy of knowledge) embodies vestiges of the visual impetus of inductive method: detached observation, exactness, accurate imitation—even in regard to the warmest intuitions, the fuzziest feelings. (Thus we say, your discussion is *clear, precise,* and *brilliant.*) If description is reinterpreted as interpretation in New Physics and Reader Response Criticism, interpretation still entails description—a spatial, referential understanding of meaning and knowledge *contained in* language and experience. (Thus we say, your interpretation is *deep, insightful,* and *revealing.* [For other visual and spatial metaphors we perceive, understand, and know by, see Lakoff and Johnson.])

As a manifestation of a logocentric mindset, an incarnation of visual method, interpretation assumes that experience (any kind of experience), no matter how probable, relative, contingent, uncertain, resides in and needs to be extracted from form (including the "form" of experience) as a condition of knowing. In a way that resembles Heidegger's discussion concerning the ideological nature of technology,[32] Susan Sontag points out in "Against Interpretation" that "[to] interpret is to impoverish, to deplete the world—in order to set up a shadow world of 'meanings'. . . . Interpretation, based on a highly dubious theory that a work of art is composed of items of content, violates art. It makes art into an article for use, for arrangement into a mental scheme of categories" (98–99). As a technology—even a "soft" technology (cf. Porush)—interpretation operationalizes experience, functionalizes it, renders it an object for use. Thus, the ideology of technique endemic in our scientific and technological society perhaps dominates our thinking, research, and practice in literature as it does in science. No matter what the epistemological thrust of the theory, our methods can be understood to "contain" within themselves formalistic imperatives of direct observation, accuracy, and completeness, and concomitant rationalistic imperatives of spatial containment and logical relation, imperatives that tend to bend inquiry (even this one) back to their own logocentric ends.

In retaining interpretation as its primary method, therefore, and (re)defining knowledge according to it, Reader Response Criticism perhaps also can be understood to reduce affective experience to a specialized (and spatial) object of study for the development and application of method. It is because of the imperative to *describe* affect in empirical and rational terms that we continue to interpret responses and so construct spatial categories, heuristics, schemata, and standards for doing so. Insofar as interpretation of hard to observe phenomena is based on the parameters of the "experimental apparatus" used, interpretation must reconstruct and determine experience according to its own criteria in order to "comprehend" it and so interpretation replaces subjective experience as the tangible "object" of study. As a method, interpretation inevitably turns the phenomenal field (whatever that might be) into visual objects and structural relationships, into observable instances of method for the purpose of investigation. For Bleich, the "literary artifact" is *totally* consumed in the resymbolization of subjective and social response statements (*Subjective Criticism* 213, passim).

It is perhaps for this reason that Bleich does not attempt to deal with the sensuous nature of language that we find discussed in Cassirer, whom he relies on for his understanding of the affective nature of symbols. While Bleich and other Reader Response critics recognize and attempt to deal with the emotional foundation of human language and knowledge, they (like everyone else) are more or less locked into logocentric assumptions about emotions, language, and knowledge by the imperative to interpret them. Thus, while interpretation (symbolization and resymbolization) may be central to human experience, we may still miss an important dimension of affective response: the nature of language as a physical, sensuous, oral form—as an affective, indeterminate form of knowledge in itself. Interpretation even may to some degree undermine rather than enhance the subjective experience of literature and writing.

As Bohr seemed to be aware (39), in what Gadamer might

call the hermeneutic circle of undecidability, we must rely on the "context of justification" to rationally reconstruct the process of discovery, explain our methods, and verify our results according to those explanations, those methods. Yet, as Gerald Graff has suggested, when literary method becomes tautological, literary study becomes self-referential and literature becomes irrelevant. Interpretation (even reinterpreted) may therefore represent what Polanyi (51) calls "destructive analysis," by which we attempt (and inexorably fail) to get at particular, "tacit" skills, yet must continue to engage in to check out "spurious observations," "specious practices," and "false interpretation." But are observations, practices, interpretation, all of which in this statement imply some objective standard of correctness, the best way to apprehend affective experience?

Just as yet unknown aspects or dimensions of subatomic reality may not be amenable to or explainable by our current, spatially oriented methods, unknown aspects or dimensions of feeling and emotion *as experienced* may not be wholly amenable to or explainable by them either. Affective experience in reading and writing may involve more than interpretation, even as Bleich understands it—as resymbolization of experience into a more subjectively and socially satisfying form (cf. Harding, "Psychological Processes" 54). That is, what Bleich calls "affective logic" may be a different sort of logic altogether. In fact, interpretation, used to describe and explain affective logic, may not be anything like affective logic, and it is doubtful that any Reader Response critic, including Bleich, would say so. If emotions do not occur in a determinate, observable space, if affective experience can be diffuse, inchoate, unfocused, would they be better understood and "described" as nonspatial, as a form of temporal knowledge?

The temporal dimension of experience is not well understood. Even in New Physics, time is conceptualized and only understood in spatial terms. For all the paradoxes it proposes to common sense, Einstein's relativity theory too was predominately visual: energy is a "field"; multidimensional points are still "points" (if no longer on a straight line); time is another "coordinate" *in* "space-time." Based on Kant's a priori categories of intuition, the concept of time, like the concepts substance, space, and causality, appears to be lodged in a spatial ontology of textual culture. This inability to comprehend time other than spatially may represent the limits of our knowledge of indeterminacy and is another significance of the parallel between New Physics and Reader Response Criticism. It's as if having led us to the brink of feeling, to the edge of indeterminacy, New Physics is unable to take the plunge into the "temporal abyss." We will discuss the problem of time in relation to describing affective experience in reading and writing in chapters 4 and 5, and appendix D.

If affective logic may not be so much spatial as temporal—or at least better understood that way—is it possible for us to back away from a scientific approach to the study of affective response, to shift metaphors and get out of our logocentric and into a phonocentric episteme, to understand emotions not referentially, as spatial meaning, but nonreferentially, as temporal experience? The temporal dimension of affective response to language may be more fundamental to, and more indicative of, an oral mindset. It may also be a primordial stage of response that cannot be known to consciousness. Even the prescient Eliot knew that consciousness of experience and feeling (even of time itself) is already an abstraction (*Knowledge and Experience*).

But the temporal dimension of language as sensuous sound may offer us a way of understanding the affective experience of language as an indeterminate form of knowledge, one that is neither wholly referential nor wholly rational. And that dimension of response is grounded not in the spatial, referential meaning of language, but in the temporal, nonreferential dimension of language as sound—not in interpretation, but in performance. Of course, here we merely shift the focus of study from heuristics and student responses to the sensuous form of language as the empirical object of study; but it is an empiricism based on the ear, not the eye. And while we still don't get at the black box of the mind but rather logically deduce effect and affect from the "outer environment" of language as sound, response to the sensuous nature of language as sound, as nonreferential, nonrational action, may be a little closer to tacit activities rooted in the physical nature of response, perhaps somewhere between linguistic and non-linguistic thought (see Weiskrantz); it may be a kind of knowing that *interpretation of knowledge* does not lead us to, a way of knowing grounded not only in the dimension of space but in the dimension of time—not spatial time, but "real" time.

Perhaps what we need, then, is a description of the non-formalistic, nonrationalistic, temporal dimension of affective response (or, if that paradox is not possible, of language as temporal action). Before we try to describe the temporal dimension of affective response to language, it would help to understand the sensuous nature of language as an affective, indeterminate form of knowledge. For this understanding, we now turn to the sophists and Cicero, who, living in a more oral culture, seem to have based at least a part of their epistemology of uncertainty and relativity on "the music of rhetoric" and thus built an early reader response theory on language as sensuous, physical experience. The physical dimension of language as sensuous experience, as the performance and reception of sound, can perhaps move us one step closer to understanding the temporal dimension of affective response. If we listen.

And we need to. For although Sypher was correct in pointing out that the visual preoccupation with method in literature and science was lessening, allowing "the recognition of the actuality of the contingent, the accidental" (241), he did not see that even in the investigation of indeterminate knowledge the imperative to describe formalistically and rationally is still operative in twentieth-century science and literature. In Reader Response Criticism and composition, as in New Physics, the attempt to discover "a unified field theory" that will describe "the universe of discourse" continues unabated. However, although it would appear that interpretation is the basis of knowing not only in science but the humanities[33]—even the uncertain arts of reading and writing as we currently understand them—perhaps Reader Response Criticism is not as bound by necessity to this logocentric metaphor and method as science is (though the latter too is debatable; we will touch on some conceptions of time in New Physics that may eventually lead us out of the space of our dilemma).

As Feyerabend suggests in regard to science (*Against Method* 30, 47, 52–53, 171), a plurality of rational and nonrational methods may be fruitful in exploring and describing indeterminate experience. As we continue to examine the limits of indeterminacy in scientific and literary practice and attempt to develop what we hope will be a better understanding of the temporal nature of affective experience and of the brain itself, we may find that we have to redefine literacy (cf. Ochsner, *Physical Eloquence*) and even knowledge itself—not only in terms of "shifting relations between speech and writing" (Elbow, "Shifting") but in terms of the relations between space and time as well. For the logocentric imperative to describe empirically and rationally—to analyze and interpret according to spatial modes of knowing only—reflects and represents the methodological limits of Reader Response Criticism and of the epistemic-social trend in rhetoric generally. For now, the need and desire to analyze and interpret are like a black hole from which nothing, not even light, can escape.

Three

Cicero as Reader Response Critic: Sophistic Rhetoric and the Epistemic Music of Rhetoric

From Poetry to Prose: The Sensuous Epistemology of the Sophists

Much revisionist scholarship in classical rhetoric has been concerned with sophistic epistemology, and the relationship between this epistemology and the social-epistemic trend in contemporary rhetorical theory has been noted (see Katz, "Epistemic Trend"). The revised understanding of the epistemology of the sophists of ancient Greece is also directly relevant to Reader Response Criticism and composition. In fact, the sophistic tradition in rhetoric is much more in line with contemporary theory and practice than we have been led to believe. The sophistic philosophy of language and knowledge, which can be understood to culminate in the rhetorical treatises of the Roman Cicero, can provide us not only with the techne of rhetoric that we associate with this tradition but with a theory of style as a sensuous, indeterminate form of knowledge. This theory, derived from a primary, oral rhetoric, in many ways constitutes an early reader response criticism that lends historical support for contemporary practice but also goes beyond it in making experience and performance rather than interpretation central to knowledge. (While oral interpretation as taught in speech departments also makes performance of literature central, by and large it regards these as aesthetic or cultural rather than "epistemological experiences" [see Bacon, *Art*; Beloof et al.; Gottlieb; Schrivner; Veilleux; but cf. Bacon in Fernandez]; we will discuss the value of oral interpretation later.)

The sophistic controversy concerning the relationship between epistemology and rhetoric—a battle over *paideia*, the correct philosophy of education and knowledge that has raged between "scientists" and "humanists" throughout history— has been traced back to the struggle between the sophists and Plato for the mind of ancient Greece (Hunt; Jaeger). Plato held that "True" knowledge exists in the realm of Ideal Forms. This abstract realm is outside of and prior to language and the senses; thus, rhetoric has no subject matter of its own. Only philosophers could attain this realm—and apparently they had to be philosophers of Plato's ilk and liking. For Plato, rhetoric (read style) cannot lead to knowledge. As he sets forth in the *Phaedrus*, only when rhetoric is founded on the scientific principles of dialectic can it be useful in communicating knowledge to those not capable of philosophical method. Ironically, then, Plato perhaps gave greater girth to rhetoric in the long run than he may have intended. But at the same time, Plato restricted rhetoric by making it separate from and secondary to knowledge, splitting philosophy from rhetoric, and rational thinking from emotional persuasion, a dichotomy sanctified in Descartes's mind/body duality and institutionalized by modern science.

Enos speculates that the confusion concerning the sophists results from Aristotle's treatment of them even more than Plato's ("Rhetorical Theory" 2–3; cf. Kerferd 5). In his *Rhetoric*, Aristotle attempted to answer Plato's demand by providing rhetoric with a scientific, philosophical basis. Contra Plato, however, Aristotle granted that there was a realm of uncertain knowledge that was opposed to apodictic or scientific knowledge and so made even dialectic, Plato's pride, a counterpart of rhetoric. For Aristotle, philosophy as well as rhetoric dealt with uncertain knowledge (*Rhetoric* I.1354a1): dialectic with philosophical argument, rhetoric with political and ethical arguments (I.1356a25–23). However, although Aristotle "demotes" dialectic, he still maintains that there is a realm of certain knowledge that rhetoric cannot deal with. Like Plato, Aristotle claims that rhetoric has no subject matter of its own. Thus, Aristotle too assumes a split between knowledge and language, between subject matter and words (*Rhetoric*, I.1358a21–24; 1359b5–18). Even though he allows somewhat for the social nature of philosophical and rhetorical knowledge because they deal in uncertainties, he obviously wishes it were not so.

This can be seen in Book III of the *Rhetoric*, where Aristotle somewhat grudgingly takes up a cursory discussion of style and delivery—in the same breath, as it were. Here Aristotle makes clear his distinction between reason and emotion, between objective knowledge and persuasion, between "raw facts" and style, and his preference for the former in every case. Style, Aristotle says, is "a necessary evil" "owing to the defect in our hearers"; the language arts have some "small but real" effect on intelligibility, says Aristotle, but are not as important as people think; we should really make our case with nothing but the "bare facts" (III. 1404a4–12). Even Aristotle's treatment of emotion in Book II is thoroughly rational and systematic. As Enos argues, Aristotle puts much more credence in abstract reasoning and systematic theory than he does in language, the senses, intuition, and emotions ("Rhetorical Theory"). The result of Aristotle's rapprochement between dialectic and rhetoric, says Enos, is that rhetoric becomes a philosophically rigorous and systematic art for the production of knowledge by rational heuristics (4). Given his view of rhetoric as "an explicit, rational process," it is not surprising that, according to Enos, Aristotle misunderstands and distorts the sophistic contribution to rhetoric (2–3). Despite uncertainties surrounding Aristotle's text itself, this is the view of the sophists that has been received and accepted throughout history and that has influenced the teaching of reading and writing.[1]

The philosophical strain between the sophists, Plato, and Aristotle, like that between literary and scientific theory and method, can at least in part be understood to have its origin in the rise of logocentrism in ancient Greece. For Ong, Havelock, Enos, Lentz, and others, there seems to be a connection between the introduction of the visual phenomenon of writing and the rise of the formalistic, rationalistic epistemology of Plato and Aristotle in which objectivity, autonomy, and discreteness become paramount considerations. In an oral culture, says Ong, knowledge is more additive rather than subordinated, aggregative rather than analytic, redundant and copious rather than innovative and sparse, formulaic rather than original, agonistically toned rather than neutral, empathetic and participatory rather than objective and distanced, situational rather than abstract (*Orality* 31–57).

It was the coming of writing that Ong, Havelock (*Preface, Muse*), and Lentz understand as underlying Plato's attack on the sophists and poets in general. Indeed, the philosophy of Plato and Aristotle can be seen as the metaphysical foundation and precursor of the formalistic and rationalistic philosophy that informs contemporary science as well.[2]

> Plato's entire epistemology was unwittingly a programmed rejection of the old oral, mobile, warm, personally interactive lifeworld of oral culture (represented by the poets, whom he would not allow in his Republic). The term *idea*, form, is visually based, coming from the same root at the Latin *video*, to see. . . . Platonic form was form conceived of by analogy with visible form. The Platonic ideas are voiceless, immobile, devoid of all warmth, not interactive but isolated, not part of the human lifeworld at all but utterly above and beyond it. (Ong, *Orality* 80)

This is not without paradox and problems, however. For in Plato's *Phaedrus*, Socrates also denounces writing. Yet, "Plato could formulate his phonocentrism, his preference for orality over writing, clearly and effectively only because he could write" (Ong, *Orality* 168). As Ong writes: "Plato's relationship to orality was thoroughly ambiguous" (167; see Havelock, *Preface*; Lentz (12–34).

But neither Aristotle nor Plato willingly accepted the sophistic belief in the central role of sensuous language in shaping our perception and knowledge of reality. Unlike Plato and Aristotle, the sophists held that all knowledge is subjective, and thus probable, relative, contingent, and uncertain, and could only be created in and through style. And they applied this epistemology to their pedagogy. True peripatetics (see Hunt), the sophists were wandering teachers and orators (much like composition teachers today) who made rhetoric the center of their educational philosophy and practice. Our true progenitors (cf. Jaeger 46), the sophists also made teaching the basis of their livelihood (if only they had asked for a little more money). But the philosophy and teaching of the sophists seem to hinge on a sensual, oral philosophy of language and knowledge that is opposed to the more abstract, "literate" one of Plato and, possibly with the exception of the elocutionary movement in the eighteenth century, to most of the subsequent rhetorical (and literary) tradition from the Renaissance down to the present.[3]

As W. B. Stanford noted in *The Sound of Greek: Studies in the Greek Theory and Practice of Euphony*, classical scholars and rhetoricians continue to ignore and dismiss the affective, sensuous dimension of language as unworthy of study (80). Except for Richard Leo Enos ("Rhetorical Theory," "Composing Process," *Greek Rhetoric*), few contemporary rhetorical scholars have recognized the epistemic music of rhetoric, the sensuous substance of words as sound in relation to thought, and the probable role it played in sophistic philosophy and composition. If this dimension of language, rooted in sound and physical delivery and/or response, has been denigrated and neglected in rhetorical theory since Plato and Aristotle, who rejected the affective, sensuous forms of language—at least in theory—in favor of formalistic method and rational heuristics, then perhaps in the history of rhetoric Plato and Aristotle can mark for us points in the transition from the poetic, nonrational prose of the sophists to the nonpoetic, rational prose of the subsequent rhetorical tradition in which sophistic style has been seen as excessive, deceptive, showy, unethical, and useless, and prose a mere shear medium for communicating facts.

In the history of rhetoric, then, the sophists too can be understood as representing not only an opposing epistemology to that of Plato and Aristotle but the beginning of an opposing tradition of writing as well, one that links poetry and rhetoric in sensuous oratorical prose and thus is directly relevant to "understanding" the affective experience of language. As Enos argues in *Greek Rhetoric Before Aristotle*, the development in rhetoric of writing—the transition from the poetry of the poets and rhapsodes to the poetic, nonrational prose of the sophists to nonpoetic, rational prose of Plato and Aristotle—was made neither simply nor cleanly and was intimately tied to the "shift" from orality to literacy (also see Thomas Coles; Enos, "Composing Process"; Lentz; Welch). Without having to accept the "Great Leap" from orality to literacy, an understanding of the possible relationships between sophistic epistemology and orality therefore may help us out of the methodological cul-de-sac that we now face in our attempts to apply Reader Response Criticism to literature and composition to teach affective experience as an indeterminate form of knowledge.

In fact, the poetic tradition of rhetoric that developed from early oral verse and song through oratorical eloquence to sensuous written prose, in which the music of rhetoric was epistemic—a way of coming to know—can be traced from the pivotal first sophists up through Cicero, whose later rhetorical treatises may represent the mature culmination of the sophistic "literary" tradition. This tradition can be read as an oral theory of reader response criticism, a forerunner of contemporary Reader Response Criticism, but one rooted in the physical nature of language as sound. Like Untersteiner, we do not "wish to retrace the whole history of the concept of 'sophist' " (xv); like Untersteiner, we also do not deny the real differences among the sophists in looking at their similarities (cf. Marrou 79; Schiappa). However, in this chapter we will not only explore the sophistic movement generally and as a whole but also extend it to Cicero and examine its relationship to Reader Response Criticism in order to use the former movement as a corrective and a touchstone for the latter.

In tracing the development of the sophistic tradition as a "history of reader response," we need to remember that our understanding of that epistemology and that tradition (especially in terms of response) is based on our current *episteme*, as Jarratt suggests (xv–xxiv), that our understanding is itself a rational reconstruction of essentially unknown experience and little understood processes, and so in the true sophistic sense, will be limited and uncertain. History is full of contradictory narratives that, like the paradoxical statement "everything I say is a lie," involve a infinite regress of reinterpretations (cf. Hofstadter for an entertaining romp through this and other paradoxes). Furthermore, our understanding of sophistic epistemology and tradition is based wholly on "secondary orality"—on the ability to read and write. Any understanding of a culture that was primarily oral must be partly speculative, if for no other reason than the fact that written records were not kept. But as Ong also points out: "We are so literate that it is very difficult for us to conceive of an oral universe of communication or thought except as a variant of a literate universe" (*Orality* 2). Although we can never really know what the sophists thought or experienced except in terms of literacy, literacy does provide us with the means to reconstruct orality in a way that orality could not, even though that reconstruction may be imperfect (*Orality* 15).

It is now well known and generally accepted that before the invention of the Greek alphabet around 720–700 B.C.E., and its interiorization around 500 B.C.E., poetry was central to Greek education and culture. Based on the work of Parry and Lord, Eric Havelock has demonstrated that in the oral culture that existed in early Greece, poetry was the primary mode for the retention and transmission of knowledge. As Havelock discusses in *Preface to Plato* (145–64), rhythm and meter served to fix knowledge in the memory through its pleasurable affiliation with music, as well as through the somatic response of motor reflexes. That is, the production of *and response to* rhythm and meter involve not only sound but the manipulation of speech organs and stimulation of muscles and nervous system and so serve to make knowledge sensually physical. According to Havelock, an audience under the spell of a recitation by poet or rhapsode was able to physically identify with and participate in "the message" and "imitate" it in a remembered mimesis of music. Rhythm and meter inscribe knowledge not only in memory but also "in the muscles." Likewise, Stanford discusses in great detail "the power of words to imitate and embody ideas and emotions" (115) in ancient Greek literature, investigating not only rhythm and meter but other musical qualities of ancient Greek language as well, such as speed of delivery, intensity, timbre-quality or sound texture, and pitch variation or word melody.

In a way that somewhat counterbalances charges concerning any sharp dichotomy between orality and literacy, Havelock suggests that in the chronological march from orality to literacy, the sophists began the search for a "new level of discourse (*logos*) and a virtuosity of conceptual vocabulary" (*Preface* 304). But he also states that the attempt "to rearrange experience in categories rather than events was first attempted and long continued within the confines of rhythm" (294–95). Ong states that manuscript culture felt works of verbal art to be more in touch with the oral plenum and never very effectively distinguished between poetry and rhetoric" (*Orality* 133). Lentz more or less confirms this when he explores the tension between oral (poetic "making") and written modes of composition.[4] Stanford too points out that the early sophists explored the sounds of words in great detail and depth and how a "prose-speaker could use effects of rhythm and assonance to influence his audience" (9).

More important, however, is the notion that response to the affective, sensuous dimension of the language of the poets was fundamental in shaping perception, understanding, and knowledge for the early sophists. In "Rhetorical Theory and Sophistic Composition: A Reconstruction," Enos explores the relationship between the sophistic conception of style as indirect knowledge and their epistemology that emphasized "relativism, sense perception, and probability" (1): "The sophistic tradition . . . did not stress an abstract system of heuristics but gave pre-eminence to poetic composition" (4). With their denial of a pure realm of Being and their distrust of the human mind and the senses, the sophists appear to have believed that knowledge could not be "discovered" by either empirical induction or rational deduction but rather was persuasively created in (and through response to) poetic arrangement and style—through "cadence and *kuntsprosa*," through the physical properties of language as sound (Enos, "Rhetorical Theory" 11). Thus, says Enos, the *dissoi logoi* (or two-opposed logoi in which one argued both sides of an issue) "was a convention for coming to know, not rationally but stylistically. Similarly, analogical thought in general, and metaphor in particular, is not realized through a rational process but, if effective, is apprehended immediately" (10).

This is a theory of response as well as composition. In an oral culture, experience seemed to be arranged according to what Havelock calls "the language of senses" (*Preface* 210). But the sense through which language enters is the ear, not the eye. The orality of speech, not the visuality of text, was the ontological basis of the sophistic philosophy of knowledge—of composition and of response. "Meaning could be realized through antithetical and analogical thought indirectly, while the cadence of the poetic discourse could be experienced to such an important degree that sophists could invent words as a 'song without the chord and the lyre' " (Enos, "Rhetorical Theory" 11). The music of rhetoric is rooted in the substance of words as sound. Alliteration, assonance, consonance, rhythm, meter, rhyme: repetition and variation of sound in time.

It is also well known that Gorgias, like many of the sophists, adopted and exploited the highly rhythmic, paratactic style of the poets and rhapsodes, to which the ancient Greeks responded enthusiastically, as evidenced by the popularity of plays, the recitals by the rhapsodes, and the centrality of poetry in daily rituals and ceremonial affairs (Carter). Interpreting Gorgias's dictum—Nothing is; that even if it is, it cannot be known; and even if it were known, it could not be communicated—Enos demonstrates that Gorgias's use of the poetic style was also related to questions concerning knowledge. This dictum on the uncertainty of knowledge is itself fraught with uncertainty,[5] and it was vehemently attacked by Plato as a denial of reality and an assault on Truth in his treatise derisively named after this sophist on whom the falsity of rhetoric was forever to be blamed (*Gorgias*).

But interpreting this dictum, Enos says that for Gorgias, all knowledge is incomplete, relative, contingent, and uncertain: There is no certain knowledge; if there were, we could never know it anyway because of our limited senses and mental capabilities; and if we could know it, we wouldn't be able to communicate it because of the inadequacy and limitations of human language itself ("Epistemology" 45–48; *Greek Rhetoric* 81–83). Since there is no Platonic realm of Ideal Forms to which to refer, all knowledge for Gorgias is based on speech, which, according to Enos, enters at the level of the senses, stimulates sensory reactions through the metaphorical [and musical] power of words, and thus evokes personal, emotional responses that are necessary to "deceive" the senses and persuade the listener into believing that one argument is truer than another ("Epistemology" 48–49; *Greek Rhetoric* 78–83). For Gorgias, emotional response to style is fundamental to knowing, rather than an " 'irrational' sensation," as it is for Plato (Enos, "Epistemology" 42), or "a defect in our hearers," as it is for Aristotle (*Rhetoric* III.1404a8–9). Poetic style is necessary given the human condition (cf. Untersteiner, esp. 191–92).

The problem of knowing subjectively, then, was for the sophists intimately related to an understanding the sensuality of style as an indeterminate but necessary form of knowledge. Espousing the belief that "man is the measure of all things," Protagoras apparently held that contradictory statements (is-is not) were both true (i.e., valid). But according to G. B. Kerferd, this doctrine of the *dissoi logoi* concerns propositions about qualities of phenomena, the predication of attributes, rather than actual phenomena, Being itself (94). As in New Physics and Reader Response Criticism, the epistemological problem is the nature of phenomena, not the ontological status of nature; it is one of knowledge about characteristics based on language, perception, and prior experience, not the existence of reality. (When that proverbial tree falls in the forest, there is a sound— at least insofar as we understand—whether we hear it or not; the question is how we experience it when we do hear it, what characteristics we attribute to that experience, and what we don't sense at all.)

Thus, contradictory statements about phenomena (i.e., the wind is cold, the wind is not cold) are both true in that they refer to individual perception and experience rather than reality or essence or Being. Since statements of predication only refer to individual human experience, no person's statement can be actually refuted (Kerferd 90–92). Knowledge of reality is subjective, uncertain, and mutable, and results in social value, not truth, as the criterion for determining which statement is better (Kerferd 105–06). But since it is in and through language that one predicates and responds to the nature or qualities of things, the epistemological issue depends on the definition and understanding of *logos*, the correspondence between word and thing.

The dominant assumption in Greek philosophy was that the word and the thing were one and the same (Kerferd 73). Thus, in the *Cratylus*, Plato explores the theory of origin and nature of language as sound, which held that the sound of letters and words were directly related to the objects they represent, a theory Socrates ultimately dismisses in the *Cratylus* as inconsistent and ludicrous (esp. 422b–440d). For Plato, there *is* a one-to-one correspondence between word and thing, but it is between *name as visual sign* and essence (or idea), *not sound* (389d–393d).

As Kerferd states, for Plato, "to each segment of reality there belongs just one *logos* and to each *logos* there answers just one segment of reality" (71). (Kerferd notes the similarity between this epistemology and the one held by the logical positivists: the logical positivists were concerned with the correspondence between the structural relations of language and the structural relations of reality; the ancient Greeks were concerned with the one-to-one correspondence between words and things themselves, between names and essences [73].)

However, for Gorgias, there was apparently no correspondence between reality and language, either as visual sign or sound (Kerferd 98). At first this may seem surprising, since we generally associate the symbolic power of language with referentiality. But for Gorgias, contradictory statements about phenomena were possible and equally valid (though not necessarily true) precisely because words bear no physical resemblance or direct relationship to the properties of the phenomenon they purport to describe or explain. Thus, Kerferd believes that Gorgias's dictum, like Protagoras's, is also a problem of predication. What Gorgias is addressing, Kerferd argues, is not whether some thing is or isn't but what characteristics it possesses. Again, the problem is not the existence of nature, but how we create, respond to, and know it. We do so through the emotional and associative power of language itself.

The same problem pertains in the relationship between phenomenon and thought. For Kerferd, what is most interesting about Gorgias's argument is that it

> opens up a contrast, indeed a gulf, between cognitive mental acts (thoughts, perceptions and so on) and the objects about which they are or purport to be cognitive. It seems to be being held that for anything to be known or thought it must have (i.e., repeat or reproduce and so itself possess) the appropriate characters of the object cognized. . . . [T]here is no attempt to abolish thinking, only to deny that we can say of thoughts that they are—likewise there is no attempt to abolish things. Indeed, the whole argument depends completely on the retention of both thinking and things. (97)

According to Kerferd, Gorgias could not accept Protagoras's belief that contradictory statements were equally valid. He could not because thoughts refer only to individual experience in which contradictions between phenomena and thought are inevitable, since the latter cannot be of the same nature or quality as the objects thought about. Because all statements refer to thoughts about phenomena that are inherently contradictory, they are in a sense equally invalid. We can neither think about nor communicate "knowledge" of an object in reality but rather must "deceive" listeners (and ourselves) into believing one statement over another through the evocative power of language—not as referential symbol but as *sensory experience* (cf. Enos, *Greek Rhetoric* 80–83).

The separation of thought and language from reality might make any knowledge and communication seem impossible. This is perhaps a basis of the charge that Gorgias was a nihilist (cf. Hunt 790). But for the sophists, knowledge and communication were possible, just highly affective and uncertain. It is the belief in the split between language and reality, and between feelings/thought and reality, that underlies sophistic relativism. And as Mario Untersteiner suggests, this relativism is the basis of a tragic perception of the human condition. Because thought and reality are separate, we can never know reality with any certainty; we can only know our own predications of it or our subjective responses to the language of others. And because language and reality are separate, we can never communicate that reality adequately, even if we could know it. We only communicate language itself.

Thus, the belief in the split between language and reality, and thought and reality, is conceivably the basis of the sophistic philosophy of style as epistemic music, and affective responses to it as subjective, indeterminate knowledge. Gorgias's dictum as interpreted by Kerferd only involves a gulf between thought and reality, and between language and reality, not between language and thought (redefined to include the affective, the sensuous, the physical). It is the *unity* of language and feeling/thought that makes predication, communication, response, persuasion, and belief—in short, knowledge—possible at all, albeit affective and uncertain. And it is the *power* of language as a sensuous form to create feeling, thought, reality by evoking sensory reaction—to fill the void between thought and reality and language and reality—that makes rhetoric the subjective (and social) basis of knowledge. In this radical epistemology of the sophists, the power of poetic language to create the sensory illusion of attributes in a powerfully persuasive simulacrum of reality, not through referential verisimilitude but through emotional response to the metaphorical and musical property of words, appears to be *necessary* for belief, knowledge, and action.

The orality of poetic style perhaps played a central role in this epistemology. In an "oral culture," thought is intimately related to speech. In an oral culture, to think at any length is to communicate (Ong, *Orality* 34). Even in a literate culture, says Ong, all language must be translated into sound to be fully understood (*Orality* 8). But in an oral culture, the unity, the power, and the necessity of poetic language derives from the essential orality of language, from sound as well as, if not more than, referential meaning. However, it may be that the sound of language (as opposed to silence of the page) is itself more sensory and leads to heightened sensory reaction, which is somewhat lost in the visual "abstraction" of writing (even in poetry when it is not read out loud).

Without having to necessarily accept the radical epistemology of the sophists or deny the referential function of language, then, we can begin to recognize the slighted importance of the epistemic music of rhetoric in response. When orally performed, language as sound is not separated from thought by the eye but is heard and apprehended simultaneously, holistically, immediately, and perhaps responded to more spontaneously, emotionally. As Ong argues, unlike sight, which dissects, separates, sound surrounds, penetrates (72). Ong on the interiority of sound: Sound has "a unique relationship to interiority when sound is compared to the rest of the senses. This relationship is important because of the interiority of human consciousness and of human communication itself" (*Orality* 72).

It would seem, however, that orality may be at the heart of the sophistic philosophy of the production and reception of style (as opposed to Plato and Aristotle, who believed in the efficacy of systematic theory and thus represent a move away from oral modes of thought and expression). Of course, orality was not the sole possession of the sophists. Orality permeated Greek thought and culture. "As in Homeric education, there was the essential Homeric element of music, which was central to the whole culture and acted as a link between its various parts, connected with gymnastics through dancing and through singing with poetry" (Marrou 38–39; Marrou further discusses the importance of music in Greek thought when he states that the Greeks "looked upon themselves first and foremost as musicians. Greek culture and education were artistic rather than scientific, and Greek art was musical before it became literary and plastic" [70]). Plato's philosophical dialogues were a product of orality too.

However, we have already touched on the paradox of orality for Plato (Havelock, *Preface*; Ong, *Orality* 167–68; Lentz 12–34). And Aristotle, even more so, moved away from oral modes of thought and expression, though there are borrowings and paradoxes in his work as well (Enos, "Rhetorical Theory; Lentz 165–74). But the sophists can be understood not only to have been influenced by oral modes of thought and culture around them but to have made them integral to their philosophy of thought and teaching. The unity, power, and necessity of sound: a sophistic credo of composition and response. For the sophists, the centrality of response to the emotional power of oral, poetic language in shaping human understanding and perception seemed to be fundamental. Not only did the sophists in general accept the limitations of reason and the senses, they reveled in them, epistemologically celebrated them, and built their philosophy of oratory (and response) around what they believed was the only "true" form of knowledge—a saturnalian style that has in history come under repeated attack.[6]

Isocrates: The Sophistic Connection

Given the gaps between language/reality and thought/reality, the essential unity of language and feeling/thought in oral, poetic style as an aural, sensory, and necessary form of knowledge is also crucial in understanding the sophistic philosophy of language and knowledge as it is incarnated in the rhetorical treatises of Isocrates, and perhaps Cicero, and applied to prose.[7] Indeed, Jaeger identifies Isocrates, who wrote contemporaneously with Plato, as "a genuine sophist" (48), "the post-war representative of the sophistic and rhetorical culture which had flourished in the Periclean period" (49). In fact, Jaeger attributes the virulence of Plato's attack on the sophists to the fact that sophistic rhetoric was still alive and well in the person of Isocrates—despite the fact that he was a writer and teacher rather than an orator; Jaeger states that when Plato attacked sophists, he was also, if not primarily, attacking Isocrates (47–48).

In fact, based on the sophistic epistemology, Isocrates (and Cicero) can be understood to have developed a philosophy of oratory and eloquence founded partially on oral and partially on literate modes of thought, one that forms a *reader* response criticism and that can inform our theory and teaching of affective experience in contemporary reading and writing. For whether we believe in the radical epistemology of the sophists or not, the sentient, somatic, and rhythmic reaction to the sensual, aural feel of language in relation to the evocation of memory, emotion, and thought may be an important element in creation and response, one that we either miss completely or attempt to describe formalistically, rationally, and abstractly by interpreting it.

Like the original sophists, Isocrates was not a mere "technician," nor a teacher who promised to teach "virtue" through rhetoric, as Plato's caricature of the sophists would have it (Jaeger 60). He was a sophist who wrote (cf. Enos, *Greek Rhetoric* 113–17). Again, any misinterpretation and misunderstanding of Isocrates may be due to differences in political and educational philosophies he has with Plato, which ultimately hinge on a fundamental difference of epistemology. And again, these differences of epistemology probably hinge on differences in and tensions between modes of thought inspired by orality and literacy. Following Havelock, Tony Lentz argues that Plato attacked writers for the same reason that he attacked poets and sophists: they only possessed the appearance of wisdom, not wisdom itself (11–34; 109–21). In the case of poets, the appearance of wisdom came from divine madness; in the case of the sophists, the appearance of wisdom came from speeches and techne that students memorized and used verbatim; in the case of writing, it came from the fact that "the speech-writer sells or gives written words to others to employ as if they represent the thoughts of the speaker" (114; cf. Enos, *Greek Rhetoric* 1–10).

Lentz dubs Isocrates the "first writer" (124). But although Isocrates wrote and published his speeches and only declaimed hem for his students, it is generally acknowledged that Gorgias's poetic style (and thus, we may reasonably suppose, Gorgias's philosophy of style) heavily influenced Isocrates (Jaeger 49; Lentz 131–33). (Cicero himself discusses how Isocrates adapted Gorgias's poetic style to rhetoric [*Orator* lii.175–liii.177].)

> Just as the sophists believed themselves to be the true successors of the poets, whose special art they had transferred into prose, so Isocrates too feels that he is continuing the poets' work, and taking over the function which until a short time before him they had fulfilled in the life of his nation. His comparison between rhetoric and poetry is far more than a passing epigram. Throughout his speeches the influence of this point of view can be traced. . . . Dynastic succession of rhetoric to poetry remained the true image of the spiritual process in which rhetoric arose as a new cultural force. (Jaeger 62)

Like the sophists, Isocrates believed in the power of literary style and adapted it to rhetoric. Like the sophists, Isocrates believed in the power of speech (both the production and reception of) to shape perception, thought, and civilization itself (Isocrates, *Antidosis* 253–57). And like the sophists, Isocrates also believed that the teaching of this style as knowledge would never be more than a contingent and uncertain process (*Antidosis* 274–76; *Against the Sophists* 9–13).

Plato was a writer too. As Lentz discusses, while Plato advocated the search for wisdom through oral dialogue, he did so in writing. But Lentz (22–23) argues that though the dialogue form retains the oral mode of thought, dialectic breaks what Havelock calls "sympathetic self-identification" (see *Preface* 145–46, 197–233) in which speakers and listeners in an oral culture "lose themselves" in creation and response, a state no doubt facilitated by the hypnotic trance of the somatic style of the poets and sophists who performed it orally. It was this somatic style, this identification of sensuous language and affective response as knowledge in which rational, analytical thought is (to some degree) lost, that Plato rejected *in theory* (cf. Ong, *Orality* 80); it wasn't until his last treatises, where (with the exception of *Laws*) he gives up any attempt to convey his philosophy in a pleasurable style that would appeal to his readers (Hamilton and Cairn 957; see *Parmenides*, *Philebus*, *Sophist*, and *Statesmen* collected in that volume).

Thus, although "Isocrates moves writing and composition a step away from the memory, recitation, and style of the oral tradition" (Lentz 122), Isocrates, unlike Plato, retains the poetic style *and* attendant epistemology of the sophists, adapting it to rhetorical prose. According to Lentz (128–30), Isocrates was the first to realize that "The Writer's Audience Is Always a Fiction" (Ong), that the "implied reader" is created by and contained in the text (Gibson). But while writing fostered in Isocrates the ability to conceive of an abstract, general audience, Isocrates "wrote to be read aloud, perhaps even recited" (Lentz 130). Significantly, Isocrates actually used writing to adapt and reinforce the oral, poetic style of the sophists in written rhetoric (Cicero, *Orator* li. 174–lii. 176): "the measure of his famous periods, his careful attention to rhythm, and his passion for euphony all show the use of writing as a method of reviewing and polishing a work in terms of its sound" (Lentz 124). And like some composition students and most creative writers today, Isocrates used audience response to oral recitation (only a few friends or students, of course, given his congenital shyness) to revise and correct his prose for sound (Lentz 135).

Unlike Plato, then, Isocrates conceives of written composition in terms of poetry (in the original meaning of that word)—as "a kind of making itself, in that the written word preserved an image of the word in the mind, in the living intelligence of the maker. Isocrates herein took the Archaic conception of the written word as a form of preservation and molded this preservation into an art that captured the shape and form of the thought of man" (Lentz 125). It is likely with Isocrates, then, that writing becomes a way of "making meaning," of "discovering what we know." Again, we sense here the unity of language and thought in the living style that Isocrates brought to written rhetoric. But while "[w]riting, for Isocrates, was a more direct representation of his thought, with only an implicit relationship to the spoken word" (Lentz 125), that representation, that relationship, "the shape and form of thought" itself, was still one very much rooted in sound (129). So was his attention to the response to the sound of his writing, which he solicited from his intimate audience.

If Isocrates used writing to facilitate speech, he also used speech to facilitate writing. As Lentz relates, Isocrates wrote to be appropriate both for contemporary and for future audiences. However, eloquence, even in writing, does not involve fixed methods, immutable rules; rather, as Jaeger discusses, "Perfect eloquence must be the individual expression of a single critical moment, a *kairos*, and its highest law is that it should be wholly appropriate. Only in this way can it succeed in being new and original" (61). Just as John Poulakos points out that *kairos* in speaking in and response to a situation depends on good timing (38–39), Isocrates' treatises as words and deeds perhaps demonstrate that *kairos* applies to writing as well. Isocrates seems to have transferred the notion of *kairos* from speech to writing, consciously embedding "good timing" in the sensuous unity of his form and content, in the rhythm of his style. Perhaps music, that universal language, could facilitate *kairotic* response in and to writing for all time.

For Isocrates, "oratory is imaginative literary creation" (Jaeger 62). Isocrates illustrates what George Kennedy calls the *letteraturizzazione* of the sophistic strand of rhetoric, the process of "literaturization" of rhetoric in writing that Isocrates "carried to full development . . . in the fourth century" (*Classical Rhetoric* 16). But it was a fortuitous accident of personality and history that Isocrates was not a good speaker, for he facilitated and continued the transition from poetry to prose begun by the early sophists, the development of a literary rhetoric that retained the oral, "musical" modes of thought—of communication and response—in an age of growing literacy. As Jaeger discusses, "[B]oth the rivals, philosophy and rhetoric, spring from poetry, the oldest Greek paideia; and they cannot be understood without reference to their origins in it." Significantly, Jaeger adds that "as the old rivalry for the primacy of culture gradually narrows to a dispute about the relative values of philosophy and rhetoric, it becomes clear enough that the ancient Hellenic partnership between gymnastic training and musical culture has at last sunk to a much lower level" (47).

However, in Isocrates' analogy between oratory and sports (cf. *Antidosis* 180–90), we still hear the echo of a deep belief in a rhetoric, maybe even written rhetoric, rooted in physical, oral, and thus indeterminate performance of human language:

> [B]oth the teachers of gymnastic and the teachers of discourse are able to advance their pupils to a point where they are better men and where they are stronger in their thinking or in the use of their bodies. However, neither class of teachers is in possession of a science by which they can make capable athletes or capable orators out of whomsoever they please. They can contribute in some degree to these results,

but these powers are never found in their perfection save in those who excel by virtue of both talent and training. (*Antidosis* 185)

Indeed, despite the continued chauvinism,[8] for Isocrates it seems that rhetoric, and response to it, is still grounded in intuition based on sense experience, or as Jaeger states, "an aesthetic and practical faculty which, without claiming absolute knowledge, can still choose the right means and the right end. His whole conception of culture is based on that aesthetic power" (63). And this is the difference between sophistic Isocrates and Plato as writers. For while Plato's philosophy is poetic, even erotic, Plato did not make the affective response to and experience of this eroticism the basis of knowledge. On the contrary, at best, as in the *Phaedrus*, a sinuous, voluptuous style could only be displayed to convey knowledge already gained by dialectic—to clothe beautiful ideas in beautiful bodies for those unable to engage ("see") them any other way.

But for Isocrates, as for the early sophists, sensitivity to the sensory, corporeal nature of verbal language seemed to be a necessary basis of knowledge—both in creation and response— and thus a prerequisite for the student-orator. For Isocrates, "ability, whether in speech or in any other activity, is found in those who are well endowed by nature and have been schooled by practical experience" (*Against the Sophists* 14). Isocrates holds natural talent, and then practice, to be the paramount concerns in developing both speakers and writers (*Against the Sophists* 15). Last come rules, theory, and method. Isocrates makes it clear that the student must bring to the study of oratory "the requisite aptitude," have "a vigorous and imaginative mind" (*Against the Sophists* 18–19). (This of course accords with Lentz's observation that in an oral culture, teaching, like *ethos* itself, is "physical" in the sense that it takes as its referent the "presence" of the "living intelligence" of the human being.) But for Isocrates, the student also must possess and bring to his study a "musical talent." What is utmost in oratory (and in writing) is the character of the speaker and "a voice and clarity of utterance which are able to captivate the audience, not only by what he says, but *by the music of his words"* (*Antidosis* 189; emphasis mine).

Isocrates' treatment of literature thus bears the epistemological imprint of the sophists. For example, one purpose of literature for Isocrates is to teach "virtue" by example, inasmuch as that is possible (*Antidosis* 277). Like the sophists (Marrou 77–82), Isocrates thus treats virtue not as Ideal Forms, but as a practical aesthetic, one that involves the education of the intuitive faculty and leads to action that can be judged (Jaeger 49); but for Isocrates as for the sophists (Hunt 78–79), a moral education through response to literature was itself a physical, affective, and thus uncertain process (cf. Ochsner 24–25).[9] In fact, if Isocrates criticized the teachers of rhetoric (both the absolutist philosophers and the technical rhetoricians) who claimed they could teach wisdom and virtue by formal rules and methodologies of oratory, or, as H. I. Marrou states, "as a perfect machine that was bound to function without fail, no matter what the morality of the person applying it" (126), Isocrates also criticized those who thought literature could do so.

> Literature—the art (not the science) of speech—is the best instrument for sharpening the faculty of judgment. The instrument is not in itself sufficient, a certain gift is needed too, for in this field of reality—moral, human reality—*there can be no infallible system ensuring that any mind will get the right result simply because it is rational.* There was nothing more absurd in Isocrates' view than the Socratic's attempt to turn "virtue" into a kind of knowledge, a science like mathematics, that could be taught. . . . [T]his is so because the effort to find the right expression demands and develops a sensitivity of thought, a sense of different shades of meaning, which it is difficult to express in conceptual ideas, and even, sometimes, impossible. (Marrou 134; emphasis mine)

In this book, we are concerned not so much with ethics as with the physical nature of language and knowledge and the implications of this for reading, writing, and rhetorical education generally. If virtue, like eloquence, is physical, there cannot really be any separation between language and human personality, between knowledge and the human beings who speak and write and read and teach it, a point Booth (*Company*) makes in our time. As Isocrates (and Cicero) understood, that separation, that reduction, is a result of our methods. Contrary to Knoblauch and Brannon's understanding of the classical tradition (cf. reviews by Hagaman, Enos, Halloran, Robertson, and Larson), the sophistic strain of classical rhetoric constitutes a strong argument against the predominance of "objective" teaching methods in the classroom. For as Marrou (302) seems to point out, it was not specialized technique that the ancients were interested in teaching, as we in a more scientific society are, but a general theory of what it means to be human. It is not the technological *ethos* that the study of rhetoric, literature, and humanities (or, given the new philosophy of language and knowledge under consideration here, even science and technology) should impart. It is a human one. Science and technology, like rationality, are only parts of knowledge, parts of what it means to be human.

The problem of the physical nature of knowledge and the indeterminacy of method applies to the use of response to literature to teach oratory as well as morality. If for Isocrates a moral education through response to literature was itself a physical, uncertain process, it is conceivable that response to a "musical" education was as well. Interpretation was not the goal of instruction; language as physically experienced, as performed and heard, was (see appendix C; cf. Marrou 126; Enos, *Greek Rhetoric* 114). Jaeger states that Isocrates does pick up Plato's "doctrine of a rhetorical system of ideas" based on an analogy with the alphabet in which "a large number of variously assembled shapes are reduced to a limited number of basic 'elements', and thus the meaning of each of the apparently manifold shapes is recognized" (61). But Jaeger adds, "Oratory which knew no more than these forms would be as sounding brass and a tinkling cymbal. The letters of the alphabet, immovable and unchangeable, are the most complete contrast to the fluid and manifold situations of human life" (61; note the musical metaphors here). While Isocrates in general certainly does not throw out the teaching of principles and techniques (*Against the Sophists* 18–19), he seems to indicate that these are not what are most important. In fact, Isocrates actually goes so far as to intimate that in almost every case the orator with just natural talent and a charismatic personality, but with no training, would be superior to the orator with little talent or personality who had learned all the rules and principles of oratory (*Antidosis* 190).

Of course, as far as oratory goes, one reason for the uncertainty of a rhetorical education is the variability of subject and occasion: "no system of knowledge can possibly cover these occasions, since in all cases they elude our science," says Isocrates in the *Antidosis* (184). When knowledge is held to be subjective, it is the variability of the speaker that makes a formal system of rules for eloquence, like a system for response, ultimately impossible. "More than any other sphere of life, the art of oratory resists the effort of systematic reason to reduce all individual facts to a number of established *schemata*, basic forms," says Jaeger; "[i]n the realm of logic, Plato calls these basic forms the Ideas" (61). But the uncertainty of a rhetorical education for Isocrates perhaps also has something to do with the difficulty of teaching the *kairotic* unity of language and thought in speaking and writing as a physical performance of sensuous sound.

Given Isocrates' penchant for writing his speeches down and using these as well as literary masterpieces as "models" for his students to "imitate" (again, see my discussion in appendix C), this difficulty for Isocrates may have applied to reading and writing as well as speaking. In fact, there was not as much difference between reading, writing, and speaking for Isocrates as there is for us. The focus of his instruction was "speech composition" (Enos, *Greek Rhetoric* 113). Until fairly recently, orators wrote to be heard (Ong, *Orality* 10; 115). While oratorical-literary production is superficially different from reception, oratory and writing, and response to speech and reading, can be understood as similar not only in terms of the process of making (and interpreting) meaning but also in terms of the physical performance of the sounds and rhythms of speech. For reading, like speaking and writing, is inexorably oral in nature (Ong, *Orality* 8; Halloran and Bradford 191). As more scholars in contemporary composition are beginning to actively explore (e.g. Perl; Elbow, *What is English*; Schultz; Ochsner), the subjective nature of knowledge, of eloquence and of response, entails the entire physical character of the speaker-writer-reader. It must also entail the physical character of language as sound.

Cicero's Poetic Philosophy of Style as Epistemic Music

Given the differences between Isocrates and Plato as writers, in the transition from orality to literacy—in the gradual movement from "primary" (oral) rhetoric to literary (written) rhetoric—there seemed to be at least two traditions of writing. There was the nonpoetic Attic "plain style" more or less institutionalized by Plato and Aristotle that we have inherited. And there was the poetic, musical style transferred to prose by the sophists that perhaps survives and develops relatively intact at least through Isocrates to Cicero. In fact, it could be argued that Cicero himself was a sophist.[10] Although scholars have generally acknowledged Cicero's debt to Isocrates, in treatments of classical rhetoric, Cicero, unlike Isocrates, has not been thought of as a descendent of the sophists. Rather, Cicero has been regarded as a sort of neo-Aristotelian who classified and established systematic procedures for the production of eloquence (Howell 75–76). Given the enormous influence of Aristotelian rhetoric, with its rational, systematic treatment of the art (Enos, "Rhetorical Theory" 11), it is easy to understand why.

Cicero also has been categorized as a "technical rhetorician" based on his first treatise, *De Inventione*, a handbook for advocates in the law courts (Kennedy, *Classical Rhetoric* 37).[11] We will have reason to explore the connection between Ciceronian and sophistic philosophy more in the next section (also see appendix B). But the direct relationship between Isocrates' and Cicero's philosophy of style can help us begin to understand what a reader response criticism based on oral modes of thought and expression would "look like." Morris Croll understands Cicero to be the inheritor and progenitor of the classical strain of musically ornate or "Asian" prose style originated by the sophists (as opposed to the Attic, or plain, style based on writing used by Aristotle and the Stoics that flourished in the Renaissance). Croll argues that the periodic style based on units of rhythmic sound in the oratorical prose of Gorgias and Isocrates was the standard form of prose in Greece as well as Rome, reaching its fullest and most mature expression in Cicero (54–61) and that this oratorical prose style was the standard until the sixteenth century.[12]

Although Cicero lived in slightly cooler, more literate climes than did the sophists or Isocrates, "Cicero's Rome was an 'oral' society" (Enos, *Literate Mode* 4). "Yet," Enos adds, "in a real sense Republican Rome was also a literate society" (4). Thus, much as Lentz, a student of Enos, discusses the relationship between orality and writing that coexisted in Isocrates' Greece, Enos states that "[Roman] society, while understandably dominated by oral modes of expression, had integrated written discourse, even if its primary function was to facilitate and preserve oral discourse" (4). In fact, just as Lentz credits Isocrates with being the "first writer" to have actually internalized literate modes of thought and used them to enhance and polish oral expression in order to capture and preserve the speech event for audiences not bound by orality to a specific time and place (123–24), Enos argues that Cicero used writing to "facilitate [oral] modes of thought and expression. Specifically, considering abstract concepts, articulating apodictic and coexistent relationships, and structuring prose-rhythmic passages that articulate such relationships lucidly benefit from writing ability" (Enos, *Literate Mode* 35) and that Cicero's texts captured the "robustness" of the speech event (xii).

Thus, Cicero, like Isocrates, used writing to develop a more literate theory of oratory and response but one still very much animated by sound in performance. Despite the later, more literate date, Cicero, like Isocrates, seems to have conceived of prose style in terms of poetry and music. Given the virulence of the anti-Ciceronian movement in the Renaissance, there is little doubt of this, though the testaments of history are sometimes wrong.[13] Cicero's love of musical style is easily seen (and heard) in his consideration of the relationship between rhetoric and poetry in his later, more mature treatises. For Cicero, as for Isocrates and the sophists, rhetoric, historically derived from poetry, was similar to it. In Book I of *De Oratore*, Cicero says: "The truth is that the poet is a very near kinsman of the orator, rather more fettered as regards rhythm, but with ampler freedom in his choice of words, while in the use of many sorts of ornament he is his ally and almost his counterpart" (xvi.70). And oratory and poetry are historically derived from music, and are similar to it (*D. O.* III.xliv.174): both poetry and oratory rely on and employ the music inherent in language, the rhythms and sounds of words. In our time, Richard Lanham also argues against the distinction between poetry and prose based on rhythm and meter; rhythm is as fundamental to good prose as it is to poetry, fundamental to the act of reading as a rhetorical performance.[14]

Later, in the dialogue of *De Oratore*, Crassus, Cicero's mouthpiece, also allows that "the old Greek masters held the view that in this prose style it is proper for us to use something almost amounting to versification, that is, certain definite rhythms" (III.xliv.173). Though prose is written more in "free style" (III.xlviii.184), meter also acts as norm in prose as well as poetry (and in this sentence), establishing a baseline against which rhythm (and variation in cadence) can be heard: "if all sounds and utterances contain an element of rhythm possessing certain beats and capable of being measured by its regular intervals, it will be proper to reckon this kind of rhythm as a merit in prose, provided that it is not used in an unbroken succession" (III.xlviii.185). Despite the fact that Aristotle forbid the frequent use of certain meters in oratory, Crassus states that certain meters are suitable as long as it doesn't "fall into down-right verse or something resembling verse" (III.xlvii.182). In fact, Crassus reports he agrees that meters used in verse, such as anapest (dithyramb) "occur widely in all opulent prose" (III.xlviii.185).

For Cicero, the effective use of rhythm in prose actually seems to be one difference between "an inexperienced and ignorant speaker" and the orator who "links words and meaning together in such a manner as to unfold his thought in a rhythm that is at once bound and free" (*D. O.* III.xliv.175–76). Although Cicero, like Isocrates, transfers an oral conception of poetic style to prose, perhaps because he did live in a more literate time and place, as Enos demonstrates, Cicero does not unequivocally accept or adopt either the high literary style of the poets and rhapsodes or its adaptation by the sophists and Isocrates to oratory.[15] But despite some qualifications, Crassus agrees that "at all events polished and systematic prose must have a rhythm" (III.xlviii.184).

The "poetic" nature of prose is also important for our understanding Cicero's philosophy of style as a theory of affective response. For while Cicero is talking about (and writing in) Latin here, the same principles may be applicable to the performance of reading and writing in English, which is generally thought to be iambic (see Saintsbury, *A History of English Prose Rhythm*; but cf. Hoover, who argues it is not). As teachers of oral interpretation know, one reason for using rhythm and meter in prose, like melody in music, of course, is to provide pleasure (*D. O.* III.xliv.174). The origin, says Crassus, is physical: "nature herself modulates the voice to gratify the ear of mankind . . . and this cannot be achieved unless the voice contains an element of rhythm" (III.xlviii.186). Physically produced by the pulse of breathing and the rise and fall of the voice, rhythm is essential to both poetry and oratory because of its aesthetic appeal to the ear (*Orator* lx.203). For Cicero, the sensuous nature of language as pleasurable sound supersedes and subsumes the necessity of breathing (cf. Leff, Untitled 13, on beauty and necessity, discussed in the next section). While the production of style has a physical basis—the lungs, the standard of the orator's art—rhythm and meter, like that of the poet and the musician, are dictated by the ear (*D. O.* III.xlvi.181–xlvii.182).

Like Isocrates and the sophists, then, Cicero's conception of what Michael Leff calls "affective stylistics" (Untitled 2) seems to be rooted in the intuition of the physical sensation of language as performed by the voice. To his own question as to "what produces the pleasure," Cicero answers: "The same phenomenon as in verse; theory sets down the exact measure of these, but without theory the ear marks their limits with unconscious intuition" (lx.203). But it is more than a matter of pleasure. For Cicero, as for Isocrates and the sophists, rhythm seems to be a tacit, physical form of knowledge, one that constitutes a "natural" basis of response and persuasion. The following passage, from *De Oratore*, is significant for our understanding of Cicero's philosophy of style as a theory of response:

> [D]o not let anybody wonder how these things can possibly make any impression on the unlearned crowd when it forms the audience, because in this particular department as in every other nature has a vast and indeed incredible power. For everybody is able to discriminate between what is right and what wrong in matters of art and proportion by a sort of *subconscious instinct, without having any theory of art or proportion of their own*; and while they can do this in the case of pictures and statues and other works to understand which nature has given them less equipment, at the same time *they display this much more in judging the rhythms and pronunciations of words, because these are rooted deep in the general sensibility, and nature has decreed that nobody shall be entirely devoid of these faculties*. And consequently *everybody is influenced not only by skilful arrangement of words but also by rhythms and pronunciations*. For what proportion of people understands the science of rhythm and metre? yet. . . . It is remarkable how little difference there is between the expert and the plain man as critics, though there is a great gap between them as performers. *For as art started from nature, it would certainly be deemed to have failed if it had not a natural power of affecting us and giving us pleasure; but nothing is so akin to our own minds as rhythms and words.* (III.l.195–li.197; emphasis mine)

In the *Orator*, another late treatise, Cicero again discusses the importance of the musical dimension of language in communicating knowledge: "however agreeable or important thoughts may be, still if they are expressed in words which are ill—arranged, they will offend the ear, which is very fastidious in its judgement" (xliv. 150). In this treatise too, Cicero points up the power of response to the rhythm and the sound of words as a form of affective knowledge: "Not that the multitude knows anything of feet, or has any understanding of rhythm; and when displeased they do not realize why or with what they are displeased," says Cicero. "And yet nature herself has implanted in our ears the power of judging long and short sounds as well as high and low pitch in words" (li. 173).

In fact, Cicero seems to believe that the music of language, along with knowledge of subject matter, is an epistemic basis of eloquence—the "ideal" but necessary unity of form and content: "to speak with well-knit rhythms without ideas is folly, to present ideas without order and rhythm in language is to be speechless" (*Orator* lxxi. 236). Combined with knowledge of subject matter, music as an epistemic basis of eloquence is not a matter of theory or heuristics but is rooted in the ear: "the decision as to subject-matter and words to express it belongs to the intellect," says Cicero, "but in the choice of sounds and rhythms the ear is the judge; the former are dependent on the understanding, the latter on pleasure; therefore reason determines the rules of art in the former case, sensation in the latter" (xlviii. 162). As Stanford seems to have understood, the response to musical properties of verbal style constitutes a kind of tacit, affective knowledge, one that is inherent in and fundamental to speech. For Croll as well, music, not science, is the basis of studying rhythm (436).[16]

The notion of response to the music of style as a kind of instinctual knowledge is in harmony with the Isocratean-Ciceronian notion that everyone possesses "natural talent" to varying degrees, which enables both eloquence and response but which cannot be taught by theory or rules alone (Cicero, *D. O.* III. xviii. 70). This notion is thus also in harmony with some of the basic premises of contemporary composition theory concerning students' innate verbal abilities (see Shaughnessy; Elbow, *Writing*) but strikes a different chord in a related key. It is obvious that the discussion here is about the production and response to style *in speech* rather than in writing and so may seem more appropriate to oral interpretation than to reading and composition. "Delivery, I assert, is the dominant power of oratory," says Cicero (*D. O.* III.lvi.213). But the "musical training" of the voice (and ear) may help us teach "voice" in writing as well.

In the *Orator*, Cicero explicitly discusses the importance of the "music" of the voice *in delivery*: "For the voice possesses a marvellous quality, so that from merely three registers, high, low, and intermediate, it produces such a rich and pleasing variety in song." (xvii.57). Delivery is the art of rendering style audible, insofar as the human voice, by virtue of physical necessity and nature, is musical. Thus Cicero advises: "Let art follow the leadership of nature in pleasing the ear. . . . The superior orator will therefore vary and modulate his voice; now raising, now lowering it, he will run through the whole scale of tones" (xvii.58–59). But in Cicero's discussion of delivery as a kind of musical performance of three registers, we may also hear the oral inception and musical basis of the plain, middle, and grand styles that a more literate culture understood as the three "offices" of the orator and that we have applied more statically to writing. However, Cicero seems to suggest that the three styles characterize all eloquence and correspond to the fluid functions of instructing, delighting, and moving an audience in any given speech: "*at one moment* we use a dignified style, at another a plain one, and at another we keep a middle course between the two; thus *the style of our oratory follows the line of thought we take, and changes and turns to suit all the requirements of pleasing the ear and influencing the mind of the audience*" (*D. O.* III.xlv.177; emphasis mine).

In fact, in the *Orator*, the older Cicero lays out what Ochs in the prefatory remarks to his synopsis of *Orator* calls a "unified and coherent" theory of oratory, one situated in the aesthetic principle of style (136). This theory at once takes in both the literary style of the poets and its adaptation to oratory by the sophists and Isocrates and goes beyond them in a way that represents the further, more "literate" development of sophistic theory of rhetoric and response. The use of the three styles, "the plain style for proof, the middle style for pleasure, the vigorous style for persuasion" (*Orator* xx.69), is governed by propriety, which for Cicero is the "foundation of eloquence" (xx.70). Cicero says that the orator who can command the plain style "and has not conceived of anything higher, if he has attained perfection in this style, is a great orator, if not the greatest" (xxviii.98). Significantly in terms of the transition from poetry to prose, Cicero equates the middle style, to delight and please, with the sophists (xxvii.96). However, Cicero states that it is in the vigorous or grand style in which "is summed up the entire virtue of the orator" (*Orator* xx.69). "The orator of the third style is magnificent, opulent, stately and ornate; he undoubtedly has the greatest power" (xxviii.97).

The vigorous grand style can, of course, be learned from the study of poetry (*D. O.* III.x.39), the middle style from the study of the sophists (cf. *De Optimo Genere Oratorum*), and the plain from the Attic orators. But Cicero qualifies his advocacy of the style of poetry based on the maturing notion of propriety, just as he qualifies his advocacy of the style of the sophists (*Orator* xix.66). Although the greatest orator is the one who is capable of achieving the grand style, he or she must also command the middle style, which Cicero associates with the sophists, as well as the plain, or Attic, style—and know when and how to use them all in any given speech (*Orator* xx.69–xxviii.99). While Cicero recognizes the power of the grand, vigorous, copious style and considers the orator who has this "the chief," he says we should despise the orator who only has the grand style, that in fact this orator (like the ancient poets speaking in dithyrambs, touched by divine hands) will seem "to be scarcely sane . . . a raving madman among the sane, like a drunken reveller in the midst of sober men" (xxviii.99).

Ultimately, then, the power of eloquence depends on propriety, which is rooted in *kairos* and serves to make any one of the three styles so appropriate it becomes almost invisible. The invisibility of style based on propriety is also evident in Bruce Psaty's discussion of the role of metaphor in *De Oratore*.[17] Given the notion of eloquence as a unity of form and content, then, what Cicero seems to mean by plain style is not merely reporting of the facts, or by the middle style, mere embellishment. Rather, at every level, style does not only *appeal* to the senses, as Psaty correctly indicates (112); it also "shapes" and "illuminates" thought and experience in speech by making it orderly and apparent and so deceives the senses, including sight (cf. DiLorenzo 258), yet remains invisible itself at any given moment by the operation of propriety (cf. *Orator* xxi.72).

The invisibility of style—even metaphor—can be understood especially in regard to orality; in declamation, recitation, even just reading aloud, style is not "visual" (at least until it is read silently), and because it is not, it does not afford the luxury of perusal. In speech, there is no time to think about the logical relations of tenor and vehicle; in speech metaphors are immediately affective, but hidden, perhaps in much the same way that Lakoff and Johnson suggest many of the metaphors that underlie our thought are hidden in everyday speech. In this sense, style as musical sound gives order and bodily shape to thought and speech (whether oral or written) and at the same time remains invisible (nonreferential) itself. Thus, an "oral notion" of style perhaps also leads to the sophistic belief in the power of language to deceive and persuade the senses, as well as the deeply held conviction that knowledge is uncertain.

For Cicero too, style is epistemic. At every level, style involves what Susanne Langer calls "symbolic transformation," which Enos himself compares to the sophistic philosophy of language ("Rhetorical Theory" 1). In fact, the notion of holistic response to oral language corresponds to Langer's concept of presentational symbols already mentioned in chapter 2 and to be discussed in more depth in chapter 5. But perhaps, as Cicero seems to suggest (*D. O.* III.l. 195–197), holistic response occurs more often or more easily with "sound symbols," such as music or verbal language, rather than "sight symbols," such as painting. Style is perhaps even more epistemic when orally performed, where the inherent music of rhetoric heightens and reveals the power of language to evoke and affect not only ideas but emotions and the senses. And the epistemic music of style occurs to varying degrees at every level. At its best, perhaps even the plain scientific style is aesthetically pleasing, has a physical feel in the face, is musically tight in the mouth, though not always obviously so. If Enos points up the power of style for Gorgias as an indirect, affective form of knowledge to enter at the level of and deceive the senses, the *invisibility of style* based on propriety is sometimes necessary to do this: "This eloquence has power to sway men's minds and move them in every possible way. Now it storms the feelings, now it creeps in; it implants new ideas and uproots the old" (Cicero, *Orator* xxviii.97).

According to Ong, even in our high-tech society, language refers to and is radically rooted in sound (*Orality* 8). (Perhaps the reason is that the affective dimension of language, the one that conveys the most emotion, is a tacitly oral one.) As Halloran and Bradford point out, "The ultimate radical of presentation for any text is the human voice, as our persistent use of the term audience—the ones who audit—suggests." Thus, they argue that the figures of speech found even in scientific and technical writing are related to sound (though as Croll might point out [54], the *figura sententiae*, the figures of thought, are a different—and difficult—music) and that more research needs to be done concerning "the relationship between visual and auditory modes in the processing of texts" (191).

Perhaps even in a literate culture, then, if the "oral author" is to instruct, delight, and move an audience, he or she must not only have a well-developed and flexible "voice" but also must have a well-developed ear, both of which depend first on natural ability, then on training and practice, and least of all, on theory, art, and rules. And if style is to physically enter and affectively deceive the senses, whether plain, middle, or grand, perhaps it must be musical, must be sounded—even in prose— to be fully appreciated and understood. In an "oral culture," this was probably easier to understand—and do. In an oral culture, there is not much distinction between style and delivery. In an oral culture, style is performed; style is physical; style is a musical form of knowledge. As Plato and Aristotle perhaps understood all too well, in an oral culture, style leads to a sophistic philosophy of rhetoric and of response as affective, uncertain knowledge.

Cicero's Sophistic Epistemology and the Indeterminacy of Method

Just as there seems to be a "stylistic connection" between the sophists, Isocrates, and Cicero in regard to the epistemic music of rhetoric, there seems to be a "philosophical connection" between them in regard to a belief in the epistemological uncertainty of style as a form of knowledge. (For a detailed argument concerning the possible connections between the sophists and Cicero, see appendix B.) This philosophical connection has a direct bearing on our understanding of the relationship of response as affective experience and the indeterminacy of method in the teaching of literature and writing. Just as style, not rational heuristic, was the unifying element of speech for the sophists (Enos, "Rhetorical Theory"), for Cicero, "style is the unifying principle of oral discourse" (Ochs 136). Style orders speech and so is itself a form of knowledge. In fact, Cicero's more literate philosophy of poetic style constitutes a highly developed theory of reader response criticism—but one still afloat on an ontology of sound.

For example, in an unpublished paper Michael Leff argues that *De Oratore* is both in its content *and its form* a "self-reflexive" philosophical treatise on the epistemology of rhetoric that reflects in its very structure Cicero's belief in the interdependence of form and content (Untitled 2). In the dialogue of *De Oratore*, Crassus, renowned both as an orator and as a teacher of rhetoric, must repeatedly ward off the distinction between rhetoric and knowledge that is foisted upon him by his young and eager students who continually beg him to teach them his rhetorical technique. Crassus, on the other hand, seeks to enlarge their conception of rhetoric beyond mere art, or techne, and to convey to his listeners the unity of content and style in eloquence. As Marrou states, Cicero "tried hard to wean the youth of his day from this naive, utilitarian idea of rhetoric and to enlarge their conception of the ideal orator, harking back to Isocrates' original ideal in all its noble simplicity" (383).

Yet, because these students of rhetoric consider the power of oratory to come from rational art, they continue to try to divide rhetoric into parts, thereby destroying the essence of eloquence. As Leff suggests, then, the structure of *De Oratore* is twofold: "there is a linear, external sequence of prescriptive doctrine set along side an internally developed philosophical account of the ideal orator. While the technical structure divides oratory into components, the philosophical structure seeks to preserve its integrity by repeating and amplifying the thesis of the unity of wisdom and eloquence, or perhaps more precisely, the unity of *res* and *verba* in genuine eloquence" (Untitled 1). As in Reader Response Criticism, style is essential to the meaning of the text: it doesn't only embody content; it is a part of the content, and necessary for the perception of it (cf. Rosenblatt, *Literature* 44–45). Leff makes this very point as well: "To borrow a notion from the contemporary school of affective stylistics, the meaning of the text consists in what it does as well as what it states" (Untitled 2).

This point is essential in understanding not only Cicero's dialogue but one way in which Cicero was an ancient and quite feasibly the first real Reader Response critic. The multiplicity of viewpoints voiced in *De Oratore* has been the cause of much confusion concerning Cicero's own philosophy of rhetoric. For while it is generally acknowledged that Crassus is Cicero's primary spokesman, the other arguments in the dialogue concerning rhetoric as techne are given considerable space and weight, and the discussion, at least on the surface, seems unresolved.

De Oratore is not a Platonic dialogue in which the philosophical cards are stacked in favor of Socrates. In fact, Crassus's failure to teach his conception of eloquence is the point of the entire dialogue.

De Oratore is thus a literate version of a true sophistic controversy: all sides of the issue are explored, resulting in uncertainty regarding one's position, and nobody really wins. Here, however, the *dissoi logoi* are embodied in the *written* structure of the dialogue itself, as represented at various levels of style and arrangement, which reflects Cicero's more "literate," self-conscious mind. But the dialogue of *De Oratore* shows that, as in Reader Response Criticism, in Ciceronian rhetoric style and content are ideally taught as one through aesthetic (read subjective) responses to arrangement and style, and (social) debate and "consensus." The dialogue of *De Oratore* also shows that any attempt to analyze and interpret the unity of style and content must inevitably fail—and that that failure is that unity's success. For if Crassus had succumbed totally to his listeners' desire for an analysis and interpretation of his "technique" of rhetoric, he would have been forced to separate form from content, meaning from performance. Thus, Cicero succeeds precisely because Crassus fails. By not separating form from content, by making even the failure of analysis and interpretation a part of the unity of form and content of the treatise, Crassus conveys the true nature of eloquence by stylistic indirection, by response to its unity, to us, future readers, if not yet to his eager students, who continue to harangue him in order to persuade him to reveal his techniques through further analysis and interpretation.

This is where the similarities between Cicero's sophistic epistemology and Reader Response Criticism come into harmonic interplay—and where "oral modes of thought" begin in counterpoint to plumb the depths of the problem of teaching the affective experience of literature and writing as indeterminate knowledge, where the dissonance between Cicero's philosophy of rhetoric and Reader Response Criticism as it is applied to composition begins to be heard. Like the sophists, Cicero seems to hold in *De Oratore* that the *processes* of creation and response to eloquence in speech (and writing) cannot be studied and taught directly by empirical observation and analysis of those processes, or indirectly by rational heuristics and interpretation. Rather, the processes of creation and response can only be "intuited" and inferred indirectly from the unity of form and structure, as exhibited by Crassus's "model" performance, and by this, Cicero's most mature treatise itself.

While Reader Response critics make interpretation the basis of pedagogy and of knowledge, and even integrate it into the meaning and structure of content, analysis and interpretation are not enough. While they are necessary for understanding and knowledge, as demonstrated by Leff's interpretive performance of *De Oratore* (cf. Leff, "Interpretation"), analysis and interpretation can only take us so far in understanding the phenomenon of the *experience of language*; intuition and the experience of the *unity of language and thought* must do the rest—a process perhaps facilitated by the oral performance of language. This is a point made by teachers and scholars of oral interpretation as well (see Bacon; McCurdy; Neville; and Bales, all in Fernandez. For the history of oral interpretation, see Gottlieb, ch. 1; Thompson). The sound of style is the physical embodiment of the unity of language and thought that is otherwise uncertain. Unlike interpretive knowledge, the explanation of eloquence as a form of wisdom and "one of the supreme virtues" (Cicero, *D. O.* III.xiv.55) is ultimately ineffable and indeterminate. But it is not unutterable and so can be experienced.

So too, perhaps, the response to style that underlies a good part of eloquence. Like the sophists and Isocrates, and unlike Plato and Aristotle, Cicero makes no separation between rhetoric and philosophy, between style and substance, between emotion and knowledge. Indeed, in Book III, Crassus vehemently objects—on epistemological grounds—to the traditional split between thought and speech, between philosophy and rhetoric made by the Platonic Socrates (xvi.60–61), which has been forced upon Crassus by his students. This provokes Crassus to give utterance to his profoundest epistemological belief in the unity of substance and style:

> Every speech consists of matter and words, and the words cannot fall into place if you remove the matter, nor can the matter have clarity if you remove the words. . . . [A]ll this universe, above us and below us is one single whole, and is held together by a single force and harmony of nature; for there exists no class of things which can stand by itself, severed from the rest, or which the rest can dispense with and yet be able to preserve their own force and everlasting existence. (Cicero, *D. O.* III.v.19–20)

In fact, this is not only an epistemological statement concerning the relationship between language and knowledge but an ontological one regarding the nature of reality itself, one that in many ways resembles the reconstructed reasoning of the sophists, and results in a vision of reality much like that arrived at in New Physics (see appendix B).

As in Gorgias's philosophy according to Enos and Kerferd, style in Cicero's epistemology is epistemic by necessity. Leff makes this point as well concerning the relationship between Cicero's ontology and epistemology. For Cicero, as for Isocrates (Jaeger 49) and the sophists (Marrou 81–88), beauty and utility are related, and so philosophical contemplation leads to action (Leff, Untitled 11). Cicero, Leff says, "constructs an aesthetic theory that connects form with function, and beauty with utility" (13). In this, Cicero was in some ways very much a part or aware of his highly pragmatic society. Cicero too had to argue for the necessity and virtue of philosophy and poetry beyond politico-mythic proclamation or popular drivel in his day, just as we have to today.

In addition, Enos argues that Cicero's view and use of style as both aesthetic and practical were necessary given the nature of the crowds that began to gather in the Forum in his time, and which the advocate increasingly had to consider, influence, and please (*Literate Mode* 36–40). But not only was Cicero a part of his culture, he also towered above it because of his "literary" skills (*Literate Mode* 47–51). Like the sophists and Isocrates, then, Cicero, in Book III of *De Oratore*, "shows the reader how to apply the theory of rhetoric and the conceptions of philosophy to the practical life of the orator" (Leff, Untitled 17). Contemplative philosophy and socially active rhetoric are unified in the style and arrangement of the text.[18] Art is necessary to make ideas/reality apparent to the senses.

Again, the result of this unity of language and thought in style that can only be intuited is a philosophy of contingency and uncertainty concerning not only language instruction but the ontological basis of knowledge as a subjective (and social) construct as well. For Cicero and the sophists (as for the New physicists and philosophers of science such as Polanyi), reality (like speech or in response to it) cannot be separated by analysis without changing or destroying it. But for Cicero, as for Isocrates and the sophists, it would seem that the unity of form and content in rhetoric is still rooted in sound rather than visual referent. In fact, Cicero's sophistic philosophy of methodological uncertainty also can be understood to be facilitated by and at least partially grounded in an ontology of orality. For Cicero, as for Isocrates and the first sophists, the *kosmos* of speech is perhaps created in the music of language. Rhythm, like the unity of form and content, is part of the natural order of things (*D. O.* III.xlviii.186). Although Cicero does not talk about rhythm per se as "the harmony of the universe," does not see music itself as the single law governing the order of things (as Pythagoras, and Plato in modified form, did), for Cicero, rhythm is one manifestation of the relationship between beauty and utility that he observes is "of the universe," "this whole ordered world of nature" (*D. O.* III.xlv.178–79; cf. Barfield 150, who makes a distinction between music and rhythm in poetry and prose).

The distinction between rhythm as the actual principle governing the universe and a manifestation of the relation between beauty and utility is an important one in the history of rhetoric, one that perhaps can be traced back to different interpretations of Pythagorean theory.[19] For Cicero, as for Isocrates, "the correctness of a word" seems to reside not in a visual or abstract one-to-one correspondence between word and object but rather in the physical, oral harmony of style and thought, in the ability of the speaker to make as much of the "reality of his thought" as palatable and perceptible as possible to an audience through the performance of language as sound, and for the audience of listeners to hear and be persuaded as to the rightness of that perception (see DiLorenzo). Although language does not contain in any demonstrable way a one-to-one correspondence with nature, it nevertheless depends on the harmony that is intuited in nature as well as in language, where it is heightened in performance.

Thus, for Cicero, as for Isocrates and the sophists, the intuition of eloquence, and response to it, is perhaps ultimately rooted in and the result of the physical (and limited) characteristics of speaker and the listener, in delivery and in hearing. Separating words from thoughts, says Crassus, is like severing body from mind: "neither can take place without disaster" (Cicero, *D. O.* III.vi.24). Here again, we see the analogy that reflects the "material" base of Cicero's oral philosophy of language and knowledge: the disaster is not only epistemological but "ontological" as well. Thought is not bodiless but is physical, embodied in speech. The ontological basis of the belief in the unity of form and content, thought and style, *res* and *verba*, is probably an oral one, one rooted in the physical but indeterminate cosmos of language as sound.

This is quite contrary, of course, to the Platonic notion of knowledge and virtue as Ideal Forms—although as Lentz shows, knowledge of these Forms for Plato paradoxically could only be demonstrated by a "living intelligence," a belief rooted in orality as well. (It is also somewhat at odds with the "abstract" heuristics for interpretation in Reader Response Criticism.) If, as Ochs states in the preface to his synopsis of the *Orator*, Cicero "draws upon Plato's concept of 'ideas' to illustrate his conception of the ideal orator" (136), Cicero bases knowledge not in the autonomous realm of transcendental

Ideas, but in the orator, in the ideal of the physical human being. For Cicero, style (*ornatus*) as *kosmos*, the Pythagorean unity of all things in the universe, is embodied *in the music of speech*. Poetic style is not merely a matter of pleasure, then; it is also a matter of the *unity, power,* and *necessity* of style in speech that we find in the sophistic philosophy of language and knowledge. Thought must be made not merely visible, as in writing, but tangible, alluring, physically attractive to the senses, and so possibly depends on the all-embracing, sensorially synthetic, aesthetic faculty of the ear to detect it and refine it (cf. *D. O.* I.xxxii.150). It's not only a case of not knowing what we think until we see what we say but also of not knowing what we think until we feel what we say. As teachers of oral interpretation (e.g., Schrivner) are keenly aware, eloquence of style, even in prose, must be performed to be fully realized and known to the senses.

For Cicero, response to style is also a means of judging the credibility and sincerity of the speaker. Eloquence as *ornatus*, as "ornamentation" or "kosmetic," is not merely stylistic artifice or technique, but the calling up of the appropriate *ethos* and emotions through style according to subject, audience, purpose (Cicero, *D. O.* II.xlvi.195). Style cannot be considered apart from knowledge (*D. O.* I.xiv.63). (And the lack of knowledge is a true lesson in the sociology of knowledge: "style, if the underlying subject matter be not comprehended and mastered by the speaker, must inevitably be of no account or become the sport of universal derision" [Cicero, *D. O.* I.xii.52].) Based on the notion of propriety, the speaker must not only communicate "the facts" but the appropriate emotions in the appropriate styles if he or she is to persuade an audience (see *Orator* viii.24; Schrivner; Parrish esp. 97–98).

Contrary to Eliot's (ostensible) belief in the necessity of finding an objective correlative in style in order to escape from personality and emotion into art, then, for Cicero, style (sensuously symbolized if sometimes invisible due to the operation of propriety) appears to be necessary to make personality and emotion perceptible through art. Discussing style in delivery as a performance, Crassus, in a statement that is almost the exact antithesis of Aristotle's, says: "[T]here can be no doubt that reality beats imitation in everything; and if reality unaided were sufficiently effective in presentation, we should have no need at all for art. But because emotion, which mostly has to be displayed or counterfeited by action, is often so confused as to be obscured and almost smothered out of sight, we have to dispel the things that obscure it and take up its prominent and striking points" (Cicero, *D. O.* III.lvii.215). For Cicero, emotions are not "a defect in our hearers" (Aristotle, *Rhetoric* III.1404a7); we cannot make our case with "just the facts." As Reader Response critics rightly assert, emotions (and response to affective style) are essential to knowledge, and the perception and communication of "facts," though that perception, that knowledge, that communication, like our methods, be uncertain.

Sophistic Pedagogy and Reader Response Criticism; Or, How Not to Do Things with Cicero

In using language to reveal and explore personality, motives, and emotions, Cicero's views parallel somewhat those of contemporary Reader Response Criticism. In fact, there are many parallels between the rhetorical theory of the sophists, Isocrates, and Cicero, and Reader Response critics such as Rosenblatt, Fish, and Bleich. The sophists, Isocrates, and Cicero more or less held a subjective (and social) philosophy of language and knowledge: (1) language is not separate from knowledge, an embellishment on the facts, but rather is epistemic, fundamental to knowing; (2) persuasion is not peripheral to the activity of knowing but rather is the foundation of all knowledge; and (3) emotional response is not to be suppressed in the pursuit of "objective knowledge" but rather is the basis of perception and knowledge, and a kind of knowledge itself. Cicero (*D. O.* III.xiv.55; xx.76), like Isocrates (*Antidosis* 253–57) and the sophists, thus regards rhetoric as central to all knowledge.

For Cicero, education seems to be a subjective (and social) enterprise as well. Cicero believed in a tutorial system of education (cf. Murphy, "Roman Writing Instruction" 20), which could be described as subjective and "social" in nature. In fact, a subjective (and social) method of education based on holistic human interaction was the whole point of the sophistic philosophy of rhetoric and, indeed, of Greek education.[20] We can also intuit the subjective and social method of education in the form of *De Oratore* itself. That Cicero's is truly a subjective method is attested to by Crassus's insistence that the intuitive faculty necessary for eloquence cannot be taught by formal rules or theory of art, but only indirectly, by affective response to the unity of form and content in style and arrangement (even in writing! [cf. *D. O.* I.xxxii.150]). That Cicero's is truly a social method of instruction is attested to by the outcome of the dialogue: although he may have enlarged the discussion (and thus the student's conception) of eloquence, Crassus fails to totally teach or convince his listeners of the true nature of it. (And this is quite real. How much of what we say do our students really, physically absorb into their life?) As in the Reader Response classroom, the teacher's is another voice, another opinion, though an important one, in arriving at a subjective (and socially satisfying) form of knowledge.

However, there are some important differences, beyond the obvious ones that result from an oratorical versus a "literary" education, between Cicero's sophistic pedagogy and Reader Response Criticism as it is currently conceived and taught, differences perhaps ultimately based on a phonocentric rather than logocentric understanding and experience of discourse. The power of style to underlie thought and make "the facts" perceptible to oneself and to an audience more or less parallels Bleich's view of symbolization as a process of identifying and naming. Cicero understood that language is the basis of our experience of the world, including its order (DiLorenzo). For Cicero, as for Reader Response critics, this process is an affective and uncertain one and leads to affective and uncertain knowledge. But because eloquence was the primary purpose of a rhetorical education using literature, "symbolization" and resymbolization as interpretive explanation for Cicero also seemed to entail a concern with language rooted in the physical character of the speaker and the physical nature of language as sound heightened in performance. It is not only interpretation but the *power* of language as a sensuous form to create feeling, thought, and reality by evoking sensory reaction, to fill the void between thought and reality and language and reality, that makes rhetoric the subjective (and social) basis of belief, knowledge, and action.

While the role of symbolization is acknowledged in Reader Response Criticism, the *experience* of language in the process of symbolization and resymbolization is not actively taught or pursued but is merely assumed as a "given"—as if "the facts" of the case, the student's subjective motivations, are enough to make experience apparent, as if the necessary aesthetic that occurs naturally in speech also occurs sufficiently enough in symbolization or resymbolization to arrive at either subjective knowledge or social consensus and must not actively be created through style and delivery. But as the sophists seem to understand, symbolization and even resymbolization are not enough. Where symbolization for Cicero leads outward, to the eloquence necessary for emotional persuasion and social action as well as resymbolization, for Reader Response critics, symbolization leads only to resymbolization, leads back to the interpretation of texts or the subjective motivations underlying responses to texts for social exploration and validation, and by extension, survival (but cf. Bleich, *Double Perspective*).

It is not the goal of Reader Response critics, of course, to use literature to teach eloquence, although one could argue that it is—or should be—the goal of those who apply it to composition. It may be because of this that the focus of most Reader Response Criticism, and those who use it to teach writing, remains fixed on interpreting literary texts. Like literary texts, student response statements are "self-consuming artifacts." But while persuasion utilizes the analytic and interpretive faculties, persuasion, for better or worse, also occurs on a much more holistic, immediate, affective level—especially in speech. Eloquence as symbolization (and resymbolization) is the creation of thought, reality, and social action through the unity, power, and necessity of oral language to enter and deceive the senses. Eloquence is (re)symbolization with a rhetorical purpose.

Thus, if the proper use of the different "registers"—the sinuous, the sensuous, and the somatic style—is necessary to make thought physically appealing (and thus apparent) to the senses, then the power of style itself depends on the "musical" ability to produce and to hear it, whether in speech or writing (cf. Bertram, xiii, who makes a connection between listening and reading in oral interpretation). Again, this depends first on "natural talent," and second on practice and training. Like Isocrates, Cicero employs an analogy between athletic ability and speaking, between the gymnasium and oratory (D. O. I.xvi.73). Style is not merely a matter of method; it is athletic. "Symbolic action" is more than a metaphor for what happens when people speak and listen. Speaking, like writing, like language itself, is physical (cf. Ochsner).

For Cicero (D. O. III.xviii.70), eloquence—the *kairotic* harmony of form and content—cannot be taught by theory. "Theoretical abstractions . . . cannot teach propriety," says Leff; "It can only be apprehended as embodied in a particular discourse" (Untitled 16). While this might lead us to think again that that unity can be taught by analysis and interpretation of style and content, perhaps it cannot, at least not totally. As we explored in chapter 2, analysis and interpretation reduce and/or change the physical phenomenon of the experience of language, rendering it a theoretical abstraction (just as this discussion does). Even if interpretation is fundamental in the immediate, concrete, physical apprehension of experience of language at the moment of persuasion—and it almost certainly is—it is not only interpretation as we understand it: a rational reconstruction of experience according to our theories for the purpose of explanation. Rather, interpretation also includes the affective response and experience of our senses to language itself as a stylistic form of knowledge.

In this more inclusive act of "interpretation," the aesthetic faculty concerned with the affective meaning of sound, with the temporal experience of language, may be as important as the interpretive faculty concerned with referential meaning. (This will be the subject of chapters 4 and 5.) While analysis and interpretation are useful, even necessary in understanding the harmony of form and content, then, they cannot hope to get at or duplicate the holistic experience of language—a point that almost all scholars of oral interpretation make (see Fernandez). Rather, that harmony perhaps can only be apprehended immediately and holistically in the performance of a particular piece of discourse. The aesthetic faculty and musical feel for language are rooted in the ground sounds of speech, in the tuned turnings of the ear, and so perhaps cannot be very well developed by formalistic or rationalistic methods alone.

Perhaps this intuitive, aesthetic faculty can only or best be educated indirectly, then, through oral recitation and declamation. While Reader Response critics make use of oral response statements in researching processes of reading and writing, in developing heuristics, and in classroom pedagogy, the performance of style as the physical embodiment of knowledge and emotion in sound is not primary or integral to instruction. In the affective stylistics of Reader Response critics, there is little consideration of delivery as it pertains to teaching, research (i.e., the relation of sound to meaning and response), reading, or writing. (Even oral interpretation is to a large extent predicated on the value and goal of the analysis and interpretation of the meaning of a literary work and makes this its primary purpose [e.g., see Beloof et al.; Geiger; Schrivner 9–11].) But for the sophists, Isocrates, and Cicero, affective stylistics *as a form of knowledge* seems to rest on the intuition of the sense perception of words and sentences physically following another in the temporal dimension of sound, not the spatial dimension of the page.

This difference in ontology may be essential. For while language in the spatial dimension "points" primarily to referential meaning, language in the temporal dimension, like nonverbal music, only communicates indeterminate emotion embodied in sensuous sound—and that only indirectly. The affective experience of language is not only created through referential meaning but also through sound. Affect is embedded in (and conceivably can be "traced") in language itself. Against a backdrop of meter, sound and variation in rhythm, in prose as well as poetry, can stimulate emotion and relay feeling that can simulate, create, reflect, or reinforce referential meaning at the level of words, sentences, or even paragraphs. Style as an affective form of knowledge is perhaps derived more from the ear than the eye. It is rhythm, according to Cicero, that is most akin to the mind (*D. O.* III.l.195). Given the ubiquity and universality of music, this may still be true in our literate culture as well.

Thus, as we will *see* in chapter 4, affective stylistics conceived of in exclusively literate, spatial terms may miss the potentially important, physical dimension of subjective experience in language as sound. Even Perelman's important concept of "presence"—the emphasizing in language of certain thoughts or concepts "to combat the domination of sensibility by our surroundings" (35–36) and gain the "adherence" of an audience to an argument—appears to be predominantly visual, spatial, when compared to the oral, sophistic notion of poetic arrangement and style as the creator of necessary illusion, or Cicero's concept of *ornatus* as embodied in the unity of the form and content of speech. Although Perelman states that "[p]resence acts directly upon our sensibility" (35) and understands it to be created by such techniques as repetition, amplification, and other figures of speech (37–39), he does not consider how the musical aspects of language also create presence—how the sound of language makes ideas sensually present. Like almost all contemporary discussions of style, Perelman's discussion of the figures of speech centers around the creation of presence through the structuring and relationship of *ideas* rather than also through the sensory allure of language as sound (cf. Enos, *Greek Rhetoric* 86). The epistemological bias engendered by the spatial ontology of literacy is reflected even in the best contemporary rhetorical theory.

In fact, we might go so far as to assert that students develop the intuitive, aesthetic faculty despite our theories and methods rather than because of them. For the sophists, Isocrates, and Cicero, affective stylistics seems to have been much more physical than it is for us. It seems that for them style was related to physical (and emotional) development—perhaps not exactly as we understand that term, as "psychological maturity," but as the ability to adapt to rhetorical situations by invoking or responding to powerful language. (In some ways this is opposite of cognitive development as we conceive of it, since we tend to become more abstract and rational as we "mature" and so lose the musical feel for the play of language in localized situations [cf. Elbow, "Shifting" 292–93; Havelock, "Star Wars" 415].)

Reader Response critics too recognize that emotional development, personality, and immediate situation may have more to do with the way students read and respond to and write texts than teaching based on formalistic, rationalistic, a priori methods. But in treating motivations underlying response to texts as the subject of interpretation, Reader Response critics and composition teachers in some ways inadvertently but almost invariably reduce personality itself to an abstraction, an object of method. In this sense, to speak of and teach resymbolization, or even symbolization in terms of heuristics, is already to speak of and teach the physical experience of emotion, personality, and situation as an abstraction, just as to speak of or teach rhythm in terms of prosodic parsing or imitation as heuristics for analysis and interpretation is ineluctably a reduction and abstraction of the physical, somatic responses to language in actual experience.

The affective character of language as sound, even in reading and writing, must in some sense be "performed" to be felt, heard (cf. Bacon, Art 2–4; Langer, Feeling 135). The fact that for Isocrates and Cicero art or techne is just the beginning, and cannot teach eloquence, "illuminates the harmony" of substance and style that cannot be spatially separated by analysis and interpretation without in some respect destroying the experience of it. For the sophists, the ontological unity of form and content that has its analogue in the order of sound is a matter of the necessity of beauty as a fundamental basis of knowledge. And that knowledge ultimately and only can be "sensed," intuited, and thus will always remain uncertain. If there exists a gulf between language and reality and thought and reality, there exists no gulf between language and affective thought. For if it does exist, we can know nothing, arrive at nothing—a vision even more tragic than Untersteiner would ascribe to the first sophists.

It is the physical dimension of language as sound in relation to affective knowledge that we will be particularly interested in the remainder of this book. Methods of studying affective response in reading and writing must be rooted in an empiricism that is "enlightened" because the affective experience of language is tacit, physical, aural, and uncertain. "This is a deficiency from a purely theoretical perspective, but it is a great advantage to the practicing orator," says Leff in regard to teaching eloquence; "He need not learn a complex and intricate set of abstract principles; he need only understand the fundamental concepts and apply them to his intuitive practice, which is itself a reflection of the same natural harmony" (Untitled 16). Thus, a reader response "criticism" concerned with the affective experience of language may not depend so much on analysis and interpretation as intuition and imitation of the music and movement of language.

Because Cicero was concerned with eloquence (the unity of form and content in sensuous style as affective knowledge—and response to it) for the purpose of *persuasion* rather than analysis and interpretation, and because that unity was oral in nature, that unity of eloquence, that response, is perhaps best taught by "aural imitation." This involves not only reading aloud, but reading out loud (with all the implications of a performance), and the somatic response of the entire body to it (see appendix C). Again, oral interpretation, with its instructional emphasis not only on the vocalization of meaning and emotion but also with its embodiment in musculature (see Schrivner, esp. Part 3), may be able to help us here. While Reader Response critics can justifiably argue that in teaching literature through the analysis and interpretation as subjective and social knowledge, they are in fact educating the intuitive faculty necessary for eloquence and response, and while they may make a significant gesture toward persuasion necessary in arriving at social knowledge, that unifying, synthetic, "musical faculty" is not the focus of Reader Response *pedagogy*. Interpretation is.

Given his apparently sophistic epistemology, as well as the predominance of oratory in his society, it is not surprising that "Cicero thought highly of declamation" (Ochs 91). Recitation, too, seemed to be important for Cicero, though we perhaps begin to see in Cicero the beginning of a modern self-consciousness about reading out loud that accompanied the growth of literacy: "if by advice, by exhortation, by inquiry, by sharing your knowledge, if at times even by reading out loud to them or listening to their reading, if you could really improve men by some teaching of this sort, I cannot understand why you should decline to do so" (*Orator* xlii. 144). Despite the seeming self-consciousness, these "oral techniques," like orality itself, were still commonplace in Cicero's Rome.

But while they were commonplace, Cicero, like Isocrates and the sophists, may have made these oral techniques integral to his thought and teaching. Thus, there also may be a connection between Cicero's sophistic epistemology and his pedagogical methods.[21] In any case, for Cicero, writing was meant to facilitate speaking (*D. O.* I.xxxii.150), literature was oratorical, and textual criticism, itself oral, was meant to analyze the sound of the text to be read out loud (Marrou 375; Murphy, "Roman Writing Instruction" 42, 46). What Cicero seemed to mean by reading and criticism was recitation and declamation. Literature for Cicero was not only an object of pure Platonic contemplation as it is for us. The purpose of literature, even poetry, also seems to have been to teach the power of style and emotion in eloquence. In *De Oratore*, Cicero has Antonius remark that it is from poetry and the stage that the orator can learn about emotion and human character, for "no man can be a good poet who is not on fire with passion, and inspired by something very like frenzy" (II.xlvi.194). Cicero is obviously thinking about the grand, ornate style here. But the focus of both literary and nonliterary instruction seems to have been "performance."

While any speculation concerning Cicero's actual teaching methods is open to debate, Cicero, like Isocrates and the sophists, probably used a variety of oral techniques in addition to writing (cf. *D. O.* I.xxxii.150) to teach eloquence and affective response in and through physical delivery and sound: declamation (as physical performance, which included, in addition to the study of drama and poetry, training in voice, facial expression, gesture, body movement), recitation (reading *out loud*, as opposed to aloud, again stressing the performative aspect), and aural/oral imitation (which may have been more important in reading and writing as a "physical performance" than analysis and interpretation—and different from it [see appendix C]).

Contra Knoblauch and Brannon, then, some of the latest and most "radical" experiments in contemporary composition, like reading out loud, story workshop, pantomime, body movement, and dance, find historical precedent and support in the classical rhetorical tradition—of the sophists and Cicero. We will touch on these teaching techniques further in chapter 6. But here it should be emphasized that the purpose of literature and writing (*D. O.* I.xxxii.150) for Cicero, as for Isocrates and the sophists, was to teach oral performance and response. And for Cicero, what is responded to is the affective knowledge of language rooted in the rhythms of speech. "There are some people who do not feel this," says Cicero in arguing for the importance of rhythm in prose, "but I do not know what sort of ears they have, nor whether they are human at all (*Orator* l.167; Cicero cites the authority of Isocrates, as well as his senses, for support [*Orator* li.173]).

This chapter is not meant as a naive panegyric to the supposed virtues of the ancients. Cicero, Isocrates, and even the sophists did use formalistic, rationalistic methods and techniques (see Enos, *Greek Rhetoric*). Naturally, one would expect them to, given the lateness of the literary day, and the Roman temperament toward efficiency that became increasingly brutal. But as Enos points out (*Literate Mode* 4), Cicero's was still an oral culture; and as Murphy intimates ("Roman Writing Instruction" 29), Cicero in a rearguard action agitated against the formalistic, rationalistic methods of teaching that were soon to sweep through Republican Rome like the emperors. Like us, Cicero certainly did make use of formalistic, rationalistic methods, as can be seen, heard, and inferred from the treatment of oratory in his own earlier work and in other treatises of the time (e.g., *Rhetorica ad Herennium*).

Nor is this meant as a call for a return to the good old ways, such as the complex progymnasmata, and certainly not imitation as we currently understand it, though some have cited the usefulness of those methods (Corbett, "Imitation" 304; Sullivan). But the older, mature, more sophistic Cicero seems to have grasped the problem of rhetorical knowledge as response and the necessity of a sensuous, poetic style in the teaching of eloquence, and his methods of dealing with style as oral knowledge, like those of Isocrates and the sophists, while inevitably to some degree "formalistic and rationalistic," were nevertheless still couched in more oral modes of expression and thought, still took the sensuous and physical nature of language and knowledge as their foundation, and in this way at least were probably more holistic and less reductive.

Cicero's "sophistic methods" of teaching oratory in many ways represent an ancient reader response criticism, but one keyed to oratory, tuned to oral performance. If performance and response as indeterminate knowledge are rooted in the physical attributes of human beings, teaching methods must be as well. Just as the failure of Crassus to describe the ideal of eloquence in *De Oratore* preserves the integrity of the uncertain art of rhetoric, so too in the *Orator*, the failure of Cicero (here unmasked) to describe the ideal orator preserves the integrity of the uncertain human orator. If eloquence cannot be grounded in or taught by a priori heuristics, neither can the athletic attributes of the ideal orator, which are not situated in an abstract, transcendental, a priori realm of pure Form but in the variability of human beings themselves. "It is difficult to describe the 'form' or 'pattern' of the best . . . because different people have different notions of what is best," says Cicero in regard to the orator (*Orator* x.36); "the truth is masked in obscurity" (*Orator* lxxi.238).

Thus, response to style as affective knowledge, like propriety in eloquence, must ultimately be based on limited physical intuition and therefore remain forever ineffable and uncertain. But, if Leff relates that "this is not to say that propriety is unteachable, for where one method of instruction fails, another can succeed" (Untitled 16), response too may be teachable, by a variety of "indeterminate methods." While this procedure is always hit or miss, trial and error—try this method, try that method, and see which one works better for you—it indicates the necessity for a plurality of methods and an openness and willingness to try them all. Since eloquence (and response) to style as physical experience is based partly on an aural, intuitive faculty for the ancients, perhaps we should also try to teach it today as physical experience through more aural, intuitive, "physical" methods based on "secondary orality" rather than by analysis and interpretation alone.

Perhaps response to style as affective knowledge that underlies a part of the experience of reading and writing as well as speech can better be taught as indeterminate knowledge by indirection, through "music of language" itself. Thus, the problem of developing Reader Response Criticism becomes one of describing affective response to language in a way that is not spatially reductive. Perhaps we can understand better and describe more of what happens when people write and read by understanding and describing how language as physical, as sound, might relate to affective experience as an intuitive, temporal form of knowledge. In doing so, unlike Fish's successful application of Austin and Searle to Reader Response Criticism, we should try *not* "to do things" with Cicero. To preserve as best we can the integrity of affective experience as indeterminate knowledge, it is imperative that we resist the temptation to develop formalistic, rationalistic methods based on sophistic-Ciceronian philosophy of style—that we don't use Cicero to analyze and interpret the harmony of thought and style but rather to try to comprehend affective experience itself.

To do so, we may have to understand the experience of the music of language itself as a temporal as well as spatial kind of knowledge. Unlike spatial knowledge, temporal knowledge is nonreferential, and thus indeterminate (at least in the current state of physics); perhaps it is the intuition of style in the oral dimension of time, not space, that underlies the sophistic philosophy of language as knowledge. To help us reconstruct response as temporal knowledge based on the "oral ontology" of the sophistic tradition, which may be fundamental both in a historical and physical sense to understanding language as a truly subjective form of knowledge, to help us *hear* indeterminacy, we will now turn to contemporary philosophies of composition, language, and music that in many ways reverberate with, transpose, and resolve the insights of the Cicero and the sophists.

Four

The Music of Language:
The Temporal Dimension
of Affective Experience

Contemporary Composition Theory, Secondary Orality,
and Affective Experience

In recent work in composition, there has been a growing awareness of the oral dimension of writing deriving from attempts
to teach writing as a social process (e.g., Elbow, *Writing Without
Teachers, Writing with Power*; Schultz). If Havelock argues that
"a general theory of orality must build upon a general theory
of society" (*Muse* 68), perhaps a social theory of language and
knowledge also depends on or at least partially entails a theory
of orality, of reading and writing as oral performance, in which
the reader as writer, or the writer as reader, in deciding how
prose should sound, must choose a relationship with the audience and continually recreate the text for them (Lanham 100–
02). However, it is also generally understood that orality is not
necessary for social rhetoric, that indeed, writing itself, even
in the sciences, is social in nature (see Herrington; Bazerman).

In "The Shifting Relationships Between Speech and Writing," Peter Elbow makes explicit the connection between the practice of teaching composition as a social interaction and teaching composition as speech, and begins to develop the important oral dimension of writing. Like Isocrates and Cicero, who believed that the faculty of speech that underlies eloquence is a natural one, Elbow argues that "capitalizing on the oral language skills students already possess and helping students apply those skills immediately and effortlessly to writing . . . [is] a way of helping with the crucial process Ong calls the " 'internalization of the technology of writing' " (290). Somewhat similar to Elbow, Robert Ochsner considers the role of sound in writing in relation to eye and hand and recommends that

> [a]bove all, students must be taught the rhythms of producing, seeing, and hearing written language. One simple, enjoyable, and truly ancient means toward this objective is to have students read aloud. This technique not only helps students hear prose—their own and other students—but it also assimilates this sound as the students' inner voices. They begin to hear patterns of stress that correspond to patterns of meaning; they can also develop an intuitive understanding for the pace of a reader's interpretation. Antithesis, balance, and the visual symmetries of emphasizing ideas become auditory clues to understanding a writer's work. In short, all three neurological melodies coalesce in one teaching strategy. (80, cf. 148–52)

Ochsner even goes so far as to reverse the order of the five traditional rhetorical arts to reflect their relative importance in physical eloquence: delivery, memory, style, arrangement, and invention. However, Ochsner elsewhere, and perhaps inadvertently, reveals a bias against "vocalization" in reading as inappropriate behavior for "advanced writers" (55–56). Ochsner's bias against vocalization and even subvocalization would seem to undermine his suggestion that we teach reading out loud and is widespread in our culture. This prejudice is common in reading instruction, reaching its peak in speed-reading, which downplays speech as the basis of literacy—and thus the role of sensuous sound in understanding and conveying meaning—

and focuses exclusively on words as visual (referents of) meaning; speed-reading represents the extreme in a positivistic denaturing of the text (cf. Goodman esp. 34–40). Of course, the prejudice against vocalization and even subvocalization, like the prejudice against tactility in reading—pointing to or touching words as one reads them—is perhaps grounded in the hypervisuality of literacy, which accepts the text as an ontological condition at the same time that it denies its material presence.

But the attempt to completely silence the text, to muzzle the reader, is to a certain extent impossible, given the well-known fact that somatic subvocalization involving the vocal chords always occurs, even in silent reading. It seems that in a real, physical sense, writing must be converted to speech to be meaningfully understood (Ong, *Orality* 8). In fact, we can delineate at least four levels of sound that might be important in reading and writing and that correspond to certain pedagogical goals: (*a*) the phonetic level, whereby letters are associated and translated into sound and meaning, and vice versa in writing (this is, of course, a basis of literacy and the goal of the phonics approach to teaching reading); (*b*) the ability based on speech to hear how written language is supposed to be spoken, for example, speed, tonalities, pitch, which communicate feelings and attitudes of the writer and shade ideas with emotional nuance (in elementary schools, this ability is often referred to as reading with expression); (*c*) the related but little understood level at which the sound of language itself as a musical activity creates, communicates, and/or evokes emotions, which can create, reflect, reinforce, contradict, subvert, or leave unchanged semantic meaning (in other words, the level of sound as affective response, and its relationship to experience and thought); and (*d*) the formal analysis of the abstract relations of the prosodic elements of sound (i.e., alliteration, assonance, rhyme, meter, etc.), whereby we sometimes try (and inexorably fail) to get at the nature and operation of the third level.

It is this third, elusive level of sound of language as a basis of affective response that we are interested in. One way to tap the knowledge of speech that students bring to reading and writing, of course, is to conduct writing classes as social forums in which students learn to write to a particular audience by reading what they have written out loud to the class as audience and gaining feedback from them. In advocating the teaching of writing as speech, then, Elbow takes exception to and qualifies Moffett's Piagetian notion of decentering: "the assumption that 'cognitive development' or 'psychological growth' consists of movement from concrete 'oral' modes to abstract 'literate' modes" ("Shifting" 293).[1]

Elbow especially takes issue with the notion that psychological growth is reflected in and can be determined by examining student texts themselves—"which are anything but accurate embodiments of how the student's mind really operates" ("Shifting" 292; cf. Ochsner 55–75, who, based on his notion of physical eloquence as actual text production, suggests that handwriting, like spelling, provides a "neurological window to the mind" [59]; this has some interesting implications for the effect of typing on the neurophysiology of writing as well[2]). While not denying that we must teach abstract reasoning, then, Elbow believes it is overemphasized at the expense of having students write "more often in a local context to a limited and physically present audience (as when they talk)" ("Shifting" 292). It is also overemphasized at the expense of using reading out loud to teach affective response based on the sensuous dimension of oral language—as the experience of and reaction to the performance of language itself.

It is this oral dimension of affective response in reading and writing, especially in regard to the epistemic nature of sensuous sound, that has been least explored, and which we will wish to put our ear to here. For Elbow, there is a more intrinsic relationship between thought and speech than thought and writing. As Ong argues, speech is primary and natural, an acquired skill; writing is secondary and formal, and must be learned (Orality 82; also see Krashen)—a point that Ochsner seems to agree with.[3] Thus, Elbow sees another benefit to teaching writing as speech, one that parallels the oral rhetoric of Isocrates, Cicero, and the sophists: "the best writing has *voice*, the life and rhythms of speech. Unless we actively train our students to *speak onto paper*, they will write the kind of dead, limp, nominalized prose we hate—or *say* we hate" ("Shifting" 291; cf. Murray, "Teaching the Other Self," "Listening to Writing").

Few students read their work aloud during composition or revision. And it's probably safe to say that when many students read or write, they hear little or nothing at all. They don't listen to the sound of their language but rather are engaged in shuffling visual symbols around like heavy blocks of meaning on the page. Yet, as many professional writers attest, they often read aloud what they have written and *always* hear "that inner voice" when they read and write. For example, in her literary autobiography *One Writer's Beginnings*, in a section entitled "Listening," Eudora Welty ruminates on the role of her voice when she reads and writes.

> Ever since I was first read to, then started reading to myself, there has never been a line that I didn't *hear*. As my eyes followed the sentence, a voice was saying it silently to me. . . . The cadence, whatever it is that asks you to believe, the feeling that resides in the printed word, reaches me through the readervoice. I have supposed, but never found out, that this is the case with all readers to read as listeners and with all writers, to write as listeners. It may be part of the desire to write. The sound of what falls on the page begins the process of testing it for truth, for me. Whether I am right to trust so far I don't know. By now I don't know whether I could do without either one, reading or writing, without the other. (13)

In a well-known interview, Robert Frost also ponders the quality of spoken language as it is used by poets. Frost calls this oral quality "sound-posturing" or "getting the sound of sense." In a way that seems to echo Cicero's belief in that natural, intuitive faculty for understanding the sound and rhythm of the spoken words, Frost states: "[T]he sense of every meaning has a particular sound which each individual is instinctively familiar with and without at all being conscious of the exact words that are being used is able to understand the thought, idea, or emotion that is being conveyed" (261). To prove this, Frost provides the famous analogy of listening to a person talk to someone on the phone in another room. The words themselves, and thus their semantic content, are muffled by a wall. Only the emotional meanings communicated by the sound of words, by their pitch, tone, and rhythm, can be heard.

We can demonstrate this here as well. Say the following sentences out loud to yourself in your normal speaking voice: listen to the rhythm of your speaking voice. Do you hear the emotions expressed by the music of your voice, the lilt and flow of pitch and tone that seems to highlight meaning? There's no need to analyze the "expected rhythm" (meter) of these sentences (but if you insist, the first sentence is predominately dactylic; the first half of the second sentence is predominately anapestic, the second half iambic); we feel it in the "heard rhythm" (as actually spoken), and in the tension created between the expected and heard rhythm[4] that seems to underlie our experience of meaning as it is spoken. Now listen to the sentence you are reading. Iambic. But it doesn't have to be rhythmically symmetrical. We also respond to the pattern of affect created in this sentence by hearing the emotion contained in the pitch, rhythm, and tone of it. For response is the emotional meanings of sound speakers of a community share and bring to bear on written utterance.

If the emotional meanings that speakers of a community share and bring to bear on written utterances are necessary "to make sense" of them, says Frost, "it does not seem possible to me that a man can read on the printed page what he has never heard" (262). Frost therefore also asserts the need for poets to write with their "ear to the voice" (262). And many poets do. They depend on the sound of the language spoken in the mind, if not the ear where they first hear and learn it, for the finding and falling together of form and emotion (just as I did in this sentence). For some, rhyme and rhythm even become a heuristic of invention, a way of discovering what to say and how to say it by following the sound of sense as much as content

(Frost's poem "Departmental" is an obvious example of this). There also may be a direct relationship between the sound and *invention* in prose, even scientific prose.[5] The ability to use the sound of language as a heuristic, of course, rests on a writer's experience and natural abilities with spoken language, as well as the learned ability to transfer that experience into the sound of written texts in order to, as Elbow says, "get our meanings integrated into our words" ("Shifting" 298).

Since the ability to transfer spoken language into written texts applies to reading as well, perhaps the sound of sense can also be taught by affective response to reading out loud. In fact, the affective meaning of the language of a text seems to be rooted in speech. Speech is primary; speech is the musical "tonic" from which other "intervals" of sound, other "modes" of communication, derive and build their meaning. Speech has, says Elbow, "a magic that writing lacks—call it presence, voice, or pneuma—but the truth is that we tend to experience meaning somehow more in spoken words than written ones" ("Shifting" 298). Frost understood this as well: "where all the tones of the human voice in natural speech are entirely eliminated, the sound of sense [is] without root in experience" (263). Having explored Cicero's sophistic philosophy of style, we can understand that the epistemic quality of the music of speech is contained and conveyed in the sensuous form of style itself, which is heightened in oral performance (*listen* to Frost reading "Departmental"). It is the voice that Elbow says the best writing possesses ("Shifting" 299).

If we take seriously Cicero's understanding of the importance of the relationship between sound and eloquence, then the oral dimension of reading and writing may be important not only in poetry (where it is also neglected) but in all rhetorical prose styles as well, even scientific ones. Noted for his facility with language and fluidity of style, even when writing about technical matter, Norbert Wiener can provide us with an example of how tonality and rhythm can work in science. The following quote is from the beginning of a chapter entitled "Feedback and Oscillation." Read these paragraphs out loud (or really hear and feel them in your mind); pay close *aural* attention to the rhythm and movement of each sentence in relation to the content of the sentence. (Wiener uses independent and dependent clauses, coordinating conjunctions, the rhythms of word placement, and even prepositions to create the sound of sense—the rigidity and awkwardness of movement described *and conveyed* by the sound of the language, which sentence by sentence creates in language the experience Wiener describes. [One can even note the predominance of certain prepositions in each paragraph—with, on/in, of/from—which set, reflect, and play the "themes" of symptom, location, and etiology.] Conjunctions used to set up parallel coordinate clauses that create the experience of continuous movement, as in polysyndeton, are underlined; prepositions used to create a preoccupation with direction or placement are circled.)

A patient comes into a neurological clinic. He is not paralyzed, and he can move his legs when he receives the order. Nevertheless, he suffers under a severe disability. He walks with a peculiar, uncertain gait, with eyes downcast on the ground and on his legs. He starts each step with a kick, throwing each leg in succession in front of him. If blindfolded, he cannot stand up, and totters to the ground. What is the matter with him?

Another patient comes in. While he sits at rest in his chair, there seems to be nothing wrong with him. However, offer him a cigarette, and he will swing his hand past it in trying to pick it up. This will be followed by an equally futile swing in the other direction, and this by still a third swing back, until his motion becomes nothing but a futile and violent oscillation. Give him a glass of water, and he will empty it in these swings before he is able to bring it to his mouth. What is the matter with him?

Both of these patients are suffering from one form or another of what is known as *ataxia*. Their muscles are strong and healthy enough, but they are unable to organize their actions. The first patient suffers from *tabes dorsalis*. The part of the spinal cord which ordinarily receives sensations has been damaged or destroyed by the late sequelae of syphilis.

The incoming messages are blunted, if they have not totally disappeared. The receptors in the joints and the tendons and muscles and soles of his feet, which ordinarily convey to him the position and state of motion of his legs, send no messages which his central nervous system can pick up and transmit, and for information concerning his posture he is obliged to trust his eyes and the balancing organs of his inner ear. In the jargon of the physiologist, he has lost an important part of his proprioceptive or kinesthetic sense. (95–96)

Now imagine you are hearing someone speak this in another room through a muffled wall. What you would hear would be tonality and rhythm that would communicate the experiential sense of this passage without the content. What you would hear would be the sound of sense. The rhythms and tones of voice create affective meaning, which when they coincide with referential meaning (or only associational meanings, as in the poems of Dylan Thomas) make *the experience* of thought and emotion more palatable and perceptible to the hearer. It is the sounds of language voiced that "make an audience feel the meanings very much in those words" (Elbow, "Shifting" 299). What Elbow is actually proposing by his suggestion that we teach writing as speech, then, is perhaps nothing less than the education of the intuitive faculty, that natural aesthetic that Isocrates and Cicero talk about. Whether in speech or in writing, voice instills and reveals the emotional and physical character of the meaning of words. Whether in speech or writing, voice highlights and plays the speaker's feelings in words. Whether in speech or in writing, voice persuades.

Yet, despite the recognition of the importance of voice in reading and writing by poets and writers and teachers of composition, little research has been done in exploring the role of sound as a source of affective knowledge in writing or reading, or in recitation as it relates to writing and reading, and the work that has been done is textually oriented.[6] This is no doubt partly the result of the formalistic, rationalistic philosophy of language and knowledge facilitated, if not engendered, by writing and print technology, which reduces rhythm, tone, and voice to minor "technical elements" in writing. Of course, there is also the problem of studying the elusive variables of rhythm, tone, and voice. Probably one major reason for the decision not to investigate the sound of sense is the difficulty of measuring it. Certainly the methodological commitment to measure imposes constraints on what can be "looked at." (Cf. Ihde, who attempts a phenomenological study and celebration of sound in *Listening and Voice*).

In a different approach to the problem, based on the work of Eugene Gendlin, Sondra Perl, in "Understanding Composing," explores the notion of voice in writing as "felt sense." While not concerned with the sound of language itself, Perl suggests that in addition to the ideas and visual images that present themselves to the mind's eye, the process of writing also entails listening to, or more precisely, "focusing" on emotions, feelings, and attitudes toward the text that are experienced during the process of writing. For Perl, this experience, or "felt sense" is "tacit knowledge" sensed in and by the body. In this way as well, "voice" is physical; it "is anchored in the writer's body," for writing is "not solely the product of a mind but of a mind alive in a living, sensing body" (Perl 365).

While Perl doesn't explicitly deal with felt sense as sound, she does ask if voice as felt sense is that tacit knowledge that professional writers can "sense more readily than unskilled writers" and whether it can help us describe the process of writing more holistically (366). If the answer is yes, can we also focus on felt sense not only as it is intuited in the sentient body but also as it is created in and through language as a physical medium—as sound? While this would also entail the prelogical dimension of felt, or experienced, meaning that Gendlin discusses, it would also attempt to "describe" that experience as it occurs in the affective response to the music of language. That is, perhaps we can in some sense track and attend to the flow of feeling as it is created and/or embodied in language by paying attention to the sound of language as a sensuous form. Although Gendlin comments that "response most often springs from the inwardly felt experiencing without verbal symbolization" (14), he also believes that attention to experience (or certain aspects of experience) is a "symbolic process" (10), broadly defined. Thus, although the focus of our attention is somewhat different, Gendlin and Perl might agree that it is in the interaction of language and experience where meaning occurs: "Meaning is *formed* in the interaction of experiencing and something that functions symbolically. Feeling without symbolization is blind; symbolization without feeling is empty" (*Experiencing* 5). It is the interaction of felt sense and language as a sensuous form that we are interested in.

Furthermore, if felt sense is the intuition of experience that underlies voice in writing, it is reasonable to suppose that felt sense also underlies and occurs in reading. Perhaps, then, felt sense in writing can be taught by reading out loud—through imitation of oral performance. If, according to Polanyi, tacit knowledge is based on natural talent, is learned subconsciously and performed intuitively, it probably cannot be taught very well by formalistic rules but rather is learned primarily by imitation and practice (53). Where Perl applies Gendlin's notion of felt sense to writing, we will also apply it to reading. In this and the following chapter, we will focus on how felt sense is created, embodied, and experienced in the sensuous form of language as sound, how the epistemic music of language contains and communicates affective experience in reading and writing.

We will not talk about language *as* music here (see Lanier, who attempts to develop a theory of poetry as music), although there may be certain benefits to mapping the sound of language, both in poetry and prose, in terms of musical notation to supplement other traditional and invented systems of prosodic or linguistic analyses.[7] Nor will we talk about music as it is "imposed" on language, as in song lyrics, although musical notation also reveals the differences between song lyrics as music and the music of language.[8] Rather, we will talk about the music *of* language as spoken—as a sensuous movement of sound that sets up and plays off of expectations created by its own rhythms. We will talk about the music that is inherent in language and our affective response to it as a form of knowledge. Language (sung or spoken) does not have the advantages of pure musical experience insofar as language is also referential (see Zuckerkandl, Langer, discussed later). And spoken language does not possess some of the properties of music that in some sense take the place of referentiality, such as scales, intervals, melody, and harmonic progression, which is a large part of the "meaning" of music. However, language does possess some of the other important properties of music, such as tonality and rhythm, which in addition to referential or connotative meaning, perhaps play a large part in the affective experience of language.

How can we account for the affective nature of language as sound and describe the physical experience of it in a way that is not methodologically reductive, which chapter 2 argued is the major problem with investigating feeling and emotion as indeterminate phenomena? In "Piaget, Problem-Solving, and Freshman Composition," Lee Odell explores the need to get students to listen to the dissonance and disequilibrium they feel during the process of writing. Dissonance and disequilibrium underlie "all human activities" (36) and are the result of the relative nature of all human knowledge, which is "subject to continual revision" (37). Odell's assertion is doubly significant for us: not only do we hear the sophistic philosophy of uncertainty that undergirds much contemporary composition, but also an implicit, metaphorical connection between uncertainty and "dissonance," between indeterminacy and sound as a kind of knowledge. Although this is not Odell's point, disequilibrium and especially dissonance refer not only to cognitive distress but also to sound. For Odell, the ability to identify dissonance and to restore balance and harmony is the basis of formulating and solving problems, which in turn is the basis of reading and writing "sensitively, thoughtfully, and independently" (37). Although the source of disequilibrium will be unique for each student, Odell states that we can show students how to "examine their experiences and their expectations" (38).

As we touched on in chapter 2, Richards argued for the need

to have students learn to interpret their emotions, feelings, and attitudes as organic responses, which he believed were a form of intuitive knowledge that informs our understanding of and relationship to the world; for Richards, this is the value of reading poetry and literature generally (*Principles* 98–102). But if interpretation, based on the referential function of language, only leads to a positivistic (mis)understanding of feelings, as Tate and Fish charge, perhaps we can examine experiences and expectations by understanding language as a nonreferential, sensuous, physical, uncertain form of knowledge, as Cicero and the sophists seemed to—by understanding how language itself is the basis of affective response, of felt sense in the dimension of time, as sound.

Like Perl and Odell, Elbow understands disequilibrium or dissonance to be an essential by-product of the uncertainty of knowledge; Elbow understands the problem with teaching students to write as one of getting them to listen to their affective states, their emotional dissonance and harmony in reading out loud. But for Elbow, dissonance or disequilibrium (as well as resolution and harmony) entails tension between "anticipation and resolution" that "binds time" ("Shifting" 296). Elbow leaves the problem of describing this temporal dimension of the affective experience of speech for future resolution. However, as he hints, the oral dimension of language as sound in time may be essential in understanding how affective experience is created in language.

In fact, the temporal dimension of language and experience may take us beyond the epistemological cul-de-sac in contemporary Reader Response Criticism and New Physics. Although Kintgen argues that even linguistic descriptions of style may not be enough to understand a reader's perception of a text, perhaps a temporal, as opposed to spatial, approach to style can overcome some of the difficulty. And while other attempts have been made to analyze "musical time" rather than quantity in language—that is, rhythm rather than meter (Sumera refers to the prosodic work of Steele, Thomson, and Croll as "the core of what might be called the Temporal tradition in the study of verse" [105])—we will be interested here less in analysis and more in the nature of affective response to the aural dimension of language as a form of knowledge.

Thus, we will try to build on the work of Elbow and Perl by attempting to explore how voice and felt sense are also created in and through affective response to the music of language and how that response is temporal in nature. Not only is dissonance a by-product of the uncertainty of knowledge; the sound of language itself may be a form of uncertain knowledge. But is it possible to describe affective response in reading (and writing) as an indeterminate form of temporal knowledge in a way that is not inherently reductive? Can an understanding of affective response in time inform our attempts to educate the literate aesthetic faculty through oral performance? An exploration of the temporal dimension of the experience of sound in language, and the problem of teaching it, will occupy us in the remainder of this book. To begin to understand affective response to language in time, and the problems encountered therein, let's return to Reader Response Criticism, where style as a temporal form of knowledge is seen but not heard.

Affective Stylistics and the Education of the Aesthetic Faculty

Somewhat like Elbow, Stanley Fish and Wolfgang Iser understand aesthetic response in reading as a temporal process of anticipation and resolution or retrospection. In "Literature in the Reader: Affective Stylistics," Stanley Fish sets out to refute the predominant notion of the text as a static object in space. Or, to put it in terms of the discussion in chapter 2, Fish sets out to refute the atomistic philosophy in which words are held to be discrete elements that have a one-to-one correspondence with objects in reality. Rather than asking what a sentence means, Fish asks what a sentence does—to the reader: "It [the sentence] is no longer an object, a thing-in-itself, but an *event*, something that *happens* to, and, with the participation of, 'the reader' " (25). It is what happens to the reader, says Fish, that is the meaning of the sentence.

Like Elbow on the process of writing, Fish understands the process of reading as an event in time, a temporal flow in which a reader's responses to the text emerge and are confirmed or altered over time. Simply put, in the process of reading, as in the process of writing, words, phrases, sentences, paragraphs create expectations in the reader on many different levels of experience ("Literature" 27). These expectations, which are either fulfilled, postponed, or denied, lead to further expectations that are fulfilled, postponed, or denied, ad infinitum, thus building a complex of meaningful expectations in the reader. Until this complex is brought to a satisfactory closure on all levels, the result is a constant state of expectations, of flux, or, to use Odell's terms, disequilibrium and dissonance.

(I recently chaired a master's thesis on Thomas Pynchon's *V* in which, in one chapter, the student shifts back and forth in each section between an analysis of cold war discourse and an analysis of the novel. The rhythm created by the repeated and extended comparisons [the length or "duration" of the sections], as well as the parallel structure created by the lead sentences of the comparison, led me to expect that the chapter would end with a discussion of the novel; while the expected lead sentence occurred in the last paragraph of the chapter, the discussion of the novel didn't, creating both unintended confusion, dissonance, and a desire for closure. [In fact, the aperiodic rhythm of *V* itself, contained in the microlevel of sentences and macrolevel of scenes, actually grows more frenetic, oscillates more and more wildly toward the end of the novel, creating a deliberate frenzy of dissonance that mirrors the breakdown of meaning.])

Although Fish assumes the goal of response over the time flow of the sentence to be the analysis and interpretation of meaning, his understanding of the temporal nature of the reading process does begin to give us an understanding of affective response as patterns of expectation in time. In *The Act of Reading: A Theory of Aesthetic Response*, Wolfgang Iser also examines the process of response based on patterns of expectation and fulfillment. For Iser, the text consists of instructions or schemata that the reader "actualizes" according to prior knowledge and expectations. Iser adopts the notion of schemata from Gestalt psychology, particularly as it is applied to the study of art in E. H. Gombrich's *Art and Illusion*. In Gestalt psychology, schemata organize our perceptions in patterns of expectation according to the "economy principle." Schemata thus reduce the complexity of the world into patterns that constitute our perception, experience, and knowledge of the world. Somewhat like Odell ("Piaget" 37), Iser believes that the discrepancies between the reader's schemata, or expectations, and the schemata of text are a source of disequilibrium and dissonance that the reader must try to resolve by revising his or her own schemata in the light of the new experience the text presents. Knowledge, whether of text or world, is subject to continual revision and change.

However, in painting, says Iser, there is a "referential norm" that is violated in representation but that the viewer can refer to, to make sense of the painting (*Act* 91). On the other hand, in literature there is no referential norm—no visual object to which a literature can be compared—since language is symbolic. (This will be important in understanding the nonreferential nature of the music of language as well.) Thus, says Iser, "[t]he relation of the text to the world can only be discerned by way of the schemata which the text bears within itself." For Iser, this is "the repertoire of social norms and literary conventions which condition the particular 'picture' offered by the work" (92). But it is the reader's repertoire that the text either confirms, plays off of, or subverts. And it is the pressure of the difference, the tension created by the "asymmetry" between what the reader expects or believes and the text that forces the reader to continually reorganize her or his expectations and to shape the text in light of this (81). (In discussing whether texts confirm or deny readers' expectations—whether or not the repertoires "overlap"—Iser adopts the spatial terms "vertical" and "horizontal" [83].)

For Iser, this structuring of our experience within the text itself, without reference to an external visual, is accomplished by a "foreground and background" of knowledge. Unlike painting, the foreground and background of a literary text is brought about by the author's "selection" of strategies from the repertoire contained within the text. For example, "social norms . . . will automatically establish a frame of reference in the form of a thought system or social system from which they were selected" (93). Again, the result of the difference between the reader's schemata and those contained in the text, between the background and the foreground, is the creation of expectations, of tension or disequilibrium. It is this tension, Iser believes, that motivates the reader to create "the aesthetic object." (Iser distinguishes this "aesthetic object" that the reader creates from "the text" that the author creates in much the same way that Rosenblatt (*Reader*) does between "poem" and "text.") It is the aesthetic object the reader creates in which the tension created by the relationship between the schemata of the text and the reader is resolved.

In fact, the process through which this aesthetic object emerges—the process of "selection and combination"—is Iser's primary interest. (For Iser, "selection" creates the background-foreground relationship, and thus "the world of the text." "Combination," on the other hand, "organizes the chosen elements in such a way as to allow comprehension of the text. Selection establishes the outer link, combination the inner" [*Act* 96].) For Iser, then, what each of the elements selected from the repertoire and combined in the text presents are different perspectives that interact with each other. Given that the process of reading occurs over time, the result is what Iser calls "the wandering viewpoint." (In describing the shifting perspectives of the reader created by the schemata chosen from the repertoire over the temporal course of reading a text, Iser has recourse to two more terms drawn from Gestalt psychology: "theme and horizon." Theme for Iser is the perspective the reader has adopted at any particular time; horizon is the relegation of other possible perspectives of the wandering viewpoint to the background. These viewpoints "not only modify one another, but also influence past and future synthesis" [*Act* 99].)

Thus, for Iser, "anticipation and retrospection" are the essence of the process of reading as aesthetic response. As Iser puts it, "Our attitude toward each theme is influenced by the horizon of past themes, and as each theme itself becomes part of the horizon during the time-flow of our reading, so it, too, exerts an influence on subsequent themes" (99). Reading always results in a growth of the reader's schemata, "an enrichment, as attitudes are at one and the same time refined and broadened" (*Act* 99)—a change in those very social, cultural, historical, and literary systems that constitute the reader's repertoire, and thus a change in the reader's knowledge.

The connection between the change and growth brought about by the stretching, playing, and breaking of expectations in the process of writing as described by Odell and in the process of reading as described by Iser is important. As we discussed in chapter 2, the attempt to integrate Reader Response Criticism with composition is based on the assumption that reading and writing involve similar mental processes that facilitate intellectual and emotional development. But as we also discussed, there are epistemological problems rooted in the methods of Reader Response Criticism, problems that extend to affective stylistics and lead back to the predominately visual ontology of reading and writing—to reception as analysis and interpretation rather than a performance of language.

Limitations of Affective Stylistics as Visual Aesthetic

Iser's description of the reading process based on Gestalt psychology does give us an understanding of aesthetic response as a temporal flow that parallels and in some ways supplements Elbow's. However, for Elbow, this temporal flow is understood in terms of speech, is bodied forth in voice, as sound. While Iser does consider anticipation and retrospection to be the affective basis of reading, like Fish, he understands reading, and therefore affective response, in visual rather than aural terms.

Yet, according to Ong, language is first and foremost sound. "Written texts all have to be related somehow, directly or indirectly, to the world of sound, the natural habitat of language to yield their meanings. 'Reading' a text means converting it to sound, aloud or in the imagination, syllable-by-syllable in slow reading or sketchily in the rapid reading common to high-technology cultures. Writing can never dispense with orality" (*Orality* 8).

Iser's visual bias in regard to the affective process of reading can be *seen* in the wholly visual metaphors that he adopts from Gombrich's theory of visual art: foreground/background, wandering viewpoint. Iser's understanding of anticipation and retrospection—as theme and horizon—is visual as well. In fact, Iser considers the structure of expectations themselves as visual rather than aural phenomena insofar as he regards language as a visual (rather than aural) stimulus (*Act* 117). Indeed, Iser regards "mental images as the basic feature of ideation" (135). What Iser calls "the process of image-building" involves the reader's building a totality out of the partial schemata of the text: "in assembling it, he will *occupy the position* set out for him, and so create a *sequence of images* that eventually results in his *constituting the meaning of the text*" (141; emphasis mine).

In this sense, literature is a visual art for Iser. Although Iser is careful to make a distinction between the normative frame of reference in visual art and the literary frame of reference that must be created out of the repertoire contained in the literary work of art itself, he makes no distinction between painting as visual art and language as predominantly oral. Iser, like other Reader Response critics, shows no particular awareness of or acute interest in the oral dimension of language. Anywhere Iser does consider the aural dimension of literature, he does so in visual terms. In describing how we read, for example, Iser refers to the "eye-voice span," which "when applied to the literary text will designate that span of the text which can be encompassed during each phase of reading and from which we anticipate the next phase" (*Act* 110). Thus, the eye-voice span, which apprehends "syntactic units of sentences" as "residual 'chunks' for perception within the literary text" (110) is primarily visual, not aural. Iser doesn't even consider the possibility of aural perception.

Thus, while Iser understands the process of reading as a temporal process involving expectations, just as Elbow understands the process of writing, Iser's understanding is spatial rather than temporal. In fact, as his metaphors reveal, Iser's understanding of time, like ours, is heavily spatial. For Iser, reading takes place along a "time-axis" (*Act* 157); spatial "gaps" or "blanks" in the text constitute "a place" within the temporal structure of the text for the reader to make connections (*Act* 169); the temporal process of connecting or "filling in the blanks" builds up the expectations that result in *visual* ideation.[9] Iser even discusses blanks in the larger structures or pieces of the text in terms of sight: "The blank as an empty space between segments enables them to be joined together, thus constituting a field of vision for the wandering viewpoint" (197).

That Iser's is a visual understanding of the reading process, and of temporal patterns themselves, needs no further proof. And it is understandable, given the problem of comprehending time that we touched on in chapter 2 and will explore again shortly. This attention to field of vision, to image, to viewpoint, might lead one to think that Gestalt psychology itself only can be understood as visual, that we only can understand the temporality of affective response in terms of the sense of sight. But this may not be necessarily so. As Elbow states, "Because of the confusion introduced into our very notion of structure by the pervasive metaphor of space, I suspect that we are still waiting for the help we need in showing us simple and valid models of good structure in time" ("Shifting" 297). Since time is conceptualized in terms of visual ideation in affective stylistics, Reader Response Criticism may not be able to help us as much in understanding and "describing" what happens in the temporal process of reading (and writing)—not what happens in the more abstract relation between thought and language as symbol, but what happens in the more physical relation of thought and language as sound.

Based on cognitive psychology, researchers in composition also have attempted to understand affect in terms of visual schemata—how affect can constitute schemata (McLeod), and how affect interacts with or modifies cognitive schemata (Flower, "Decision Points"). While the recognition of the role of emotion in the thinking/composing process is most valuable, the attempt to understand feeling in visual, spatial terms is puzzling—and revealing. Emotion (perhaps like all knowledge) seems to be instantaneous, physical, and diffuse, and thus may be better understood as an indeterminate movement of patterns in time rather than visual schemata localized in space. Perhaps it is *in* musical rather than spatial metaphors, then—tone, not image; rhythm, not schemata; melody and harmony, not foreground and background; key and modulation, not theme and horizon; duration, not eye-voice-span; rests, not blanks—that we can better understand and describe the temporal process of reading.

But it is not only a matter of analytical terminology, of metaphors. It is a different mode of apprehension, one which points to a different dimension of knowledge. You will remember that in *De Oratore* Cicero makes a point of emphasizing that the ability to understand and judge the sound of rhythm and words is rooted more deeply in the general sensibility than is the ability to judge painting and sculpture (*D. O.* III.l. 195–97). Cicero's belief that the music of language is a more fundamental, primal, affective basis of aesthetic judgment than visual arts somewhat belies our dependence on visual *gestalten* as the basis of aesthetic response. In fact, it has even been suggested that the ability to "read" a painting, a photograph, a movie, is culturally relative, and must be learned (see Tyrwhitt, "Moving Eye"). The same may be true of music. However, as Ong reports, "[o]ral speech is fully natural in that every human being in every culture who is not physiologically or psychologically impaired learns to talk" (*Orality* 82). But Ong iterates, "By contrast with natural, oral speech, writing is completely artificial. There is no way to write 'naturally' " (*Orality* 82).

A part of this "naturalness" has to do with the nature of

language as sound. Unlike Iser, who understands language in terms of abstract, visual schemata, Ong understands language in terms of the physical sensation of voice in the body and as an acoustic medium that bears a special relationship "to interiority when sound is compared to the other senses" (Orality 71). Sound has a special relationship to consciousness in that sound must be interiorized to be experienced, understood. However, Ong more or less affirms what the ancient Cicero uttered about eloquence, and what the contemporary mathematical physicist Penrose points out about the nature of time itself: "There is no adequate model in the physical universe for this operation of consciousness, which is distinctly human and which signals the capacity of human beings to form true communities wherein person shares with person interiority, intersubjectivity" (Orality 177).

The physical experience of the sound of language, then, is perhaps the root or tonic of subjective and social knowledge: "all sound, and especially oral utterance, which comes from inside living organisms, is 'dynamic' " (Orality 32). Although "experience is intellectualized mnemonically," says Ong (36), in an oral culture, memory is not a container of schemata, as it is for Iser. Oral memorization does not separate knowledge from the knower, nor knower from learner. Rather, they are one in sound. "Sustained thought in an oral culture is tied to communication" (Orality 34). Thus, for Ong, one of the primary characteristics of an oral culture is that knowledge is not abstract, but situational (Orality 49). Unlike Iser's "abstract" depiction of how the schemata of the text alter the reader's "repertoire," then, in an oral culture it is "a listener," not a text, that is necessary "to stimulate and ground your thought" (Orality 34; cf. 176). In an oral culture, says Ong, "[p]ersonality structures . . . are more communal and externalized" (69).

But it is more than just the fact that "oral modes of thought" are more subjective and social than literate ones. The physical experience of language has something to do with the nature of sound itself, which, unlike sight, is more holistic, surrounds and incorporates the hearer with the heard (Ong, Orality 72).

Ong's belief that sight externalizes, isolates, distances, and sound internalizes, unifies, embraces is supported by recent brain research, as reported by Ochsner: "The auditory melody of hearing is an holistic task, comparable to the cognitive style of the right hemisphere, whereas the visual melody of sight permits us to fixate on something, to analyze it carefully. In this regard, looking at something carefully for details is a cognitive style of the left hemisphere" (61).

In addition to the fact that sight is sensed and appears to occur on the more external organ of the eye, while sound echoes and vibrates in the more internal organ of the ear, sound is perhaps more physically experiential than sight in another way. It travels through the air as sound waves, as opposed to light waves, which travel through the electromagnetic spectrum as photons (cf. Ong, *Orality* 71 for a discussion of the nature of light as reflected). While both sound and light are physical—one impinging on the eardrum and auditory nerves, the other on the retina and optic nerves—sound waves are considerably slower than light waves (750 miles per hour vs. 186,000,000 miles per second) and so may be more physically experiential than photons. Although many painters will disagree with the basic assumption (I'm not sure I agree with it myself), perhaps this is the reason some people can "feel" sound more than they can "feel" sight (except when their eyes hurt), why most people respond more immediately and physically to music than to painting, whose emotional response perhaps requires more "cognitive processing." (This excludes the psychological phenomenon known as synesthesia, the mixing or confusion of the senses, by which sight, for example, is experienced in terms of touch or flavor, or sound is experienced in terms of colors, etc. [see part 1 of Cytowic's *The Man Who Tasted Shapes* for a wide-ranging discussion of synesthesia as an involuntary medical phenomenon.])

Furthermore, the experience of sound as sensed exists in "its evanescence, its relationship to time. Sound exists only when it is going out of existence" (Ong, *Orality* 71). That is, the experience of sound as an indeterminate form of knowledge (not the meaning sound as a symbol refers to) exists in time, not space. Certainly, we can understand how sound waves move through space, are spatial. In fact, as Victor Zuckerkandl, whose work we will use in the next section, suggests, space too can be auditory (271–348). But as Zuckerkandl points out, even in auditory space, the experience and meaning of sound (its referent) exists in time, while the meaning of sight (its referent) exists in space.

Whatever else it might be, then, Ong's theory of orality in some sense constitutes an oral theory of response. But what is the temporal nature of sound, however transitory, when it exists in time, and what is its relation to feeling and consciousness? Ong doesn't attempt to answer this. New Physics can't. Perhaps what we need, then, is a more temporal model of sound in reading (and writing) as oral phenomena—of response in "real time" rather than spatial time. The question of what "real time" is was taken up in an interesting way by T. S. Eliot in his doctoral dissertation (see appendix D). It is also taken up by some philosophy of music, where it is developed into both a theory of knowledge and a set of temporal principles underlying affective schemata. Recognizing the abstract nature of all our knowledge, and for what its worth given our somewhat limited knowledge of the physiology and structure of the brain itself, affective schemata may in fact be more temporal than spatial in nature (or could more easily be understood that way). That is, affective schemata may not be spatial insofar as emotions cannot be localized, but rather constituted by a sensuous movement in bodily consciousness over time. As temporal forms, "musical schemata" thus might bring us a little closer to understanding affective experience in reading and writing.

Can the philosophy of music move us beyond the epistemological impasse that almost seems to be inscribed in our typographic culture and help us understand affective response to language in reading and writing as a more purely temporal flow in an oral mode in a way that is less reductive, and that will allow students to transfer more easily and naturally their ability to speak to reading and writing? Like Isocrates and Cicero, I suggest that while based on natural talent, "musical appreciation" of speech can be improved by practice and performance. Theories (like this one) are probably the least useful of all, though necessary to understand phenomena. But perhaps when we understand the temporal movement of affective response to the sensuous form of language in time, as sound in time as well as meaning in space, a true epistemological shift in methodology can occur in Reader Response Criticism and its implementation in teaching of composition, and a new sophistic more fully emerge in our scientific culture. For as long as affective response remains visually bound to the written text in the dimension of space and does not attend to the aural text in the dimension of time, Reader Response Criticism may ineluctably lead to analysis and interpretation and so be somewhat grounded in the formalistic, rationalistic epistemology that it seeks to redress.

To attempt to achieve an understanding of the aural text in time, it will be necessary to modulate from visual to musical metaphors, to syncopate and transpose the theme of our discussion from a spatial to a temporal key, which is perhaps closer to an oral ontology of thought. This shift will be accomplished only "temporarily" and with great difficulty, given the spatial nature of human reasoning and Kantian limitations of the senses. To do so, we now turn to the philosophy of music.

Reading and Writing and the Temporal Ontology of Music

> How then pray shall we enter on so great an undertaking with confidence in this capacity of rhythmical utterance? The difficulty of the thing is not so great as its importance; for there is nothing so delicate or flexible, or that follows so easily wherever one leads it, as speech.
> —Cicero, D. O.

It is interesting that although Ong discusses rhythm in relation to somatic mnemonics, such as body rocking (*Orality* 150), he never really discusses music per se. For despite Ong's claim that we can never fully comprehend the true nature of orality (*Orality* 31), based on the primacy of music for the sophists, Isocrates, and Cicero, we will take Elbow's suggestion in "The Shifting Relationships Between Speech and Writing" that we can turn to studies of music to construct a model of writing in time and apply it to reading. Indeed, music may be able to give us more insight into an "oral mindset," one based on the temporal dimension of meaning that music "describes." In the bibliography of this article, Elbow mentions two books on music, Victor Zuckerkandl's *Sound and Symbol: Music and the External World* and Leonard B. Meyer's *Emotion and Meaning in Music*. We will use the first in this chapter to understand sound as temporal knowledge and the second in the following chapter to explore affective response in reading (and writing) not as visual *gestalten*, as in Reader Response Criticism and contemporary composition, but as musical *gestalten*. As temporal schemata that slide on sound, these musical *gestalten* may give us a better, less reductive way of accounting for and perhaps eventually describing the affective response to the movement of language as indeterminate knowledge.

By way of explanation, a caveat: Given the relativity and uncertainty of temporal knowledge (our inability to understand it except in terms of space, and thus perhaps our inability to understand it at all), this theory of the music of language is not meant to be used as an a priori model in the teaching of reading and writing. Rather, this theory is meant as an indeterminate (noncausal or multicausal) model of affective response to the movement of language as sound that may facilitate our understanding of the experiential nature of reading and writing as oral performance and help us develop some approaches to supplement analysis and interpretation in the teaching of literature and writing. That is, this theory represents an attempt to study the role of time in response as a multidimensional point in the space-time of response and to construct a "temporal model" of the relationship of sound and affect as indeterminate knowledge. As Cicero states in the *Orator*, "We shall lay down no rules—that was not our undertaking—but we shall outline the form and likeness of surpassing eloquence: nor shall we explain how this is produced, but how it looks to us" (xiii.43).

For Zuckerkandl, music as an aural phenomenon is motion in time. But Zuckerkandl tries to understand motion over time as purely auditory, temporal, not visual, spatial. In fact, Zuckerkandl says the essence of motion itself is sound! "Musical motion is at the core of every motion" (138). Because it is beyond "body and place," the essence of motion cannot be seen or touched, Zuckerkandl states; it can only be heard. Just as Ong argues that sound bears a special relationship to interiority when compared to the other senses because it occurs within the organism, Zuckerkandl argues that "[c]ompared with seeing and touching, hearing proves to be the faculty that gets at the essence; that pierces to the core of the phenomenon" (146).

Thus, for Zuckerkandl, the meaning of music, like music itself, is temporal and therefore nonreferential. It refers to nothing but itself. The same may apply to the temporal nature of language as well (cf. Croll 436). "The older psychology sought to understand all psychological phenomena, including sensation and sense perception, after the pattern of physical phenomena, that is, mechanistically and atomistically," says Zuckerkandl (129). Zuckerkandl therefore believes that the misunderstanding of music has been the result of "positivistic thinking" (3). Like Ong's understanding of orality, Zuckerkandl thinks that through music "other modes of connection with the world are revealed . . . modes that are otherwise overshadowed by the dominance of the eye" (3). And like Isocrates and Cicero in regard to the "techniques" of eloquence, Zuckerkandl believes that methods patterned after the natural sciences "can be successfully employed only in the marginal provinces of music" (5).

In fact, the problem of time and space in physics is so important to understanding the temporal dimension of sound that Zuckerkandl spends more than half his big tome discussing the philosophy of music in terms of it; the interested reader will want to check out the summary of Zuckerkandl's discussion of the philosophy of music as it pertains to physics in appendix

D of this book. The central problem is that the Newtonian conception of the motion of material bodies in space, when applied to the "musical motion" of language, reduces the auditory, temporal phenomena (musical event, text, or responses to it) to spatial objects of referential meaning. But the temporal, nonreferential dimension (of music or language), like affective experience, may not be spatial at all.

Actually, the temporal dimension may create affective experience. It may be the temporal, nonreferential dimension of language that underlies the sound of sense that is heard in the wall-muffled voice. It also may be the temporal, nonreferential dimension of language that underlies a part of the sophistic philosophy of style as an uncertain form of knowledge but which even for the ancients was overshadowed by the spatial dominance of the eye (Zuckerkandl's deliberation on the ancients' conception of space and time in relation to Cosmos has implications not only for our understanding of orality and literacy but also for our understanding of the problem of motion, narration, and the relation of time to sophistic epistemology, and is also summarized in appendix D).

For Zuckerkandl, the problem of understanding music is one of understanding the nature of time itself, independent of space. The spatial understanding of time, of course, has been magnified and codified by modern philosophy and science:

> The scientific age, whose chief interest was in material-spatial phenomena and processes, saw the problem of time wholly in the light—or rather the darkness—of the problem of space. The time concept was subordinated to the space concept. For Descartes, who gave this view of the universe its classical formulation which prevailed for centuries, space is the paramount reality of the physical world; time is merely the consequence of our inability to experience the all-embracing simultaneity of things in space except as a succession. (Zuckerkandl 156)

As we explored in chapter 2, based on Kantian categories of intuition, New physicists too conceive of time as a dimension of space and so understand it in spatial terms only. [10] While time has been the subject of speculation through the ages, it was only in this century that time was even *formally* recognized in physics as a dimension of reality at all.

Zuckerkandl believes that a shift away from purely spatial, visual modes of thought is occurring, where subatomic phenomena are not spatial objects, but temporal events. Now, says Zuckerkandl, "[t]ime is recognized as the foundation of all existence; even inanimate matter is shown to be, in its core, vibration—a temporal phenomenon. The concept of time has everywhere taken precedence over the concept of space" (156). However, this may be a little premature. Roger Penrose expresses the problem this way:

> The way in which time is treated in modern physics is not essentially different from the way in which *space* is treated and the 'time' of physical descriptions does not really 'flow' at all; we just have a static-looking fixed 'space-time' in which events of our universe are laid out! Yet, according to our perceptions, time *does* flow. . . . My guess is that there is something illusory here too, and the time of our perceptions does not 'really' flow in quite the linear forward-moving way that we perceive it to flow (whatever that might mean!). The temporal ordering that we 'appear' to perceive is, I am claiming, something that we impose on our perceptions in order to make sense of them in relation to the uniform forward time-progression of an external physical reality. (443–44)

Zuckerkandl too expresses reservations concerning the efficacy and extent of the shift in New Physics: "For the physicists, finally, time has basically never been anything but a fourth dimension added to the three dimensions of space, a measurable extension" (183–84). Even Heidegger's phenomenological conception of time is in some respects spatial (see appendix D). At the Newtonian level, our understanding of time is fine; but at the subatomic level, it is perhaps a different mix. Time may be an essential, unknown component of indeterminacy (Penrose 442–47). It may be an essential component of affective response to language as well. And analysis and interpretation based on spatial modes of perception and knowing, on traditional empiricism and rationalism, may not be able to get at the nature of time.

It is only recently that New physicists like Roger Penrose have begun to recognize that our inability to understand time independently of space may be leading us to a false perception of time as flowing and thus to incomplete or illusory conceptions of reality and of consciousness itself (444). As Penrose notes, "[C]onsciousness itself will fit only very uncomfortably into our present conventional space-time descriptions!" (447). For Penrose, both classical physics and New Physics are only approximations—the precursors of a new, more complete theory that will include and go beyond them to fully account for the nature of time and consciousness (see 302–47 and esp. 442–47). In fact, in a way that supports Eliot's early insights (*Knowledge*), Penrose himself alludes to the consciousness of musical composition (and mathematical invention) as opposed to performance (or logic) in "real time" as an indicator that "the timing and temporal progression of consciousness is not in accord with that of external physical reality" (445; cf. Zuckerkandl 273, who compares and contrasts tones to thought). The true nature of time, and perhaps of consciousness itself, may be more on the order of something simultaneous rather than a flow.

Indeed, music itself, which after all seems to unfold linearly and is in its "deep structure" mathematical, may also be Kantian. As we discussed in chapter 2, the categories of pure intuition seem to be an a priori condition of our knowing. Assuming that time is not causal or spatial,[11] the spatiality of Kantian consciousness that underlies the imperative to describe time in terms of space (linearly) or causally (as related sequences) may represent the limits of indeterminacy and of knowledge generally. If so, music, like New Physics and Reader Response Criticism, would represent, to borrow Holton's phrase, another "impotency proposition," in this case a bridge over the gap of our ignorance of time. But if music is still a priori, we will explore how it is perhaps no longer visual, spatial, linear—how its logical and mathematical structures refer only to time, not space, and so may get us at least a little closer to this nonreferential, indeterminate realm of experience. If Whorf states, "Newtonian space, time, and matter are no intuitions. They are recepts from culture and language" (153), there may be a way out of the spatial dimension of Kantian consciousness. Perhaps musical modes of thinking are the key to time perception; now if we could only find the door.

Zuckerkandl's understanding of music perhaps can bring us a little closer to the temporal ontology of language as something simultaneous as well as linear. The basic element of music, of course, is tone (Zuckerkandl 12). But Zuckerkandl argues that tones not only move in time but are manifestations of time, "images of time" (248–64). Not only rhythm and meter but tone itself is constituted by and reveals time. "A true image of time must be an image for the ear, an audible image, an image made of tones," says Zuckerkandl (254–55); "[t]ones are time become audible matter. . . . What the hearer perceives in the tones—and the rests—of a musical work is not simply time but shaped and organized time" (258–59).

Although it is difficult to do so, tone as an image of time can be heard in language when language is "emptied" of its strictly semantic content, as in the poems of Dylan Thomas.[12] Indeed, Zuckerkandl's conception of tone as an image of time seems the antithesis of Iser's conception of the image as visual ideation. As Zuckerkandl suggests, "[A]n image of the nonspatial world that should not be a translation into the spatial, an image to be listened to, not looked at, an image of the flowing made of intangible material—such an image would necessarily overturn our ideas of images and their making" (255). To understand the temporal nature of language, which may help us understand better what in writing Odell calls "dissonance," Elbow "voice," Perl "felt sense," and perhaps what we teach when we teach reading as oral performance rather than silent act, we must first understand that a word is a tone, an image of time. Every utterance is an image of time, which perhaps plays a part in creating affective experience. And in a way that supports Ong's contention that sound is primary even in literate cultures (*Orality* 2), Zuckerkandl states that "[t]he black characters on the white page, the letters that meet the eye, are spatial, to be sure. But the thought that emerges from the character and comes to meet me leaves the character, and with them everything spatial, behind" (272).

But a tone does not a melody make. "A melody is a series of tones that make sense" says Zuckerkandl, "just as sounds in succession make sense as words and sentences. . . . What we hear in melodies is not tones but tone words, tone sentences" (15–16). However, Zuckerkandl argues that it is because music is nonreferential, "because there are no things and places in music, precisely *because* music has freed itself from all connection with things and places, that . . . the core of motion can be manifested in absolute purity and immediacy" (138). And Zuckerkandl adds, "It is precisely *because* hearing music is a perception of purely dynamic phenomena that the core of the process of motion can be elementally experienced in music, and above all in music" (138).[13] Like Cicero concerning the universality of the music of language, Zuckerkandl concerning the universality language of music claims: "Most people understand the language of tones without further ado; they are capable of hearing successions of tones as melodies, of distinguishing between sense and nonsense in tones" (16).

This affective movement of tones without reference to meaning in melody (and perhaps in language, such as can be heard when one listens to a speech in a language one doesn't understand) is possible because tones in succession possess a "dynamic" quality. "The single tone was simply a tone; the same tone at the end of the phrase in our melody is a *tone that has become active*, a tone in a definite state of activity": "What we hear in this way we can designate as a state of disturbed equilibrium, as a tension, a tendency, almost a will. The tone seems to point beyond itself toward the release from tension and restoration of equilibrium; it seems to look in a definite direction for the event that will bring about this change; it even seems to demand the event" (Zuckerkandl 19). Zuckerkandl's understanding of music as tones in a dynamic succession that create expectations, disturb equilibrium, demand resolution, does in some ways resemble Odell's and Elbow's understanding of affective response in writing, and Fish and Iser's understanding of affective response in reading. But Zuckerkandl's understanding of expectations and equilibrium is obviously related exclusively to the dynamics of music.[14] Can we understand reading and writing as tones in dynamic succession and learn to listen for harmony and dissonance, for affective states created by the music of language?

Perhaps the "best" readers and writers hear the dynamic succession of tones, and this is especially pronounced in reading and composition as an oral/aural phenomenon. It is the dynamic movement of words as tones in the dimension of time, as well as the considerable connotative, emotional force of the meaning of words in the dimension of space, in which some of the harmony or dissonance of language is created and resides. Take these lines that Jesse Jackson, probably one of the greatest orators of our time, chanted during the 1988 Democratic Convention: "We will go from the outhouse, to the town house, to the statehouse, to the White House. We will win! We will win! We will win!" It is the dynamic succession of words as tones, as much as the meaning of the words themselves, that creates the tension and movement of the sentence, that causes the reader to get caught up and respond to the climactic resolution at the end. Many examples of dissonance, both intentional and unintentional, also can be found in contemporary political speeches and prose (we will deal with the difference between intentional and unintentional dissonance in the next chapter).

Thus, to understand the dynamic nature of words as tones, as images of time, we must also understand that tone is "not a difference of pitch," at least not as we commonly think, but a difference "of position in the tonal system" (Zuckerkandl 34). While spoken or written language is not built on intervals of a tonal scale, the dynamics created by the position of words as tones may apply to written language as well. "The totalities that are called *Gestalten* are distinguished by the characteristic that in them the individual part does not acquire its meaning from itself (or not exclusively from itself), but receives it from the whole" (229). This observation takes the cliché that no word in a great piece of literature could be altered or its order changed without a loss of meaning and places it in a temporal context. Although the dynamic quality of tones is contained in the relationship between them, what we hear in a tone is "the *promise of a whole* that it bears within itself" (37).

This teleology of tone is possible because tones are part of a dynamic context, a whole that exists for Zuckerkandl in simultaneous time, "a temporal whole, a whole whose parts are given as a sequence, as temporal succession" (229). In other words, tones don't move (up and down) through space-time for Zuckerkandl; time moves through tones, connecting them, making them vibrate and "flow" in a harmonious whole. And not just sequential time, as counted by the metronome, but simultaneous time, which gives the tones meaning in relation to each and to the temporal whole in which they are sounded. It is in the dynamic context of sound that tone becomes a manifestation of the simultaneity of time—or as close as we can get to it. Despite the necessity of the temporal succession of tones, then, Zuckerkandl suggests it is the aural whole from which music (primarily) derives its "meaning" as a temporal phenomenon. (Indeed, it is very hard to understand the meaning of tone [either in music or language] in and of itself, divorced from context; tones necessarily derive even more of their significance from context than words do, insofar as they are nonreferential. But as those working with oral interpretation might point out, this also may apply to the rendering of language as an aural experience as well [e.g., see Schrivner 9–11; Geiger 149].)

As Zuckerkandl argues, "Hearing music means hearing the action of forces" (37). It means hearing time. "Musical contexts are motion contexts, kinetic contexts," says Zuckerkandl;

"tones are elements of a musical context because and in so far as they are conveyors of a motion that goes through and beyond them. When we hear music, what we hear is above all motions" (76). It is "the dynamic quality [of motion] that permits tones to become the conveyors of meaning" (21). In music, motion includes not only the obvious, such as rhythm and meter, but melodic motion: interval—or tone steps; scale—the "rising and falling" of tones in set progressions; and harmonic cadence— the simultaneous motion of tones (see Zuckerkandl 151–247). While language does not have established intervals, scales, or harmonic cadences (except when sung), it certainly does make deliberate use of pitch and lineal harmonic resonances set up in echoes of sound, such as in consonance, assonance, alliteration, and rhyme—internal if not end rhyme; the counterpointing of heard and expected rhythm—rhythm and meter; as well as re-verberations created by structural repetition—parallelism, metaphor, and other figures of speech, which give words aural "presence" (cf. Perelman 37).

But Zuckerkandl argues that "[t]he principal manifestation of time in music is rhythm" (157). Rhythm is the temporal force that moves through a musical work, that brings it to life. In fact, it seems that for Zuckerkandl, as for Cicero (*D. O.* xlviii. 185–86) and even some contemporary science (cf. Prigogine), rhythm is a fundamental process of the universe.[15] For Zuckerkandl, as for Cicero (*D. O.* III. xlviii. 184–86), meter acts as the norm against which rhythm plays. Zuckerkandl too suggests that regularity in music is not a merit but a norm. But meter is not static either: "if we were able to define melody as motion in a dynamic field of tones, rhythm now presents itself to us as *motion* in the dynamic field of meter" (Zuckerkandl 173–74).

We might wonder about the relevance of meter for the teaching of expository (or even argumentative) writing. After all, music depends entirely upon acoustic patterns for its meaning, and prose (and even much contemporary poetry) is not nearly as regular or metrical as music. But like Cicero (*D. O.*

III. xliv. 176), Zuckerkandl claims that "[m]elodic motion is *free motion*"; however, it is the "*norm* that serves this freedom as a standard, gives it meaning, and thus makes it possible at all" (99). In poetry, this norm is created by expected meter. In the dynamics of speech, the all-inclusive, all-embracing context of sound created by the tone and rhythm of the very first word, and all subsequent words, is perhaps the norm and a basis of affective response. But it is there in the prose as well (see *A History of English Prose Rhythm*, in which Saintsbury analyzes and divides prose rhythms into historical periods; also see, for example, Bollinger; Croll; Steele).

But this is where the distinction between time and space is particularly important. When we talk about reading and writing as an aural event in time, we too mean it as a movement not in auditory *space*, nor even temporal *space*. Rather, we mean it as an event in simultaneous time, an expression of motion, not of the rhythm of words and sentences—for particular words and sentences disappear as soon as they are uttered—but of the temporal force that moves throughout and even beyond the tonal context of the work, the temporal "field" in which the work exists, that in prose as well as verse gathers the rhythmic flux of syllables into meaningful felt motion. That force, that field, is meter. When we ignore it in prose, we miss the music of the universe of discourse.

Like Cicero, then, the level of style we are talking about is not merely matter of embellishment. It is a matter of physical, felt patterns of sound in the dynamic context of time, in the field of meter, that in conjunction with content help create affective experience in reading and writing. Of course, our analytical, spatial approach to rhythm and meter gets at this to some extent. However, when we analyze meter by traditional or linguistic methods, we unwittingly separate form from content—not only from semantic content but from musical content. That is, we separate rhythm from meter, motion from time; we reduce sound to a static, spatial analogue in order to understand it and so often miss its temporal nature, lose the aural experience as lived.[16] As Cicero says, it is "not in the number of syllables but in the length as it affects the ear, which is the sharper and more reliable test" (*D. O.* III.xlvii.183).

Affective Stylistics as Holistic Music

If the simultaneity of time manifests itself most in the dynamic context of sound, then to construct a temporal model of reading and writing as oral/aural phenomena we need to be able to explore not only the rhythm and meter of sentences but also the rhythm and meter (or proportions) of the organizational structures that create that context. We need to explore the movement of time through prose not only on the level of word or sentence but from sentence to sentence, from paragraph to paragraph, from section to section, and throughout the work as a dynamic whole. And we need to do so in temporal rather than spatial terms.

Based on the cognitive model of the writing process ("Cognitive Process"), Linda Flower's understanding of organization as establishing contextual expectations, using hierarchies, and providing visual cues (*Problem Solving* esp. 128–40) does this to some extent. But like most discussions of organization, hers is understandably a spatial rather than temporal conceptualization of these processes. Like Reader Response critics, Flower is concerned with expectations and structure in regard to how readers will interpret semantic content rather than with expectations and structure as the action of forces that create affect. Given the preoccupation with visual modes of comprehension in our culture, even poets and teachers of poetry seem obsessed with language as a visual rather than an aural object of meaning. While the spatial dimension of meaning is certainly the most important in our culture, it does not totally account for the experience of language.

Expectations are also created by the motion of time in sound as an action of forces. If in the dynamic context of music or language tone is the image of "incompleteness that we hear," then "[t]o *hear* incompleteness is to hear time" (Zuckerkandl

253). Thus, expectation is a function of the tone as a part of a dynamic system. Tone bears expectation entirely in itself. "Indeed," says Zuckerkandl, "the individual tone bears its meaning so exclusively in itself that it can only be understood at all if *no* past or future tone stands beside it in consciousness" (232). As Zuckerkandl discusses, this nonreferentiality is demonstrated by the surprise (and joy) we continually experience in listening to certain melodies. The emotions we feel are the result of the fact that when we listen to music we are not listening to events in time only, but to time itself: "Our foreknowledge is concerned with the stream of events; our hearing is concerned with the stream of time" (233). Zuckerkandl goes so far as to argue that insofar as *gestalten* consist of tones (rather than the repertoire and schemata, as they do for Iser), memory and anticipation play little if any part in the experience of the whole. "In the hearing of melodies, nothing is remembered and nothing anticipated," Zuckerkandl asserts (230).[17]

Like his view of image, then, Zuckerkandl's view of anticipation in the dynamic context of sound is quite different from Iser's conception of it. Iser's claim that the absence of actual visual referents in symbols that requires meaning be created in the interaction between the reader and the text over the temporal course of the work superficially resembles Zuckerkandl's claim that music is nonreferential. However, anticipation is, according to Iser, ultimately spatial in that it has as its object the formation of an image of the world. But according to Zuckerkandl, "[i]t is not expectation *of something*, a feeling whose object is an event in time; it is pure expectation, which has time itself, the eventuation of time, as its object." In music, says Zuckerkandl, "the self-anticipation of time can be the subject of an experience" (233). Where Iser's visual *gestalten* point exclusively toward space, Zuckerkandl's aural *gestalten* point exclusively toward time.

Yet, Zuckerkandl states that the phenomena he is describing not only appear in music but "must be demonstrable in the other arts in which time appears as a factor" (234), and he turns to literature for further proof of his philosophical claim that anticipation is nonreferential and contained in the temporal flow of the work as a whole. And he does so in a way that highlights the opposition between a spatial and a temporal understanding of *gestalten*. Zuckerkandl suggests that "it is only after the purely objective element of tension, the curiosity to know what is coming, has been disposed of that the other kind of tension and expectation can become manifest. Hence the heightened artistic pleasure one receives from rereading a great story" (234).

This seems to be the antithesis of Iser's point that the reader selects and combines elements in the temporal flow of the text to form an image of the world. For Zuckerkandl the world (of time) is already constituted by and contained in music:

> [T]he total course of a musical work is on a large scale . . . a whole that unfolds in time and is so constituted that, though its individual members appear one after another, the whole, in order to be present, does not have to wait for member to be added to member, but is, so to speak, always already there, not factually, as with the spatial *Gestalt*, but as direction, as oriented tension. . . . Audible forms are perfect temporal *Gestalten*, creatures of time, as spatial *Gestalten* are creatures of space. (236–37)

Thus, Zuckerkandl argues that referentiality and any spatial imaging of the world must be disposed of before the hearing of music (see nn. 27, 30).

Given his understanding of music existing in time as a simultaneous whole, it is not surprising that Zuckerkandl should unwittingly refute Iser's spatial notion of "blanks" as well. Like Iser, Zuckerkandl believes that gaps violate the "laws of good continuity." But while Iser considers blanks necessary to stimulate the reader's imagination and the operation of the literary schemata, Zuckerkandl maintains that there are no gaps in music: "Motion without continuity is inconceivable" (118). If, for the New physicists, space is no longer an empty void but rather a manifestation of a vast energy field of which the electromagnetic spectrum and all matter, whether subatomic particles or planets, is a part, time itself is beginning to be understood not only as a mere factor in velocity of objects but rather as the dimension of motion itself. For Zuckerkandl, "a void, a nothing, becomes the conveyor of motion" (121).

We may find it hard to entirely agree with Zuckerkandl's assertion that music (like literature for Eliot) is a self-contained whole, complete in itself, an ideal temporal realm of meaning not dependent on a listener. However, his insight here is an interesting one, for it allows us to begin to understand the purely temporal dimension of language at the level of organization. Shaking off referentiality and spatial time, "real time" may be an important element in "literary experience," and perhaps in literacy itself: "the simple fact that one can see a play twice with the same tension strikingly demonstrates that time *is* something other than a mere formality, a mere container for successive events" (Zuckerkandl 234). If tone and rhythm are events in the dynamic context of time, in the field of motion and meter, organizational structure is too. Organization is more than a container of events in time; it is an event in time itself, set in motion by sound.

The organizational structure of music, albeit nonreferential, is much more determinate than the musical structure of language insofar as melodies are built on keys that actually form the basis of the meaning of music. But perhaps the organizational structure of language (or the lack of it), even in the most mundane piece of prose, may be better *experienced* by the sense of hearing than by sight (but cf. Ochsner 77–106, esp. 93–99, for a different understanding of auditory rhythm and pacing in writing vs. speaking, and its relationship to kinetic and visual melodies). Our sense of equilibrium, of balance, is located in the ear. Though much more tenuous, various, and uncertain, the organizational structure of language in the dimension of time may also underlie and to some degree create the affective experience of its parts. We can only gesture here at how this "higher level" of musical structure, this "field" of organization that creates the dynamic context and sets time in motion through tone, rhythm, and meter, might work in language (although I would point to Peter Elbow's "The Shifting Relationships Between Speech and Writing" itself as an example of it). Thus, in a way that closely parallels Ong's work, but goes beyond it in developing a temporal model of aural experience, Zuckerkandl's philosophy of music provides a critique of the visually based understanding of structure in Reader Response Criticism. As Zuckerkandl states, "[V]iewing, beholding, is not the sole privilege of the eye" (259). "[T]he eye pushes the without away from me. . . . The eye discloses space to me in that it excludes me from it. The ear, on the other hand, discloses space to me in that it lets me participate in it. . . . Where the eye draws the strict boundary line that divides without from within, world from self, the ear creates a bridge. . . . The space experience of the eye is a disjunctive experience; the space experience of the ear is a participative experience" (291). If for Zuckerkandl "[t]he new dimension by which music enriches our image world—is *time*, and everything for which the word stands: flowing, becoming, change, motion" (260), it is from this dimension that we perhaps can return to a fuller appreciation of the experience and meaning of language. As Zuckerkandl suggests in regard to music, "if now, from this newly won level, tones again seek to be linked with words, with actions . . . they do not thereby lose any of their new freedom; on the contrary, they, in their turn, now free word and action from exclusive connection with the world of things, bring a new dimension to view in them" (260).

Perhaps Zuckerkandl's understanding of the temporal dimension of music can be a new basis for understanding affective response in reading and writing. Perhaps it even hints at a solution to the problem of time and consciousness Penrose points out in New Physics. For music, Zuckerkandl proclaims, represents nothing less than "the unity of consciousness" (264). Be that as it may, we can use Zuckerkandl's understanding of music as a temporal field to begin to develop a model of affective response in reading and writing as aural, temporal, indeterminate knowledge. For speech is referential *and acoustical*. As an acoustic environment, in the temporal dimension, the music of speech, like music itself, is not divided but all-inclusive, surrounding, embracing, uniting subject and object, outer and inner, whole with part, speaker and spoken. If "the subject enters into perceptual contact with the surrounding space," it is through sound, in time, that this occurs (Zuckerkandl 275). And if space becomes "alive as a result of sound," time is the force that makes it live (Zuckerkandl 277).

Perhaps time, and all it stands for, is the basis of the experience of language as sound, emotion a lump of time caught in the throat. Perhaps it is through time that we can know the affective experience of language as an indeterminate flux and flow. Perhaps it is in time that the essential unity, the oneness that oral cultures experienced in sound, exists. Perhaps we have not lost it. Perhaps it is still in the music of language. Could it be that voice and felt sense, that dissonance and disequilibrium, that harmony and resolution in reading and writing are musical in nature, are the epistemic basis of affective knowledge, are a temporal form of knowledge? Could it be, as Zuckerkandl believes, that "music becomes the *key* that leads to a new understanding of the world of the psyche, of organisms, even of the inorganic matter" (264)? Could it be that "what is taking place here [is] a comprehensive *musicalization* of thought, a change of orientation under the aegis of new images, of time images, a change that seems to be opening new roads to our understanding and indeed, to our logic?" (Zuckerkandl 264).

Five

Toward a Conclusion of Indeterminacy:
Reader Response as a Rhetoric
of Musical Performance

Reader Response and the Emergent Philosophy of Music

> It is . . . not hard to recognize that there is a certain rhythm
> to prose. For the decision is given by our senses; and in
> such a case it is unfair not to acknowledge the occurrence
> of the phenomenon, even if we are unable to discover its
> cause.
>
> —Cicero, *Orator*

If the simultaneity of time manifests itself most in the dynamic context of sound, then we need to construct a nonformalistic, nonrationalistic model of affective response to the temporal, indeterminate dimension of language as sound. What we
need, then, is a temporal description of phonocentric experience in reading and writing. We can't really describe (i.e., analyze and interpret) temporal experience in affective response,
for the temporal experience seems to lie beyond spatial models
or modes of understanding. But we can perhaps describe the

principles underlying temporal experience. To construct a temporal model of reading and writing, we would need nonformalistic, nonrationalistic principles that can more holistically account for affective response to the sound of language in time, principles that may apply at all levels of musico-linguistic experience (word, sentence, paragraph, chapter) and all kinds of rhetorical music (prose, poetry, play; fiction, non-fiction, scientific and technical writing).

For these temporal principles of affective response, we now turn to *Emotion and Meaning in Music* by Leonard Meyer, whose work in the affective stylistics of music forms a foundation for a whole school of musical theory. Unlike Zuckerkandl, Meyer does not consider the experience of music apart from human experience but rather focuses on the principles underlying aural *gestalten* as the basis of affective meaning in music.[1] In fact, Meyer's book is premised on the similarity of *gestalt* patterns in music and literature (viii). Meyer may provide, then, a useful alternative to Iser's visual approach to Gestalt psychology and perception in literature, as well as a necessary antidote to Zuckerkandl's somewhat "positivistic" approach to language. Taken as a whole, these patterns and principles could constitute the beginning of a reader response criticism situated in the temporal dimension of language, a rhetoric of musical performance.

For Meyer, the meaning of music cannot be considered apart from its cultural context (ix). Of course, this is true in literature as well as music. As we discussed in chapter 4, Iser believes that the social and cultural "norms" of literature are contained in the "repertoire" of the work that interact in various ways with the reader's expectations. However, Meyer believes that emotional meanings must learned. Thus, while the Kantian categories of intuition, or the natural aesthetic faculty that underlies music and speech, are innate, perhaps the meaning of aesthetic responses and their appropriateness in particular contexts are not. This also seems to fit well with the sophistic and Ciceronian notion of eloquence as a natural talent that everyone possesses to varying degrees but one that must still be developed by practice and training. Although we possess the innate propensity to create and understand music and speech, and although emotions themselves may be universal (De Rivera 677–81), using Krashen's distinction between acquisition and learning,[2] the emotional meanings of music and of the music of language, like vocabulary and grammatical rules, probably must be learned. Like the sound of sense, then, the emotional meaning of music is at least partly social.

Meyer understands this in a way that not only parallels but seems to echo Moffett: "Musical meaning and significance, like other kinds of significant gestures and symbols, arise out of and presuppose social processes of experience which constitute the musical universes of discourse" (Meyer 60) Indeed, in his discussion of musical meaning, Meyer, like Moffett, refers to the work of George Herbert Mead concerning the acquisition of the affective stylistics of music as a process of internalization. It is internalization "which enables the creative artist, the composer, to communicate with listeners," says Meyer (40–41). And in a way that echoes Murray's concern with teaching the other, critical self ("Teaching"), Meyer adds that it is because the composer "is continually taking the attitude of the listener that the composer becomes aware and conscious of his own self, his ego, in the process of creation" (41). In fact, just as Murray believes that the critical voice is internalized, we can understand that from a social perspective the creative voice is one that is internalized as well (cf. Elbow, *Writing with Power* 7–12, who makes a distinction between creating and criticizing as opposing mentalities in the process in writing).

In addition, unlike Zuckerkandl, for whom music has no meaning apart from structure, Meyer argues that there is no difference between musical style and affective experience. And because there is no difference between musical style and affective experience, there is no separation between emotion and meaning in music, between feeling and cognition (39). Like Odell ("Piaget"), Meyer says: "It is . . . evident that thinking, the overcoming of difficulties, and expectation are one process" (88). Fish makes a similar point concerning the identity of cognition and emotions ("Literature in the Reader"). However, unlike Fish, Meyer understands affective expectations to be not only the cognitive result of aesthetic structure but also that structure, that thinking itself, to be musical, to be an aural form of temporal knowledge. This also seems much more probable than Zuckerkandl's claim that the meaning of music exists independently of the hearer. Although the tree may have fallen in the forest and made a sound, we do not know what sound it made unless we hear it or extrapolate from the experience of having heard other trees fall.

Meyer's view of the aural, temporal unity of emotion and thought also has implications for how we view the role of memory in musical expectation, as well as how we view memory itself. If the sense perception of immediate experience (or consciousness for Penrose) exists in a different time order than the object perceived, as Eliot believes (*Knowledge* 109–11, discussed here in appendix D), the sophistic belief in the dichotomy of language/reality and thought/reality, but not language and thought, makes the unity of emotion and thought in the same time order phenomenologically possible. Thus, just as the unity of language and thought makes communication, belief, and knowledge possible, albeit uncertain, the unity of emotion and thought makes aesthetic experience possible, no matter what order of reality the music actually exists in. That is, the aural unity of language and thought, or emotion and thought, is a temporal unity.

Unlike Zuckerkandl, Meyer believes memory plays an essential part in the temporal process of musical hearing: "Expectation depends in very important ways upon memory processes. As we listen to a particular musical work we organize our experience and hence our expectations both in terms of the past of that particular work, which begins after the first stimulus has been heard and is consequently 'past,' and in terms of our memories of earlier musical experiences" (88). This may also be important in understanding one value of reading out loud in the teaching of writing: the musical memory is not limited to the sound of one piece, but rather involves in important ways the memory of other musical experiences that have been heard, retained, and learned, and can be perhaps be imitated in the student's written composition. (More about this later.) In this way, previous musical performances that are remembered in the body and mind constitute that wider field of temporal organization Zuckerkandl talks about in which a particular work sits.

Memory also may be important in understanding the interaction of thought and style. As Enos intimates ("Epistemology" 49; *Greek Rhetoric* 80), for Gorgias it was perhaps in memory where the music of style evokes emotions that deceive the senses, where language stirs with the past into the concoction we believe to be present and true. It is in memory where the sensory reaction to music evokes past experience to create a simulacrum of a sensuous but nonreferential reality. For Meyer, like Iser, memory plays a vital role in affective experience, in the creation of expectations, and thus in the shaping of knowledge itself.

However, the difference between Meyer and Iser is that Iser conceives of the reader's memory qua repertoire as a kind of storage/retrieval unit from which old information can be called up and against which new information can be compared. While the new information modifies the images contained in the reader's repertoire and alters the structure of the schemata there, it does nothing to memory itself. Memory for Iser merely *contains* schemata, mental representations that are built up from learned experience. On the other hand, memory, or at least musical memory, for Meyer, is itself constituted by the "traces" of affect created by musical experience. It is "[t]he traces left in the memory by experience" themselves that "are constantly changing" (Meyer 89). These traces of affect that determine musical process are physical forces rather than abstract schemata (91). Thus, expectations, like thinking itself, seem to be more rooted in bodily experience, more physical, felt for Meyer (39) than they do for Iser, for whom memory is a spatial container of ideas.

Meyer's *gestalt* approach to aesthetic response should therefore be able to elucidate some of the principles underlying the response to language as a musical trace of emotion in sound, rather than only as visual ideation, the imaging of meaning. It should be able to help us begin to understand the relation between voice and felt sense as musical patterns of expectation created in our response to language, which in turn may help us recontextualize Reader Response Criticism within a temporal ontology in order to teach reading and writing in oral as well as visual terms. Without further wrestling with the epistemological controversy concerning the meaning of music, which beyond this point is not relevant here anyway, let's briefly discuss Meyer's understanding of the relationship between musical patterns and emotional experience.

The Emotional Meaning of Music

Like Reader Response critics such as Bleich and Iser, Meyer believes that emotion and the patterns of meaning that manifest themselves in human communication are the result of the inhibition of sensory drives and their subsequent release in symbols. As in language acquisition and development in Reader Response Criticism, motivational symbolism seems to play a part in the creation and comprehension of music for Meyer, though he does not use this term. Based on the work of Piaget and Langer, Meyer like Bleich believes that emotion rises into consciousness because of a sensory or instinctual conflict. "Emotion or affect is aroused when a tendency to respond is arrested" (Meyer 14). And this can happen at any level of language, at any level of consciousness.

In a way similar to Odell, Meyer remarks that the result of these conflicts

> is not only affect, as a product of inhibition, but doubt, confusion, and uncertainty as well. These latter concomitants of conflict are of importance because they may themselves become the basis for further tendencies. For to the human mind such states of doubt and confusion are abhorrent and when confronted with them, the mind attempts to resolve them into clarity and certainty. . . . Thus confusion and lack of clarity, growing out of conflicting tendencies, may them-

selves become stimuli producing further tendencies—tendencies toward further clarification—which may become independent of the original conflicting tendencies. (15–16)

Thus, there is no need to reference referential meaning in the affective patterns created by music. As a "stimulus," says Meyer, music "activates tendencies, inhibits them, and provides meaningful resolutions" (23). Just as the foreground/background and theme/horizon determine the "wandering viewpoint" over ideational time for Iser, for Meyer musical patterns determine the direction of the emotional tendency over auditory time (24).

Of course, if and when the tendency to act is satisfied, there is little or no awareness of emotional conflict. When this happens, the impetus to seek release through symbolic forms is dissipated: "If the pattern reaction runs its normal course to completion, then the whole process may be completely unconscious. . . . The more automatic behavior becomes, the less conscious it is" (24). When wholly adapted and harmonious, the style is invisible. But when the patterns, musical or otherwise, create, direct, and then in some way inhibit or disturb the completion of the natural drives and tendencies, these drives and instincts are brought into consciousness as conflict, as frustrated expectations (24).

Perhaps it is these expectations that Odell and Elbow think we should teach our students to recognize, for they can indicate a conflict or a problem (not always a bad thing) that needs (or creates the desire for) a solution. But these expectations, and the frustration that results and demands resolution, are not only created on the visual level of style as ideation, as Reader Response critics have correctly perceived, but also on the auditory level of style as sound. We can recognize them by listening—if we know what to listen for.

In music, expectations as conscious or self-conscious inhibitions may be blocked by being directly inhibited, complicated with other expectations, totally reversed, temporarily delayed, indefinitely suspended, ambiguous, nonspecific, or doubtful either originally or in their fulfillment (Meyer 25–30). One can immediately *see* the similarities and consequences for this understanding of expectations in the traditional terms of reading and writing: introduction, organization, clarity, style, conclusion. But for Meyer, as perhaps for sophists such as Gorgias, "expectation is largely a product of stylistic experience" (35). And style is "[a] sound or group of sounds (whether simultaneous, successive, or both) that indicate, imply, or lead the listener to expect a more or less probable event" (45). Morris Croll too touches on the temporal dimension of meaning in rhetorical language when he mentions "the release of the rhythmic impulse" (348), the "psychological bases" of rhythm in terms of "principles of resolution" (351), "the energy of utterance" that "accompanies, interprets, stimulates energy of emotion" (353), "the momentary conflict between the rhythmic pattern and the actual run of words that fill it" (392), and "the principle of *resistance* to rhythm" which controls rhythm and creates significant variation (433–34).

Thus, there is a symbiotic rather than antithetical relationship between style and substance, between aesthetic response and problem solving, between uncertainty and knowledge. Expectation operates on the level of *style as sound*, as the felt sense of language, as well as content. And Meyer's understanding of style as both musical and ideational can be applied to prose as well as to poetry. For example, here's a paraphrase of a sentence from a Hemingway novel (I can't remember where I heard this, which one), where the principle under discussion seems readymade: "Pulling the sled behind him, he began climbing up the hill, going higher and higher, until he finally reached the top, then coasted down." Note how the dependent clause (of the sled) must be pulled up the slope of this sentence in stages, until reaching the top (the climax of the sentence), after which the sentence (the voice and the sled) quickly fall off, descend. Through sound, rhythm, and structure of style, language builds up expectations that demand resolution and so creates the experience of its meaning. This sentence, when said out loud, even changes the reader/speaker's breathing pattern, actually makes one pant a little with exhaustion.

In the next section, we will explore in some detail the principles that for Meyer describe how emotions are created, inhibited, and released through patterns that are the manifestation of the auditory movement of music through time (14). Expectations, and the conscious effects that aural patterns give rise to, such as suspense, surprise, joy, frustration, doubt, anxiety, and certainty, are the emotional meaning of music (Meyer 35). But we also will understand how the relationship of sound to meaning is always built on temporal uncertainty. In fact, in discussing affective uncertainty, what Zuckerkandl and Meyer are describing is temporal indeterminacy. Temporal knowledge is always uncertain knowledge. Perhaps this is how dissonance is related to uncertainty, how the experience of sound itself can be a form of knowledge. And the discomfiture with uncertainty and our innate desire for the fulfillment of expectations, for closure, could be the very reason we tend to dismiss this uncertainty as irrelevant to and even destructive of knowledge. Like Odell ("Piaget"), Meyer states: "From the outset ignorance arouses strong mental tendencies toward clarification which are immediately affective. If ignorance persists in spite of all, then the individual is thrown into a state of doubt and uncertainty" (27). The dilemma, then, may be getting our students (and ourselves) to understand the experience of ignorance as a form of knowledge. For the experience of this paradox drives us to immediately set up rational heuristics that exclude or at the very least hide temporal uncertainty in the spatial cloak of reason, that disguise the affective dimension of our intellectual experience in logic.

The Indeterminate Shapes of Aesthetic Response as Musical Gestalten

In *Emotion and Meaning in Music*, Meyer attempts to account for the nature (if not the cause) of musical experience by exploring the relationship between temporal patterns of sound and aesthetic response. Meyer thinks that what is perceived in music are *general* auditory "shapes," patterns of musical *experience*. Like physicist Erwin Schrodinger (22), Meyer considers these shapes or *gestalten* to be "a process of mind rather than a thing" (92) and therefore merely serve to "confirm our expectations," though "its consequents can be envisaged with some degree of probability" (157). Although Kant thought the shape of time is difficult to discern (and he was right, given our attempts to do so spatially), these general shapes of experience may help us understand the affective but indeterminate level of response to language as sound.

Because they are too indeterminate to describe directly, Meyer tries to account for the shapes of musical experience by summarizing what he calls "The Principles of Pattern Perception," which include "The Law of Good Continuation," "Completion and Closure," and "The Weakening of Shape." What he is in a sense cataloging are the principles that underlie our experience of uncertainty as it is created and/or exists in the temporal states of harmony and dissonance. In these general principles Meyer may in fact be describing "the laws" that underlie the shape or order of indeterminacy itself (or our experience of it), laws that may even apply to physical phenomenon (cf. Prigogine). In any case, we will briefly review these principles here in the belief that they can constitute a general but powerful theory of response, the beginning of a rhetoric of auditory reception and oral performance that may prove beneficial in "illuminating" our experience of the physical, temporal level of language as sound in reading and writing. Although theory for Cicero was the least effective in teaching eloquence, theory, like other mental frameworks, is necessary to articulate and comprehend what it is we are experiencing.

One of the fundamental principles underlying temporal, musical perception is The Law of Good Continuation. Meyer states, "A shape or pattern, will, other things being equal, tend to be continued in its initial operation" (92). For Meyer, The Law of Good Continuation underlies expectations, whereby "the motion" of a "process" is continued (as in this sentence). Or reversed it can be (thus). Reversal may be either sudden or subtle, such as in a modulated sequence where tension is gradually built up by a series of small changes in which expectations are only slightly reversed (like so). Good continuation can also be "weakened" (Q.E.D). But we must remember that Meyer is talking about patterns of sound; expectations are created not only at the level of meaning but also at the level of sound.

The principle of good continuation in sound can be heard and felt, for instance, in the first paragraph of Hemingway's *A Farewell to Arms*:

> In the last summer of that year we lived in a house in a village that looked across the river and the plain to the mountains. In the bed of the river there were pebbles and boulders, dry and white in the sun and the water was clear and swiftly moving and blue in the channels. Troops went by the house and down the road and the dust they raised powdered the leaves of the trees. The trunks of the trees too were dusty and the leaves fell early that year and we saw the troops marching along the road and the dust rising and leaves, stirred by the breeze, falling and the soldiers marching and afterward the road bare and white except for the leaves. (3)

Although there is no reversal (such as anastrophe) in the passage above, in the last sentence the reader detects a weakening of shape (discussed more below) in the change of rhythm in the sentence that creates and mirrors the stirring breeze and falling leaves, after which good continuation is resumed to good effect: the identification of leaves and soldiers through association in structure and sound. These general principles operate at "higher" levels of structure as well. While hard to get at, we should, as Cicero says, acknowledge the occurrence, even if we are unable to discover the cause (*Orator* liv. 183).

Meyer also distinguishes the Law of Good Continuation from Repetition, the musical phenomenon in which "[a] figure which is repeated over and over again arouses a strong expectation of change, both because continuation is inhibited and because the figure is not allowed to reach completion" (135). (Based on "the law of return"—"it is better to return to any starting point whatsoever than not to return" [151]—Meyer makes a distinction between two kinds of repetition: recurrence, "which takes place after there has been a departure from whatever has been established as given in the particular piece" [151], and reiteration, which, "whether exact or varied, is the successive repetition of a given sound term" [152]. Because of the principle of good continuation, recurrence leads to expectations that the pattern itself will be again repeated, not to expectations of change; recurrence, when it occurs, creates a feeling of completion and closure; reiteration creates the expectation and desire for change.)

When repetition is no longer affectively meaningful, "saturation" occurs (135–38). However, says Meyer, even good continuation is itself contingent: "we expect continuation only so long as it appears significant and meaningful in the sense that it can be understood as motion toward a goal. If meaning becomes obscured, then change will be expected" (93). That is, saturation may set in when continuation becomes reiteration (93). Reiteration creates saturation. Reiteration creates dissonance. But saturation also may occur even though variation is present—when variation becomes reiteration (136), and so variation too can lead to a desire for change, for a good continuation of repetition. The following paragraph from a page near the end of *A Farewell to Arms* is perhaps an effective example of how reiteration (of variation) leads to saturation, builds a desire for change:

> It is very dangerous. The nurse went into the room and shut the door. I sat outside in the hall. Everything was gone inside of me. I did not think I could not think. I knew she was going to die and I prayed that she would not. Don't let her die. Oh, God, please don't let her die. I'll do anything for you if you won't let her die. Please, please, please don't let her die. Dear God, don't let her die. Please, please, please don't let her die. God please make her not die. I'll do anything you say if you don't let her die. You took the baby but don't let her die. That was all right but don't let her die. Please, please, dear God, don't let her die. (312).

Again, it is not only content that builds this desire for change but the style as an aural movement of sound in time. In the juxtaposition of this example with the first, we also get a hint of how Hemingway structures the movement of the chapters of the novel as a temporal whole, moving from calm descriptive chapters based on good continuation to emotionally anguished chapters based on reiteration.

In prose as well as poetry, we can also understand the use of repetition of sound not only in terms of internal rhyme, such as alliteration, assonance, and consonance, but in certain figures of speech as well: parallelism, antithesis, anaphora, anastrophe, epistrophe, polyptoton, polysyndeton, asyndeton, climax . . . An example of significant repetition as an aural movement of figures that builds a desire for change, but then satisfies that desire with "recurrence," is contained in Martin Luther King, Jr.'s, use of anaphora: "We are moving to the land of freedom. Let us march to the realization of the American dream. Let us march on segregated housing. Let us march on segregated schools. Let us march on poverty. Let us march on ballot boxes, march on the ballot boxes until the race baiters disappear from the political arena, until the Wallaces of our nation tremble away in silence" (in Corbett, *Classical Rhetoric* 437–38). And then there's repetition of sound itself, that leads to intentional saturation, to a dissonance that is not immediately satisfied by change, as in Harding's nomination speech for Howard Taft: "Progress is not proclamation nor palaver. It is not pretense nor play on prejudice. It is not the perturbation of a people passion-wrought nor a promise proposed" (also in Corbett, *Classical Rhetoric* 436). In all these cases, we cannot help but notice how well the music of rhetoric suits the content and intent.

In the example from Wiener's *Cybernetics* in the last chapter, we experienced the auditory effect of the repetition of prepositions and conjunctions that call attention to and create the feeling of disequilibrium and dissonance—of oscillation and feedback. In fact, returning to that example (pp. 142–43), we can understand those paragraphs more as an aural, temporal phenomenon by applying Meyer's principles to them. We hear good continuation in the parallel movement of the sentences, weakened in the first paragraph by the phrases "a peculiar, uncertain gait" and "he cannot stand up, and totters to the ground"—a weakness that mirrors the patient's condition; but in tandem with the reiteration of prepositions, this good continuation eventually builds a desire for change: a cessation of the parallel coordinate clauses that swing like loose limbs on conjunctions. This desire is finally satisfied by the refrain "what is the matter with him?" that, repeated in the second paragraph, becomes a recurrence that returns the piece to good continuation in a different key, so to speak: the music of the paragraph on diagnosis, which resolves the example with aural as well as clinical closure.

As we can *hear* in these brief "analyses" of the music of rhetoric, what Meyer's principles give us is an auditory understanding of organizational *gestalten* in terms of general patterns of temporal expectation and affect. While we cannot help but understand continuation or incompleteness or closure or repetition or saturation in reading and writing in terms of ideas, given the essential referentiality of language, we should remember that given the unity of language and thought, of emotion and knowledge, these affective processes may occur in style at the level of sound as well. While both Reader Response Criticism and composition theory deal with the role of expectation in comprehension and problem solving in relation to meaning, Meyer's principles may provide an understanding of those expectations in relation to the aural shape of a sentence, the auditory pattern of a paragraph, or the temporal organization of the whole. The movement of auditory time through language may be essential in understanding the progression of affective experience not only as a process of spatial ideation but also a parallel process of aural experience.

Like Zuckerkandl, Meyer believes that rhythm is a fundamental element of musical expression and experience. As we also hear in the examples above, rhythm is the most important kind of continuation (Meyer 102). Rhythm is necessary "in achieving and disturbing continuity" (102). As the movement of sound "sensed" over time, it may even underlie all other forms of continuation. Like good continuation, the "mental groupings of unaccented beats" that constitute rhythm "may, of course, be more or less clear. And within any given meter they may vary indefinitely" (103). Of course, this too has much to do with the affective experience of language. As Elbow intimates, and as we are all aware, when rhythm is weakened, "voice" may be weakened as well. The weakening of rhythm results in an "ambiguity of shape."

However, to say rhythm is weak is not necessarily always negative; weak rhythm may be useful. As Meyer states in regard to the Law of the Weakening of Shape: "The words 'good' or 'strong,' 'poor' or 'weak' as used in the discussion of shape are not to be construed as implying value judgments. On the contrary, weak, ambiguous shapes may . . . perform a valuable and vital function in creating and molding the affective aesthetic musical experience. For the lack of distinct, tangible shapes and of well-articulated modes of progression is capable of arousing powerful desires for, and expectations of, clarification and improvement" (160). In other words, weak rhythm, like repetition and dissonance in general, can be intentional, can be used for good effect. On the level of sound, the result of the weakening of shape can lead to subliminal differences. It also can lead to musical misunderstanding and incoherence. For rhythm, between words, sentences, or larger parts, like other elements of the music of language, such as alliteration, can create connection and cohesion through sound. The weakening of shape through a lessening or lack of rhythm, and the ambiguity, doubt, and uncertainty that arises from it, might be just what the writer intended; or it may be the result of musical inexperience or a tin ear. A good writer can succeed in building expectations and a desire for clarification (through a variation of rhythm—or a lack of it, as in the examples above); the poor writer may only create confusion and undirected doubt, not only in content but through sound.

The tendency of the mind to impose organizational structure

when one is not apparent (or even when one is apparent) in order to make sense, understand, interpret, is well known in both Reader Response Criticism and composition theory (cf. Flower, *Problem Solving* 128–40). But perhaps it also works at the level of sound, in rhythm. That is, rhythm influences perception and understanding as well. Take the following famous example (again, found in Corbett, *Classical Rhetoric* 434): "I came, I saw, I conquered." The grammatical music of this phrase is in large part created by the strong rhythm of the asyndeton, the absence of conjunctions, which presents the march of events (also communicated through the tones as images of time) as series in which one event immediately follows another and in which each event is coequal with the other (Caesar's seeing and coming is as powerful as his conquering); the strength of this phrasing is also created by the musical emphasis on the word *I*. (Again, we are not only talking about meaning, but also about the physical effect of sound on a listener, the experience of language in conjunction with the apprehension of meaning.)

Now let's try some permutations:

1. "I came and I saw and I conquered."
2. "I came, saw, conquered."
3. "I came, saw, and conquered."

In the first permutation (polysydeton), the rhythm is changed, the events (the tones as images of time) seem simultaneous, the action is dance-like, diluted; here, instead of iambic we have anapestic meter—the meter of comedy. Here, Caesar comes skipping into town (perhaps more appropriate for Caligula rather than Caesar.) In the second permutation (ellipsis), there is little rhythm at all. That is, the rhythm is weakened, and so the events (as time images) seem quick, simultaneous, undifferentiated; and there is very little emphasis through subject or sound on Caesar. In the last permutation (probably the way most competent writers would write it, as a series with commas with "and" before the last item), the rhythm (and thus the tones as time images) is still weak, and therefore the events these words describe are still somewhat diminished, not (only) grammatically but by the music of the language. The point here is that different rhythms, created by different figures, create different effects; we have a choice of how we construct affective experience through sound.

Of course, good shape, as well as weak, ambiguous shape, also depends on the ability of the listener/reader to recognize and respond to them. This is where reading and writing as oral activities, as performance and reception, coincide. Listening research, with its focus on increasing the aural attention, perception, comprehension, and memory of the listener, may be of some help here; although it focuses on imaging meaning rather than the affective level of the experience of sound we are talking about, some of the exercises developed by these researchers could be applied to the temporal experience of sound (see Lundsteen; Rost 29–31; Ur). Perhaps readers could be taught to recognize and experience the effect of auditory shapes on their "musical comprehension" of a text. As Meyer states, "[I]f we do not understand a given style, if we lack the proper habits of responses, we will either fail to apprehend shape or, if we apprehend it in terms of another style, we will fail to comprehend it" (160). The apprehension and the comprehension of musical shape are always relative to the listener's "musical knowledge." Somewhat like Isocrates and Cicero, Meyer thus says in regard to musical education: "It is important to recall that the norms of style, of tonality, important as they are, can be altered through training and knowledge" (160).

However, the apprehension and comprehension of rhythm is also contingent on the context of the work itself. Like Zuckerkandl, Meyer states, "Rhythmic organization does not operate as an isolated independent variable without reference to other aspects of the total musical organization" (149). But Meyer also elucidates the psychological principle underlying the operation of rhythm in the organizational field of meter. Good continuation of rhythm depends on the principle of Completion and Closure: "the mind . . . is continually striving for completeness, stability, and rest" (128). But what constitutes good continuation is contingent on the principle of completion and closure as it operates in the work as a whole: "what represents completeness will vary from style to style and piece to piece. . . . For the individual musical work also establishes norms which condition our feelings and opinions as to completeness and closure, and these norms of the individual work may be unusual within the style" (Meyer 128, 138).

This parallels the need for norms Iser perceives within the text because of the nonrepresentational nature of literature, but does so in terms of auditory phenomena. For example, unlike Iser, Meyer believes that a "structural gap" in music is not "a blank" inserted into the work by the author in order to be "filled in" by the reader. "In fact," says Meyer, "it might be better to consider such a break as a disturbance in continuity rather than as a structural gap" (130). Thus, while Meyer understands these gaps as activating processes latent in the listener the way that Iser does the reader, for Meyer the affective process caused by a disturbance in continuity is purely an auditory experience rather than a visual imaging of meaning. And the *affective value* of structural gaps is directly related to our need for completeness and closure: "Though a temporal process can be broken off and then continued again, the subsequent continuation does not in any real sense fill the gap thus created. Such a break in process may arouse the keenest expectation" (Meyer 131).

But significantly, Meyer suggests that the interrelationship of our desire for good continuation and our desire for completion and closure points up "the difficulties involved in setting up any accurate distinctions between various laws of perception" (129). The laws are in fact "corollary," "since all incompleteness is, in some sense, a lack of good continuation and since that which is complete must have been well continued" (Meyer 129). What we really have here, then, is a principle of musical indeterminacy. Because completion and closure involve the creation of expectation through the shape of music, and then its fulfillment, "neither continuity nor completeness create shape or pattern. Rather, they are the products of shape or pattern" (130).

Meyer's book, with its general principles describing the shapes of sound that are created in the musical experience, thus can constitute a theory of reader response grounded in aural, temporal *gestalten* that are themselves the product of indeterminacy. These principles are therefore not meant to solve the problem of interpreting affective experience in reading and writing; perhaps the problem cannot be solved. But these principles do bring us a little closer to understanding that experience in more nonformalistic, nonrationalistic terms. In fact, these aural *gestalten* reveal that part of the subjective experience of language that is nonreferential, nonrational, rooted in temporal uncertainty. That is, these *gestalten* as aural metaphors do not so much describe as circumscribe, do not depict some empirically verifiable meaning but rather merely delineate the indeterminate shapes of temporal processes. The uncertainty of subjective experience is not only recognized here but embedded in the very nature of the principles involved. While these principles do not get us to the quantum level of thought—or beyond—they perhaps point us in the right direction: toward the temporal dimension of reader response and writing.

And while the problems of causality (the inference that these principles underlie affective experience) and of time (the notion that the motion of time is linear) remain, Meyer's model of indeterminacy perhaps brings us one step closer to understanding affective logic in relation to sound (cf. Witkin). Perhaps it is these general, nonformalistic, nonrationalistic shapes and patterns created by response to sound that are inherent in and most akin to affective logic, to the temporality of consciousness itself, and that we teach when we teach reading and writing as oral performance. If we accept this model as underlying reading and writing as an aural, temporal phenomenon, it will be necessary to partially let go of, or at least temporarily suspend, the need in our scientific culture to analyze and interpret response in terms of referential meaning. In a rhetoric of musical performance, literary, nonliterary, and student texts would become auditory models of temporal experience as well as spatial models of meaning. But how are these shapes and patterns of sound learned? How is oral performance reproduced in consciousness?

Affective Response as the Imitation
of Sensuous Forms in Consciousness

Meyer's discussion of the role of learning and memory in musical experience suggests that the internalization of affective temporal experience might be important here. In fact, the internalization of affective experience created in the music of language may be more closely related to the acquisition and retention of both language and knowledge than heretofore believed. Perhaps in the musical hearing of style, felt sense can even be understood as temporal sensation breaking from memory into consciousness. In this case, stylistic invention is not divine intervention, disembodied voices speaking Ideal Forms, or the conscious employment of formal heuristics, as much as the remembrance of the experience of the physical movement of language as sound, experience that reading and writing as oral performance may teach.

Both Zuckerkandl and Meyer provide a basis for understanding the auditory and temporal dimension of language and thus provide a needed and useful counterbalance to more formalistic, rationalistic conceptions of reading and writing. But neither Zuckerkandl's phenomenology of music nor Meyer's stimulus-response approach to the formation of musical *gestalten* brings us close enough to understanding how this auditory and temporal dimension is related to the learning of verbal language, to the referential component of language, or to "higher" levels of thought and consciousness. In trying to return to the spatial dimension of consciousness without losing the temporal, to understand the essential relationship between the affective and referential levels of language and the role of sound in linguistic consciousness, we need to turn again to the work of Ernst Cassirer and Susanne Langer.

In *The Philosophy of Symbolic Forms* 1, Cassirer develops a philosophy of language as a unity of sensuous form and intellectual content that at once supplements and goes beyond the sophistic and Ciceronian view of language as a unity of substance and style in sound. In conjunction with Zuckerkandl's and Meyer's philosophies of music, Cassirer can help us understand imitation not only as the analysis and interpretation of meaning in the spatial dimension of the written/printed text but as the response to and internalization of the sound of language as spoken. It is both interesting and significant that unlike most philosophers of language Cassirer develops a philosophy of language that is based on the orality of language. In this sense, as well as in terms of philosophical principle, Cassirer, like Langer (cf. Enos, "Rhetorical Theory" 1), seems to be very close to Cicero and the sophists. (In fact, Cassirer and Langer philosophically could be considered contemporary sophists.)

It is also interesting and significant that Reader Response critics like Bleich, who invoke and rely on Cassirer in their work, do not deal with the oral aspects of his work. As we discussed in chapter 2, Cassirer argues that language is not only referential signs for objective reality but also "emotional signs for sensuous drives and stimuli" (148). For Bleich (as well as Meyer), this is the process of symbolization. But Cassirer goes one step further. Contrary to Zuckerkandl's view of language as wholly referential, and thus of a static relationship between sound and meaning that results from the positivism of print, Cassirer cites nineteenth-century philosophers of language for whom the relationship was dynamic: "language was considered in terms of the dynamics of speech, which in turn was related to the dynamics of feeling and emotion" (150). Cassirer is not adopting here the "correspondence" theory whereby words are directly related to their referent by sound. But Cassirer does believe that in its sensuous origin language attempts to capture the sensory quality of objects it apprehends.[3] It appears that for Cassirer sounds are related to feeling in the dynamic movement of expression in language and consciousness, a movement that is both sensual and abstract, natural and cultural; thus, the meaning of sound is both acquired and learned.

Like Meyer, Cassirer concedes that feelings are originally the result of natural drives and motivations that are somehow inhibited and thus raised into consciousness. However, Cassirer argues that these feelings, drives, and emotions are also "imprinted" on and embodied in language as a physical, sensuous form. Cassirer considers this as fundamental in language as an organic form of thought. Language is not made, but *"grows* in a necessary process from within" (Cassirer 153). Thus, language is not merely a set of signs that refer to an independent reality, *there*, as Zuckerkandl believes. In a way that both predates yet moves beyond Bleich, Cassirer believes not only that knowledge is not autonomous but also that it is not merely subjective; in the sensuous form of language as sound, it is physical as well. Cassirer believes that language is a *sensuous symbolic form* both in speech and consciousness, through which objects are first apprehended and perceived. Language is "the synthetic structure of consciousness itself, through which the world of sensation becomes a world of *intuition*" (Cassirer 153).

Thus, affect perhaps can be experienced, if not traced, in the sensuous form of language as well. In fact, Cassirer also goes beyond Kant insofar as Cassirer believes that language itself, as a sensuous form, is the basis of the categories of intuition. Language constitutes the "impure" categories of experience. That is, our intuitions of time, space, motion are sensuous categories of thought and feeling that are imprinted both upon our minds and upon reality in and through language and are in fact "inseparable from . . . language" (Cassirer 159). In its insistence on the inseparable unity of sensuous form and intellectual content, and the inadequacy of method in getting at this unity, Cassirer's philosophy in some ways parallels the epistemology of Cicero and the sophists; indeed, Cassirer thinks the scientific "abstraction and analysis" of language "deadening" (160). Just as Zuckerkandl understands the dynamic quality of tones in music to be manifested not through tone alone but also through their relationship in melody, Cassirer understands that the dynamic relationship between thought and speech does not occur on the level of words, where most atomistic analyses of language and meaning as a one-to-one correspondence lie. Rather, the dynamic relationship between thought and speech occurs within sentences.

Based on his understanding of the dynamic relationship in sound between sensuous form and intellectual content, Cassirer states that the most important musical quality of language essential in the process of language acquisition and intellectual development is rhythm: "To the qualitative differentiation and gradation of sounds is added a dynamic gradation by stress and rhythm" (185). This is similar to Meyer and Zuckerkandl's assertion that rhythm is the most important element of music. Contrary to Zuckerkandl's positivistic, spatial view of language, however, sound, stress, and rhythm for Cassirer represent the sensuous beginnings of the dynamic of feeling and thought as it enters into new and more abstract relations. These relations are expressed in sound by the phonetic sequence (185; cf. Sumera).

It is the sentence, then, that demonstrates the synthesis of consciousness in language for Cassirer, "for the sentence reveals the original force of *syntheses* upon which all speech and all understanding are essentially based" (160). As sensuous form, sentences represent an expression of the relation between language and consciousness, just as melody represents an expression of the relation between tones and time for Zuckerkandl. For Cassirer, however, this relationship itself is brought about by the synthesizing power of consciousness (rather than an autonomous whole, a self-referential *gestalt*, as for Zuckerkandl). This synthesizing power of consciousness finds its physical manifestation in speech and cannot be separated from it: "The two, content and expression, become what they are only in their interpenetration," says Cassirer; speech is not just "a mediated product" of consciousness; speech is fundamental to consciousness: The "seeming externalization" of consciousness in speech "is an essential factor in its own formation" (178–79). Thus, what Cassirer calls the "expressive movement" of feeling and thought is not only a movement of speech but a movement in (or of) consciousness as well.

In fact, this expressive movement in speech perhaps gets us

a little closer to affective response as a physical, temporal form of knowledge, something between nonlinguistic experience and linguistic thought (cf. Weiskrantz). Could it be that this expressive movement in consciousness is the basis of the felt sense of language, which perhaps can be described as auditory and temporal patterns of music, and that this expressive movement underlies both the process of imitation in reading out loud and of voice in writing as speech? Could it be that imitation as the response to and internalization of the sound of language as spoken is a response to and internalization of the temporal patterns of the music of language? While these questions are not easily answered, Cassirer does provide support for the view of imitation implicit in them.

> [T]o regard movement and feeling of movement as an element and a fundamental factor in the structure of consciousness itself, is to acknowledge that here again the dynamic is not based on the static but the static on the dynamic—that all psychological 'reality' consists in processes and changes, while the fixation of states is merely a subsequent work of abstraction and analysis. Thus mimetic movement is also an immediate unity of the "inward" and "outward," the "spiritual" and the "physical," for by what it directly and sensuously is, it signifies and "says" something else, which is nonetheless present in it. Here there is no mere "transition," no arbitrary addition of the mimetic sign to the emotion it designates; on the contrary, both emotion and expression, inner and its discharge, are given in one and the same act, undivided in time. (Cassirer 179)

Thus, for Cassirer, and perhaps for Cicero and the sophists (see appendix C), imitation is not understood in Lockean terms as the objective analysis and rational interpretation of nature or text, but in terms of the inner production of symbolic forms that are at once mimetic and conceptual, sensuous and symbolic: "imitation itself is on its way to becoming *representation*, in which objects are no longer simply received in their finished structure, but built up by the consciousness according to their constitutive traits" (184). As Cassirer points out, "Even Aristotle calls the sounds of language 'imitations,' and says that the human voice is of all organs the best suited to imitation (Rhetoric, III, i)" (Cassirer 184).

But as Cassirer understands it, for Aristotle "this mimetic character of the word is not opposed to its purely symbolic character; on the contrary, Aristotle stresses the symbolic character of the word by pointing out that the unarticulate sound expressing sensation, such as we find in the animal world, becomes *linguistic sound* only through its use as a symbol." Thus, concludes Cassirer, the terms *sound* and *symbol* "merge, for Aristotle here uses 'imitation' in a broader, deeper sense: for him it is not only the origin of language, but also of artistic activity" (183). (As noted in chapter 3, however, the sensuous aspect of language was not a happy fact for Aristotle, as it was for the sophists who relished the physical nature of language and style as a form of knowledge. Nor is imitation held in high esteem in contemporary thought, where it is conceived of as the internalization of visual-verbal structures.[4])

Given his "oral philosophy" of symbolic forms, Cassirer believes internalization actually entails the imitation of sound as sensuous form, an expressive movement in consciousness that simultaneously and necessarily involves the production of intellectual content: "the apparent 'reproduction' . . . actually presupposes an inner 'production'" (183). In fact, as language moves away from direct representation of the sensory apprehension of objects imitated in sensuous form to the inner production of intellectual content, two things happen for Cassirer. On the objective side, language now becomes capable of serving not only as an expression of contents and their qualities but also and above all as an expression of formal relations; on the subjective side, the dynamic of feeling and the dynamic of thought are imprinted upon the expression of formal relations (185). Even at its logical purest, language for Cassirer retains its sensuous origins, expressing not only intellectual form but also the subjective emotions and drives that first motivated its formation (158–59).

Whether or not one accepts that there is a direct physical

connection between the sensuous form of sound and sensory impressions of "an object," there does seem to be a connection between emotional experience and the sound of a word, even if this relationship is localized, cultural, or otherwise learned. If there is no one-to-one correspondence between word and thing or thought and thing, but only between word and thought, as the sophists seemed to have believed, the sensuous nature of language as sound is no less valuable in evoking a simulacrum of reality. Like the question as to whether the intuitive categories of experience are innate or learned (or whether they are pure or symbolic), if one accepts their effect in perception and experience, then their origins ultimately perhaps do not matter at all. (Note that for Cassirer, as for the sophists and Cicero, the categories of experience created by and embedded in language are predicated on the qualities of things, not things themselves, which may also be the ontological basis of the sophistic epistemology of relativity and the ontological necessity of style as a physical form of knowledge.)

If we understand imitation as the reproduction of the sensuous form of sound in consciousness by which a physical representation of meaning is built in language and consciousness, as Cassirer does, we can understand that the aesthetic faculty that underlies the intuition of sensuous form, the natural affective response to the music of language, is basic to language acquisition. In fact, for Cassirer, imitation is the basis of language learning.[5] Although the childhood period of sensuous language acquisition has long passed for our students, perhaps we can make use of the sensuous nature of language already acquired in the dialectic development of thought and speech in teaching reading and writing as oral performance. Research in linguistics, rhetoric, reading, writing, literacy, oral interpretation, and listening have hardly touched on this aspect of language development, and much more could be done.

If the sensuous dimension of language as sound is fundamental to the process of learning language, it also may be elemental in the process of reading and writing at several levels and justifies an oral as well as visual approach to texts. Even

Cassirer, who holds that the higher categories of intuition occur at the level of synthetic structure rather than sensuous sound and that synthesis reveals itself most in the spatial intuition (198–99), also holds that even the more abstract symbolic forms still contain within them the trace of their sensuous origins as forms of speech by virtue of their being a product in and of human consciousness. As Odell implies ("Piaget"), language learning and problem solving are not only intellectual, not only cognitive structure, but also aesthetic play (cf. Lanham 101–02). Indeed, play can be regarded as the basis of all intellectual and cultural activity (see Huizinga, *Homo Ludens*). In reading and writing, language can become a toy played by all the physical organs of speech: the diaphragm, the chest, the lungs, the throat, the vocal chords, the nasal passage, the mouth, the teeth, the tongue, the face. The physicality of speech is almost sexual in its holistic nature.

And imitation is an affective process of recreation (or representation) that underlies the process of resymbolization—not only as interpretation, as abstracting, spatializing activities, but also as the production of physical and mental categories of experience in sound. Imitation as the resymbolization of *both* sensuous form and intellectual content in language and consciousness is thus perhaps a basis of affective response as well. As a unity of sensuous form and intellectual content, perhaps affective response in reading and writing can best be taught by the performance and imitation of the sensuous music of rhetoric. For if the sensuous categories of intuition in language include time, as Cassirer seems to believe, then what is experienced and resymbolized (imitated) in reading and writing as oral performance are perhaps the shapes of temporal experience itself.

The concepts of resymbolization implicit in Reader Response Criticism and of imitation in contemporary composition are both understood as analysis and interpretation based on the spatial ontology of literacy. But Cassirer's concept of "resymbolization" as an imitation of the movement of sensuous form and intellectual content in language and consciousness may constitute the psychological basis of a rhetoric of performance, one that enables us to understand affective response in reading and writing as temporal knowledge, and to teach it through the music of language. Imitation may be a more direct, albeit indeterminate, avenue to teaching affective response to language than are the spatial methods of analysis and interpretation.

It is this sensuous form of language and knowledge as a temporal movement in speech and consciousness that we may want to investigate and tap more in reading and writing. The music of language is not just aesthetic play for poets, nor is it the vestiges of mnemonic devices left over from the good old oral days. Rather, tone, stress, rhythm, rhyme are aural *gestalten*, nonrational topoi that are rooted in the physical nature of language and consciousness and may be central to verbal harmony and dissonance as a form of affective, uncertain knowledge. This is, perhaps, how the sophists intuitively understood declamation and recitation and why they used imitation to teach it.

"Presentational" Language as Musical Performance

Although we can never really understand what the sophists experienced, thought, and felt, in *Feeling and Form*, Susanne Langer, building on the work of Cassirer, discusses the relationship between music and language as "presentational" patterns, as opposed to discursive, or referential, patterns, in a way that might further allow us to understand reading (and writing) as a musical performance. (All Langer references in this section will be to *Feeling and Form*.) For Langer, presentational (i.e., nondiscursive) meaning is the feeling expressed through nonreferential symbols as logically articulated form.

As a presentational pattern, then, an artistic symbol "is . . . deeper than any semantic of accepted signs and their referents, more essential than any schema that may be heuristically read" (22). Langer's understanding of music as articulated form—as sensuous symbol—also allows her to take the step that Zuckerkandl refuses to take, a step that allows us to understand the relationship between the dynamics of music as articulated form and the aesthetics of feeling in consciousness.

> The tonal structures we call "music" bear a close logical similarity to the forms of human feeling—forms of growth and attenuation, flowing and stowing, conflict and resolution, speed, arrest, terrific excitement, calm, or subtle activation and dreamy lapses—not joy and sorrow perhaps, but the poignancy of either and both—the greatness and brevity and eternal passing of everything vitally felt. Such is the pattern, or logical form, of sentience; and the pattern of music is that same form worked out in pure, measured sound and silence. Music is a tonal analogue of emotive life. (27)

Langer thus understands the movement of music as the movement of feeling. Music is nonreferential for Langer, just as it is for Zuckerkandl: "although we do receive it [music] as significant form, and comprehend the processes of life and sentience through its audible, dynamic pattern, it is not a language because it has no vocabulary" (Langer 31). But like Meyer, Langer believes that form is a logical (i.e., presentational) expression of emotional states, of expectation and closure, tension and release, balance and disequilibrium, harmony and dissonance. And because music has no vocabulary, "the congruence of the symbolic form and the form of some vital experience must be directly perceived by the force of the *Gestalt* alone" (59).

Based on this understanding of music as symbolic expression of emotional states, it is reasonable to speculate that there is a connection between the presentational pattern of music and the presentational pattern of prose as sensuous speech, between musical performance and reading out loud. Indeed, unlike Zuckerkandl, Langer does see a relationship between music and language insofar as they are both presentational patterns. Music is *like* language in that it is an articulated form in consciousness: "Its parts not only fuse together to yield a greater entity, but in doing so they maintain some degree of separate existence, and the sensuous character of each element is affected by its function in the complex whole" (31).

For Langer, language is presentational too by virtue of the fact that separate words, which have assigned meanings (both denotative and connotative), are usually used in combination, not singly, and derive their meaning by association in that combination. A couple of homegrown, poetic examples will illustrate, I think, the way the combination of individual words fuses into a new experiential symbol, a presentational symbol, through the association of their meanings: the fire engine screamed red; lime and sunblown cheeks. The nonsense sentence, often used by linguists to show how syntax creates meaning, demonstrates this as well: "clear green ideas sleep furiously." The result is a complex structure (or pattern) of meaning whose totality is more than the sum of its parts. "A word or mark used arbitrarily to denote or connote something may be called an associative symbol, for its meaning depends entirely on association. As soon, however, as words taken to denote different things are used in combination, something is expressed by the way they are combined. The whole complex is a symbol, because the combination of words brings their connotations irresistibly together in a complex, too, and this complex of ideas is analogous to the word–complex" (30).

Just as Cassirer believes that the expressive movement of language is a synthesis of sensuous form and intellectual content in consciousness, Langer believes that it is when words are combined into sentences that "logical" relations, that is, a mimesis of relationship of objects reproduced in consciousness, are constructed. But unlike Cassirer, in *Feeling and Form* Langer concentrates on the logic of symbolic forms as presentational rather than their development into higher modes of thought. As an articulated form, language, like music, is on one level anyway, presentational, exists in time as well as space. In a chapter entitled "The Image of Time" in which she discusses music from a phenomenological perspective in much the same way that Zuckerkandl does, Langer states that time is not only passage, transience, the "interval between selected moments" that we scientifically (discursively) measure by clock-time. Rather, time is also "filled with its own characteristic forms, as space is filled with material forms" (112).

But Langer's phenomenology, unlike Zuckerkandl's, is psychological. What are these forms, these images of time? "The phenomena that fill time are *tensions*—physical, emotional, or intellectual. Time exists for us because we undergo tensions and their resolutions" (113). Complementing Meyer's discussion of shape, Langer adds: "Their peculiar building up, and their ways of breaking or diminishing or merging into longer and greater tensions, make for a vast variety of temporal forms" (113). The temporal (as well as spatial) arts are the "dynamic forms of subjective experience" (114). Thus, the "expressive symbol" is also an "image of time" (115). Therefore, we might safely say that affect not only results from the association of meaning but is also embodied in the temporal forms of the physical structure of language itself.

Like Cicero, Zuckerkandl, Meyer, and Cassirer, Langer regards rhythm as the most important temporal form (126). Just as knowledge is subject to continual revision for Odell, Iser, and Meyer, for Langer this permanence "is really a pattern of changes" (127). And it is temporal in nature: "even in its highest operations, the mind still follows the organic rhythm which is the source of vital unity: the building-up of a new dynamic *Gestalt* in the very process of a former one's passing away" (Langer 128). Given this connection between time and knowledge (or the uncertainty of it), Langer could also provide a psychologically based phenomenological view of presentational logic as physical feeling in the realm of time.

As to be expected, she does this in terms of music. In a chapter entitled "The Musical Matrix," Langer states: " 'The language of music' as we know it has evolved its own forms, and these are traditional like the structural elements of speech" (124). If the movement of audible forms includes "the recognition of related tones" (125), Langer also adds that one of the principles governing music "has been the intonation of speech"

(125): "The essence of all composition—tonal or atonal, vocal or instrumental, even purely percussive, if you will—is the semblance of *organic* movement, the illusion of the indivisible whole. Vital organization is the frame of all feeling, because feeling exists only in living organisms; and the logic of all symbols that can express feeling is the logic of organic processes" (126). However, as also to be expected, the relationship between music and speech as presentational symbols is for Langer not without problems. Her discussion of these problems is directly relevant to our understanding of affective response to the music of language in reading and writing as a rhetoric of performance.

Despite the similarities between music and language as articulated forms, Langer does not readily accept the similarity of language and music, as she makes clear in a chapter entitled "The Living Work." Nor does she accept language as a presentational pattern in time without qualifications. As with Zuckerkandl, the major difference between language and music for Langer is that the former has recourse to a vocabulary while the latter is "wholly articulated" and presents its meaning without recourse to a vocabulary. For Langer, the fact that language is referential while music is not results in the hearing of music as an entirely different order of aural experience.

But for Langer, the difference between language and music lingers around the distinction between "imaginary vs. real hearing," between silent reading and performance. "To a person who can read music as readily as most people read language," Langer allows, "music becomes audible by the perusal of a score, as words do in ordinary reading. So one is naturally led to ask: Is silent reading of music the same sort of experience as silent reading of literature?" (136). Refuting the claim made by Calvin Brown in *Music and Literature: A Comparison of the Arts* that "[m]usic and literature . . . are alike in that they are arts presented through the sense of hearing, having their development in time, and hence requiring a good memory for their comprehension" (11),[6] the answer to the question above for Langer is a qualified no. "Having remarked that silent reading of music is possible," says Langer, he [Brown] considers it proof enough that the tonal structures and word structures are 'presented to the ear' in the same essential way" (134–35).

However, for Langer "there is a radical difference" between language and music; in music, the passage of time is made audible by purely sonorous elements. That is, the temporality of music as an articulated form is wholly realized in sound. The sonorous elements of music "exist for the ear alone; all the musical helps to our actual perception of time are eliminated and replaced by tonal experiences in the musical image of duration" (135). On the other hand, Langer argues, "the elements of literature" are not sounds in and for themselves; words are not meant for the ear alone: "instead of being pure sense objects that may become 'natural' symbolic forms, like shapes and tones, they are symbols already, namely assigned symbols" (135).

Thus, Langer argues that "[t]he phenomenon of silent reading" occurs in literature and in music but possesses "different values" (135). As the sophists knew, all art deceives and creates the illusion of experience—meaning. But because of the difference in illusion that language and music each make as presentational patterns, the problem for Langer is not only the partially referential nature of language but also a difference of purpose as well. Written music is meant to be performed and is most fully realized as articulated form when it is performed. The whole purpose of reading music is performance: "Performance is the completion of a musical work, a logical continuation of the composition, carrying the creation through from thought to physical expression" (138). Thus, the performer of music is thus a cocreator with the composer: "Real performance is as creative an act as composition" (139). In contrast, Langer argues that language does not need to be performed by the reader to be fully realized, even as a presentational form.

Thus, we have arrived at what is perhaps the crux of the problem in regard to how we perceive the relation of language and music and how we understand the role of oral performance in reading. There are two issues concerning the relationship between performance in music and performance in language that need to be examined. First, as discussed in chapter 2, Reader Response Criticism, like much contemporary composition theory, has done much to dispel the notion of the passive reader. While there are differences between them, at the very least Reader Response critics agree that the reader actively makes or composes meaning through transaction with the text. The text is not a finished product, a complete *gestalt*, but must be completed by a reader.

Even in this limited, text-bound sense, then, the reader, like the musician with a score, *is* a performer of the text, in that he or she must interpret and complete the text in order to understand it, just as a performer does the work of the composer (cf. Bacon, "The Act of Literature" 2, who cites Langer to argue for the oral performance of literature as a form of knowledge rather than mere experience). In fact, in his reader response criticism, Umberto Eco actually uses the term *performer* to describe the relation of the reader to the text, and the act of reading itself as a kind of semiotic performance (*Role of the Reader* 53). By her dismissal of this kind of performance in literature, it is obvious here and elsewhere that Langer does not see the reader as a cocreator with the author.[7]

The second issue concerning Langer's view of the relation of music and language in regard to performance that needs to be addressed is that like other literary critics, including Reader Response critics, Langer does not think of language, either poetry or prose, in terms of oral performance (cf. Bacon, McCurdy, Neville, and Bales [in Fernandez], who argue for the oral approach to teaching literature). It is clear from her discussion of language and musical performance that Langer does not regard literary language in terms of auditory sound, does not recognize the (potential) role of oral performance in fully realizing the presentational patterns of language as an articulated, temporal form. But for Wallace Bacon, even the silent reader must embody and perform the text to experience and know it ("Act of Literature" 4).

What is so interesting here—and so problematical—is that while Langer recognizes the nondiscursive elements of poetry, including musical ones, she does not discuss the role of these musical elements in the illusion created by poetry as a presentational form. In fact, not only does she not hear the nondiscursive, musical elements of poetry in the same way that she does the articulated form of music, but like Iser, she discusses poetry by comparing it to the art of painting! But doesn't it seem more logical that poetry as a nondiscursive symbolic form relies more on articulated forms of music rather than painting for its emotional import and its artistic effect? Doesn't it make more sense to regard speech as closer to music than to painting? Apparently not to our logocentric minds, which regard language as a spatial phenomenon.

Perhaps the only real difference between poetry and music in performance, then, is that music is "pure" articulated form, while language, though presentational, is "impure" because it is also discursive. In language, the temporally clear, pristine tones of music are cluttered and stained with referential meaning. Thus, Langer argues, the exclusively acoustic phenomena of music—tone, duration, timbre, volume, consonance and dissonance, stress—can only be heard in real, not imaginary, hearing (134–37): in "mental hearing, as it is experienced in silent reading," says Langer in regard to music, "those tonal properties which are most definitely given to the physical ear, surviving even inattentive listening, are the very ones that may be quite vague or even completely lacking to the inward ear" (137).

Therefore, Langer postulates that performance, actual hearing, is the purpose and final result of reading music. It is only in performance that the sensuous, sonorous nature of music as an articulated form can be fully realized and comprehended (141). But based on the previous discussion, perhaps the same applies to the oral performance of language. For just as "in music the relation of inward hearing and actual hearing underlies a whole phase of artistic production: the work of the performer" (135), so too in writing and reading; it is only when reading is performed semiotically, interactively, *and orally*, that the meaning of a written text is wholly understood; and it is only when the written text is performed orally that its sensuous, sonorous, physical nature as presentational pattern, as sound, can be fully realized, and the text completely comprehended in all its sensuous aspects.

And just as "the final decision of *what every tone sounds like*" resides with the performer (Langer 139), so too the decision as to how the tones, rhythms, and other acoustic features of the text are to sound resides with the reciter of the text. Lanham makes these points as well.[8] This was also the purpose of parsing and declaiming texts for the ancients (Lanham 101; Marrou 375; Murphy, "Roman Writing Instruction" 42, 46). Reading silently to oneself, with one's inward ear, can come only after one has internalized and become aware of the sensuous nature of sound, and is perhaps never completely successful. This obviously has implications for the teaching of writing as well. If, as Cassirer suggests, even the most abstract concepts have their roots in and retain some of their sensuous origins in speech, language as an articulated form is never as fully realized as when it is spoken.

We know that "the reader" in an oral culture not only conveyed information, but performed it, and often in the process added to it. In addition, many contemporary poets are returning to the belief that poetry is not only meant for the printed page but is meant to be performed—sometimes in a way that incorporates all the other arts (see, for example, Vincent and Zweig, *Poetry as Performance*). And we know the importance Cicero and the sophists placed on delivery in creating the sensory allure of verbal reality, the illusion necessary to create knowledge, persuade an audience. Indeed, we know that there is a subconscious and uncontrollable process of subvocalization that occurs even in silent and speed-reading, though the latter tries, to the detriment of the sensuous nature of sound, to minimize this automatic physical response, just as body rocking, finger pointing, and the like, were eliminated by the former. That is, there is vocal performance even at this "low level" of reading. Like the composer or musician with a score, then, the reader or writer of a text is in fact always a performer, whether the performance is real or imaginary, whether the text is read "silently" or aloud.

Despite these problems, however, Langer does discuss performance in a way that might help us understand how to teach reading and writing as a musical performance. In the chapter entitled "The Living Work," Langer examines the problematic relationship between language and musical performance in a discussion of voice as an instrument of "artistic utterance," that is, musical utterance versus "personal utterance."

> Artistic utterance always strives to create as complete and transparent a symbol as possible, whereas personal utterance, under the stress of actual emotion, usually contents itself with half-articulated symbols, just enough to explain the *symptoms* of inward pressure. Where music serves the primary purpose of direct emotive expression, the feeling of utterance is not altogether controlled by inward hearing, but is confused by unmusical gesture that is only imperfectly assimilated to the process of tone production. (139–40)

This distinction between artistic utterance and personal utterance is an interesting one. For while the experienced performer does not add emotion to the work of art, since the emotions are already contained within the music of the work as an "objective" articulated form, the inexperienced performer will add his or her personal emotions to the work, and those emotions are not necessarily controlled by hearing (cf. Parrish, "The Concept of Naturalness").

The distinction between artistic and personal utterance is thus important for two reasons. First, everyone has experienced someone's reading a text out loud in a way that actually diminishes rather than enhances the text, usually a student, often a scholar, sometimes even a poet. Sometimes they do this by mumbling or garbling a text; sometimes they do this by exaggerating the rhythm and sound of a text. In regard to the latter, the result of a poor performance, says Langer, is that the "dynamic stresses of every passage are exaggerated beyond the requirements of the melodic and harmonic tensions, which, logically and artistically, they should illuminate" (140). Langer herself sees in speech "a similar discrepancy between meaning and its passional emphasis called 'oratorical' ": "It is usually attributed to a lack of restraint, but that is not really its source. A performer whose utterance is inspired entirely by the commanding form of the work does not have to restrain anything, but gives all he has—all his feeling for every phrase, every resolving or unresolving harmonic strain in the work" (140).

Langer's discussion here immediately brings to mind Cicero's discussion of delivery in *De Oratore*. For Cicero (qua Antonious), the speaker must display or imitate the emotions he wishes his audience to feel—emotions that the best writing perhaps already must contain, articulated but latent in its form. But later in *De Oratore*, Cicero (qua Crassus) also makes it a requirement that the best orator will have control over his style, being able to shift from plain to middle to grand in following the flow of thought and in accordance with the occasion. Thus, Langer's distinction here between artistic and personal utterance might be useful in preventing students from exaggerating or overdramatizing the music of a text—which is especially noticeable in poetry writing classes, where students deliver their verse either in singsong fashion or like song lyrics. Rather, we must get them to respond to the music that is "in" the language of the text (cf. Schrivner 79; 125; Geiger 139).

This is not necessarily to adopt an essentialist view of the music of language. It is fairly well known, for example, that the difference between the music of poetry and song lyrics is that poetry employs the music inherent in language as speech (such as alliteration, rhyme, rhythm, meter, etc.) while song lyrics rely more on externally supplied music (such as time notation and melody). In fact, the application of music to lyrics often alters or distorts the "natural" pronunciation and rhythms of language, extending a word through several notes, for example, or syncopating or speeding up entire lines (see ch. 4, n. 8). In addition, as Parrish points out, the oral rendering of a text is controlled less by what feels natural than by what seems so to the audience (97–98). For Cicero too, style is dictated by the requirements of the audience and occasion. Aside from the question of what the "objective" music of the text might be, in our culture there is a definite bias not only toward the plain style in writing but toward the plain style in reading and speaking as well. Many people are put off by any display of emotion, especially excess emotion and verbal antics in performance, preferring instead that the text be read almost in a monotone. The prejudice created by the printed page thus can be understood to extend to speech, to oratory, and to the music of language itself.

The second reason the distinction between artistic and personal utterance is important is that it might apply not only to response as a performance of a musical work—to reading, but to its creation as well—to writing. Can we, and should we, distinguish between artistic utterance and personal utterance in the musical process of composing a text? That is, should we make a distinction between sound meant for others and sound meant for self—the first under conscious control of hearing, inner or otherwise, and meant for the ear, the latter under less control, and more the result of inward emotional pressure to express, regardless of the musical form this expression takes? Cooper and Odell ("Considerations of Sound") suggest that the consideration of sound in writing for an audience is important for professional writers. But if we follow Langer's cue, it seems that in also asking students to become aware of voice, of felt sense, of dissonance in language in order to facilitate their ability both to solve problems and to write well, we are asking them to be aware of and use sound both for themselves and for others. Thus, both personal *and* artistic utterance might be important in teaching writing. The music of language as outward expression as well as inner hearing, then, would become central in a rhetoric of performance.

The music of language as outward expression might be important for another reason as well. In a way that parallels Cicero's regard for the importance of delivery, Langer says that the power of hearing what is in the work and translating it into manifested symbols, into physical form, is not always present, even where inner hearing is: "The possession of what I can only term 'muscular imagination,' the basis of vocal or instrumental technique, does not always accompany the power of inner hearing which is the foundation of all musical thinking" (140). The ability to listen to and hear music in the imagination, then, is not necessarily correlated of the ability to produce it. Even some composers, Langer remarks, cannot perform their own compositions very well: "the composer's natural gift is fully sensuous" (141).

Based not only on the relationship between music and language but also on much research into the process of writing that attempts to correct the often problematic practice of writers' composing in their heads, the same may hold true for verbal composition. As the imitation of the sensuous form and intellectual content in language and consciousness, the teaching of the music of rhetoric as outward expression, as artistic utterance, may be essential in teaching the music of rhetoric as inner hearing, as personal utterance (cf. Bertram xiii). And this, in turn, again suggests the need to teach response to reading, as well as writing, as an oral, temporal performance—as epistemic music—to develop voice as the felt sense of language itself.

Langer's distinction between artistic and personal utterance in musical imagination is also based on her understanding of the relationship between musical instruments and human voice. Indeed, Langer discusses the relationship between musical instrumentation and the physical apparatus of the human voice. In doing so, she seems to provide yet another basis for understanding the importance of teaching reading and writing as sensuous, musical speech: the codevelopment of the physical voice itself with inner hearing. For Langer, musical instruments contain "the quality of impassioned utterance": "This quality belongs naturally to the human voice. But the voice is so much more an instrument of biological response than of art that all actual emotions, crude or fine, deep or casual, are reflected in its spontaneously variable tone. It is the prime avenue of self-expression, and in this demonstrative capacity not really a musical instrument at all" (141). For Langer, then, intonation in language serves the practical (i.e., discursive) function of expression, whereas in music, it serves the nonpragmatic function of harmony and melody (141). "Music," says Langer, "begins only when some formal factor—rhythm or melody—is recognized as a framework within which accent and intonation are elements in their own right, not chance attributes of individual speech" (142; cf. Barfield 150, who discusses the development of music as distinguished from rhythm in the evolution of poetry and prose).

Because musical instruments represent a development of the objectification of intonation for Langer, "instruments furnish a standard to which vocal pitch may be held" (143). Thus, "vocal music can only approximate to the flexibility, the distinctness, the tonal and rhythmic accuracy of instruments" (143). (It is safe to suppose that in the ancient and medieval worlds, before the proliferation of musical instruments, voice and thus language were more integral to all musical performance, and in this way closer to music, than they are now. With the development of musical instruments, "instrumentation" overtook human voice as the new, "objective" standard [as technology did so many other things], eventually relegating voice to a minor element in music, making language a supplement to musical sound. In this way too the development of instrumentation in the history of music is similar to the development of a rhetoric of writing, in which more visual modes of thought and expression supplanted those based more on sound [see Croll, esp. 45–102], and voice, like the art of delivery itself, became a relatively minor technical element.)

Langer does allow that it is also possible for speech to become music, as it does in song, in which "the sound of the utterance rather than the discourse, becomes the notable phenomenon" (142). And despite her preference for musical instrumentation based on a desire for objectivity in musical utterance, Langer admits that because voice is primary, it actually constitutes the basis and standard to which musical composition and instrumentation—if not music itself—aspire. "The voice as an instrument, free from all interference by the physiological duties of the lungs, emotional constrictions of the throat, or the non-musical habits of the tongue, is the ideal that governs his (the composer's) tonal imagination and work. By listening and by practice he purifies the element that is the dangerous, but chief and irreplaceable asset of vocal music—the element of *utterance"* (143). Thus, even while musical instruments, modeled after the imperfect human voice, strive to obtain an objective, purer sound, "[i]nstrumental music strives for the expressiveness of song, the sound of direct utterance, 'voice' " (144).

Perhaps this is the understanding of voice so many have been searching for. In fact, it is the increasing flexibility of the organs of speech, and the supple expressiveness of the human voice, that Cassirer believes underlies and allows the corresponding articulation and development of thought in consciousness (184–85). Perhaps it is this flexibility and expressiveness of voice, then, as opposed to the objectivity of instrumentation, of techniques and heuristics, that we should strive for in the teaching of reading and writing—that will lead to the recognition by the ear of the tones, rhythms, and harmonies of speech as an aural framework in which affective experience is imitated and understood. And this flexibility and expressiveness of thought and speech can perhaps best be taught in reading and writing as the performance of and response to the music of language. Writers perhaps should be the performers of their own work in order to write well—or better—just as the reader should perhaps perform a work in order to fully *experience* and understand it as presentational as well as discursive logic.

Based on the sophistic understanding of language as an oral unity of form and content in consciousness, perhaps the flexibility and expressiveness of voice can be taught by imitation through the performance of and response to the music of language: of literature, of poetry, of essays, student or professional, nontechnical and technical; performance and response as the articulation of presentational patterns of language, the movement of the sensuous form of language in consciousness, as felt sense of language, as eloquence, as sound. But how? How teach the intuition of musical sound? "The first principle in musical hearing is not, as many people assume, the ability to distinguish the separate elements in a composition and the ability to recognize its devices, but to experience the primary illusion, to feel the consistent movement and recognize at once the commanding form which makes this piece an inviolable whole" (Langer 147).

Like the sophistic and Ciceronian conception of eloquence, rhetoric as a musical performance cannot be taught by rules or techniques nor by analysis and interpretation alone. Rather, as Langer states, we must be quiet and listen like children (147). Thus, the prerequisite to learning the music of language is to be quiet. We must put away our noisy heuristics for a little while. We must put our ear to the page and attend to what in the course of this discussion has been variously referred to as voice, felt sense, harmony and dissonance; the temporal shapes of musical experience; the dynamic unity of sensuous form and intellectual content; the presentational pattern of articulated form; the expressive movement of consciousness. For "listening is the primary musical activity. The musician listens to his own idea before he plays, before he writes. The basis of all musical advance is more comprehensive hearing" (Langer 148; cf. Bertram; Anderson and Lynch; Ur).

Six

Postscript: Teaching Indeterminacy? Methods, Fears, Politics, Curricula, and the Problem of Epistemology

Teaching Play, Researching Expectations, Listening to Indeterminacy

This book attempts to demonstrate that there is a relationship between literary and scientific theory; that as part of an emerging sophistic in our culture, Reader Response Criticism shares the same epistemology of probability, relativity, contingency, and uncertainty as New Physics; that in their continued visual emphasis on analysis and interpretation they also share the Newtonian imperatives to describe and explain affective experience in empirical, referential, and rational terms; that formalistic, rationalistic method, solidified and institutionalized in the theory and practice of New Criticism and Newtonian science, represents the limits of our understanding of indeterminate experience in texts and in nature; and that efforts to understand and teach reading and writing using Reader Response Criticism based on analysis and interpretation tend to undermine somewhat its philosophical agenda.

We therefore turned to the rhetorical tradition of the ancient sophists, Isocrates, and Cicero to explore language itself as an indirect and uncertain form of knowledge, one grounded in an oral culture's need and desire for a sensuous, poetic style that could form a nonformalistic, nonrationalistic basis of affective response; speculated that nonformalistic, nonrationalistic knowledge in both literature and science, like indeterminacy itself, is somehow related to the nature of time which we don't as yet understand; discovered in some contemporary philosophies of language and music a nonreferential theory of the sensuous movement of aural, temporal forms in consciousness; suggested that imitation as symbolic reproduction of these forms in speech and consciousness could perhaps best be described and understood according to the musical principles that underlie the sensuous shapes of prose as sound; touched on the notion (discussed more in appendix C) that aural imitation, because more physical and less reductive, may provide a basis for a better method of educating the aesthetic faculty involved in affective response; and demonstrated that based on this notion of imitation we could perhaps best teach the affective, physical, temporal dimension of reading and writing through a rhetoric of the musical performance of language.

Suggestions for teaching the response as a rhetoric of performance include approaches and methods found not only in Reader Response Criticism, composition theory, and rhetoric but also oral interpretation, listening research, and musicology itself. The work in speech departments on oral interpretation, for example, although focused on the re-creation of the "meaning" of a text, could with its attention to style, delivery, gesture, drama, and group dynamics certainly contribute to teaching reader response as a musical (and social) phenomenon (e.g., see Bertram; Bowen; Cohen; Gottlieb; Haas; Long; Sloan; Veilleux). These studies might also be useful for applying reading performance to the teaching of writing, provided we eschew as much as possible the formalistic, rationalistic approach to analyzing both meaning and sound found in them.

For example, in conjunction with Elbow's suggestion (*Writ-*

ing with Power 304–13), we could teach voice (physical and mental) through the performance of dialogues and other essays—the student's or someone else's. We could have students orally "interpret" their work and have the class *listen* for shifts of intonation, speed, and pacing as temporal movements, and how these create, maintain, and affect emotions. They could also listen for places where the voices stumbled, where the timing faltered, where the emotional energy faded, and then try to identify the source of the emotional dissonance and how to resolve it through oral revision. They could exchange dialogues (or essays), and, based on a dramatistic reading similar to method acting, we could ask them to relate the work to an emotional experience, dwell on and evoke some relevant past emotional experience, and then act out the work in that emotion (see Schrivner 79; cf. Parrish).

Schultz and others have been exploring the use not only of voice and visuals in teaching the performance of language but also of drama, gesture, body movement, and even dance, which the ancients knew was intimately, physically related to speech, and which oral interpretation also treats (e.g., see Stewig; Heinig and Stillwell; Gray and Mager; Spolin). While the focus in oral interpretation is not generally affective response to language as an epistemic experience, it too may be valuable in helping us concentrate on the felt sense of language as a form of knowledge in the body, as a physical movement in time as well as space. Students would not only hear their work in their own voice and in the voice of others (cf. Murray, "Teaching the Other Self") but would hear, see, and feel their words in other physical forms, in different kinds of music, in various emotional states.

With these techniques, students could experience the temporal relation between language and emotion, which emotion is best suited the style of the work, and whether this was the affective music and movement the writer intended (cf. Parrish; Geiger; Elbow, *Writing with Power* 262). For students who are suffering from writer's block, parts could be cast and recast, appropriate emotions called up for the unfinished piece, and then—carried by the emotional state and the timing of the style, the expectations the writer had begun to create—the students could act out the work beyond the point at which the writer had stopped, got stuck; thus, writers could get some idea of how, based on their voice as felt sense, on the expectations created by their style as a musical phenomenon, their piece could be developed, continued, extended, or changed.

In addition, affective response in oral performance could be used to teach organization as the experience of aural, affective, temporal expectations rather than purely visual, spatial, cognitive ones. Linda Flower's concepts of writers and readers creating contexts, chunking related information, establishing hierarchy, and providing cues to create organizational expectations (*Problem Solving*) might also be useful here. However, the focus would now be on *hearing* the paragraph breaks, the chunking, the hierarchies, the cues, through the rhythm of the sentences as well as the temporal organization of the essay (cf. Gendlin, *Focusing*; Perl, "Guidelines"). Students would try to listen to the expectations set up by the flow of the piece in time, to their affective states, to auditory cues, and then, based on Meyer's principles, discuss what aural expectations had been created by sound, and whether they had been resolved, delayed, or thwarted (cf. Elbow, *Writing with Power* 256–59). Students would not be given recourse to the visual text but rather be forced to *listen* to the sound of the language for these expectations and their affective responses to them.

No doubt students will have a hard time focusing on the sound as felt sense of language, on the rhythm of expectations, and will revert to content and meaning for cues. In this regard, despite the preoccupation with analysis, testing, and measurement, some of the exercises developed in listening research might be valuable in getting students to more closely listen to language itself (see Anderson and Lynch; Rost; Ur); they might also be valuable in helping us understand better the relationship between listening and other language skills such as reading and writing (Lundsteen). Through such exercises, we may be able to get students to pay attention to the affective dimension of style long enough to begin to feel the temporal structure of the text.

These exercises, and the aural, temporal response to reading and writing, then, should probably be well incorporated into the course, become a major focus of attention. What we need in contemporary composition theory and Reader Response Criticism, perhaps, is a way to use oral performance as a required, integral part of the entire course. In addition to analysis and interpretation and the other things we do in the classroom, students should probably continually read pieces—published and their own—out loud, articulating and responding in oral performance to the dynamic music and movement of language in time (and internalizing its relation to content) in order to facilitate the development of inner hearing and outward expression, of problem solving and audience adaptation. More pedagogical research and application need to be done here. (For other techniques on teaching writing as "physical eloquence," also see Ochsner [128–37].)

Since one major assumption is that reading out loud improves writing in basic as well as higher level courses, an area of research that probably needs investigation is whether there is in fact a correlation between the reader response as oral performance and the development of writing ability—defined not only in terms of spatial skills, such as clarity and organization, but also temporal ones, such as style and emotion. It might also be interesting to see if there is any correlation between musical and linguistic development, between musical inclination and voice in writing.

Research in this area might include ethnographic studies, using the classroom as a research site of performance and response (cf. Bleich "Identity"). The advantage of this research method, of course, is that in its relationship to narrative and its situation in the research setting ethnography is in some ways more subjective and oral by its very nature, rather than objectively empirical or strictly rationalistic. In studying the affective experience of language, it would be especially important not to violate the unity of the phenomena under study with our methods. Comparative protocol analyses also might prove useful in studying (and supplementing the analysis of) the specific effects of oral performance and response on thinking and writing processes—on the role of sound in invention, in word choice, for example. Despite its limitations, protocol analysis might be especially valuable in that it too is an oral methodology, embodies and uses "reading and writing out loud" in the study of the phenomenon itself. In fact, it is possible that read- and write-aloud protocols can actually be employed to teach reading and writing as oral performance. This suggests a whole other avenue of pedagogical research.

In addition, there are a number of nonformalistic, nonrationalistic "techniques" that are being used or could be used to understand and teach affective response to the oral performance of language. Based on the work of Gendlin (*Focusing*), for instance, Sondra Perl ("Guidelines") has developed a nonformalistic, nonrationalistic set of "instructions" for helping writers focus on their reactions and feelings, on felt sense as they write. These guidelines may be applicable to reading as well. Don Gallehr has applied the ancient and seemingly universal practice of meditation (in a nonreligious way) to the teaching of writing as a way of clearing the mind for fresh linguistic experience, for new thought. If tones for Zuckerkandl clear the mind for musical hearing (cf. Suhor, "The Uses of Silence"), these techniques may also clear the mind for musical reading and response.

Reading Affectively Versus Reading Critically?

All the techniques and approaches discussed also serve to call our standard methods of teaching reading and writing, and notions of literacy and knowledge itself, into question. In our culture, much attention has been paid to reading critically, especially as of late. With the poor literacy rates and lack of academic skills epidemic in the United States, educators, politicians, textbook publishers, the media, and the general public have all joined in the chorus of complaints. Given the problems with the reading and writing ability of students, that attention is warranted, though one has to wonder about the effectiveness of the methods for correcting these problems: more analysis, more interpretation. In fact, institutionalized in New Criticism as the model of teaching critical, social, and cultural awareness (see Leavis, *Culture and Environment, Education*; Hirsch et al., *Cultural Literacy*; cf. Eagleton 27–53), reading (and writing) critically has been the focus of our pedagogy for many years.

In a hyper, meta, mutated form, reading critically can be understood to be carried on in poststructuralist theory as well. Yet, teaching methods that grew out of the sixties, with their emphasis on student rights, personal creativity, and free electives, have been blamed for the plummeting standards and skills (Bloom). With their emphasis on the open-ended, political nature of knowledge, Reader Response Criticism, expressive writing, and poststructuralist theory generally can be understood to be related to, if not actually an outgrowth of, the educational and cultural movement of the sixties.

But putting nostalgia aside, perhaps we should stop for a moment. How effective were the methods of mass education that came before this movement—formal analysis, rational interpretation? Are the "looser" methods that grew out of the sixties really to blame, as Bloom maintains? Will a return to "the basics," founded on a formalistic, rationalistic epistemology, be any more effective than what we had then, or have now? Are what are now perceived as the basics any more basic than affective experience, which, even in its primitive but absolutely fundamental form, curiosity, must underlie knowledge, and which directly affects a student's ability and desire to learn? Are we caught in the myth and metaphors of logocentric methods embedded in our scientific and technological culture—myths and metaphors used by politicians and administrators and policy makers and fostered and strengthened by the educational establishment to justify itself in such a culture?

Aside from a host of other possible social and cultural causes (cf. Lasch, esp. 125–53), is it also possible that the new, less restrictive methods now under attack from all quarters don't work in theory or practice as well as we would wish them to precisely because they are grounded in the very formalistic, rationalistic epistemology they seek to counteract? Could it be that sophistic methods don't work because we simultaneously hold a Platonic notion of knowledge—because we employ formalized, rationalized versions of sophistic method?

While we have talked much of "reading critically," we have not talked much about "reading affectively." This is one area where Reader Response Criticism has been invaluable: in stressing the importance of affective logic, Reader Response Criticism has helped keep alive in a scientific and technological culture the notion that emotions are the basis of all knowledge and a kind of knowledge in themselves. But reading affectively? The latter would appear to be a relatively minor concern compared to reading critically, one easily relegated to the backwaters of teaching. And yet, if we, like Reader Response critics, the sophists, and Cicero, believe that feeling and emotion are the starting point and the foundation of all knowledge, perhaps reading affectively, and writing affectively too, is more important than we currently think.

Perhaps we should not continue to make the distinction between reading critically and reading affectively at all. In some sense, all knowledge is a physical experience. But "affective logic" (an oxymoron that unites feeling and cognition) perhaps underlies both. Only our methods may make us think it does not. The methods we use render what we look at an object of method are themselves an abstraction, rather than a part of the phenomenon. Yet, even our methods are part of the human experience, just as objectivity is a human phenomenon, a scientific project, a social contract, a stylistic proclivity, an *ethos*, a state of emotion. We think of methods as something other than human because we define them according to the imperatives of method itself—imperatives that we create and that our methods then require as a condition of their efficient operation and efficacious use. But the teaching of reading and writing (and perhaps science itself) is not necessarily bound to the imperatives of science as currently conceived. There are different levels of experience, different kinds of knowledge. All are important, and all may be essential in understanding the nature of human knowledge and to teaching reading and writing.

Fear and Loathing and
the Teaching of Reading Out Loud

One assumption of this book has been that reading out loud as a musical performance and response to a text can get us closer to the affective experience of language as a temporal phenomenon, and preserve it as an indeterminate form of knowledge, than can analysis and interpretation. But as Lanham laments, "Reading aloud is precisely what no one in America does anymore. To an American university student, the prospect of reading a literary text aloud in class produces a response akin to lockjaw. Reading aloud. An alien concept" (100). Why? Why don't we do more reading out loud in our classrooms? Perhaps we are afraid. Afraid of our students' reactions, and perhaps the reactions of our colleagues. As we are only too aware, many university students seem to loathe English, whether literature or writing. And most are used to the security of formalistic, rationalistic methods of study, and expect them. They are also afraid of reading out loud: of exposing their personalities (see Elbow, *Writing with Power* 306–11), of being different (cf. Gilligan, *In a Different Voice*), of taking responsibility for their language (cf. Berry, *Standing by Words*), all of which oral performance requires. This fear is especially heightened when - students are reading out loud unfinished drafts, works in progress.

Although students in general have some initial misgivings about reading their own work out loud, almost all do eventually overcome their fear. Many actually come to appreciate the value and importance of the method and think it helps their writing. Their fears dissipate somewhat. But what about ours? How will we appear, advocating and practicing such an ancient, antiquated form of teaching in a scientific and technological culture? Will we lose in credibility if we don't maintain our professional (i.e., formalistic, rationalistic) *ethos* (cf. McCormick)? How will students, most of them majoring in the sciences and engineering, and all of them wary of writing and suspicious of the value of the humanities as they are presently constituted and taught (as a pseudoscience—perhaps because they are taught this way), react to such a nonmethodological (as opposed to unmethodical) way of teaching? To paraphrase Bleich (*Subjective Criticism* 104), to some extent we are all epistemologically inhibited. If we took Cicero's advice (*Orator* xlii.144), we would even read to them out loud.

Further, it is one thing to have students read their drafts out loud and quite another to have them perform literature or poetry on a regular basis—without benefit of a method of analysis and interpretation like New Criticism that can be taught (though not easily), or the intellectual rigor and appeal of poststructuralism. Their fear and our fear, and the potential loathing of our colleagues in literature and in other disciplines, keeps us from doing more of that. But as Elbow, as well as Murray, points out, this fear and loathing—theirs and ours—is another legacy of the traditional, "New critical" way of teaching reading (and writing) as a formalistic, rationalistic enterprise. And the epistemology underlying this enterprise, and the formalistic, rationalistic method itself, has become an ideology that permeates our entire culture (cf. Eagleton 17–53). In our society, reading and writing, like making love in a urban room, are something do be done quickly and without sound. It is doubtful whether a one-semester stand can overcome years of epistemological loathing and fear. Yet we continue to try, sometimes having students read their drafts out loud, and reading pieces of literary or other works out loud ourselves in class to go over them, perhaps with apologetic explanation or embarrassed hesitation, for any benefit that might accrue, and the sheer joy of it.

The Problem with Reading Out Loud
and the Play of Indeterminacy

Perhaps the biggest problem with reading out loud is that it is such an uncertain technique for teaching affective response in reading and writing and, even more so, literacy—something more akin to play than teaching. Given the uncertain nature of the affective experience of language, this method of instruction has to be. To the degree that we specify the method anymore, we risk narrowing the focus of response, risk making method rather than experience the focus of response. As Lanham states, the problem with reading out loud is that

> [p]rose, in such a proceeding, cannot be approached with the scientific attitude alone. Preoccupation with form, with the play attitude, is immediate and continual. A performance is played. The text must be re-created. Surely, some such pedagogy as this is desperately needed in English classes in America today. Students are sometimes asked to memorize a passage of verse. But I have never heard . . . of a student being asked to memorize and declaim a passage of prose. The debater's training, like Freshman Composition, emphasizes invention, finding arguments, rather than stylistic surface. This is movement precisely in the wrong direction. And the speed-reading course is plain lunacy. Its mere premise horrifies: reading is something to be gotten through. Seldom has the American dislike and suspicion of words shown so clearly. Words are to be gotten over with. (101–02)

Play? Except for those who write poetry or fiction or drama, or who take a creative writing class (and sometimes not even there), most students have not played with language since their childhood. Most have had the sensuousness of language, the physicality of style, beaten out of them as early as elementary school by the formalistic, rationalistic methods used to fulfill the technological, ideological, and economic imperative to communicate clearly, precisely, efficiently. And they certainly have not learned the play attitude in other writing classes, for as Lanham laments, most writing classes are conducted on a scientific model of instruction that is antithetical to play. It is perhaps because of this that we need to teach reading (and writing) as oral performance. "Every course in composition ought to be a course in Slow Reading. To read a prose text aloud, again and again, is the most important single act you can perform, if you are to understand style" (Lanham 102).

The play attitude is necessary if we are to cope and deal successfully with the uncertainty of temporal expectation, with the indeterminacy of affective knowledge. For the open-ended nature of language as an endless play of shimmering significations and temporal forms without a final signified, which deconstructionists are fond of pointing out, also necessitates open-ended methods of handling and instruction. And those "methods" depend on the ability to play. If there is no ultimate signified, but just a powerfully real, necessary, linguistic, and social one (or one imposed by political fiat), the endless ring of language, the play and interplay of the forms in time and space, is everything. The problem, then, becomes living with uncertainty, something we've never been able to do very well.

Play, Literacy, and Indeterminacy in a Technological Culture

The teaching of rhythm and sound is not only a matter of the play attitude, however. Or rather, play is more important than we think. Before he died, Eric Havelock considered the implications of his work on orality in ancient Greece for the teaching of reading and writing and literacy in modern society. In "Orality, Literacy, and Star Wars," Havelock, like Cassirer, argues that orality is closer to sensory experience than is written discourse and that the rhythmic oral word is central to intellectual development. Yet, he says, "[i]n education, as formally conducted and institutionalized, these are treated wholly as fringe benefits, as extracurricular" (415). The problem with literacy,

Havelock suggests, is that "[a]s we learn to use abstractions, we also learn to distance ourselves from this level of experience, and so learn to distance ourselves from physical and emotional reality" (415). Based on the fact that abstract language is endemic in our highly scientific, technological, bureaucratic culture, Havelock too concludes "that oral and poetic training should be coupled with training in reading and writing and composition at all levels of the educational process" (416).

All this perhaps suggests the need to broaden and perhaps redefine literacy itself, something that Ochsner's book on physical eloquence has begun to do (also see Bizzell, "Arguing about Literacy," "Beyond Anti-Foundationalism"). Literacy, the ability to read and write, is usually thought of in terms of "skills" necessary to understand content and be a "productive" member of society. Thus, literacy is taught primarily through the analysis and interpretation and production of texts (in academia, "capitalistic production" is the publication of the texts themselves). However, based on the subjective and social philosophy of language and knowledge emerging in our scientific culture, we may also want to begin to think of literacy in terms of secondary orality: as the ability to create and comprehend written texts in terms of affective responses to the temporal modes of language as sound. We may want to think of reading and writing not only as a set of abstract skills but also as the ability to understand and create texts that are physically persuasive, that are as affective as speech.

It might be argued that these affective linguistic skills are acquired rather than learned. But that is the point here. What Elbow, like Havelock, argues in "The Shifting Relationships Between Speech and Writing" is that we must bring writing and speech closer together to make writing a more naturally *acquired* rather than a learned skill. Ochsner argues this point as well. But an understanding of writing as acquired rather than learned will necessitate a shift of epistemology away from a formalistic, rationalistic conception of language and knowledge to a truly subjective and social one, a shift from a visual to an oral ontology of literacy. Enos ("Composing Process") perhaps provides us with a historical basis (and cautions) for this shift (also see Enos, *Oral and Written Communication*). Zuckerkandl and Meyer suggest parallels in musical education that might help us with it. Cassirer and Langer give us a philosophical basis for it. The next step into indeterminacy is ours.

Indeterminacy, Politics, and Curricula

There are many implications for academic specialization and curriculum design that such a shift in epistemology and ontology would entail, both large and small. All of the discussion of the philosophical, rhetorical, pedagogical, and cultural implications perhaps suggests that there is a possibility, a need, and a basis for the unification of reading and writing, of literature and composition and rhetoric, and even of the humanities and the sciences (see Holton, esp. 461–84). This is contrary to the recent trend in all disciplines, including English, to split even further. In the oral and temporal realm of language, the inherent relationship of poetry and prose is obvious. In oral performance, the relationship between rhetoric and poetry, which Cicero and the sophists recognized, is not only acknowledged but is utilized. And the oral performance of literature can be better used to teach writing if both are taught not only as inherently social but also as oral in nature. As the sophists and Cicero seemed to believe, the beauty and power of the music of language may not only be necessary for emotional persuasion but to thought itself. If Halloran and Whitburn's reconsideration of the plain style is taken into account, this may apply to scientific and technical communication as well.

But it is not only a matter of reading out loud. In oral performance as a physical, epistemic act, the bodily nature of all knowledge is perhaps better recognized and fulfilled. This suggests the possibility, the need, and the basis for the unification of all the language arts—composition, rhetoric, literature, drama, speech, listening. Indeterminacy tends to break down our walls of artificial division, be they methods or disciplines.

As Cicero proclaimed, all knowledge, like the universe itself, is interrelated, one. However, we cannot be naive enough to think that, given the intense specialization that has been occurring in all disciplines in this century, we can actually bring these separate departments of knowledge back together anytime soon. The bureaucratic imperative, like the technological imperative to which it relates, remains, and is possibly here to stay. However, I do think that we can make more fruitful connections and contributions to each other's work than we do now. Cicero said the ideal rhetor must have "grasped the principles and nature of every subject and every art" (D. O. I.xvii.80; see I.i–xix.) The synthesis, though slow, may be beginning.

Dissonance and Secondary Divine Madness

The question that remains, however, is whether we can actually ever describe and teach affective experience as an indeterminate realm of knowledge, even with the temporal principles of response drawn from music theory. Can we describe and teach the principles that underlie the uncertainty of affective experience as a form of knowledge without analyzing and so reducing them? Can we teach intuition? The answer brings us back to problem of epistemology and of culture—a problem we have never left. Formalistic, rationalistic method has dominated the metaphors and modes of thought in the twentieth century. In its parallelism to New Physics, poststructuralism perhaps presages the critical theory and pedagogy of the twenty-first century. But as Roger Penrose points out, because of the paradoxical and anomalous nature of our knowledge, it is becoming increasingly clear that New Physics, and perhaps poststructuralism as well, must move on to new metaphors, methods, and modes of thought based on future discoveries concerning the nature of time and its relationship to space, a relationship we are only now beginning to understand.

But we should also realize and remember the inherent limitations of human methods and understanding. Our theories—

like the indeterminate phenomenon under study—always out-strip our research and our practice. If the affective experience of style as a sensuous form of knowledge exists in and is created by time, we cannot analyze it with our spatial methods and may never wholly grasp it with our intellect. The division of time and space, of affect and cognition, like the division between wave and particle, reveals the indeterminacy of our methods and our knowledge. Language and consciousness seem to con-demn us to referential and rational modes of thought at the same time that they free us to speak and think.

Music itself may be Kantian in nature. Although music can be understood mathematically, if it is not in its Pythagorean essence mathematical—can be understood as affective mathe-matics, as the calculus of response—music may not get us any closer to describing or measuring the quantum, indeterminate level of experience. Meyer's concept of the temporal *gestalten* of music, seemingly grounded as it is in a stimulus–response theory of response, is ultimately causal—a problem Zucker-kandl tries to deal with by locating the effect and meaning of music outside the realm of human experience. And so we are thrown back into the abyss between Ideal Forms and quantum happenstance, from which the dissonance of indeterminacy be-gins. Although music perhaps does get us closer to the non-referential, temporal dimension of affective response, our no-tions of the nonreferential, temporal dimension of response, like our notions of time and space, of orality and literacy, are themselves constructions of a predominately spatial con-sciousness.

In researching, describing, and teaching affective response as a rhetoric of musical performance, the best we can do is to develop methods based on secondary orality. Although an un-derstanding of temporal expectation based on secondary orality certainly seems to get us closer to the affective experience of language as a sensuous, nonreferential, indeterminate form of knowledge, like the secondary divine madness we experience when performing a text, this too may be a deception, an illu-sion created by language and consciousness itself. But this deception, this illusion, this madness, is all we've got. An understanding of style as affective, physical, temporal experience based on secondary orality doesn't solve the problem of teaching indeterminacy, but it elucidates it by calling into question the nature of human knowledge itself. It helps us understand the problem of method and so perhaps moves us a step closer toward the temporal dimension of affective experience.

We may never totally succeed in developing a method for researching, describing, and teaching affective response to temporal experience as indeterminate knowledge. This statement of the strong principle of indeterminacy will not be popular. Like Crassus's students, we clamor for techniques, for methods, for explanations, for answers. Only slowly, and with much consternation, do we understand that there are none that will suffice to teach the indeterminate realm of language and knowledge. As Mario Untersteiner suggests (xvi), this is a true sophistic position, the tragic human condition reflected in Gorgias's dictum: Reality does not exist; if it did exist, we could not understand it; if we could understand it, we could not communicate it.

Given the failure of Crassus in De Oratore to teach his students the true nature of rhetoric and the fact that the ideal of eloquence can be taught only by indirection, it is perhaps only fitting and appropriate that the affective level of performance and response ultimately remains ineffable—but not unknowable to experience. Although this too may be a rationalization, an illusion, the failure to develop a formalistic method of teaching the affective, subjective, physical experience of language is actually a success. To the degree that our methods for studying this experience are *not* determinate, to the degree that our knowledge is uncertain, we leave open the temporal door of consciousness.

And so we wait for indeterminacy like a ghost to come.

Appendixes

Notes

Works Cited

Index

Appendix A

The Problem of Affect and Interpretation: Allen Tate Versus the Logical Positivists

In *Reason in Madness*, Allen Tate explicitly explores the philosophical relationship between scientific and literary theory in a way that illuminates the problem of studying affect in interpretation. It is both significant and ironic that in "The Present Function of Criticism," Tate, the archetypal New critic, begins by attacking the science of logical positivism that he sees underlying historical and biographical criticism. That Tate even discusses literary criticism in terms of science is significant in that it perhaps attests to the close philosophical relation between literature and science. And that Tate sees historical criticism in terms of logical positivism is ironic in that in arguing against logical positivism as a scientific basis for literary criticism, Tate ultimately adopts and advocates an epistemology for New Criticism that seems to underlie science as well: that of Newtonian physics.

For Tate, "positivism is not only a scientific movement, but also a moral attitude; it is "a spiritual disorder" of our scientific, technological, industrial society ("Present Function" 4). Applied to language, logical positivism dictates that for every proposition, that is, true statement, there must be an external, visual, objectively verifiable referent in reality. Thus, Tate argues, in this philosophy the function of language is reduced to accurate description of external reality, which becomes the only valid use of language. In the positivistic philosophy of knowledge, language is a problematical but necessary container of propositions about external reality. In the positivistic philosophy of knowledge, poetic statements about emotions are untestable. Because they are not subject to empirical proof, poetic statements, like metaphysical ones, are eliminated from consideration as valid propositions.

For example, in *Language, Truth, and Logic*, A. J. Ayer maintains that "no statement which refers to a 'reality' transcending the limits of all possible sense-experience can possibly have any literal significance; from which it must follow that the labours of those who have striven to describe such a reality have all been devoted to the production of nonsense" (34). According to Ayer, the problem is one of "a rule which determines the literal significance of language" (34): "The criterion which we use to test the genuineness of apparent statements of fact is the criterion of verifiability. We say a sentence is factually significant to any given person, if and only if, he knows how to verify the proposition which it purports to express—that is, if he knows what observations would lead him, under certain conditions, to accept the proposition as being true, or reject it as being false" (35).

Ayer therefore makes a distinction between verifiable statements and those dependent on future experience, which are "if not a tautology, a mere pseudo-proposition;" although it may be "emotionally significant," it is not "literally significant" (35). He thus also makes a distinction between verifiable statements and poetic statements, which, while they may not have literal significance according to the criterion of verifiability and so can be neither true nor false, "express, or arouse, emotion, and thus [can] be subject to ethical or aesthetic standards" (44). Significantly, Ayer admits that most literary statements are in fact verifiable, but he makes a sharp distinction between scientific and poetic statements, the first "concerned with the expression of true propositions, the other with the creation of works of art" (44). But based on the belief that the truth criterion can and must be applied to all propositions, poetic statements about feelings and beliefs are merely aesthetic at best.

Therefore, Tate states in "Literature as Knowledge" that in our positivistic age, meaning in poetry "has been replaced with operational validity" (26). Reviewing Charles W. Morris's work in the semiotics of language, Tate argues that because Morris must consider poetry to consist of iconic, that is, self-referential, signs, Morris is forced to conclude that as propositions,

> poetry is in the realm of values; and . . . since the values are not attached to reality, they are irresponsible feelings. They are, in fact, rhetoric. And it is also significant that for Mr. Morris the study of rhetoric is a branch of pragmatics; it is even a kind of technological instrument. For, in the essay "Science, Art, and Technology," poetry seems to acquire its main responsibility in the technological function of telling us what we *ought* to want and do. Here again, neo-classical didacticism appears in terms of a rigorous instrumentalism. (44)

In the work of Morris, then, Tate finds what he considers to be the central problem in our time with the positivistic approach to literature, and with language and knowledge in general: caught in the sign/referent trap set by the logical positivists, in which there is supposed to be an atomistic one-to-one correspondence between proposition and phenomena, they have eliminated the role of cognition by replacing intelligence with a *scientific methodology, a technique,* for ascertaining the truth of any given proposition. As Tate states: "By implication there is an interpreter, a person, a mind; but Mr. Morris is consistently vague about him: he is not a technical factor, he is a superfluous entity, in semiosis. That is to say, not only is he not needed in order to explain the functioning of signs; he would embarrass the explanation" (31). For Tate, logical positivism goes beyond commonsense empiricism that underlies scientific procedure in that positivism eliminates universals, knowledge, and thus cognition altogether. Only that contained in language which can be reduced to "exclusively perceptual terms" can be proven to exist (Roelof qtd. in Tate, 32). "In this positivistic technique for the analysis of language, the interpreting mind, the cognizing intelligence, is lost in the perceptual account of its external behavior" (33; cf. Booth, *Modern Dogma*). (Tate finds the same problem with I. A. Richards insofar as Richards reduces poetry to unverifiable statements about feeling.)

For Tate, then, the function of literature (and literary criticism) is the preservation of intelligence. But in the first in a series of ironies that may reveal the profound influence of Newtonian science on New Criticism, what Tate admits as "intelligence" and uses to counter the pernicious effect of logical positivism, is itself based solely on a formalistic, rationalistic conception of cognition. The move comes when, in "The Present Function of Criticism," Tate attacks the positivistic Doctrine of Relevance: "The Doctrine of Relevance is very simple. It means that the subject-matter of a literary work must not be isolated in terms of form; it must be tested (on an analogy to scientific techniques) by observation of the world that it 'represents' " (14). But for Tate, there can be no separation of language and subject matter in poetry. However, Tate's purpose is not so much to focus attention on the affective unity of form and content as it is to eliminate the need for external (or internal) referents from discussion altogether. To counteract the pernicious effects of logical positivism that reduce language to a linguistic gesture toward a definitive reality, Tate declares that there is no subject matter outside of form. That is, all is form. If poetry cannot consist of referentially valid propositions about the world or about emotion and value, Tate has eliminated the need for language to refer to anything at all except itself.

The obvious problem here is that in his focus on form Tate precludes the study of the affective experience of the reader. As for Eliot, for Tate, it is the critic's function only to analyze and interpret form. Subjective emotions and other "external" considerations, as well as positivistic method, are to be replaced by objectivity, logic, and the text itself. Tate's conception of cognition, of intelligence, then, is like Eliot's: formalistic, rationalistic, and *seemingly* Newtonian. For Tate can no more allow subjective interpretation into criticism or admit emotions and beliefs are a part of intelligence than Morris can accept "an interpreter, a person, a mind." "We must return to, we must never leave, the poem itself. Its 'interest' value is a cognitive one; it is sufficient that here, in the poem, we get knowledge of a whole object. If rational inquiry is the only mode of criticism, we must remember that the way we employ the mode must always powerfully affect our experience of the poem" (Tate, "Literature" 61). Unlike Eliot, then, who at least in this regard "appears" to be more committed to empiricism, Tate, like us, admits and accepts the necessity of rational hypotheses in interpretation and expresses an awareness of the consequences of this rationality on our understanding and experience of affect in interpretation. Nevertheless, Tate is apparently willing to endure this for a blow against the rough referential treatment of literature at the hands of the logical positivists.

For Tate, literary form, like Plato's Idea, seems to be a kind of pure category of experience, neither mimetic (i.e., referential) nor affective or innate in the mind, but an ideal order. Citing with approval Richards's later work on Coleridge, Tate states in "Literature As Knowledge" that " *'Poetry is the completest mode of utterance.'* It is neither the world of verifiable science nor a projection of ourselves; yet it is *complete.*" For Tate, "the order of completeness" achieved "in great works of the imagination" is distinct from the "experimental completeness aimed at by the positivist sciences, whose responsibility is directed towards the verification of limited techniques. The completeness of science is an abstraction covering an ideal co-operation among specialized methods." For Tate, the completeness of literature "is not of the experimental order, but of the experienced order: in short, of the mythical order" ("Literature" 59–60).

In this essay, Tate does not explain what this mythic order of literary experience is. (In "Tension in Poetry," Tate tries to account for the meaning of poetry as "the full organized body of extension and intention that we find in it" [72], but this essay does little to clarify the problem. In fact, his solution is not so different from that of Morris, whom he criticizes on this point. To account for how meaning in poetry was possible at all if all signs were icons—only referred to themselves—Morris postulated that there was also "syntactic meaning," that is, some referential signs in combination with icons that allowed for communication. But Tate's ideas about extension and intention seem to be the same concepts applied at the level of words themselves, similar to the relationship between denotation and connotation, and do not solve the problem of affect in reading; only the terminology has changed. Tate moves from the order of experience to the mythic order without explaining the connection.)

Like Eliot, like us, then, Tate must assume the mythic order exists in order to proceed with investigation, to grant that poetry is a kind of knowledge at all. But in declaring that poetry has no subject matter outside of form in an attempt to eliminate the need for external (or internal) referents demanded by the positivists ("Function" 19), Tate can be seen to go to *logical* extremes (i.e., toward rational idealism) while seeming to remain within the confines of a Newtonian epistemology. Although not as extreme as logical positivism, Tate's is also a visual epistemology. Tate has merely shifted the focus of accurate description from the external world of reality or internal world of affect to the work itself, the analysis and interpretation of which leads to the mythic order of experience ("Literature" 59–61; cf. Iser, *Act* 15; Eagleton 47).

With his emphasis on literary form as a pure category of experience that can be known formalistically and rationalistically, Tate can be seen to be creating a "Platonic" as well as an empirical basis for literary criticism (26, 32) in order to escape the problem of referentiality and of affect without ever resolving the inherent contradiction: how can we describe something we can't see? This contradiction seems to be less reprehensible than logical positivism in that it is both empirical *and idealistic*: it involves not only objective perception but also rational cognition. Facts, truth, reality of a great literary work are exhibited in form; but now, the ideal forms wherein true knowledge resides are in language itself rather than in a transcendental Platonic realm, or some shadowy external world of nature or reader.

Having shown us the problematic relationship between language and reality in poetry, Tate collapses language and subject matter, pleasure and truth, into form, covering over the classical dilemma as to whether the poetic, affective element is "objective feature or subjective effect" ("Literature" 49). Having stated what kind of knowledge poetry *is not*—positivistic— Tate effectively brushes aside the question of what kind of knowledge poetry *is*. It is enough that we can get knowledge of the whole object from the form. This is an assumption that cannot really be proved but which, for Tate, is necessary for criticism to proceed on something other than a positivistic or subjective basis and for the preservation of "intelligence" itself. "However we may see the completeness of poetry, it is a problem less to be solved than, in its full import, to be preserved" ("Literature" 61). And thus, again, given Tate's definition of intelligence, the reader's experience of the text, like the role of emotions themselves in knowledge, is neither considered nor explained by the theory.

Appendix B

Philosophical Bloodlines:
The Sophistic Ontology
of Cicero's Epistemology

The idea of Cicero's being a sophist may seem unexpected, even radical, to some and so deserves appendicular explanation. In "The Critique of Socrates in Cicero's *De Oratore*: *Ornatus* and the Nature of Wisdom," Raymond DiLorenzo discusses how the Ciceronian concept of *ornatus* is embodied in a metaphor Crassus uses in his attempt to explain eloquence, the relation of style and subject matter: "*Verba* are the *lumen*, the light, which falls upon *res*; and *res* give, as it were, *sedes*, seat or place, to *verba*. The metaphor suggests that words cast light upon things. They reveal things, and, through that, receive place" (250). While this metaphor is obviously visual (perhaps a reflection of an age of growing literacy in which Cicero lived) and points to a relationship between words and reality (which is very unsophistic), the relationship can indirectly be understood in terms of a "musical," uncertain order as well. In this appendix I would like to examine how, and how this relates to sophistic epistemology.

As DiLorenzo states, "Cicero himself once used the word

ornatus to mean *kosmos*, the order which is the universe" (253). DiLorenzo is thus led to consider the relation between *ornatus* and the Greek concept of *kosmos*. The universe is *kosmos*, or order, because "all in it is interdependent"; for Crassus, "*Res* and *verba*, like the things of the world above and below, belong together. We infer speech, like nature, is also *kosmos*" (253). The vision of reality as *kosmos*, as a synthetic unity in which all elements are interdependent, can be traced back to both Socrates and the sophists, and to the pre-Socratics. DiLorenzo states that it was Pythagoras who first called the universe *kosmos* "because of the order in it." It is well known that Pythagoras conceived of this order in mathematical-musical terms. However, the sophist's conception of *kosmos*, and thus of course *ornatus*, is somewhat different from that of Socrates and Plato. The difference between Plato and the sophists was a difference not only of epistemology, of how we know, but of ontology, the nature of reality itself, which again may hinge on differences between orality and literacy.

Contrary to received opinion (cf. Marrou 82), Kerferd shows that the sophists *were* interested in the physical universe and the science of their day. Kerferd (39) even cites Cicero (Diels and Kranz, *Fragmente*) as attesting to this fact, which is significant, given my argument concerning the connection between the sophists, Isocrates, and Cicero. As Kerferd states, Socrates refused to talk about "the nature of the universe, how the cosmos arose, and the necessary laws governing the heavenly bodies, arguing that those who thought about such matters were out of their minds" (39). The sophists, on the other hand, were willing and able to speculate, argue about, and debate the origin and action of things unseen as well as seen without the need of any "visual," ontological absolutes to which to refer as a higher authority.

As Kerferd discusses in a chapter entitled "The Theory of Language," the difference in ontology, like the difference in epistemology, also hinges on the definition of *logos*, the relationship between word and thing, just as it did for the sophists. And again, this definition of *logos* may hinge on the difference between oral and literate modes of thought. Kerferd traces the two opposing bloodlines of thought concerning the origin and nature of the universe to the earlier pre-Socratics. According to Kerferd, one line of thought "held that all things are the offspring of flow" and included such figures as Homer, Hesiod, Heraclitus, and Empedocles. The other line of thought "held that every thing is one and stationary within itself" and included such thinkers as Xenophon and Parmenides (49). We know that Pythagoras and Parmenides inform Plato's philosophy and cosmology (Cornford). Kerferd himself states that Plato was aware of this division of thought among the early philosophers and cites references in Plato's work to prove it (49). We also know that there is a somewhat direct philosophical line from Heraclitus to Protagoras to Gorgias to Isocrates (see my rough schemata at the end of this appendix); and except for the questionable relationship between Protagoras and Gorgias, the former was the latter's teacher in every case.

Significantly, Kerferd begins by citing Cratylus's belief in a one-to-one correspondence between word and thing rooted in sound: "Everything has a right name of its own which comes by nature, and a name is not whatever people call a thing by agreement, simply their own voice applied to the thing, but there is a kind of constituted correctness in names which is the same for all men (*Cratylus* 383a–b)" (73). But as I discuss in chapter 3, later in the dialogue Plato has Socrates knock this position in favor of a referential one; it is a visual, rational, abstract order that obtains between word and thing and makes "the correctness of names" possible, not a physical one of sound. This seems to concur with Kerferd's interpretation (74–77).

Given my discussion in chapter 3 concerning the disjuncture between language/reality and thought/reality that seems in part to underlie sophistic relativism, it is obvious that this view of the unity of word and thing in sound also flies in the face of the sophists—and perhaps Cicero—who maintain the primacy of language as both a subjective and social force in determining reality. While Kerferd does find some evidence to suggest Protagoras believed in this doctrine of "the rightness of names," he says it may have been related to the doctrine of the *dissoi logoi*—the need to make one *logos* appear more correct than another—and thus only a matter of the degree of the relation between sound and thing (perhaps like onomatopoeia in modern times); as Kerferd states, "[I]n the absence of details, we can only speculate as to how all this was fitted together" (76).

A unity of word and thing in sound also flies in the face of some of the pre-Socratic and Socratic philosophers as well. The central problem that haunted Greek philosophy in its search for ontological truth was that something cannot be and not be simultaneously. According to Kerferd, in attempting to find "the natural correctness in things," Heraclitus himself sought to discover the fundamental laws underlying the flux of reality upon which to base human laws, "whether or not Heraclitus understood that this was what he was doing" (113). Heraclitus too sought the truth, laws that would hold both for reality and for language, as well as the relationship between them. While Heraclitus dismissed what most people held to be correct knowledge of reality and argued that his own account was correct, "[t]his correct account is for him an account of states of affairs that are contradictory—the apparent world that language is about is found to be full of objective contradictions" (Kerferd 71).

Because Heraclitus held reality to be in a state of continual flux, the result of his attempt to find the natural correctness of things in a one-to-one correspondence between language and reality could only lead to a view of language in continual flux as well—and to the very contradictions that Plato and subsequent philosophers (such as the logical positivists) tried to eradicate. As Reader Response critics and New physicists seem to understand, if one holds that language must reflect and contain reality and that the reality one observes continually changes, then inevitably language, that is, statements about reality, will change too.

This philosophical position would seem particularly well suited to an oral culture, since language existed and was conceptualized as sound and thus was itself subject to change. (In a related discussion, Ong demonstrates that memorization was not a verbatim activity devoted to exact reduplication of aural texts, but rather formulaic, devoted to the passing down of aural mnemonic patterns [*Orality* 34]. Citing Frances Yates, Lentz also makes a distinction between "memory of things" and "memory of words" and suggests that the ancient Greeks as well as Cicero "may not require memory of words, or verbatim recall, but may necessitate only accurate reproduction of the arguments or events in a particular recitation" [92–93].) One can only speculate how the ontology of orality influenced the perception of the relationship between word and thing. Without positing another, rational realm of existence— Being—to which language can refer (or an absolute empirical reality, as Newtonian scientists do, or an ideal rational empiricism in form, as Tate and the New critics do), there is no way to obtain the single and absolute Truth underlying being.

One solution to this problem is to posit another realm to which language can refer. Thus, according to Kerferd, the pre-Socratic Parmenides was led "to sunder the world of appearances from the world of being" (71), to postulate a higher "visual" reality that could be the basis of *Logos*, to which *Logos* could refer. This, of course, is one basis of the Platonic Forms as well. "Plato's solution . . . was neither that of renouncing language, nor that of abandoning altogether the world of experience, but rather the manufacture of a 'third' world, that of the Platonic Forms" (Kerferd 76). Therefore, says Kerferd, Plato "resolved the problem of correct language by altering reality to fit the needs of language, instead of the reverse" (77). Plato never allows either contradiction or opinion into his philosophy of knowledge.

But posit a higher, unchanging realm of existence upon which all reality could rest but that is itself unprovable, the sophists would not do. As Kerferd states, the sophists could not follow Parmenides, who denied "the reality of the phenomenal world; rather, for them, the starting point was the phenomenal world itself, regularly seen as constituting the whole of reality and consequently the only possible object of cognition" (72). Like Heraclitus, the sophist Protagoras "had actually described the physical world as in a state of flux, with emissions continually replaced by accretions which made good what was lost" (Kerferd 72). Plato thus accused Protagoras of "holding theories which exclude the possibility that things have some fixed being of their own" (Kerferd 72). Gorgias too, notes Kerferd, "went at least some distance in the same direction in that he explained perception of physical objects in the same fashion as Empedocles, namely by positing continuous efflu- ences from objects which enter or fail to enter various pores of the body" (72).

Thus, in the sophistic view of science, as in the sophistic view of language, everything is in flux, but interdependent, one, and thus all method is reductive. (The philosophical blood- lines here traced from the pre-Socratics can be seen to generally form and inform not only the philosophical foundation of Pla- tonic and sophistic doctrine but Newtonian and New Physics as well [though this is a bit of a simplification]. But whether it's Empedocles' effluences or Democritus's atoms in a fiery void, whether Newton's gravitational attraction between mass points or Lorentz's stationary ether, whether Einstein's energy/mat- ter or Heisenberg's particle/wave, the dual conceptions are more or less the same; only the metaphors have changed. [For a discussion of the atom-continuum controversy that has raged throughout the history of science, see Toulmin and Goodfield's *The Architecture of Matter*. Also see pages 482–92 and the "Epi- logue," 493–520, of Gillispie's *The Edge of Objectivity*].) In fact, in its vision of reality as a synthetic unity in which all elements are interrelated and in flux (as opposed to autonomous, fixed, and stable) and the attendant belief that they cannot be separated without irreparable damage, this sophistic ontology and the epistemology based on it are remarkably similar to the vision of subatomic reality revealed by the New Physics. Fritjof Capra perhaps summarizes this holistic vision of reality best in *The Tao of Physics*:

> The exploration of the subatomic world in the twentieth cen- tury has revealed the intrinsically dynamic nature of matter. It has shown that the constituents of atoms, the subatomic particles, are dynamic patterns which do not exist as isolated entities, but as integral parts of an inseparable network of interactions. These interactions involve a ceaseless flow of

energy manifesting itself as the exchange of particles; a dynamic interplay in which particles are created and destroyed without end in a continual variation of energy patterns. The particle interactions give rise to the stable structures which build up the material world, which again do not remain static, but oscillate in rhythmic movements. The whole universe is thus engaged in endless motion and activity; in a continual cosmic dance of energy. (211)

The ontological belief in the interdependence and interaction of all things in speech and in nature that can only be intuited, not known, perhaps underlies Cicero's philosophy of language and knowledge as well. While the philosophy concerning the interdependence of res and verba might seem to contradict the sophistic dichotomy between reality and thought, and reality and language discussed earlier, it may not. The key word in DiLorenzo's discussion is "like." For res and verba are "like the things of the world" (253). Res, "things" are not the objects of the world but thoughts about objects, which inhabit a parallel world of mind and language. Because the senses are limited and the truth imperceptible for Cicero (Enos, Literate Mode 39) as for Gorgias (Enos, "Rhetorical Theory"), Cicero's philosophy does not necessarily involve a unity of thought and reality, or a unity of language and reality, but only a unity of language and thought based on an intuition of a unity in a reality that is uncertain. That is, the "intuition of the unity of things in the world, in the arts and sciences, and in the forms of eloquence" ("Ornatus" 249) is, as DiLorenzo states, "an analogue, in the order of discourse, of what obtains in the physical order of things. The principle itself is the fact, intuited by some of the ancient Greeks, and seen by Crassus himself, that all things both above and below are something one (unum). Crassus seems to mean here by unum a unity of dependence among different things. He does not speak as if this unity of dependence were a conclusion of reasoning. It is something seen, intuited by the mind" (250).

Eloquence as ornatus, then, as a kosmos itself, makes this "order of things conceived by the mind" "perceptible," "a cosmetic whole" (254). As Reader Response critics such as Fish and Iser seem to understand, affective stylistics is a necessary aesthetic that illuminates thought by its own order and so cannot be divided (DiLorenzo 255). The Ciceronian unity of language and thought thus might also seem to contradict the third statement of Gorgias's dictum, that "even if we knew it, we couldn't communicate it" because of the inadequacy of language to express thought. However, we must remember that according to Kerferd, Gorgias is here talking about the inability to think about and communicate Being, Platonic essences, not being, the reality of our thoughts. The unity of language and thought, like the unity of reality that is obtained through the senses, can only be intuited and made apparent in the style of discourse and argument, not determined or expressed by formalistic, rationalistic methods. While style illuminates thought, it is not identical with thought. The result is that affective response to style provides an indeterminate form of knowledge, which is all we may know.

Beginning with the common problem of flux noted by Heraclitus, the rough flowchart below is meant to summarize the two lines of opposing thought, which for convenience I call the "rational idealists" and the "enlightened empiricists," in the history of rhetoric (cf. Enos, *Greek Rhetoric* 69).

Two Philosophical Bloodlines:
A Highly Reductive Schema of the
Classical View of Language and Knowledge

"Rational Idealists"   "Enlightened Empiricists"

Heraclitus (535–457 B.C.E.)—Held that everything in the universe was in fiery flux; also believed in the one-to-one correspondence between word and reality; thus fundamental laws of nature were themselves contradictory.

Pythagoras (c. 580–500 B.C.E.). Material objects describable in mathematical terms; universe constructed in numerical ratios.

Democritus (460–370 B.C.E.). Material world consists of infinitesimally small atoms, fundamental units of reality that are invisible and can thus only be known rationally.

Parmenides (fl. 5th cent. B.C.E.). Sunders temporal world of appearance from Reality, an eternal third realm of essences to which words refer without contradiction.

Plato (429–348 B.C.E.). Pupil of Socrates. Posits realm of Ideal Forms, where true knowledge exists and can only be reached by dialectic; rhetoric a means to communicate knowledge after the fact to those unable to engage in philosophical method. Thus separates philosophy and rhetoric, knowledge and emotion. Rhetoric has no subject matter of its own.

Aristotle (384–322 B.C.E.). Pupil of Plato. Picks up

Empedocles (490–430 B.C.E.). Know not rationally, but through the senses, stylistically, through music of language rather than heuristically.

Protagoras (c. 480–410 B.C.E.). Pupil of Empedocles. Contradictory statements equally true. Cannot know essences, only qualities; do not agree about these. Problem of predication, not Reality; basis of sophists—arguing both sides of an issue. If all statements valid, then persuasion necessary to decide on course of action. Early sociology of knowledge.

Gorgias (c. 485–380 B.C.E.). Mind and senses limited. We cannot know Reality; if we could, we would not understand it; if we did, we would not be able to communicate it. Rhetoric, emotional persuasion, literary style necessary for any knowledge at all. Language has the power to "deceive" the sense, evoke reality in the minds of hearers.

Isocrates (436–338 B.C.E.). Pupil of Gorgias, contemporary of Plato. Continued so-

Plato's suggestion for a true rhetoric based on philosophical principles. However, both rhetoric and philosophy deal with probable knowledge, as opposed to apodictic, or scientific knowledge of material world, which is certain and can be known objectively. Emotion, style in rhetoric a necessary evil "owing to a defect in our hearers;" bare facts preferable.

phistic tradition, adapted literary style to written rhetoric. No science of rhetoric. Natural talent primary, theory and technique secondary. Everyone possesses aesthetic faculty that can be educated only indirectly. Rhetoric the basis of knowledge, society, culture. Orator must be morally good.

Cicero (106–43 B.C.E.). Roman orator and rhetorical theorist heavily influenced by Isocrates. Everyone possesses an intuitive faculty for rhythm and sound of words. Style as *ornatus*: unity of form and content necessary to make ideas and feelings perceptible and persuasive to self and others. *Ornatus* as kosmos: language exhibits unity intuited in the universe, but which we ultimately cannot know. Not atoms in a void, but all interdependent. Words do not necessarily correspond to reality, but must correspond to thought. *Ornatus* occurs at all levels of style—plain, middle, as well as grand. Eloquence the basis of knowledge. All knowledge the province of rhetoric.

Appendix C

Analysis, Interpretation, and the Aurality of Imitation: A Reconsideration

It is well known that imitation was the primary method of writing instruction in ancient Greece and Rome. Edward P. J. Corbett believes that imitation was the primary method that the sophists used to teach oratory and literature. For Corbett, imitation is divided into: (1) theory, "a set of rules that provide a definite method and system," (2) imitation, "a studied method" for analyzing and emulating models held up as standards, and (3) practice, "assiduous exercises and experience" ("Imitation" 304). Following this method of "prelection," a rule or general precept of invention, arrangement, or style is demonstrated and discussed through the analysis (and interpretation) of a model discourse that the student then imitates following the rule; finally, the student practices the rule without the model.

Corbett's model of imitation then entails the objective analysis and interpretation of good models in order to internalize precepts and rules. For Corbett, prelection consists of "elaborate commentary" by the teacher of the invention, organization and style of the text "designed to expose the strengths (and sometimes the weaknesses) in selection, structure, and style" (306). Indeed, Corbett states that the ancient practice of imitation is similar to New Criticism: "Doubting that his student will detect these strengths and weaknesses from a mere exposure to the text, the teacher explicitly points out the excellences, explains how and why they are functioning, and relates them to the rhetorical principles his students have been studying in the abstract. What the prelection is comparable to is the Brooks-and-Warren method of explicating a poem that many of us learned in graduate school right after World War II" (306).

In discussing Isocrates' view of rhetoric in contradistinction to Plato's, Jaeger also cites imitation as the primary method of instruction:

> Isocrates holds fast to its empiricism. Therein he clings to the principle of *imitation* established by his predecessors—the principle which in the future was to play such an enormous part in rhetoric and (as literature came more and more under the influence of rhetoric) in every branch of literature. Here we know more of his method of teaching than we do of his attitude to the rhetorical doctrine of ideas; for all his great speeches were meant to be models in which his pupils could study the precepts of his art. ("Isocrates" 65)

Marrou too discusses Isocrates' method of having pupils study principles in "the abstract" and then apply them in practice to their own exercises: "The essential part of his apprenticeship was the study and criticism of first-class models. As an inheritor of the oldest tradition, Isocrates adapted to literature the fundamental ideas of Homeric education: 'example' and 'imitation.' " Thus, Marrou concludes: "By doing so he inaugurated a tradition, and one which was to last: this classical idea of imitation of literary models now has a long history behind it" (*History* 126).

But doesn't the analysis and interpretation of models for imitation based on the study of abstract rules or a priori precepts somewhat seem to contradict Isocrates' and Cicero's belief that eloquence cannot be taught by formalistic, rationalistic techniques? Is there a contradiction here, as in Reader Response Criticism, between the epistemology professed and the methodology practiced? Perhaps. Contradiction seems to be a part of the human condition. It was certainly part of the sophistic position. But perhaps we should also ask whether the sophists, Isocrates, and Cicero may have had a different understanding of imitation—of empiricism—than the logocentric one we attribute to them. In this regard, it may be significant that Quintilian is a major source for our understanding of imitation in the ancient world. It is Quintilian's understanding of classical rhetoric that informs the work of Hugh Blair (Kennedy, *Classical Rhetoric* 103), who also had a major influence on the twentieth-century current-traditional approach to teaching composition through the analysis and interpretation of literature (see Berlin, "Rhetoric and Poetics"). Both Corbett and Marrou at least partially derive their understanding of the practice of imitation in the ancient world from Quintilian. So does Murphy ("Roman Writing Instruction").

A part of the problem, of course, is the lack of extant texts from the sophists (see Diels and Kranz; Freeman; Sprague). And despite the fact that we know more about Isocrates' teaching method than anything else about him (Jaeger 65), even his major treatise on teaching, *Against the Sophists*, is incomplete. As Kennedy states, "The system of technical rhetoric which Quintilian expounds from Book 3 through Book 11 contains many details which we might not otherwise know" (*Classical Rhetoric* 101; cf. Murphy, "Roman Writing Instruction" 29–30). In addition, Quintilian wrote more about pedagogy in his epic work on the education of the orator, the *Institutio Oratoria*, than even Isocrates or Cicero. And he wrote about it in a much more formalized and systematic way than either of them. This is an important point. For given the degree of rational formulation and systematic treatment of rhetoric exhibited in Quintilian's *Institutio Oratoria*, the question is, did he have the same understanding of imitation as did the sophists, Isocrates, and Cicero? I think not—and would like to speculate why here and suggest an alternate "reading" of imitation. Murphy marks the turning point from a tutorial to a systematic education in Rome in Cicero's century ("Roman Writing Instruction" 20). But Murphy takes Quintilian, not Cicero, as the transitional figure and starting point of his discussion. In fact, Murphy cites Cicero's *De Oratore* as "the last major objection against a well--organized, discourse centered teaching program which was clearly already rooted in Roman society" (29). Quintilian certainly seems to have held the same philosophy of rhetoric as Isocrates and Cicero in that he regarded rhetoric as central to education, and eloquence as central to rhetoric. In developing a curriculum vitae for the ideal orator, Quintilian was for the most part following Isocrates and Cicero concerning the practical value of a rhetorical education in society. Like Isocrates and Cicero, Quintilian believes that "the study of literature is fundamental to the study of rhetoric and the education of an orator" (I.iv. 5). And like Isocrates and Cicero, Quintilian did not believe that the study of rhetoric had the power to implant morality and wisdom in characters where it was not naturally present or to foster talent in those who did not have it (XII.i.30).

But despite these shared rhetorical doctrines and even writing style, Quintilian may be seen to differ from Isocrates and Cicero in the emphasis he places on technique and rules in developing the natural abilities of the orator (cf. Murphy, "Roman Writing Instruction" 34). While Quintilian specifies that the orator must be a good man skilled at speaking (I:Pr.9), and often cites nature as the best judge, it is *the art* of rhetoric that constitutes the twelve books of the *Institutio Oratoria* and governs the entire education of the orator from cradle to grave. Thus, while I do not agree with Kennedy's classification of Cicero as a technical rhetorician, I would agree with his classification of Quintilian as one (*Classical Rhetoric* 100–02). In a way, Quintilian is the Aristotle of the sophistic tradition. Although he follows in the philosophical footsteps in Cicero and Isocrates, Quintilian formalizes into a more or less rational system what was for Isocrates intuition and practice, and was for Cicero ultimately ineffable.

Quintilian thus approaches literature in a rhetorical education from a more technical standpoint as well. In chapter 1 of Book X, Quintilian reviews at length the role and value of reading great works of literature for developing *copia*, fecundity of thought and vocabulary, and discusses in some analytical detail the different genres and particular works within them that would be most helpful to the orator. In chapter 2 of Book X, Quintilian discusses both the problems of imitation—knowing what to imitate and what to avoid—as well as the value of imitating literary models as a method for learning style. Thus, while Quintilian still conceives of literature as the foundation of oratory as did Isocrates and Cicero, we can perhaps begin to detect in his treatise a division of style and content and a corresponding view of literature as a source for stylistic "technique." In Quintilian's work, style is no longer a heuristic of invention, a mode of thought, a form of knowledge, but rather an ornament of composition.

Quintilian's understanding of imitation, under the increasing spread and influence of literacy, may reflect an increasing concern with textuality, what Kennedy might call literary imitation. Unlike the sophists (Enos, "Rhetorical Theory" 10), Quintilian has begun to treat imitation separately from declamation, which he primarily conceives of as training for the law courts (though ultimately, imitation still led to declamation, which was "the cap, the culmination of the whole process" [Murphy, "Roman Writing Instruction" 61]). Unlike the sophists, Isocrates, and Cicero, then, in this formalization of the sophistic rhetorical education, Quintilian has begun to make distinctions between the rhetoric and literature. And in this early formalization we perhaps recognize a method of teaching literature that is closer to our own than the more unformulated methods of the sophists, Isocrates, or Cicero. Kennedy himself states about Book X that "Quintilian's discussion here of what the student should read borders on literary criticism," though the emphasis remains on "what literature can help the orator" (*Classical Rhetoric* 101).

Given this interpretation of Quintilian's place in the history of literary rhetoric, it is understandable how imitation in sophistic theory and practice has been thought of in terms of analysis and interpretation. But for the sophists and Isocrates and Cicero, imitation may not have been nearly so technical, declamation and imitation not nearly so distinct. In "primary" as opposed to "secondary" rhetoric, imitation was oral. As George Kennedy states, "The sophist spoke and only occasionally perhaps reduced his technique to rules: the student listened, admired, and imitated, sometimes verbatim" (*Classical Rhetoric* 117). And according to Marrou, although the sophists developed techniques for teaching rhetoric, "[i]n the fifth century the teaching of rhetoric was not so precise: the rules were very general and students got on to practical exercises" (85). The teacher did prepare models for his students to copy and study and later use as models for their own compositions (Marrou 85). But despite the appearance of what Marrou calls an "intellectual, literary element," he states: "[W]e are still a long way from 'the peoples of the Book' " (70); "in ancient Greece, and especially in its political life, the spoken word reigned supreme" (84).

Isocrates, too, conceived of both rhetoric and literature, whether read or spoken, as an oral art. Isocrates "helped raise oratory to the level of a literary art," says Marrou, "and, on the other hand, preserve that influence of the spoken word on literature, which, helped by the custom of reading out loud, was to remain the dominant feature of Greek literature" (122). In the Greek secondary school, the treatment of literature had four stages: criticism of the text, reading, exposition, and judgment (Marrou 229–30). However, criticism of the text was not interpretation as we understand it, but rather correction of copies of a manuscript, which in an oral culture were often at variance with each other (Marrou 230). "Real interpretation" in the literary education of the Greek secondary school "took a long time to pass beyond the tentative gropings of practice and take on a scientific form" (Marrou 229).

As Marrou describes it, then, criticism of the text was "merely introductory; the proper study of the authors only began with

'expressive reading' " (230). The purpose of "expressive declamation" was to "take account of the sense of the text, the
rhythm of the verse and the general tone of the work" (230).
Stanford's study of Greek euphony supports this contention as
well. In the higher education of the ancient Greeks, this study
of the sound of the text represented what Marrou calls "close
study" of the text (231), which is obviously different from the
way we understand the term based on the New Criticism—as
the analysis and interpretation of form. "What else could be expected in literature? . . . Reading was done aloud, so that there
was no borderline between the written and the spoken word;
the result was that the categories of eloquence were imposed
on every form of mental activity—on poetry, on history, and
even . . . philosophy. Hellenistic culture was above all things a
rhetorical culture" (Marrou 369).

For Marrou, the practice of declamation, of "reading with
expression a passage that was corrected beforehand," also provided the basis for secondary and higher education in rhetoric
and literature in the Roman schools (375). Marrou cites the
ambiguous state of manuscripts as the basis of this practice.
Murphy too notes the relative scarcity of texts as one cause
of oral instruction ("Roman Writing Instruction" 42). Now,
in his account of Roman education, Marrou, like Murphy
("Roman Writing Instruction" 46), does lay more stress on
close reading as we know it: analysis and interpretation (375).
Roman educators certainly did analyze and interpret, using
methods available to them from technical rhetoric such as the
figures of speech (see *Rhetorica ad Herennium*). But as Marrou
states, "This was supposed to explain the rhythm of the verse,
rare or difficult words, glossemata, poetic turns of phrase"
(375). Murphy too suggests that "the exercise also trains the
'ear' of the student for later exercises in analyzing the oral arguments used in orations" ("Roman Writing Instruction" 46).

Despite the obvious separation of form and content, then,
the parsing of the texts was probably not so much concerned
with literary form as with sound. Roman educators were still
concerned with literature as read aloud, with writing as spo-

ken. "In theory the rhetor was the person who taught the art of speaking (and writing, for the Ancients looked upon the two things as inseparable)" (Marrou 238). However, although Marrou recognizes the role of recitation in the rhetorical and literary education of Greece and Rome, he seems to attribute much of the practice of reading out loud to the ambiguous state of the manuscripts then in use. The parsing of the text had to be done aloud because "the phrases and sentences had to be found, questions had to be distinguished from plain statements by the tone of voice, and lines had to be made to scan according to the laws of prosody and metre" (230). Based on his careful research and examination of schoolboy papyrus, this is undoubtedly correct. But to cite the material cause for a practice without acknowledging the epistemology that results is to perhaps overlook a significant rhetorical and cultural dimension. Marrou may exhibit here a bias indigenous to our society, one that favors literate modes of expression and thought.

As has often been noted in regard to poetic prosody, the analysis of sound is reductive, turns the sensuous experience of sound into an abstract object of study, and is in this sense more formalistic, rationalistic. In fact, Marrou states that in Roman education, the secondary level became increasingly technical (239). Marrou goes so far as to state that in higher rhetorical education in Rome, students were taught "the complex system of rules, methods, and customs that had gradually been perfected in Greek schools from the time of the Sophists" (382). Students then practiced what they had learned in theory and rule by imitating speeches that were like those they would have to deliver in assembly or law courts (Marrou 276). (But Marrou also states that the topics of the imaginary speeches studied through imitation and declamation themselves became increasingly fantastic, bizarre, and removed from the real life— the actual circumstances of the assembly or courts of law [374], a point supported by Murphy as well ["Roman Writing Instruction" 66].)

This technical insistence on precepts and rules (and speeches) as primary in themselves would seem to run counter to the teaching of both Isocrates and Cicero. In fact, rhetorical education in Rome increasingly ignored the ideals of eloquence established by Isocrates and Cicero. As Marrou states, Isocrates' belief that theory be kept to a minimum was ignored—teaching grew in the "direction of an ever greater technical perfection" (271). So too: "Cicero convinced neither his young contemporaries nor succeeding generations. Nor was Quintilian listened to either, when, a century later, he taught practically the same doctrine, basing his neo-classicism on Cicero's authority" (Marrou 382–83). Given Quintilian's ideals, it is perhaps significant as well as ironic that he himself moved in the direction, if not technical perfection, of systematic thoroughness. For the tendency to do so was an imperative not only of his increasingly literate society and culture but of Western civilization itself.

However, as Murphy ("Roman Writing Instruction") demonstrates, the highly complex technical apparatus of the progymnasmata, in which imitation played so large a part, still ultimately led to declamation, which was the highest point and purpose of study. That is, although the practice of imitation in Rome may have been more formalistic and rationalistic than in ancient Greece, it was a preferred method of instruction in what was still an oral culture. While there are traces of the growing literacy in ancient Greece as well as in Rome, "in Western classical antiquity, it was taken for granted that a written text of any worth was meant to and deserved to be read aloud, and the practice of reading texts aloud continued, quite commonly with many variations, through the nineteenth century" (Ong, *Orality* 115). In fact, in Greek and Roman antiquity, texts of speeches were recorded after the fact, says Ong, and it was considered disgraceful for the orator to read from a text (10).

There is no doubt that the sophists, Isocrates, Cicero—even the more technical Quintilian (Kennedy, *Classical Rhetoric* 119)—essentially conceived of rhetoric as speech. There is also little doubt that the sophists, Isocrates, and Cicero essentially conceived—to lessening degrees—of rhetoric in terms of poetry. Only a century between Cicero and Quintilian. And Quintilian has uncoupled rhetoric and poetry. Although Quintilian still regards the rhetorical study of literature as essential for the orator, he does not seem to conceive of literature in the same way Isocrates and Cicero do—as a sensuous form of speech. Nor does he seem to conceive of rhetoric in these terms either. For Quintilian, sophistic rhetorical education has already become a more rationalistic enterprise.

Given these apparent differences between Cicero and Quintilian and the stylistic and philosophical relationship between the sophists, Isocrates, and Cicero, is it not possible that Cicero also understood imitation not as the object of visual analysis and interpretation in and for itself but as the imitation of the music of the spoken word for the purpose of persuasion? May we not suppose with some confidence that for Cicero reading and discussing aloud was still primary (see the discussion in chapter 3)? Given that our understanding of the practice of imitation in the ancient world is based almost wholly on Quintilian's, is it not possible, then, that the sophists, Isocrates, and Cicero also conceived of imitation as an oral/aural process, in which declamation was central, rather than the end product of the process only? Despite the lateness of the day in terms of the passing of what Walter Ong understands as the oral culture into the chirographic, literate one, could it not be that Cicero's concept of eloquence as the unity of style and substance, which depends on natural talent based on the physical nature and intuition of language as speech, could only be taught indirectly by imitation? As Enos observes, "Cicero's legal preparation stressed observation, imitation, and a mentor-apprentice relationship. Such methods are well suited to acquiring proficiency in orally dominated expression, and, in fact, are similar to techniques of education for oral composition. Bards and rhapsodes frequently learned techniques of oral composition by modeling experts after intense, sustained observation, and Cicero appears to have done much the same in his legal preparation" (*Greek Rhetoric* 7).

For Cicero, even the pen points to this end. In *De Oratore* Crassus states that the practice of writing leads to eloquence: "the pen is the best and most eminent author of oratory" (I.xxxii.150). But if speech is the basis of style for Cicero, written style can also be the basis of speech: "when written notes are exhausted, the rest of the speech still maintains a like progress, under the impulse given by the similarity and energy of the written word" (*D. O.* III.xxxiii.153). The principle of aural imitation, then, obtains here as well. Style as an oral phenomenon can be learned through imitating writing as well as reading out loud. Like Isocrates (and certainly Quintilian [Murphy, "Roman Writing Instruction" 20]), Cicero believed writing could improve eloquence and used writing to develop a highly literate oral style. But it was the orality of speech that writing was to imitate. And it was the unity of the literary *De Oratore*, not the divisions of the technical *De Inventione*, that Cicero wanted students to emulate.

What I wish to tentatively suggest here, then, is essentially a revision of our formalistic, rationalistic notion of imitation as the visual analysis, interpretation, and internalization of objective structures, a notion that has played such a dominant role in the teaching of reading and writing throughout history. Indeed, I would hazard to say that prelection *is* comparable to the methodology of the New Criticism because we have understood imitation (and Quintilian himself?) in terms of New Criticism. It is this formalistic, rationalistic notion of imitation as analysis and interpretation leading to the internalization of rules and principles of good form and structure that underlies at least one method of using literature to teach writing. But this notion of imitation is based on the privileged ontological status of the textual consciousness, one that we perhaps begin to find in Quintilian. As Ong points out, there is a "persistent tendency, even among scholars, to think of writing as the basic form of language" (*Orality* 5).

Given their philosophy of style as music, which I explore in chapter 3, I would submit that for the sophists, for Isocrates, and for Cicero, imitation was not merely mimesis of objective textual structures of model speeches, was not taught by the analysis and interpretation of style as visual. Rather, for the ancients, imitation was more likely a mimesis of the affective music of speech, taught more through the somatic response of the body to the rhythms and sounds of language than through analysis and interpretation. Even Aristotle conceives of imitation as aural mimesis (Cassirer 183; see my discussion in chapter 4). But as Enos hints, ("Rhetorical Theory" 10), for the sophists and, by extension, Isocrates and Cicero, imitation more than likely involved somatic response to the music of language as sung, recited, read out loud, and that affective response to the sound of language as it enters the senses and underlies perception, thoughts, and convictions constituted a kind of intuitive, epistemic form of knowledge. In an oral culture, imitation is the internalization of style as an aural, physical experience. As a method of indirection, it was perhaps essential in educating the intuitive aesthetic faculty necessary for performance and persuasion, a faculty rooted in the oral, physical, but indeterminate, unity of language and knowledge as speech.

Appendix D

Time, Space, and Music: Some Philosophical Speculations

The relation between space, time, and music is so important to a deeper understanding of the epistemological issues treated in this book that some philosophical speculation about the nature of time seems warranted here. Our primary task cannot be to describe time, since we do not know what it is, but rather to touch on some notions about it; nor will we accept any one theory of time, but rather only point to our indeterminate knowledge of it. But as these theories reveal, though we do not understand its nature, time may be fundamental not only to the external world and our knowledge of it but to consciousness itself. Time also may be the epistemic basis of affective experience, which we can at least partly know in and through the experience of music—and perhaps in and through the music of rhetoric.

In *Knowledge and Experience*, Eliot states that "the problem of time in knowledge and in reality" (109) involves the fact that universals are out of time, while our perception of an object appears to be in time; that is, as Penrose points out, temporal consciousness is not in sync with external reality (444–45).

Further, Eliot adds: "[I]f existent objects are wholly in time, the very persistence of our attention upon them will involve the holding together of various moments of sensation by a common meaning, and that meaning will not be within the time to which it refers" (109). Thus, for Eliot, there appear to be "two-time orders which are not reducible to each other, or the possibility of a continuum of various time-orders from the immediate order of experience *sensa* to the object itself, which, so far as it is *that* object, is not in time at all" (110). Eliot therefore concludes "that which is purely in time cannot be said to exist at all"; "any object which is wholly real is independent of time" (110).

Likewise, for Eliot, "perception isn't in time; but there are several time-orders, and the collision occurs only when we arbitrarily assume that one is real and that there is a separate order of perception which must somehow correspond to it . . . real time seems to be as much an inference as real space" (111). Obviously, this is something we do all the time: we assume that linear, spatial time is the correct time, to which everything, in life, in literature, in writing, must conform. But, Eliot states, "time-order . . . will vary according to what we take as the object," and the object will consist of "the same sense-data in different relations" (110). Thus, too, Eliot would reject consciousness as the phenomenological basis of knowledge; reality does not exist in the object or in consciousness but in our analysis of their relations. (Cf. Levinas, esp. 37–95, on Husserl's phenomenology of internal time consciousness as the basis of "transcendental subjectivity.")

Physics, of course, has always attempted to deal with the problem of time in terms of space. But as Eliot intimates, even the notion of space is problematic. As we discussed in chapter 2, Newtonian physics attempts to measure movement by calculating the velocity of mass points in what is considered empty space. Thus, a body in motion can be measured according to points along some line. The actual points traversed between are of little relevance, since only the starting and finishing points are needed for the calculation. It is just assumed that there are "gaps" of empty space between the points of place through which a body travels (just as Iser assumes there are gaps in literary schemata, spaces that the reader must actively fill). As soon as the interaction of forces—one body affecting another across empty space by gravity, for instance—comes into play, however, the notion of empty space becomes immediately problematical. If we say that space is empty, what is the nature of these forces? How can we account for the physical interaction of bodies at a distance?

In the early years of modern science, the idea of space as an ether (or filled with ether) that could propel or attract was used to account for the force between physical objects. But as we also discussed in chapter 2, in Einstein's theory, space is conceived of not as an static, empty field (or as an ether), but as an electromagnetic field. With the advent of Einstein's Special and General Theories of Relativity, the idea of the ether is replaced with a view of space that curves or bends around the mass of objects (the heavy ball resting in a net). The primary concern of physics now is finding a theory that will unify all the forces discovered in nature and simultaneously account for the temporal origin of the universe (see ch. 4, n. 10). Despite the altered view of space in relativity theory, in celestial calculations time is merely another dimension of space, though a more essential one.

In fact, the problem of time seems to have much to do with the problem of motion in space. Quantum mechanics introduced the notion of subatomic as well as atomic particles (electrons, protons, neutrons) whose exchange accounted for the attraction and repulsion of the larger particles of matter they constituted. And of course, this occurs "over time." However, one problem that physicists face is that in trying to arrive at the most elemental level of reality, they find they can divide subatomic particles into ever smaller, infinitesimal particles, ad infinitum. The problem, says Zuckerkandl in the context of music, is that "[t]hings move in space. Space has no gaps. The course the moving thing follows is a line in space, a continuous series of places" (127). The logical question, then, is: what is between the places? More places? And between those?

Zuckerkandl traces the problem all the way back to Zeno and the Eleatics, who declared "that the whole universe of motion was an illusion" (124) because space as an object could be endlessly divided, and thus an object theoretically shown never to be able to move. For Zuckerkandl, the confusion comes in the identification of space with motion: "[T]hey equated the 'between' of motion with interspace. They assumed that the process of motion could be entirely comprehended in spatial data . . . they failed to maintain the distinction between motion and spatial track" (128). Thus, Zuckerkandl locates the problem in Zeno's paradox in the assumption that "everything that was true of the spatial path of motion had also to be true of motion itself." But "motion *cannot* be entirely comprehended in spatial-local data," Zuckerkandl states (128).

The problem is large—larger than space itself. Where does motion (of music) occur, Zuckerkandl asks. "If things and places do not suffice to make us understand the process of motion, then this process must in some essential aspect extend beyond the realm of things and place" (Zuckerkandl 128–29). For Zuckerkandl motion occurs in time. And not the passage of spatial time, which we divide up (154), and *in* which objects and events (including music) seem to move, but of pure time, which flows *through* objects and events. Eliot's distinction between "perceived time" and "real time," then, perhaps can be understood as a distinction between time as something moved in and time as something that itself moves. That is, the problem is the identification of motion and time. For Zuckerkandl, time is not the "*form* of experience," but the "*content* of experience." Time is not a measurement of events; it "*produces* events" (202). For Zuckerkandl, this is the temporal nature of both music and universe (see my discussion in ch. 4, n. 11).

Zuckerkandl's notion of time as the cause and content of events in some ways also resembles Heidegger's conception of time (*Existence and Being, On Being and Time*), discussed below, as standing behind and constituting Being, just as Heidegger's conception of time as a unity of past, present, and future resembles Zuckerkandl's conception of time as a dynamic system of auditory interplay. This may be essential in understanding language as temporal motion as well. The metaphysics of music may momentarily shift our ontological attention from the visual, referential dimension to the auditory, temporal dimension that in the future could be, as Zuckerkandl (264) and Penrose (442–47) suggest, at the heart of a new physics of reality and a new philosophy of knowledge and consciousness.

Like some scholars working on a revisionist theory of the sophists and Cicero, Zuckerkandl traces his understanding of the relation of space, time, and music back to the ancients' conception of Cosmos. "Those who believe that music provides a source of knowledge of the inner world are certainly not wrong," says Zuckerkandl; "[b]ut the deeper teaching of music concerns the nature not of 'psyche' but of 'cosmos.' The teachers of antiquity who spoke of the music of the spheres, of the cosmos as a musical order, knew this" (147). In a way that is reminiscent of Ong's discussion of the evanescence of sound as an event in time (*Orality* 32), Zuckerkandl states: "[I]n the present too the flux of time does not stand still; in the present too the future steadily and irresistibly becomes the past. The present, of which alone we can say that it *is* and that in it *we are*, shrinks to an immeasurably small instantaneous section of the everlasting process of change from what is not yet to what is no more, from one nonbeing to another nonbeing" (155).

This is not only similar to Ong's discussion of sound but also may provide insight into the oral mindset of the sophists. Does it not sound like the speculation of the ancient Greeks, perhaps even the ontological basis of Gorgias's and Protagoras's epistemology of nonbeing, and of the ontological necessity of uncertainty of the sophists? "What a precarious situation, balancing on the hairline of the present, which, itself evaporating into immeasurability, separates two oceans of nonbeing," says Zuckerkandl; "[t]he existence of man is inevitably drawn into the uncertainty which surrounds time; and so it is not surprising that the problem of time has long been one of the principle themes of theological and philosophical speculation" (155). In fact, temporal modes of thought and being may be at the heart of phonocentric expression, sophistic epistemology. According to Zuckerkandl, based on Plato and Plotinus, medieval thought attempted to solve the problem of time, motion, and change by considering time as subordinate to eternity, motion to rest, and change as the imperfection of the world after the fall as well as the earthly manifestation of prelapsarian perfection and proof that God exists. The ontological subordination of time to space, which perhaps can be traced all the way back to the debates of the ancients, may in some way be central to the dominance of formalistic, rationalistic epistemology in Western culture.

The problem of time is also manifest in the nature of narration in relation to orality and literacy. Jarratt, for example, argues against simple divisions of orality and literacy based on the problematic presence of narrative modes of thought, which participate both in *mythos* and *logos* (31–61). To cast it in our own terms here, narrative is both temporal and rational. As Jarratt points out, narrative as a more abstract, rational mode of temporal thought was present very early in human history. Narration is the basic mode of human understanding and discourse. For Walter Fisher, the narrative paradigm—the story of life—represents the basic logic of human meaning and value that underlies *all* rational discourse, what Fisher calls "narrative rationality" (48–49).

Of course, one accepted characteristic of narrative rationality is that it is temporal—primarily organized according to a sequence of meaningful (and perhaps causally related) events, rather than primarily inductive or deductive modes of reasoning, though these modes of reasoning certainly play a part in both the creation and understanding of narration. (For a discussion of the opposition between the narrative configuration of knowledge in the human sciences and the research model of the natural sciences, see Polkinghorne, *Narrative Knowing and the Human Sciences*.) However, we also can understand that narration, while grounded in concrete, temporal events, is already abstracted by a spatial understanding of time as a linear progression. In fact, narration can be seen to represent an earlier manifestation of spatial reasoning, though, because it is based on the temporal sequence of events, a less formal and rationalistic one. Thus, narration can be understood to represent another, more subtle stage in the slow transition from orality to literacy that Havelock and Ong do not deny—one in which, in the development of literate consciousness, thinking is still embedded in concrete events, but in which those events are sequenced in a spatial abstraction of time.

This, then, is perhaps to revise our notions of narrative time itself. Narration is a representation of concrete events in time rather than reasoning based on logical categories in abstract space (see Polkinghorne, esp. 37–69). But the logical configuration of time in narration is linear and sequential, spatially divided time, and thus may be illusory in regard to time (Penrose 442–47). Here again, there is perhaps an identification or confusion of motion with space—this time, narrative motion with narrative spatial track. Narrative motion (the physical movement of time through a narrative) may not be identical to spatial motion (the spatial organization or track of the narrative). In any case, as the narrative configuration of time illustrates, the only way humans seem to be able to understand time is spatially—as motion through space, one event following another, as points on a line. If narrative rationality is temporal rationality, temporal rationality is spatial. Temporal rationality, then, perhaps represents the spatial limits of our understanding of time and, therefore, of indeterminacy; temporal rationality may be the "technology" or "hardwiring" of our Kantian consciousness, beyond which we cannot think.

In *Existence and Being* and *On Being and Time*, Heidegger does manage to venture a little beyond the concept of spatial time as a series of present moments that we find in Plato, Aristotle, Kant, Descartes, Hegel, and Bergson insofar as he posits the unity between past, present, and future (the "ecstasies" of Temporality that produce time but that are "Outside-itself" [Brock 81]); thus Temporality is the "transcendental horizon" for Dasein, or Being, "in its relations to things in the world, non-human and human" (Brock 19), which includes intentionality, or "Caring." For Heidegger, Dasein is not a subjective reality nor an ontological one; rather, it is one located outside the mental and the physical but manifested in the phenomenon of the world itself as Being. (In this way Heidegger differs from Husserl, who holds transcendental consciousness rather than Being to be the phenomenological object of study [Brock 19; cf. Levinas]. And Heidegger differs from Eliot [*Knowledge and Experience*] in that while the relationship between the mental and the physical is utmost for Eliot and is constructed as a fact by the analysis of experience [111, 157], that relationship for Heidegger is only one facet of experience and is given as a fact in the phenomenon of the world as Being.)

However, even Heidegger's phenomenology of time, like Husserl's, can in some ways be understood to be based on linear, sequential modes of thought insofar as the future is held to be the primary mode for the intentionality of Being, or consciousness, respectively, which includes death as its terminal point and which is always moving toward itself. (See Brock, esp. 18–26; 52–106; Heidegger, *On Time and Being*; cf. Lakoff and Johnson 7–9, on time metaphors.) In fact, to escape the trap of spatial time, to find a "purer" temporal rather than spatial mode of being, we may have to go all the way back to prehistoric humans, who, according to Erich Neumann, experienced no separation between their skin and surrounding environment, but rather experienced them as one (what Neumann called "the participation mystic," esp. 262, 269).

If there was no conceptual spatial division between body and world, then (as in the beginning, everything, including time and space, were one) there was no need for causality either (cf. Stambaugh viii); like Burke's rhetorical consubstantiality, which we need because we are divided from each other, we need causality because we are divided from the world; if we existed as one substance with each other and the world, there would be no need for language *or causality* and thus no need for time as we understand it—spatially. We would live in time as simultaneity, rather than space-time, which is divided. (However, see Whorf (142–54) and Dorothy Lee for a discussion of what can perhaps be considered "vestiges" of a "purer" temporal mode of being and understanding in the relation between verb tenses of various Indian tribes and their nonlinear codification of time.)

The notion of time as a simultaneous stillpoint in which the universe is apprehended in its essential unity is of course the basis of many Eastern religions as well. Even T. S. Eliot utters: "[I]mmediate experience . . . is a timeless unity which is not as such present in either any*where* or any*one*. It is only in the world of objects that we have time and space and selves. By the failure of any experience to be merely immediate, by its lack of harmony and cohesion, we find ourselves as conscious souls in the world of objects" (*Knowledge and Experience* 31). Immediate experience as a timeless unity is thus unknowable except in brief mystical moments of poetic and religious experience, since it is always already divided by temporal consciousness. It is thus perhaps also knowable, though imperfectly, through the temporal experience of music—and the music of language.

Notes

2. Reader Response Criticism, Writing, and the New Physics

1. To a reader familiar with the philosophical distinctions between science and technology, I may seem to be committing the error of conflating them here. In one sense I am, but deliberately so. Although science and technology are radically different enterprises, there are ways in which science and technology are similar, related, though these are not as obvious as their differences. In "The Structure of Thinking in Technology," Henryk Skolimowski defines technology in opposition to science. Technology, Skolimowski states, is neither applied science nor science itself but rather can be differentiated from science and understood by looking at the difference between scientific and technological progress (372). However, Skolimowski's notion of technological progress that he uses to define technology is itself based on what can be considered technological values—efficiency, speed, productivity, durability, and so forth—and in this sense his concept of technology and the distinction between scientific and technological progress is only tautologically defined.

In "Technology as a Form of Consciousness," Carolyn Miller also, and to my mind more successfully, defines technology in opposition to science. For Miller, "[t]echnology can be provisionally defined as the manipulation of the contingent and local to achieve material results, to distinguish it from science as the study of the universal to achieve verifiable understanding" (228). Thus, the essential distinction for Miller is one of "knowing" versus "doing." However, knowing in science has increasingly become dependent on the "doing" of technology (especially in advanced sciences like biogenetics, subatomic physics, etc., which would be impossible without technology); that is, scientific advance—and science itself—is inextricably intertwined with and dependent on technology for its very existence. Rather than science being the basis of technology,

technology can be understood to be the basis of science (Ellul 7–11). Insofar as technology "uses" scientific knowledge for its own ends, to advance and perfect technique, Ellul claims that "science has become an instrument of technique" (10) rather than the other way around; and for Ellul, this use of science to perfect technological procedure is occurring in every discipline. Thus, as Ellul states, "the border between technical activity and scientific activity is not at all sharply defined" (8). I use the terms "science" and "technology" *not synonymously*, since science also includes the investigation of nature and technology the creation of machines, each for its own sake, *but in conjunction*, because of the common basis of science and technology in method, that is, technique or procedure.

But the belief in the cultural hegemony of technology is not universally accepted. For a debate concerning the nature of technology and technological values, see *Philosophy and Technology*, Mitchum and Mackey, editors. Also see "Men and Machines: The Computational Metaphor," where Earl MacCormac seems to provide a way out of technological domination by what Colin Turbayne in *The Myth of Metaphor* would call the "unmasking" of the technological metaphors by which we understand human reasoning.

2. For example, while Robert Connors does examine the epistemological relationship between composition studies and science in his award-winning essay and is correct in seeing scientific method as a limitation, he is wrong in his positivistic assessment of Kuhn's influence as pushing composition research toward "scientific forms of inquiry" (1); Kuhn's understanding of science is essentially social and humanistic and is a part of the epistemic trend in our culture that regards science itself as rhetorical (see Bazerman; Brummet).

3. In a postindustrial, technological society, according to Habermas, the values of the traditional institutional framework (for example, those proscribed by religion) are replaced by technological means–ends relationships of the rational–purposive subsystem (for example, those of classical economics) that subsumes it. In other words, technological values like efficiency and productivity fuse with capitalism and become the driving force not only of science and society but of human relationships as well. In a technological society, says Habermas, "symbolic interaction" in the subjective and social spheres of life is replaced by "instrumental or strategic" action (Habermas 93). In the dominant "purposive-rational system," subjectivity is replaced by formal technique, and social interaction is replaced by rationalistic procedure.

Thus, rationalism constitutes what Wayne Booth (*Modern Dogma*) calls "motivism," which, he argues, underlies "dogmatic science," and that Carolyn Miller ("The Rhetoric of Decision Science") says underlies decision science: the ideological belief that rationalistic methods (those based on scientific procedure, including quantification) are the only valid form of reasoning and knowing. Following Booth, in critiquing the decision science of Herbert Simon, Miller makes a distinction between rationality and reasoning—the first based on technical criteria only as the basis for decision making, the second on reasoning that includes rhetorical deliberation based on and about human values, which would also, then, include belief, intuition, personality (ethos), and emotion. But compare Feyerabend, *Farewell to Reason*.

4. I am thinking immediately here of how Murray Gell-Mann admitted getting the name of the hypothetical particles believed to be the foundation of the universe, "quarks," from James Joyce's *Finnegan's Wake* (Zukav 261); but there are many other more subtle, profound, and interesting ways in which the literary and scientific imagination are one.

5. For Gillispie, the Newtonian epistemology is the basis for the scientific enterprise—the cutting "edge" of every science as it matures and moves further into areas previously occupied by and reserved for moral and religious belief: physics in the seventeenth century, chemistry in the eighteenth, biology in the nineteenth. Significantly, perhaps, in this book Gillispie only deals with Einsteinian relativity in the twentieth century and does not touch quantum mechanics at all; as we will see, Einstein claimed that Newtonian mechanics was a special case of relativity. However, we can also understand the knife of science to be cutting into the last frontiers of "sacred" human space with cognitive science and biogenetics. For traditional scientists such as Gillispie, scientific investigation would be impossible without this edge.

6. Holton cites the characterization of the hypothetico-deductive, or inductive, method of science given by the physicist Friedrich Dessauer as representative of "both general and popular understanding."

> (1) Tentatively, propose as a hypothesis a provisional statement obtained by induction from experience and previously established knowledge of the field. . . . (2) Now, refine and structure the hypothesis—for example, by making a mathematical or physical analogon. . . . (3) Next, draw logical conclusions or predictions from the structured hypothesis which have promise of experimental check. . . . (4) Then check the predicted consequences (deduced from the analogon) against experience, by free observation or experimental arrangement. (5) If the deduced consequences are found to correspond to the "observed facts" within expected limits—and not only these consequences, but all different ones that can be drawn . . . then a warrant is available for the decision that "the result obtained is postulated as universally valid." Thus, the hypothesis, or initial statement, is found to be scientifically "established." (47–48)

7. Like Holton (47–53), Turbayne argues in *The Myth of Metaphor* that although Newton declared *hypotheses non fingo*—that he did not make any hypotheses but rather relied on pure observation—he did "frame

hypotheses," worked deductively as well as inductively (40–45). However, unlike Turbayne, Holton is trying to elucidate the role of cultural and religious "themata" in science by showing not only that Newton made hypotheses but also suppressed those he could not prove but which were nevertheless essential to his theory, such as "that God was the cause of gravity" (52).

8. For example, in "Criticism, Inc." John Crowe Ransom discusses what "the proper business of criticism" is:

> [I]t is from the professors of literature, in this country the professors of English for the most part, that I should hope eventually for the erection of *intelligent* standards of criticism. It is their business. Criticism must become *more scientific, or precise and systematic,* and this means that it must be developed by the collective and sustained effort of learned persons—which means that its proper seat is in the universities. . . . It will never be an exact science, or even a nearly exact one. But neither will psychology. . . . (328–29; emphasis mine)

In such influential books on the teaching of literary analysis as Brooks's *The Well Wrought Urn: Studies in the Structure of Poetry*, Wimsatt and Beardsley's *The Verbal Icon: Studies in the Meaning of Poetry*, and Wellek and Warren's *Theory of Literature*, the "science of literature" is established both by precept and by literary example; although goals, terminology, and procedures are learned more or less by osmosis, as tacit knowledge (just as they are in science [Polanyi]), they are necessary to minimize subjectivity and maximize precision.

9. The Lockean assumption that seems to be present in Eliot's criticism is that ideas are not innate in the mind but rather are reflections on sensation derived directly from sense experience; sensations are impressions made by objects upon the senses; thought is reflection upon the relation of sensations. In this union of empiricism and idealism, the "data" of the literary object thus become a pure object of Platonic contemplation. "The end of the enjoyment of poetry is a pure contemplation from which the accidents of personal emotion are removed; thus we aim to see the object as it really is" ("Perfect Critic" 14–15).

However, in his dissertation, *Knowledge and Experience*, a younger Eliot gives us a different, deeper philosophical basis for New Criticism. Because he denies the possibility of immediate experience through sense data of an object in reality, arguing that sensory experience and the object in reality exist in different "time-orders" (discussed in this book more in chapter 4 and appendix D), Eliot believes neither in idealism nor realism (153). Because knowledge of immediate experience and knowledge of universals exist in different orders, he holds that knowledge of both of them is impossible. Thus, even "feeling" is already an abstraction from experience, and an inconsistent one at that, and so cannot be the object of knowledge (20). Rather, for Eliot, all knowledge consists of our analysis of the relation between immediate experience and universals. For Eliot, it is this analysis that is real (157). Eliot's "revised" Lockean view is the basis of his empiricism and the grounds on which he rejects the "investigation into the processes of knowing or the nature of an external world" (157).

(In fact, in the conclusion to *Knowledge and Experience* (see esp. 161–65), Eliot ruminates on the implications of this philosophy for the difference between description and interpretation in science and criticism in a way that somewhat resembles the metaphysical discoveries of New Physics and Reader Response Criticism to be discussed next. For the early Eliot anyway, the difference between description and interpretation is merely a matter of degree, since our knowledge of any object is already a reinterpretation, and so every statement is an interpretation beyond which objects are not reducible: "the thing is thoroughly relative . . . it exists only in the context of experience, of experience with which it is continuous" [165]. While Eliot maintains that absolutes exist, they are for him a coalescence of individual experiences, a sort of social idealism. In this book, as in his poetry, Eliot was way ahead of his time—or perhaps more accurately, continuous with it.)

10. In contemporary particle physics, this observational problem is further complicated by the high-speed particle accelerators that are used to smash subatomic particles into each other; not only does the experiment create the results as a condition of (perceiving) the event at all but the results are often random and uncontrolled; when particles are accelerated and shot into each other, they often change their very nature, or "switch" identities. Measurement becomes a statistical probability of random occurrence. In addition, new particles are often created in the process as well. But the fact that particles change into unexpected things when they are accelerated and collide is a part of the condition of discovering them. Further, in these high-speed accelerators or bubble chambers, physicists only see subatomic particles as traces, which is one reason why they can determine only position or velocity, but not both at once (Capra 187).

11. In the *Prolegomena to Any Future Metaphysics*, Immanuel Kant attempts to establish a metaphysical foundation that accounts for all knowledge of the world, making a pure science of nature possible. In doing so, Kant had to refute the assertions of both idealists and empiricists regarding the nature of our knowledge of the world, rescuing science from the ultimate subjectivity of Cartesian idealism and the empiricist belief in undifferentiated sensations acting upon the mind but unacted upon by it, which culminated in the skepticism of David Hume, discussed later in this chapter. A science of nature cannot be based on innate ideas, since these ostensibly tell us nothing about the world and, indeed, cast doubt

on its very existence. Innate ideas cannot be tested empirically, for as Kant points out, one can never be sure if what is being perceived by the senses is an object in the world or an a priori idea projected onto the world. If a science of nature based on a priori knowledge of the world is not possible, neither is a science based on knowledge a posteriori—that is, empirically, since what we experience is the existence of things, not the laws of nature. In order to possess absolute certainty, these laws would have to exist independently of our experience. And, even if they did, empirical verification of these laws outside our own experience would be impossible.

However, for Kant, we can, and do, always know our own sense experience of the world, as distinguished from the world itself. Thus, we can say with some certainty that what we experience is not the world itself but the world as it appears to our senses. But in order for this subjective sense experience to constitute knowledge of the world, a pure science of nature, Kant must postulate categories of understanding that are prior to experience. These categories of experience—time, space, causality, substance—are themselves not subject to sense experience, or intuition, because they cannot be discovered in experience or tested empirically. Rather, they exist only as pure concepts that are predicated of experience and united with sense experience in order to understand it. According to Kant, these a priori concepts form the basis of our judgments concerning our experience, to which concepts of experience must be submitted.

A priori judgments may be of two kinds: analytic propositions or synthetic propositions. Analytical propositions, such as "the ball is round," do not give us any *new* knowledge, since the concept of roundness is contained or entailed in the concept *ball*. Thus the statement "the ball is round" is an analytic judgment; it does not add to, or expand, our knowledge of the concept *ball* but merely explicates it. If, however, we say that "the ball has mass," we have done more than merely explicate the concept *ball*; we have in fact predicated, or added, the concept *mass*, which is not entailed by the concept *ball*, to it. By adding the predicate "has mass" to the subject "the ball," we have expanded our knowledge of the ball by a concept that is a priori; this is a synthetic judgment. Synthetic judgments based on a priori categories of pure intuition constitute for Kant the universal principles by which all experience can be judged and understood insofar as they establish the necessary conditions under which experience may occur. It is this notion of a priori synthetic judgments with which Heisenberg has trouble.

12. The terms *context of discovery* and *context of justification* were first introduced by Hans Reichenbach in *Experience and Prediction*

to mark the distinction between the way a scientific or mathematical result is discovered and the way in which it is presented, justified, defended, and so on, to the scientific or mathematical community. . . . According to Reichenbach, problems in the context of discovery properly are the concern of psychology and history, not philosophy; epistemology is occupied only with the context of justification. According to this view, which has been held by almost all adherents of the Received View, a philosophical analysis of theories may ignore factors in the genesis of theories, confining its attention to theories as finished products. (Suppe 125)

Thus, in *Logical Foundations of Probability*, Carnap attempted to develop a method of explicating scientific theories by reconstructing them in accordance with the correspondence rules of logical positivism, which he himself helped to develop. These rules govern the relationship between word and referent based on the distinction between observational terms (those that refer to phenomena) and theoretical terms (those that are axiomatically defined within the theory according to the correspondence rules); when a scientific theory is *rationally reconstructed* according to these axioms or rules, theoretical terms are systematically defined and replace the observational terms that are more sensory and imprecise. According to the rational reconstructionists, the theoretical terms thus can constitute the basis of "exact statements" (in terms of the data and the solution) as well as yield universal (or general) statements. This process is also known as "theory reduction" (Suppe 54, 64). According to Suppe, the observational-theoretical distinction in logical positivism also led to the view of rational reconstruction as the basis of the "historical" view of scientific progress. (For a brief discussion of the context of discovery vs. the context of justification, see Suppe 125–27; for an extended discussion of the Received View, see Suppe 3–118).

13. On the right (according to Feyerabend) are the "critical rationalists" such as Karl Popper (see *Conjectures and Refutations*), who subscribe to a rational program of systematic falsification as the only basis of science (*Against Method* 93–94, 176; also Overington 151–52). Also on the right are the "rational reconstructionists" such as Carnap and Lakatos, who, while allowing for "ad hoc hypotheses" in the "historical account" of scientific research, hold that the explication of scientific research requires the replacement of "faulty concepts" (those based on commonsense experience or terminology) with more rational, systematic ones based on the rules of positivism. Thus, explication is only possible in regard to the context of justification, (i.e., rational reconstruction), not the context of discovery (the actual processes and/or language in which scientific concepts are created; Feyerabend, *Against Method* 165–214; Carnap 1–18; Lakatos 138, 177–80; Suppe, esp. 12; 57–58; 125–26). On the left (according to anybody) are the "epistemological anarchists" such as Feyerabend himself, who argues that any systematic, rational method restricts sci-

entific freedom, creativity, and progress. Insofar as Feyerabend believes that scientific progress is primarily, if not completely, dependent on "irrational" processes, he denies the possibility of "normal science" that for Kuhn makes up the bulk of scientific research (Feyerabend, "Consolations" 197–214). In Feyerabend's "anarchist epistemology," Kuhn's notion of the history of science is itself a rational reconstruction of irrational processes.

14. The late H. R. Pagels was absolutely euphoric in his optimistic belief that physics would indeed arrive at a complete picture of the universe in the not too distant future. And while Stephen Hawking recognizes and reveals the human and political dimensions of physics, he too holds out the possibility that a complete theory will be discovered, at which time we will know "the mind of God" (175). While we may understand some of this optimism to be a "deontological appeal"—the appeal to wonder that is the result of what Jeanne Fahnestock has called "accommodation" as scientific information moves from an expert to a public forum, this optimism and belief in the eventual certainty of knowledge can also be seen to underlie the work of New Physics itself.

For example, based on the assertion that indeterminacy exists only at the classical, Newtonian level of observation and that determinacy (defined as the ability to predict the behavior of a system of space-time based on data given for one region of it—and the objectivity and precision that accompanies determinism) actually holds in both relativity theory and at the quantum level, Hawking's coworker in cosmology, Roger Penrose, in a book written to the public but admittedly less accommodated (viii), makes a distinction between the determinism of New Physics (such as in *Schrodinger's equation* governing the development of a wave packet in time) and the indeterminism when this development is magnified and measured at the Newtonian level (250). For Penrose, both are needed for agreement between theory and fact—and both are approximations, the precursors of a new, more complete theory (cf. 214–16; 225; 255–56; 268–70; 280–99; 367–68). Thus, for Penrose, it is at the as yet undiscovered interface between determinism and indeterminism where some more complete, but as yet undiscovered, theory will be discovered (297).

15. 1. The validity of interpretation is derived not only by reference to external "facts" but by reference to the interpretive strategies or procedures the community holds (Fish, "Demonstration" 364–65; Kuhn, *Scientific Revolutions* 94).

2. Different procedures result in different interpretations; the assumptions of competing communities will be that the others are not perceiving the facts correctly (Fish, "Introduction" 15, "Variorum" 171; Kuhn, *Scientific Revolutions* 94).

3. The stability of interpretive communities is made possible by strategies and rules that are instilled in each member of the community primarily through education, textbooks, and training (Fish, "*Variorum*" 171; Kuhn, *Scientific Revolutions* 19–20; 80).

4. Personal responses must be discounted; solutions must satisfy the community as a whole (Fish, *Intro.* 7; Kuhn, *Scientific Revolution* 168).

5. Interpretive communities are not completely stable and are overthrown when anomalies occur that cannot be solved by the current model (Fish, "*Variorum*" 171–72; Kuhn, *Scientific Revolutions* 66–76).

Fish therefore identifies two models of interpretation in literature: the demonstration model, "codified in the dogma and practices of New Criticism," "derived from an analogy to the procedures of logic and scientific inquiry . . . in which interpretations are either confirmed or disconfirmed by facts that are independently specified"; and the persuasion model, "in which the facts that one cites are available only because an interpretation (at least in its general and broad outline) has already been assumed" ("Demonstration vs. Persuasion" 365). Fish perhaps sums up best the two models of knowing in both scientific and literary theory we have been exploring when he states:

> In the first model critical activity is controlled by free-standing objects in relation to which its accounts are either adequate or inadequate; in the other model critical activity is constitutive of its object. In one model the self must be purged of its prejudices and presuppositions so as to clearly see a text that is independent of them; in the other, prejudicial or perspectival perception is all there is, and the question is from which of a number of equally interested perspectives will the text be constituted. In one model change (at least ideally) is progressive, a movement toward a more accurate account of a fixed and stable entity; in the other, change occurs when one perspective dislodges another and brings with it entities that had not before been available. ("Demonstration vs. Persuasion" 365–66)

16. Langer accounts for the ostensible differences between symbols in science and art by distinguishing between "discursive forms," symbols that refer to external referents, and "presentational forms," symbols whose meaning is articulated and "understood only through the meaning of the whole, through their relations within the total structure" (*New Key* 97). The presentational forms of the senses and art, as distinct from language proper, are not comprehended sequentially, bit by bit, but simultaneously,

as an integral, qualitative whole; poetry and other art forms are not merely nonsensical, or quasi-scientific statements about feeling, intuition, emotion, but present their own sensuous logic, which "is in the service of its vital import" (*Feeling* 59). Thus, Langer is able to break out of the bondage of traditional logic in her discussion of what constitutes a symbol and to revise the notion of rationality itself. Affective symbolization is basic to thought; even rationality is subjective.

17. Reader Response Criticism is flanked on the right by formalists such as E. D. Hirsch, Jr., who in the past maintained that for knowledge to be valid and anarchy prevented in the profession of English, literary interpretation must be objective and deterministic (*Aims*) and writing skills separable from content (*Philosophy*); as everyone knows, Hirsch has now adopted the opposite but equally formalistic (and popular) position in prescribing what content Americans need to know (Hirsch et al., *Cultural Literacy*; see Cain, *Crisis* 15–30). Reader Response Criticism is flanked on the left by deconstructionists like Derrida, for whom the interpretation of any system of meaning is necessarily open-ended, given the incomplete, contingent, and recursive nature of language and the "absence" of an ultimate "transcendental signified" to which language can refer; language only defers and replaces meaning as a "trace" or "supplement" in a "chain of signification" without a final signified (141–64; 269–316). Reader Response critics thus tend to locate the source of uncertainty in interpretation in the subjective transaction between reader and text, while deconstructionists locate it in the nature of language itself in which meaning is "deferred" and "disseminated," and texts are inevitably "grafted" onto one another in a multitude of unpredictable relations; in this process, even readers are "written" (cf. Neel 112–19; Eagleton 134).

In examining the relationship between literary and scientific theory, we can even see a certain parallel between the rational reconstructionists in the philosophy of science who hold that "scientific theories have canonical formulations" (Suppe 57) and Hirsch; and between epistemological anarchists like Feyerabend and Derrida, for whom the multiplicity and proliferation of theories/meanings attest to the incomplete, open-ended, and pluralistic nature of any system, and so affirm an anarchy of possibilities against the limitations of reason, language, and method. However, I would not want to push this parallelism too far.

18. Cf. Greene, who explores how readers are actively involved in creating meaningful structures and relating and incorporating what they read into what they already know as part of the process of understanding and responding to a text just as students do in the process of writing and revising their own text, and Iser's phenomenological account of reading ("Reading Process"), in which the starting point of knowledge is human consciousness centering itself in the world through language in the continual act of self-identification. Green also mentions James Britton, who,

says Greene, "lays stress on human beings' creative capacity, especially where the construction of representations is concerned" (124). In fact, Britton's division of writing into the categories of poetic, expressive, and transactional ("Composing Processes") is itself based on the early reading theory of D. W. Harding. In "The Role of the Onlooker," Harding argues that both the "passive onlooker" and the "active participant" are involved in comprehending a situation, whether real or fictional; in "Psychological Processes in the Reading of Fiction," he goes on to postulate that readers are actively evaluating a situation by representing reality to the self according to a perception of similarity based on prior experience (134; 147). The difference between the categories of "passive onlooker" and "active participant," over which Britton's scale of poetic, expressive, and transactional writing slides, is thus a matter of degree rather than kind.

These categories also resemble Rosenblatt's distinction in *The Reader, the Text, the Poem* between "efferent" and "aesthetic": an efferent evocation would, in Britton's terms, be concerned more with the "transactional" or informational value of the text, aesthetic more with the poetic, the text itself. However, for Rosenblatt, it is the attitude that the reader brings to the text that determines the purpose or function of a text (though the text can and does provide various signals and clues as to which would be more appropriate). For example, it is possible for a novel (*Moby Dick,* for instance) to be read for its informational value, just as it is possible for a technical document to be read in terms of its aesthetics. (A stylistic proclivity, objectivity does have an ethos and a flavor). Again, the difference seems to be only a matter of degree, not of kind.

Furthermore, just as Bleich understands the process of reading as an active process of exploring and discovering the motivations and drives that underlie all knowledge as a process of resymbolization that results in increased awareness and intellectual growth, James Moffett (*Teaching The Universe of Discourse*) also understands the process of writing as a process of "symbolization" (or resymbolization). It is this act of symbolization as a part of human consciousness that both the act of reading and the act of writing have in common. In fact, Moffett's theory is built on the work of Piaget in developmental psychology and language acquisition, just as Bleich's theory of subjective criticism is. For Moffett, the spectrum of discourse in which the relationships between speaker and subject matter become more distant as the ego becomes increasingly "decentered," socialized, and capable of higher and higher levels of abstract thinking is correlated with the higher and higher levels of abstraction in cognitive development that Piaget and Inholder traced (*The Psychology of the Child*). "Cognitive growth, according to Piaget," writes Moffett, "depends on expanding perspective by incorporating initially alien points of view. This 'decentering' is the principal corrective to egocentrism (and ethnocentrism, geocentrism, etc.)" (71). Thus, for Moffett, response to reading can be used to teach writing as a process of intellectual growth and socialization (208). In "Discerning Motives in Language Use" and elsewhere, Bleich himself argues that, since subjective and social motives underlie all language use, the study of these motives should be the purpose of writing instruction using literature. (For recent general collections of essays exploring the relationship between and the integration of reading and writing instruction, see *Composition and Literature: Bridging the Gap*, edited by Horner, esp. Bleich's essay "Discerning Motives"; *Convergences: Transactions in Reading and Writing*, edited by Petersen, esp. the essays by Dougherty and by Sternglass. Also see Anson; Biddle and Fulwiler; Blake; Farnan; Fenstermaker; Moran; Salvatori; Schatzberg-Smith.)

19. Despite differences of philosophical orientation and methodology, Linda Flower ("Writer-Based Prose: A Cognitive Basis for Problems in Writing") distinguishes between writer-based prose and reader-based prose in a way that corresponds to Rosenblatt's aesthetic and efferent evocation of the text in reading theory, or Britton's distinction between the spectrum from expressive to poetic and from expressive to transactional in writing theory (Peterson, "Unified Model" 461–63); for Flower, writer-based prose is "a verbal expression written by a writer to himself and for himself. . . . [It] reflects the associative, narrative path of the writer's own confrontation with her subject. . . . [I]t reveals her use of loaded terms and shifted but unexplained contexts for her statements" (20). Drawing on the similarities of these theories of reading and writing, Petersen asserts that "personal associations, prior cognitive schemes, previous emotional responses, and private images and memories" (461) seem to shape both the reading and writing processes.

And in "Writing as a Mode of Learning," Janet Emig argues that learning itself "is the reorganization or confirmation of a cognitive scheme in light of experience" (124) that is then reinforced. Thus for Emig, too, the process of writing is like the process of reading for Iser (*The Act of Reading*), which correspond to the process of learning (cf. Odell, "The Process of Writing and the Process of Learning"). For Emig, however, writing is distinct from reading in that "writing is originating and creating a unique verbal construct that is graphically recorded. Reading is creating or recreating but not originating a verbal construct that is graphically recorded" (123; cf. Ochsner 10–11). But despite Emig's insistence here on the "uniqueness" of the writing process as a mode of learning superior to reading or listening or talking, both reading and writing are dependent upon prior cognitive schemes and are thus alike at least in this regard. In the process of reading as in the process of writing, we are actively involved in changing the structures of our perception and understanding, and how we subsequently view the world. For Iser (*Act*), this is how reading "adds" to our experience and is the value of literature. (For a different but related rhetorical understanding of this process, see Boulding's *The Image*, especially chapter 1, and Young, Becker, and Pike's *Rhetoric: Discovery and Change*, especially chapters 8, 9, and 10.)

20. Because Reader Response Criticism has in the past been primarily used in the composition classroom to teach "expressive" (as opposed to "critical" or "academic" writing), the issue of whether cognitive strategies are universal or different in different disciplines (Odell, "Process of Writing"), and whether literature-based writing can teach the intellectual strategies used in other disciplines, does not come up much (e.g., see Petersen, *Convergences*, where the emphasis is on general reading, writing, and rhetorical abilities, intellectual and emotional development, and language arts curriculum reform).

21. The four primary categories of response delineated by Purves (*Elements*) are personal, descriptive, interpretive, and evaluative. The intellectual strategies classified and described by this T-unit analysis are focus, contrast, classification, change, and reference to time sequence or logical sequence or physical context (Odell and Cooper 207). Developing specific guidelines and questions for each of these strategies, Odell and Cooper sought to answer the following questions: "What intellectual processes guide [the student's] efforts to formulate a particular response? When, for example, he attempts to interpret a literary text, how does he go about it? What intellectual strategies does he use? What habits of thinking and feeling underlie his response? Are there ways in which he might use a given strategy so as to respond more fully?" (207).

22. "[The] probability function represents a mixture of two things, partly a fact and partly our knowledge of a fact. It represents a fact in so far as it assigns at the initial time the probability unity (i.e., complete certainty) to the initial situation. . . . It represents our knowledge in so far as another observer could perhaps know the position of the electron more accurately. . . . When the probability function in quantum theory has been determined at the initial time from the observation, one can from the laws of quantum theory calculate the probability function at any later time and can thereby determine the probability for a measurement giving a specified value of the measured quantity. . . . It should be emphasized, however, that the probability function does not in itself represent a course of events in the course of time. It represents a tendency for events and our knowledge of events. The probability function can be connected with reality only if one essential condition is fulfilled: if a new measurement is made to determine a certain property of the system. Only then does the probability function allow us to calculate the probable result of the new measurement. The result of the measurement again will be stated in terms of classical physics.

"Therefore, the theoretical interpretation of an experiment requires three distinct steps: (1) the translation of the initial experimental situation into a probability function; (2) the following up of this function in the course of time; (3) the statement of a new measurement to be made of the system, the result of which can then be calculated from the probability function. For the first step the fulfillment of the uncertainty relations is a necessary condition. The second step cannot be described in terms of the classical concepts; there is no description of what happens to the system between the initial observation and the next measurement. It is only in the third step that we change over again from the 'possible' to the 'actual' " (Heisenberg 45–47).

23. Penrose, an admitted Platonist, would not agree with the latter (cf. 400–49; Boulding 17). And this is where Penrose and I part company. Penrose's appeal to Platonism appears to me to be a crutch to account for what we now do not comprehend, to be what Holton calls an "impotency proposition," "a bridge over the gap of ignorance" (Holton 52–53), but one based on rationalism.

24. For Simon, the "disparate components" of "human purpose" and "natural laws" (6) are related by effectively reducing all objects and phenomena, including human behavior and cognitive processes, to "artifacts." An artifact, says Simon, is an "interface . . . between an 'inner environment,' the substance and organization of the artifact itself, and an 'outer environment,' the surroundings in which it operates. If the inner environment is appropriate to the outer environment, or vice versa, the artifact will serve the intended purpose" (9). Thus, Simon can reduce all process—in economics, psychology, AI design—to cause/effect, feedback/response relationships that control the adaptation of an inner environment to an outer environment, a process that can be studied empirically (based on rational assumptions about the inner environment). "[T]he first advantage of dividing outer from inner environment in studying an adaptive or artificial system is that we can often predict behavior from knowledge of the systems goals and its outer environment, with only minimal assumptions about the inner environment" (11).

25. For Dreyfus, who follows the philosophy of science developed by Michael Polanyi in *Personal Knowledge*, much human knowledge and behavior is situational—possessed by virtue of being conscious, sentient beings, knowledge of our own bodies, alive to and aware of their physical relationship to their environment, to space, time, matter, motion, and to language, society, and culture—which is too extensive to be stored in computer memory, using existing technology. Further, like Polanyi, Dreyfus questions whether this knowledge is amenable to empirical observation or rational heuristics—whether it can ever be programmed into binary code, since this code assumes only two discrete states—on, off. (He also questions whether the belief that the synapses of the brain operate by binary opposition is not the result of a model of neurons based on computer technology, rather than the other way around [cf. MacCormac]).

Computer programs cannot capture or simulate the totality of human experience, although it may seem that they are doing so based on the empirical observation of "rational behavior" in the "outer environment" (cf. Turing; Weizenbaum). Despite the problems involved, Abraham Moles has managed to apply information theory to the aesthetic perception in an interesting way.

26. For example, it has been noted that there is a direct relationship between smell, memory, and emotion (at least insofar as they are located in close proximity in the brain). How do we measure or even begin to understand the role of someone's sense of smell in relation to the "quality" of his or her memory and affective experience of a text? This question is asked with only partial tongue in cheek, for the role of the senses in language experience is real but beyond our current methods of inquiry (see Corbin, *The Foul and the Fragrant*, for an excellent discussion and critique of the role of smell in French history, sensibility, and culture).

27. For example, in *Subjective Criticism*, Bleich advocates the use of a response statement that "aims to record the perception of a reading experience and its natural, spontaneous consequences, among which are feelings, or affects, and peremptory memories and thoughts, or free associations" (147). In "From Story to Essay: Reading and Writing," Petrosky uses Bleich's response statements to get students to make explicit unarticulated feelings, beliefs, and perceptions, and assumptions, interpret them, and make critical connections so that they may learn through a process of socialization how to adapt their private discourse for others (26). Contrary to Petrosky, who believes freewrites do not encourage students to examine their responses critically, in "Writing about Responses: A Unified Model of Reading, Interpretation, and Composition," Bruce Petersen advocates freewritten response statements as developed by Peter Elbow in *Writing Without Teachers*. Student essays begin in subjective responses and then are developed in the classroom as social knowledge using Moffett's language arts curriculum.

28. Although it may seem nonsensical, the imperative to analyze and interpret can be seen in poststructural approaches to knowledge as well. For example, as has been generally noted, despite its commitment to indeterminacy and nonreferentiality of meaning, deconstruction attempts to describe the closed system of language itself in "rational" terms and so undermines its agenda by subscribing to a priori assumptions about "systems" of meaning it seeks to analyze or deconstruct. In deconstruction, the paradoxical absence of meaning that language replaces becomes itself the object of analysis and interpretation. Thus, like all antifoundationalist theory (Bizzell, "Foundationalism and Anti-Foundationalism" 40), deconstruction posits method in place of absolute meaning. In this sense, the whole structuralist and poststructuralist enterprise can be understood

to entail methods of analysis and interpretation even more formalistic, rationalistic, and rigorous than either New Criticism or Reader Response Criticism, and so represents an advance in the "science of literature."

29. In fact, we can perhaps recognize in the history of interpretation increasing degrees of formalism and rationalism, perhaps varying in relation to their object of study: biblical hermeneutics, concerned with revealing mystical, nonreferential knowledge of God or Divine Law; Newtonian, concerned with uncovering the laws of nature that underlie the structure of appearances; positivistic, concerned with verification of data according to axiomatic rules (see note 30 below). For a brief discussion of the development of hermeneutics in religion and history, and its relation to the belief in certain knowledge and to science, see Connolly and Keutner, *Hermeneutics Versus Science?* 4–16.

30. No matter what the epistemological paradigm, no matter what the model of research, no matter what the degree of certitude or aggressiveness, interpretation, like analysis, to some degree necessitates and commits us to induction, and thus to empirical observation and/or to the systemization of observational terms (those that refer to phenomena themselves) into nonobservational terms (those axiomatically defined by the theory), which can constitute both the basis of "exact statements" as well as yield universal or general statements (Suppe 57–58). Thus, interpretation also to some degree necessitates and commits us to deduction and thus to rationality inherent in the ideal of logical explanation. (But see Katz, "Kabbalah," where in a new line of research I discuss an epistemological paradigm that is very different from the one discussed here, a paradigm in which "observational and nonobservational terms," universal statements, and interpretive logic empirically reference the nonreferential and the nonrational in the material elements of language—the sounds, shapes, size, order, and number of Hebrew letters themselves—which are held to embody the transcendental.)

For example, Suppe says that in "the received view" of science, which began in Vienna in response to the "developments" in physics in the 1920s and directly or indirectly underlies logical positivism—"and even outlasts logical positivism as a general epistemology" (6 n. 7): "The *theory of the data* specifies how the raw experimental data is to be converted into canonical-form data specified in terms of the experimental parameters of the physical theory (which, typically, are the parameters of the theory of the experiment). . . . [T]hen this canonical data can be compared with the possible data specified by the theory of the experiment for agreement" (108). Although Reader Response Criticism is certainly not nearly as positivistic, mathematical, rigorous, or extreme (no literary criticism is—yet), employing Suppe's terms we can understand that, in Reader Response Criticism, knowledge undergoes a similar conversion: "the raw experimental data" (the text or subjective response statements) is "converted" (resymbolized) in accordance with the "theory of the experiment" (in the case of Reader Response Criticism the subjective and social theories that attend the development of the heuristic itself) into "canonical-form data" (response statements or socially validated and useful knowledge), which in turn confirms the theory of the experiment (resymbolization).

31. "[T]he temptations of a rigorous technical vocabulary induce occasional lapses into a sort of scientism. Reading and writing become at such moments instances of regulated, systemized production, as if the human agencies involved were irrelevant. The closer the linguistic focus . . . the more formal the approach, the more scientistic the functionalism. Definitions, more often than not, point the reader back toward the method, since one aim of functionalism is to perfect the instrument of analysis as much as any understanding of a text's working. . . . Critical ingenuity is pretty much confined to transporting the work into an instance of the method" (44–45).

32. Just as Sontag says that interpretation compels us to separate content from form, "to deplete the world—in order to set up a shadow world of 'meanings' " and so "makes art into an article for use" (98–99), Heidegger says that modern technology is an "enframing" that turns everything into a "standing reserve" without regard for "bringing forth its Being," a "challenging" of nature "that it supply energy than can extracted and stored as such" (*Question* 14–19).

33. The technological imperative may in fact drive the formalistic, rationalistic epistemology that underlies analysis and interpretation as the paradigm of knowledge in Western culture. While Rorty, Brown, Hernandi, Gadamer, Miller ("Rhetoric of Decision Science"), and others distinguish between technical and humanistic conceptions of rationality and interpretation and affirm their role in "the human sciences," (re)definitions may not be enough; interpretation, like reasoning itself, may be moving toward increasing rationalization in our technological culture, whether we want it to or not. Indeed, if Habermas is correct, the technological imperative has already become the basis of all knowledge and values in our postindustrial capitalism without our even knowing it—for Habermas, one of the signs of the complete ascendancy of the technological ideology. But as Carolyn Miller suggests in "Technology as a Form of Consciousness," there is some hope because we are still arguing about it (236).

3. Cicero as Reader Response Critic

1. The contradictions and shifts in the tone of the text of Aristotle's *Rhetoric* open up questions as to when its various parts were written, and even by whom. There are also a number of issues raised by translation

(see Kennedy's new translation of the *Rhetoric*). But Aristotle's text, as a form and source of "social knowledge," has perhaps influenced the development of rhetorical theory and practice down to the present (Enos, "Rhetorical Theory" 2; but cf. Conley 17, who suggests Aristotle's *Rhetoric* had little influence in the history of rhetoric until the twentieth century). In this sense, questions concerning the authenticity of the text or the timing of its composition are "academic." In any case, Aristotle's formalistic, rationalistic approach to rhetoric has at least influenced our understanding and teaching of the subject (cf. Jarratt xvi–xvii).

2. As Lentz, citing Havelock, comments, "Plato . . . was a spokesman for a new scientific and abstract view of knowledge that grew out of the written tradition" (118), one that Toulmin and Goodfield (73–91) demonstrate was mathematical in nature. And in a chapter on "Aristotle and the Origin of Scientific Thought," Lentz states, "Aristotle has a deep impact on succeeding thinkers and scientists precisely because he is the first to identify a method of inquiry that relies heavily on the awareness of linear cause and effect reasoning" (165), which Toulmin and Goodfield argue underlies all contemporary physical sciences that depend on empiricism.

Indeed, in positing an absolute realm of empirical knowledge, Aristotle can be understood to have shifted Plato's realm of Ideal Forms from an idealistic (or a purely rationalistic) basis to an empirical basis (much as Tate tried to shift literary criticism back to a Platonic basis). It was a move continued in the Renaissance by Bacon (e.g., 394–411) and Descartes (e.g., 51–52), who rejected the medieval tradition of disputation based on scholastic logic ironically founded in Aristotle's dialectic (Murphy, "Medieval Background" viii–ix), and by Sprat (e.g., 61–62, 111–16), who can in retrospect be understood to have taken Aristotle's ambivalent attitude toward style expressed in Book III of the *Rhetoric* one step further by rejecting it altogether in favor of the "naked facts." But as Kerferd notes, while the ancient Greeks (the pre-Socratics up through Plato) were interested in discovering the essence of things, modern science (beginning with Aristotle) has been interested in their logical (causal) relations—on how things interact, and that this is the primary difference between ancient and modern science (73, 86, 95). However, while Newtonian science has more or less called off the search for essences, this search again can be seen to be on in New Physics; as we will see, this parallel is not insignificant in the history of thought.

3. In the *Lectures on Elocution*, published in 1762, Thomas Sheridan attempted to revive oratory by focusing on the neglected art of delivery in rhetoric. Sheridan argues that language is not only concerned with the communication of meaning, with the nature of words as "symbols of our ideas," but with "the nobler branch of language, which consists of the signs of internal emotions"; for Sheridan, "tone, looks, and gesture" are

"the language of the passions," which spontaneously result from the pressure of inner emotion in language and form the basis of affective response (*Lecture VI*). Oddly enough, Sheridan spends much time talking about animal tones to get at this dimension of meaning in sound and delivery; but from a contemporary point of view, his study is highly significant in that it is an early expression of philosophy of language that stresses the role of drives and motivations in cognitive development, such as that of Piaget and Bleich, and how these drives and motivations are imprinted on language as a sensuous form of sound, such as in the philosophy of Cassirer (I will discuss these philosophies further in chapter 5). In *Chironomia*, Gilbert Austin actually goes so far as to develop a formal system for notating the music of speech and gesture in delivery. Although highly mechanical, this work may be of interest to those in composition working with language and body movement. Although it was highly influential in eighteenth- and nineteenth-century curricula, the elocutionary movement itself has been relatively neglected, both in the history of rhetoric and in contemporary composition.

Other early attempts to develop a musical prosody include work by Joshua Steele, John Thelwall, P. Barkas, James Chapman, Richard Roe, James Lecky, Sidney Lanier, J. P. Dabney, William Thomson, E. A. Sonnenschein, Thomas Taig, and W. Young (Sumera 100). More recent attempts include Saintsbury's, whose study of prose rhythm is perhaps one of the most famous in this century, Hoover, and Bollinger. But the role of sound in rhetoric *in relation to knowledge* has been paid scant attention since the Renaissance (Farnsworth has recently investigated theories of musical rhetoric in the baroque period and, citing the work of linguist Ray Jackendoff on phonology and cognition, has called for an examination of the musical properties of rhetoric in relation to thought.) In *Style, Rhetoric, and Rhythm*, Morris Croll argues that since the Renaissance "the neglect of this study has been due to the tendency to avoid oratorical modes on which all the theory of rhetoric is formed, and to consider prose chiefly as it is addressed to the intellect, rather than as language spoken and heard" (327–28). But for Croll, the beauty of sound is the basis of all artful prose styles (even the *genus humile* of ancient rhetoric, although its presence is less uniform and harder to detect in modern "essay prose" [358]), and the neglect of this "is a prolific source of aberration of both theory and practice" (61).

4. Lentz (90–108) divides the transition from poetry to prose into three categories: (1) "oral preparation, preservation, and publication"; (2) "oral composition, written preservation"; and (3) "publication by reading out loud from written texts." The first involved oral composition (in poetic form), memorization, and recitation; the second involved writing as an aid for memorizing oral compositions; the third, the oral recitation of written texts—reading out loud. As Lentz concludes, in this transition

the spoken word retains considerable power over the new writing. . . . [E]ven the "writers" of Hellenic discourse apparently research and compose their creations in memory with little or no aid from writing, in the best style of the oral tradition. . . . Clearly in ancient Greece, the "making" of the poets melds with the new technology of writing to yield the "making" of intellectual discourse preserved in writing. Throughout the Hellenic period, however, "making" is still the word for composition, and that word was spoken. (108)

5. This revisionist interpretation of Gorgias's dictum is by no means held in all quarters (Hunt 70; Kennedy, *Classical Rhetoric* 31). Given the limited, anecdotal, biased, and even hostile evidence concerning Gorgias and the sophists in general, this dictum is the subject of controversy and debate. However, Enos's interpretation of Gorgias's dictum does find support in G. B. Kerferd's *The Sophistic Movement.* Kerferd interprets Gorgias's dictum not as a satire on Plato's belief in Being (Forms), nor as a nihilistic denial of the existence of being (reality). Rather, Kerferd traces Gorgias's dictum back to Protagoras's doctrine of the "two—opposed-logoi," which Kerferd sees as the heart of the sophistic philosophy of rhetoric in fifth century B.C.E. (85). The *dissoi logoi* was the basis, Kerferd says, of the sophistic practice of training students to argue both sides of an issue. It was this practice that Plato denounced as substituting opinion for truth, as teaching students to make the worse seem better, the better worse, and thus of corrupting Greek youth. (Of course, one has to believe in the ontological reality of truth to make this accusation. The sophists did not. And this is the one place where the sophists appear to be "absolute.")

6. Regardless of one's opinion of rock music, one can perhaps consider Allen Bloom's attack on the somatic, irrational, and harmful effects of rock music (and of contemporary culture generally) as another incarnation and revival of the feud between "the literate Platonists" and "the oralistic sophists" who believed in response to sensory experience as the only valid form of knowledge. Bloom is heir apparent of the Apollonian philosophy of restrained, quiet music, not the Dionysian raucous of dithyrambic rhapsodic revelers. This note is not meant as an endorsement of Bloom's views or of contemporary culture but only as an interesting aside. As we will explore in regard to Cicero's style, the charge of a disruptive, ornate style seems to be a perennial one in a culture that prizes a formalistic, rationalistic philosophy of language and knowledge more than any other (see Sprat; the logical positivists, and the subsequent embodiment of their insistence on clear language in scientific and technical communication, are also cases in point. Cf. Lanham; Halloran and Bradford; also see notes 12 and 13 below).

7. There is a direct stylistic and philosophical connection between the sophists and Isocrates, one that I believe leads from the sophists to Cicero. The connection between Isocrates and the sophists has been generally recognized. Although Isocrates lived the century after the original sophists, and although he was not, like them, an itinerant teacher, but rather founded a permanent school, there are many connections, both historical and philosophical, between them. Isocrates was a pupil of both Protagoras and Gorgias (Jaeger 48; Lentz 124). In the past, it has been supposed that Isocrates' treatise *Against the Sophists* was a repudiation of the sophists. But Hunt sees this treatise as an attack on Plato and the Socratics, whom Isocrates labeled as "sophists" because of their habit of engaging in what he regarded as useless philosophical speculation and because of their belief that truth and virtue were based on certain knowledge (71). (Jaeger even sees Isocrates' *Against the Sophists* as an extended counterargument to Plato's *Gorgias* in defense of his former teacher [55–59].) I will discuss the connections between the sophists, Isocrates, and Cicero in the following sections of this chapter.

8. Despite the important relationship between sophistic style, political philosophy, and contemporary feminism (Jarratt 63–79), women were not allowed to speak publicly either in the *agora* or the Forum. Like Cicero, Isocrates, and the sophists, I obviously believe in the power of language to create perception and underlie thought and action, and would rather not repeat the male chauvinism of the classical era. However, for the sake of historical accuracy, in subsequent quotations from Isocrates and Cicero I will refrain from changing the male pronoun to a neuter one, or bracketing it with the feminine, but ask the reader to change history on his or her own.

9. On the one hand, Isocrates (*Antidosis* 276–80) believed the orator would imbibe morals, become more virtuous, by the habitual exposure to literature that depicted virtuous action, as well as the habitual compulsion to persuade an audience, which was a moral as well as rhetorical facilitator. For the ancient Greeks, morality was linked to habitual action. As Grimaldi suggests in his discussion of the role of *ethos* in enthymemic arguments, ethics are based on and always lead to action. Based on Aristotle's teleological conception of knowledge and virtue, Grimaldi (144–51) argues that just as virtue for Aristotle involves natural disposition or appetite as well as choice informed and led by intellect (*Nichomachean Ethics* VI.xii. 11443b16–xiii. 1145a14), *pathos* (emotion) and *ethos* ("the moral element in character") play a crucial role in enthymemic arguments, providing the essential link between deliberation and action (146). Grimaldi argues that while *logos*, or reason, "considers the means necessary" to reach some end in deliberative rhetoric, it is *pathos* and *ethos* that provide the impetus to act.

Thus, just as *ethos* as character is created and demonstrated in rhetoric as a form of "symbolic action," ethics as virtue is created and demonstrated in outward, observable behavior (cf. Lloyd 214–17). This view of ethics also in some ways can be understood to underlie the *virs bonus* (the "good man") theory of Roman rhetoric found in the treatises of Cicero and Quintilian as well (but cf. Enos and McClaran, "Virs Bonus"). For the ancient Greeks and Romans, character (personality) was not understood in terms of abstract psychology, as it is for us, but was created and embodied in concrete, physical acts. This ethical understanding of psychology is also contained in Aristotle's notion of the soul, whose distinguishing characteristic is activity. It is the presence of the soul that separates animate beings from inanimate objects, and the location of this activity that separates the beasts from humans, in whom the highest activity of the soul is the ability to reason (see Lloyd 181–201).

On the other hand, Isocrates' view of the role of literature in a moral education is not so naive or overly idealistic. In many ways, Isocrates anticipates and in part answers questions concerning the efficacy of literature in a moral education when he states: "I consider that the kind of art which can implant honesty and justice in depraved natures has never existed and does not now exist" (*Antidosis* 274; cf. Steiner; Booth, *Company*). Contrary to the impression Plato creates concerning the promises of a sophistic education to teach wisdom and virtue, "the true" sophistic position is that it probably cannot. Although Isocrates does not deny that training and practice, that methods and rules, can help orators who have natural talent choose the right course of action quickly or wisely (*Antidosis* 292), based on his sophistic relativism, he does not grant any one method a high degree of certainty: "it is not in the nature of man to attain a science by the possession of which we can know positively what we should do or what we should say," says Isocrates (*Antidosis* 271).

In this way, Isocrates (and later, Cicero) perhaps differed from the earlier sophists, who, according to Plato, professed they could teach virtue. But given the source and suspect nature of our knowledge of this period, and Plato's bias against the sophists, this charge is controversial and open to debate as well. It seems far more likely that the sophists believed that virtue, like knowledge, was relative and uncertain and could only be created and taught through rhetoric insofar as rhetoric (not philosophical absolutes) was the only means of creating/obtaining any knowledge at all. (Cf. Hunt 72–73; Kerferd 105–06; Untersteiner xv.)

10. Bowerstock demonstrates the thriving existence of the latter-day sophists in Cicero's Rome, and that Cicero was aware of them (9), but there is little evidence to suggest that Cicero was influenced by them. Rather, it is more likely that Cicero absorbed the teachings of Isocrates and the first sophists during his long sabbatical in Athens, Asia Minor, and Rhodes, where he studied logography, philosophy, and declamation (Enos, *Literate Mode* 8). In his mature rhetorical treatises—*De Oratore*,

Orator, and *Brutus*—Cicero borrows heavily from and acknowledges his debt to Isocrates and the early sophists (as well as Plato and Aristotle, with whom he also fundamentally disagrees [compare *D. O.* III.iii.15, and v.21 with xvi.60–61, and xix.72]).

11. Kennedy's view appears to be the result of his attempt to classify the classical rhetorical tradition into three kinds of rhetoric, technical, sophistic, and philosophical, based on whether the text, speaker, or audience, respectively, is of primary importance. Kennedy sees the handbooks of the time, such as the *Rhetorica ad Herennium*, as examples of technical rhetoric; the rhetoric of Isocrates, with its attention to the character of the speaker, as an example of sophistic rhetoric; and the treatises of Plato and Aristotle, with their high degree of theoretical "conceptualization" and systemization of the art that serves to advance knowledge, as exemplars of philosophical rhetoric. In his treatment of these various historical strands of rhetoric, it is obvious that Kennedy holds the highest form of rhetoric to be a philosophical (formalistic and rationalistic) rhetoric that can serve to advance knowledge of the art [rather than dwelling in its uncertainties, as the sophists did]. Thus, Kennedy does not grant that Cicero's later work, which professes that eloquence cannot be taught by rational systemization or formal techniques alone and that knowledge of the art cannot be directly advanced by theory, is also philosophical (cf. Jarratt, xvii).

In *De Oratore*, Cicero himself dismisses *De Inventione* as an immature product of his youth (I.i.5). And as Ochs states: "The rigid, pompous, and didactic manner of presentation more than warrants his apology" (97). Although Kennedy does admit that *De Oratore* "is a much more thoughtful work" and that "it brings together . . . some strands of philosophical and sophistic rhetoric," he also states that it "contains much of the tradition of technical rhetoric in a nontechnical form" (*Classical Rhetoric* 90). And the problem is not only with scholars in the history of rhetoric. Rhetoricians too "seized this manual as their guide and their criterion for excellence" (Ochs 97). It was *De Inventione*, not *De Oratore*, that was copied, studied, and commented upon (Marrou 383; Murphy, "Medieval Background" ix). Even today, anthologies continue only to represent the more formalistic, rationalistic parts of Cicero—even of his later treatises—overlooking or ignoring those parts that do not fit the paradigm (see Benson and Prosser; Bizzell and Hertzberg).

12. According to Croll, the Ciceronian, oratorical prose style, which was marked by the use of the "figures of sound" (the schemes), was replaced by the Attic style, which was marked by the use "figures of thought" (the tropes); the emphasis, argues Croll, was no longer on sonorous periods of sensuous sound for a public audience but on private thought processes closely reflected in written language (209–10). According to Halloran and Whitburn, the ideal of a "mechanical" plain style,

one that would mirror nature without distortion, intensified with the scientific revolution in the seventeenth century. These styles are not unrelated. For although the Newtonian scientific revolution came a century after the Renaissance, the styles of each period, one accurately reflecting individuality, originality, and spontaneity, the other objectivity and exact description, were profoundly affected by, if not based on, the invention of print technology and the spread of literacy (Ong, *Orality*; Croll).

However, Croll shows how, because of the transition from Latin to vernaculars and the difficulty of imitating the rhythms of Latin in those tongues (185), the oratorical style of the Renaissance really had its roots in "medieval schematic prose" (237). It was not the Latin rhythms of Cicero (nor those of Isocrates) that were imitated by the "Asian" writers of the Renaissance, but rather the custom of ornamentation. Discussing Euphuistic rhetoric, Croll argues that the schemes of "rhyming prose" were used more frequently and differently in the Middle Ages, not to create rhythm as in classical rhetoric, but in and for themselves. Ornamentation became the entire focus of style (264; 266; 278). Croll's distinction between "the music" of classical and medieval prose thus corresponds to Ong's observations concerning the increasing visualization of ornamentation. The net effect of Croll's essays is to revise our understanding of Cicero's position in the history of rhetoric, a position that was misrepresented by his contemporaries, misconstrued during the Middle Ages (Murphy, "Medieval Background" ix–x), and misunderstood from the Renaissance to our own time.

13. As Croll demonstrates so well, the anti-Ciceronian movement itself was based on a misunderstanding. Croll's book supplements Ong's work in its exploration of the rise of nonoratorical prose in correlation with other historical, social, political, and linguistic forces in the Renaissance (as well as changes in the personal lives and careers of the writers that Croll examines). Croll places the discussion of positivistic style and rationalistic thought that rose in the Renaissance and took root in the seventeenth century in the context of a popular moral and political philosophy of the time, a philosophy whose roots Croll traces to the Stoic philosophy of Seneca and Tacitus. While Rankin sees a philosophical (and political) relationship between the sophists and the Stoics, Croll argues that Stoic philosophy was the root cause of the anti-Ciceronian movement in style that occurred in the sixteenth century. In fact, the writers of the period considered the Ciceronian style to be immature, unmanly, and ill-suited to a life of Stoic inner detachment from the world (86). (Plutarch's favoring in *Lives* [1070–72] of Demosthenes over Cicero on the basis of courage of action and of oratorical style would seem to confirm Croll's assertions. And both Demosthenes and Plutarch were among the preferred sources of classical authority and models of oratorical style for the anti-Ciceronian movement in the Renaissance [Croll, 77–78; 97, 124, 145, 154, 180–81].)

The result was an aurally opaque (rather than accessible) prose style that was in accord with the Stoic belief in obscurity not only as a political necessity but also as a philosophical virtue. One of Croll's major arguments here is that the *figura sententiae*, the figures of thought and wit, such as antithesis, paradox, metaphor, and the aphorism, were the primary Senecan, Attic forms of stylistic expressions that rose to counter the *schemata verborum*, the "figures of sound," of the earlier oral, Ciceronian, and medieval tradition of rhetoric (54). Again, this complements Ong's study of the shift from an oral to a literate culture by demonstrating how the formulaic nature of thought and expression in what was still an oral culture was used to support the growth of a more literate prose style. The Attic or baroque prose style, with its *figura sententiae* that sought to break symmetries of thought and sound while visually tracking through syntax and form the process of the mind grappling with thought, was just as formulaic and ornate—and often more difficult—than the sonorous, oratorical prose of the "Asian," Ciceronian style it sought to displace.

14. In *Style: An Anti-Textbook*, in a chapter entitled "Poetic Prose," Lanham states:

> Rhetorical performance, of course, was what reading once meant. A Greek or Roman schoolboy did not whiffle through his assignment at a pace inculcated by Jet-Speed Dynamic Reading Institute. He first studied it intensively. He isolated and remarked the figures of speech. He analyzed the imagery. He studied the shape of a sentence and devised a speech rhythm to elucidate that shape. He selected appropriate gestures for significant junctures. He rehearsed the stages of the argument until the thought moved with a rhythm of its own. Then he memorized the passage, rehearsed it a dozen times. He was then ready to perform it—aloud. Under such a pedagogy, rhythm cannot be a separate study. It grows naturally from the way the prose is addressed. (101)

15. As we will shortly discuss, Cicero takes poetic style in oratory one step further by applying the more literate concept of propriety to it. This is most evident in the *Orator*, where Cicero lays out the criteria and "form" of the ideal Orator. In this treatise, Cicero continues the defense that he started in the *Brutus* against the charge that he advocates the Asiatic, or ornate and copious style, rather than the preferred Attic, or plain style. (This is similar to the attack made against "rhetorical" style by Sprat's Royal Society in the seventeenth century and against language in general by the logical positivists in the twentieth century.) Cicero credits Isocrates with nourishing eloquence and says "it was not amiss to speak of what we may call the cradle of the orator" (xiii.42). Cicero admires Isocrates' "sweet, fluent, copious style, with bright conceits and sounding phrases," although he says it is more fit for epideictic, or celebratory, rhetoric than it is for the forum (*Orator* xiii.42). In a discussion of rhythm, Cicero also

notes that Isocrates is generally esteemed for his introduction and use of rhythm in prose: "For when he observed that people listened to orators with solemn attention, but to poets with pleasure, he is said to have sought rhythms to use in prose as well" (li. 174).

Yet Cicero quickly adds that although Isocrates demonstrated the greatest skill in using rhythm in prose, it was the sophist Thrasymachus who invented it, and "his work shows even an excess of rhythm" (lii. 175). Gorgias also used rhythm in his prose, Cicero says, "but he used these devices somewhat immoderately" (lii. 175). Thus, Cicero praises Isocrates not for his originality but for his adaptation of poetic style to rhetoric; for Isocrates showed "greater restraint" than his sophistic predecessors (lii. 176). Cicero states that the "oratorical style" he seeks must be distinguished from "the similar style of the Sophists mentioned above. . . . [T]heir object is not to arouse the audience but to soothe it, not so much to persuade as to delight" (*Orator* xix. 65–66). It is not the metered style of the poets and the sophists that induces hypnotic trance that Cicero wants, but "the terse and vigorous language of the orator," a tight but powerful style that will arouse and move an audience (*Orator* xix. 66). We will touch on Cicero's notion of propriety again in the next section.

16. In his discussion of rhythmic rhetoric from Cicero through the Renaissance, and the anti-Ciceronian movement that followed, Croll never explicitly connects rhythm and cadence with epistemology or acknowledges the music of language as a form of knowledge. He does, however, recognize the epistemic nature of rhythm and cadence. In part III of *Style, Rhetoric, and Rhythm*, "Oratorical Cadence and Verse Rhythm," Croll turns to examine the nature of oratorical cadence in prose, the nature of rhythm in verse, and finally to reconsider the relation of music and metrics themselves. In these essays, Croll gives us a method, some of it new, for thinking about and analyzing cadence in prose based on a liberal application of the "cursus"—composition based on patterns of rhythmic clauses (303). He also develops a prosody based on a system of musical notation. Of course, the oft-noted problem with prosody based on the scansion of accents or the quantity of syllable length is that it is highly reductive. Even Croll initially seems to believe in the possibility of establishing a science of cadence (323), although he intimates that no science will be discovered (332, 429) and finally concludes (351), as Cicero does (*Orator* xliv. 150), that the ear is the final arbiter of sound.

17. According to Psaty, based on the unity of form and content, Crassus argues that metaphors should become "indistinguishable from facts" (112). (Psaty argues that in *De Oratore* itself, as elsewhere in Cicero's writing, metaphors become "a part of the content of the argument" [107; cf. Leff, Untitled].) Furthermore, metaphors are a matter of instinct, and as such, their propriety is ultimately determined by "good taste" (109). As Psaty states: "In the final analysis, style and content are not united by

appealing to the senses, or by being careful about resemblance, or by observing moderation and proper distribution—all of which are standards
of propriety—they are united when, as in the case of certain metaphors,
a word or group of words functions at once as fact and as metaphor, when
the conventional distinction between tenor and vehicle is rendered invisible" (112).

18. Not only does language aid our perception of reality; it underlies
our shared knowledge of it as well. As Raymond DiLorenzo discusses,
ornatus—the intuited unity of content and form in the *kosmos* not only of
nature but in language, in which substance is illuminated and style finds
a seat, making matter perceptible, though imperfectly, through ornamentation, "kosmetics"—is a social as well as subjective aesthetic by virtue
of the fact that language is a social medium necessary for communication
and persuasion as well as perception.

> Crassus insists upon it because *ornatus* partakes of the nature of
> wisdom. This is the essential point of his critique of Socrates. From
> all that he says in it, we are bound to infer that wisdom is not per-
> fectly itself which does not become perceptible to others through
> words and alluring through ornatus. It is, in fact, of the nature
> of wisdom to be *kosmos*, to be *ornatus*. Wisdom is not knowledge
> simply for Crassus. Wisdom is knowledge embodied in speech
> which, by attracting others at the level of their senses, enters into
> them at the level of their convictions and becomes the impetus of
> their actions. (DiLorenzo 258)

This of course also echoes Enos on Gorgias concerning the power of
(oral) language to enter at the level of the senses and become the basis of
belief and action. As for the sophists, it would seem that for Cicero the
only solution of the natural flux of language and reality is to understand
knowledge as a subjective response and social consensus about the nature
of reality that is arrived at through persuasion (cf. Enos, *Literate Mode*
39). As both subjective and social, the allure of style as *ornatus*, as a
"kosmetic" whole, is necessary to deceive the senses into believing that
one statement is truer than another. The difference between Socrates and
Crassus, says DiLorenzo, is that "Socrates would emphasize the potential
in words for deception. Crassus would emphasize the necessity of speech
which properly adorns" (255). In a passage that resembles that of Isocrates
(*Antidosis* 253–57) Cicero makes it clear that eloquence is what Burke
might call the "consubstantial" basis not only of human consciousness
but of society and civilization itself (*D. O.* III.xx.76). Rhetorical consubstantiality reflects the cosmic interdependence of all physical things.
"Men, like the things of nature, are related to one another, and words are
their chief means of communing and relating" (DiLorenzo 254). For fur-

ther discussion of the sophistic underpinnings of Cicero's epistemology, see appendix B.

19. Whereas Pythagoras posits music as the mathematical Essence of reality (and Plato says that Essences are knowable and the true objects of philosophical contemplation), for Cicero, rhythm is a practical aesthetic. Like the sophists, Cicero makes no assumptions about the Essence, or truth of things (Enos, *Literate Mode* 39), but talks only about the intuition of appearances. Thus, while the Pythagorean concept of *kosmos* obtains in both Plato and Cicero, how they differently understood and used this concept is of the utmost importance. Plato took Pythagorean belief in a mathematical-musical order in the universe as an ontological base on which to ground pure Forms *outside language*. Cicero, on the other hand, like the sophists, apparently chose to emphasize the essential unity of form and content as it is intuited *in language*.

But the "order of rhetoric" in which we intuit the order of the universe is aural (or aurally more obvious) and thus an indeterminate one. Rather than separating Knowledge from the shadowy, shifting content of language and reality that can only be known ("seen") as Ideal Forms by an elite band of philosophers, Cicero, like the sophists, maintains that *kosmos* operates and can only be intuited in the "natural" order of rhetoric, in the probability afforded by rhetorical argument (Enos, *Literate Mode* 39), and in the arrangement and style of speech understood by an aesthetic sense that everyone possesses. Thus for Cicero, eloquence—the unity of thought and style in speech—like propriety, like the music of style itself, perhaps rests on an intuition of the physical unity of the universe, the order that obtains in *kosmos* itself, which is related to the physical character of the speaker and so can't be known or taught with certainty (*D. O.* I.xxviii.132–xxix.133).

20. "Their method, not unlike that of early times, might be described as collective tutoring," says Marrou (80). That this was truly a subjective and social philosophy of education is also attested to by Marrou (302). Although Isocrates, unlike the itinerant sophists, established a permanent school, and in this sense institutionalized education, he too maintained this subjective and social basis of a rhetorical education. Marrou makes this point about the classroom as a social community in later antiquity as well: There were universities, and students would go from one teacher to another, "[b]ut the principle of a personal relationship between teacher and pupil—a principle dear to antiquity—still held good. . . . [A] group of disciples centering round the same master was often described poetically as a chorus" (271). (In this regard, the difference between, say, the sophists and Plato, can be understood to be the degree to which they put stock in philosophical method; this, in turn, was based on whether or not they held certain knowledge to be possible. For although Plato believed that the presence of a "living intelligence" is necessary to instruct—and

was in this sense opposed to writing (*Phaedrus*)—his is more a matter of interaction based on dialectic method for the purposes of ascertaining and arriving at True Knowledge, than a matter of emulating language, emotion, and human character for the purposes of emotional persuasion. For the sophists, that's all we've got.

21. Take, for example, the advice Cicero has Crassus give in *De Oratore*: "We must . . . read the poets; acquaint ourselves with histories, study and peruse the masters and authors in every excellent art, and by way of practice praise, expound, emend, criticize and confute them; we must argue every question on both sides and bring out on every topic whatever points can be deemed plausible" (*D. O. I.* 109). Certainly, study and perusal of masters and authors entailed something like literary criticism (though much less formalized than ours); but as Marrou (375) and Murphy ("Roman Writing Instruction" 42, 46) suggest, the purpose of textual criticism, even in the more literate ancient Rome, was to analyze the sound of the text to be read out loud, and as Cicero seems to point out here, "by way of practice" to "praise, expound, emend, criticize, and confute," not only to explain the "meaning" of the text in and for itself. In the statement that we should argue the point from all sides, we perhaps hear the echo of the sophistic technique of the *dissoi logoi*. And in the notion of "emending" we perhaps recognize the changeable nature of the "text" in an oral culture; like Isocrates, Cicero realized that language was "changeable matter" and must be adapted "to the general understanding of the crowd (*D. O. I.*xxiii. 108–09). (Perhaps we also perceive here the particularly popular pedagogical practice of parody that became progressively perverse in publican-pickled Rome [Marrou 374; Murphy, "Roman Writing Instruction" 66].)

4. The Music of Language

1. As we discussed in chapter 2, James Moffett has suggested, based on the work of George Herbert Mead, that the mature self is a decentered ego, a composite of many social roles that have been internalized: "thought involves incorporating the roles and attitudes of others and addressing oneself internally as one would address another externally" (Moffett, *Teaching* 67). Taking a different tack on the issue, Havelock accepts the movement from orality to literacy as a movement toward abstraction but argues that the teaching of rhythmic prose and poetry (the sensory level of language) is necessary to counter increasing abstraction of language, and thus thought, in an ever-increasing scientific and technological society: "It is my contention that if we skip over the oral stage in the educational process too hurriedly, if we slight its importance, we do damage to those very conceptual powers we aim to develop. We impair

the quality of the abstractions we are teaching ourselves and others to use" ("Star Wars" 415).

2. As Robert Ochsner (*Physical Eloquence and the Biology of Writing*) himself hints, however, the correlation between writing ability and neurophysiological development is highly controversial, and we may find many of his conclusions concerning the correlation between handwriting—messy versus neat handwriting, manuscript (printing) versus cursive handwriting, and small versus large handwriting—and cognitive writing ability to be highly questionable. As Ochsner states, this may have more to do with a teacher's perception of writing abilities than the cognitive abilities themselves (59).

It is also interesting, then, that in his discussion of the relationship of graphic shapes to kinetic, auditory, and visual melodies (55–75, 107–25), Ochsner never mentions the role or effect of typing on the (neuro)-physiology of writing. Ochsner cites Luria, who states that "[i]n the initial stages . . . *writing* depends on memorizing the graphic form of every letter. It takes place through a chain of isolated motor impulses. . . . [W]ith this practice, this structure of the process is radically altered and writing is converted into a single 'kinetic melody' " (Luria, *Working Brain* 33, cited in Ochsner 55). Certainly, typing represents an abstraction of the "kinetic melody," whereby the mechanical, repetitive keystrokes are even further removed from the auditory and kinetic melodies of handwriting than is handwriting from the different auditory and kinetic melodies of speech (discussed in note 6 below; see chart 5.4 in Ochsner 93–96). While most children do not learn to write on a typewriter, typing is the means by which most students and professionals do the majority of their writing now—including, with the popularization and affordability of word processors, drafting. Thus, depending on individual ability, typing also can be understood to change the speed at which people both can write and can capture their thoughts as they compose. Given that the speed at which people type is one of Ochsner's criteria in determining physical eloquence, one should ask how the physical act of typing changes the biological process of writing.

Ochsner's claim that the "melodies" in speech and in writing are radically different—at least in regard to sound—is also questionable. Although there certainly is a relationship between the physical ability to write and writing ability in advanced writers (in terms of the speed and pacing of thought in writing, for example [see Ochsner 77–106]), we will explore in this chapter that at all levels the sound of language as a sensuous form may have as much to do with eloquence as does the physical ability to write. In other words, I do not accept Ochsner's correlation between the physical ability to handwrite and the cognitive ability to write as the definition of "physical eloquence." Ochsner takes the written text as the ontological radical of language. While I too believe eloquence to be physical and basic to reading, writing, and knowledge generally, this is one place where I fundamentally disagree with Ochsner's view. For Ochsner, physical eloquence involves the neurological coordination of ear, hand, and eye (auditory, kinetic, and visual melodies) and is located primarily in the physical production of a written text. For me, physical eloquence involves the physical sensation of and affective response to sound (the physical production and hearing of sensuous form) and is located primarily in speech. (In this regard, it is significant that Ochsner never considers the physiology of hearing).

Thus, just as the sensuous shape of sound in speech is minimized in writing, the tactile shape of letter in writing is minimized by the mechanical production of the keystroke in typing in that, except for the positioning of the fingers over the keys, every letter entails the same, repetitive movement, the same tactile response. As Ochsner himself states, "Handwriting permits auditory attention to form, a right hemisphere function, when rhythmic shape rather than edited meaning is the purpose of subvocal feedback" (61). The minimalization or abstraction of sensuous response in typing can be extended to typing on computers. However, we can also understand that typing creates patterns of keystrokes, rhythmic "gestures," and thus, as Cassirer might argue, represents a new level of abstraction, of tactile response at the level of the word, phrase, or sentence (I discuss Cassirer in the next chapter).

3. Ochsner too takes issue with the notion that writing thus must be taught formally (rather than acquired like a second language), with the emphasis on writing as a form of cognition, and with the preoccupation with writing as the expression of ideas (13). This is a point that I *do* agree with. Based on Krashen's distinction between acquisition and learning, Ochsner claims that the acquisition of prose, like speech, is a subconscious, physical (if different) process; the writing curriculum he suggests, based on the neurological connections between eye, ear, and hand, is an attempt to counter and suggest alternatives to our formalistic, rationalistic approach to writing instruction (see 127–43). However, just as Ochsner argues that physical eloquence has been increasingly denigrated and divorced from the writing process in our formal, rational approach to teaching writing, I would argue that the same has happened to sound, even in Ochsner's otherwise insightful book.

4. This distinction between heard and expected rhythm, discussed by Perrine in *Sound and Sense* (176), is an interesting one, and often a major obstacle to a student's ability to scan and to read metered poetry. The expected rhythm, the one created by meter, is often at variance with the heard rhythm, the rhythm inherent in the language as "normally" spoken, because meter will redistribute accents of single-syllable words according to the context of the meter being established (the rhythm of two-syllable words is more or less established by usage and can be found

in the dictionary). For example, the first two lines from Browning's "My Last Duchess" could be recited thus:

⏑　⏑　—　—⏑　—⏑⏑⏑　—
"That's my last duchess painted on the wall,

—　⏑　⏑⏑　⏑　—　⏑—　⏑　—
Looking as if she were alive. I call"

But as blank verse, the lines scan iambic pentameter thus:

⏑　—　⏑　—⏑　—⏑　—⏑　—
"That's my last duchess painted on the wall,

—　⏑⏑　—⏑　—⏑—　⏑　—
Looking as if she were alive. I call"

(We note the emphasis on the word "looking" that is created in the poem by the variation in meter caused by the normal rhythm of the two-syllable word "looking," which Browning used to his own, thematic ends.)

While students often cannot find the meter of a poem because of the way the line is naturally spoken, and/or because of variations in strict meter, they often read strict meter in singsong fashion and so miss "the meaning of meter" created by the difference between the heard and expected rhythms, which are often musically "counterpointed" (Perrine 174). This was something Frost was good at as well: getting the natural speaking voice in meter, and then not only playing heard rhythm off expected rhythm, but expected rhythm off heard rhythm, as in his reading of "Stopping by Woods on a Snowy Evening": "He gives his harness bells a shake / to ask if there is some mistake" (note the shaking of the bells in the strict iambic tetrameter); "The only other sound's the sweep / of easy wind and downy flake" (although still strictly iambic tetrameter, here Frost's voice relaxes again into the "heard rhythm" of the natural speaking voice he uses in the rest of this poem).

5. In "Scientific Composing Processes: How Eminent Scientists Write Journal Articles," Jone Rymer found that at least one of the scientists she studied used sound frequently to help select the right word (225, 234); however, Rymer concludes that this is an inefficient and ineffective method, which seemed to make little difference in the quality of published article (237). The possible importance of sound in invention, even in technical writing, is supported by Cooper and Odell. In "Considerations of Sound in the Composing Process of Published Writers," Cooper and Odell posited the notion "that the act of speaking may directly assist the act of writing" (103). To explore this hypothesis, they examined the composing process of several professional (i.e., technical) writers to determine whether these writers are "concerned about the sound of their writing" and whether they consider such elements as volume, pitch, timbre, speed, inflection, and voice quality (103). They also asked whether these concerns

enter into consideration during the process of writing. Cooper and Odell were "not concerned with sound as echo to the sense, but whether the sound implied in writing was appropriate for the speaker-audience relationship" (103). They found that the technical writers they studied "were concerned with the oral qualities (volume, speed, inflection) implicit in their writing, and whether those qualities were appropriate for the speaker-audience relationship they were trying to maintain in their writing" (114).

Despite these studies, just as there has been relatively little study of the relationship of sound to thought in regard to the epistemic nature of rhetoric, there has been relatively little study of the role of sound in invention. Even linguists have tended to ignore the relationship between phonology and cognition. With the exception of Jackendoff's consideration of semantics and music, most linguistic studies of sound have tended to focus on phonetics rather than syntactic rhythm and thus have paid scant attention to sound units larger than morphemes and words. Despite the epistemological problems with empirical method, it is obvious that the relation between phonology and cognition as it operates in invention is a next needed, logical step in research.

6. Earlier studies (e.g., Sticht et al.) recognized and sought to study the role of oracy in language processing in an attempt to develop a model for teaching adult literacy (this would more or less correspond with the first level and second level of sound discussed in this chapter). A renewed drive to develop methods of reading based on sound is also reflected in the more recent *Reading Voices: Literature and the Phonotext*. In this book, Garrett Stewart develops a linguistically based method of analyzing "voice" in literature, which he argues is inhibited, suppressed, and in a sense sublimated in silent reading. But although Stewart starts with phonemes, his analysis is an enterprise in deconstructive phonology or, perhaps we should say, phonological deconstruction of the silenced text. Thus, while *Reading Voices* ostensibly is about the third level of sound as physical experience noted above (n. 2), it actually corresponds to the fourth level, in which sound is dealt with as a spatial abstraction, as an object of method. In fact, while Stewart recognizes the important "somatic quotient in the reading of writing" (3), based on the literate ontology in deconstruction that all knowledge is "written," inscribed on the world, he dismisses any "sensual ontology of music" that might exist before writing (17). (The phenomenon of language as sound is perhaps not as antithetical to a deconstructive enterprise as it at first might seem. Even Bakhtin acknowledged the necessary materiality of every sign, both in outer expression and inner consciousness, though Bakhtin was interested the social, ideological nature of the semiotic content it contained [cf. part 1, chapter 1, of *Marxism and the Philosophy of Language*]).

In *Physical Eloquence and the Biology of Writing*, Ochsner is concerned with the role of sound as "auditory melodies" (ear) in the writing process and how these relate to the "visual melodies" (eye) and "kinetic melodies"

(Luria's metaphor for hand/brain): "A *melody* results when neurons co-alesce into a patterned behavior, that is, when they have learned something as an engram and can repeat it" (Ochsner 55). However, Ochsner understands sound exclusively in terms of neurology rather than physical sensation—that is, if one can make such a distinction, in terms of cognitive rather than aural patterns—and thus "abstractly" (as if experience of sound was not already an abstraction, didn't already involve cognition). In not attending to the actual nature of sound, Ochsner perhaps misses an important dimension of reading and writing. However, not everyone would agree that fluency of speech leads to fluency of writing. Based on the notion of a neurological "biogrammar" that precedes speech and writing, Ochsner claims that "speech can help a student learn to write, initially and temporarily, but after the connection with inner language has been established, prose should become a secondary system, independent of speech. If prose remains tertiary, with speech serving an interlanguage function, then students will transfer features from speech to prose that do not belong there. Many writing problems, perhaps the majority of those produced by unskilled writers, result from these speech-to-prose transfers" (86).

Furthermore, Ochsner is not as interested in reading as he is in writing, since he believes one does not necessarily help the other (10–11); rather, he is more concerned with developing a writing curriculum based on the notion of extended, physical interaction with written texts. And because he does not attend to the nature of language itself as sound, Ochsner defines this interaction (even in listening) as interpretation (11, 150). While Stewart's and Ochsner's are important books, they thus exhibit some of the epistemological problems we explored in chapter 2 and will not help us construct a theory of affective response to the sound of language in reading and writing as indeterminate knowledge. Cf. Ochsner, esp. 10–12 and 77–106, for further discussion of the difference between biological and motivational "filters" in speech and writing. Some of the notes below contain further discussions of Ochsner's views.

7. For example, take these lines from Sylvia Plath's poem "Mirror," which scan as predominately anapestic tetrameter with much variation.

∪∪ —∪ ∪ ∪— ∪ ∪ — ∪ ∪ — ∪
I am silver and exact. I have no preconceptions.

∪ —∪ —∪ — ∪ ∪ —∪∪—
Whatever I see I swallow immediately

— ∪∪— ∪ —∪ ∪ —∪ ∪ —
Just as it is, unmisted by love or dislike.

To indicate the music of this lyric as spoken rather than sung, we can sketch in traditional musical notation, which goes beyond the gross taxonomy of accent and unaccented syllables (here somewhat problematical) and shows subtle differences and nuances of pitch, or degree of accent and volume; and speed, or the duration of syllables on the context of the line *as spoken* (cf. the linguistic analysis of prosody in Williams 178–81). I reverse the tradition of placing lyrics below words, and present the music below words to privilege the lyrics as speech.

I am sil-ver and ex-act. I have no pre-con-cep-tions.

What-ev-er I see I swal-low im-me-di-a-tely

Just as it is, un-mist-ed by love or dis-like

    In addition to getting around the problem of accounting for the extensive variation here of the meter, musical notation can reveal the *relation* of pitches to syllables, both accented and unaccented. (It doesn't matter at what pitch one begins the notes on the staff, since the natural pitch of each reader's voice will vary; it is the relation of pitches, the differential between them, that counts more. Likewise, one could conceivably start with any time signature [i.e., 3/4, 6/8, or 2/2, 4/4,] so long as the time *relation* of notes is consistent. There is perhaps a correlation as well as a difference, however, between meter and time signature, between duple and triple meters—iambic and trochaic vs. anapestic and dactylic—and "duple" and "triple" time signatures, that probably needs to be observed in order to musically scan a poem successfully [cf. Sumera on Croll, 104–11]. This may be less an issue in the musical scansion of prose, although one would have the problem of settling on a time signature that could mathematically account for the duration and relation of the pitches, in which case the musical notation and time signature would have to be worked out simultaneously.) Cf. Austin; Barkas; Steele; Thelwall; Chapman; Roe; Lecky; Dabney; Thomson (*Illustrations of English Rhythms, Rhythm and Scansion, The Rhythms of Speech*); Sonnenschein; Taig; W. Young; Saintsbury; Croll. However, like Gendlin, who asks us to focus on the physical experience that he talks about, I would only ask you to focus on the physical experience of language as sound.

8. To illustrate this, let me use two simple examples from popular music here. Take these two words from "Tommy" by The Who.

Touch me.

Spoken, these two syllables have one accented beat, and scan as trochaic. However, as sung, they are noted musically something like this:

Touch   me ———

Musically, there are three beats on the syllable *me* for a total of four in 4/4 time; it's not only a difference of pitch, then, but also of time relations in music that can stretch and distort the natural rhythms and meters of speech into a different, musical relation.

These examples could be multiplied indefinitely. One more example of the opposite effect of music on language should suffice. Take these two words from "I Know What I Know" from Paul Simon's *Graceland*, which scan:

cinematographer's party

In these two words we have eight syllables, four beats, which scan dactylic. But as sung, these words are noted something like this:

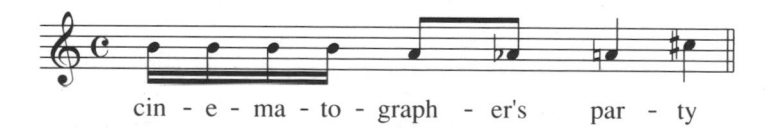

cin - e - ma - to - graph - er's   par - ty

Here, of course, the natural rhythm of the word "cinematographer's" is sped up and condensed—almost as if in a time warp—by the music, while the first syllable of the word "party" is again stretched out. Again, the natural meter of the words is altered by the music.

9. "The blanks break up the connectability of the schemata, and thus they marshall selected norms and perspective segments into a fragmented, counterfactual, contrastive or telescoped sequence nullifying any expectation of *good continuation*. As a result, the imagination is automatically mobilized, thus increasing the constitutive activity of the reader, who cannot help but try and supply the missing links that will bring the schemata together in an integrated gestalt" (Iser, *Act* 186).

10. See Hawking's *A Brief History of Time* for an in-depth understanding of the origin and relation of time to the spatial expansion of the physical universe. But as Penrose, Hawking's coworker, suggests,

> This symmetry between time and space would be even more striking for a *two*-dimensional space-time. The equations of two-dimensional space-time physics would be essentially symmetrical with respect to the interchange of space with time—yet nobody would take space to "flow" in two-dimensional physics. It is hard to believe that what makes time "actually flow" in our experiences of the physical world we know is merely the asymmetry between the number of space dimensions (3) and time dimensions (1) that our space-time happens to have. (444n.)

Also see *Motion and Time, Space and Matter: Interrelations in the History and Philosophy of Science*, Machamer and Turnbull, eds., for a philosophical and historical overview of the concept of time in scientific thought.

11. I am assuming here that time is not causal, either because it does not exist as the physio-spatial event in the world as it is currently depicted in both Newtonian physics and relativity theory, or because it represents a different kind of causality, a relationship that we do not yet comprehend. In fact, Zuckerkandl's vision of time in music suggests that it is the dimension of time that binds and unifies space: because time moves through different dimensions of space at once, it may allow different dimensions of space to exist as a simultaneous whole. Without time there would be no space (see n. 10 above). Perhaps this is what Einstein had in mind in making time a fourth dimension of space. Hypothetically, then, we should be able to travel great distances, not only by warping (crumpling) space but by accessing the dimension of time that flows through all the dimensions of space concurrently (unless there are multiple dimensions of time as well).

Or perhaps time is how we negotiate through space. Perhaps it is in and through time that we move through space—or rather, that time moves in and through us. This is Zuckerkandl's point, I think, when he probes the problem of motion resulting from the confusion of space and motion that I discuss in appendix D. Yet each dimension of space must affect time—or time manifests itself differently in each dimension of space. This could also be the reason that physical objects and consciousness seem to exist in different time orders, as Eliot and Penrose and Zuckerkandl all suggest: consciousness constitutes a different field, another dimension of space.

And yet we apprehend reality only spatially, with time being a spatial dimension (the dream of time travel itself is spatial—sequential). It would seem, then, that Kantian intuition is itself spatial—that space is a kind of master trope of the categories of pure intuition. However, this presents us with another problem: how can we even intuit that time is not causal or spatial? As Thomas Farrell discusses in his excellent review of *Orality and Literacy* in which Ong (166) makes reference to a discussion of Kant in an earlier work (*The Presence of the Word* 74):

> Ong suggests that Kant's distinction between phenomenon and noumenon is the byproduct of extreme visualism. This point of Ong's is worth explaining in some detail. Kant said that we can know only sensory data about a phenomenon, not the real thing already out there now (the noumenon). Now Ong notes that sight involves seeing only so far. There is always some point beyond which one cannot see. If one unwittingly used sight as the analogue for all knowing, one might say, as Kant does, that there is always something beyond that which we see/know, and one might then conclude that there is a noumenon we do not know. But if Kant knows there is a noumenon, then the noumenon can be known, contrary to his claim. On the other hand, if Kant does not know the noumenon, then on what grounds can he support his claim? Ong suggests that his claim presupposes sight to be the analogue for all knowing. I would suggest that modern idealism from Descartes to Derrida arises from extreme visualism: the over-dominance of sight results in the denigration and doubting of other sensory data, which in turn can lead one to doubt the existence of the already out there now real world. (364)

The "vision" of time told above is obviously beyond spatial sight, though perhaps not hearing. Thus, given the overdominance of sight, once again in history we are forced to choose, like Descartes, between our senses and our minds.

12. I think immediately of Thomas's poem "Fern Hill," whose theme is the passing of time, but much of whose meaning is affectively created not only by an inductive synthesis of images and metaphors related by associated concepts but also by the music of its language, the *tone* of each syllable as a sound image—pitch (the "highness" or "lowness" of a tone according to the number of vibrations per second); duration (the "length" of time the tone vibrates); dynamics (the "force" of a tone, i.e., the volume

of the vibration as described by decibels); timbre (the "quality" of the tone as vibration)—*in relation to each other.*

To help us tune our ears to words as tones, to understand tones singly and aside from their alliterative or rhythmical as well as semantic relations, one could begin by scanning the poem like this:

Now/as/I/was/young/and/ea/sy/un/der/the/ap/ple/boughs/
a/bout/the/lil/ting/house/and/hap/py/as/the/grass/was/green/

While there's no set pitch or scale in spoken language (though there seems to be one in the way Thomas performs this poem), one could present the pitch, duration, and dynamics of each tone through musical notation (see notes 7 and 8 above; cf. Bollinger 8; Croll; Lanier; Steele); one could even comment on the timbre, or the unique "sound-content"—not meaning, but letters, sound-shapes—of each word. However, to *hear* time of this poem, the tones must be heard in relation to each other. Listen to Thomas read this poem—or any poem—from another room with the door closed, at a volume where all you hear is tonality. As elementary as this level of understanding may seem—and is—it is important in that it already gives us a sense of words as phenomena of time, rather than as visual phenomena in space.

13. There are two epistemological problems with Zuckerkandl's book that are rooted in his phenomenological approach, and that for the sake of accuracy must be addressed, the first in this note, the second in the note below. The first problem concerns Zuckerkandl's understanding of the relationship between music and language. In asserting the nonreferential, temporal nature of music, Zuckerkandl unfortunately feels the need to assert that language is almost wholly referential. Now, it can be argued that his position on the nonreferentiality of music is necessary, since he must refute all the various claims that music is programmatic—that music refers to specific scenes or emotions—in order to examine the meaning of music on its own grounds, as a phenomenology of sound. But in arguing against what he sees as the positivistic approach to music, Zuckerkandl adopts a positivistic, spatial view of verbal language in which words have a one-to-one correspondence to referent (67). This view of language is reflected in his atomistic approach to word and meaning, which is the hallmark of the positivistic ideal: "the number of words, of the smallest meaning units of language, corresponds roughly to the number of things" (68).

For Zuckerkandl, the difference between language and music is that the word indicates or stands for its referent, while the tone can only indicate or stand for itself. The primary difference, then, between language and music "would appear to lie in the different capacity of word and tone to act as the medium of time perception" (Zuckerkandl 220). Tone "clears our sight for the perception of time as such, of time as event. The word has no such virtue" (220). While not denying that language has a strong referential component, I must disagree with Zuckerkandl's assertion as it stands. Language perhaps could clear our sight for the perception of time if approached differently, temporally rather than spatially (cf. Gallehr, "Writing and Meditation"). Zuckerkandl does seem to make an exception for poetic language, "where other musical relations come into play" (67). But the effect of this distinction is then to continue the positivistic notion of language and knowledge.

Zuckerkandl states as proof of the exclusively referential nature of language that languages can be translated while music cannot. Yet it is a well-known fact that something is always lost in translation. Perhaps a part of what is lost is the affect and nuance of meaning contained in the music of the original language as a sensuous, temporal form. This of course is especially true in translations of poetry. But, based on the relation of poetry and prose in the theories of the sophists and Cicero, it is true of all language in that all language is sensuous, a resymbolization of experience that is auditory and physical, as well as spatial and referential.

Zuckerkandl drives a wedge between music and language, between feeling and thinking: "Thinking and music are not made for each other; music is for feeling, not for thought" (6). Given the new philosophy of language and knowledge that is emerging, I find this wedge untenable. For if, as Elbow intimates ("Shifting"), writing as speech involves temporal as well as spatial patterns and relationships that underlie structure and coherence, we can begin to understand those indeterminate temporal patterns and relationships—indeterminate because knowledge in time and time itself are indeterminate—as a musical experience, one that can help us understand the disequilibrium and dissonance we feel in reading out loud and facilitate the transfer of this understanding to the felt sense of writing. We can begin to understand voice as multidimensional, as the sound of time, rather than three- dimensional, as a page of space.

14. The second problem is that for Zuckerkandl music is wholly external. That is, Zuckerkandl refuses to consider the temporal meaning of music in terms of human perception and human emotion (as well as in terms of the science of acoustics, as a physical phenomenon). For Zuckerkandl, terms like *expectation, equilibrium, tension,* and *attraction* are based on associations and can only give us a general conception of the phenomenon of music as a dynamic system (36). In fact, in a section on "Associationism," Zuckerkandl seeks to refute the very idea that we learn by association. Zuckerkandl defines association as "typical connections and sequences that we continually accompany with corresponding sensations of tension and relaxation, expectations and fulfillment"; thus, says Zuckerkandl, "the entire tonal system is understood by most psycholo-

gists as a projection of variously oriented and graduated expectations and fulfillments" (113). Based on his phenomenology of music, Zuckerkandl will have none of this.

This denial of associationism, however, threatens to undermine the attempt to find the musical principles that underlie temporal affective processes in reading and writing as oral phenomena. For clearly, reading and writing do not exist independently of reader and writer. (Neither, I would argue, does music from the listener or the composer as performers.) Language must be understood in relation to referentiality and/or affective experience to have any meaning. So must music. But Zuckerkandl makes a clear distinction between the emotion that results from the sensation of a tone and "the dynamic qualities that appear in musical tone" (58). Zuckerkandl repeatedly asserts that it is *not* "the hearer who makes the music" (44).

Given this assertion, Zuckerkandl is forced to continue the split between inner and outer, between the subjective and objective that Plato and Descartes maintained, a split that Zuckerkandl himself decries (274–75; 368–70). Because Zuckerkandl holds that musical tone cannot be described by either physical or psychological terms, he is forced to posit a third realm between the two, a phenomenological realm of pure dynamics (60–61), just as, in denying the world of the senses and of language, Plato had to posit an ideal realm of Forms. Ironically, in reacting to the positivistic approach to music, then, Zuckerkandl can be seen to be making the same kind of epistemological move in music theory that Eliot and Tate made in literary theory (discussed in ch. 2 and appendix A). In denying the referentiality of their art and collapsing form and content into Form, they all posit a pure dynamic realm of value.

Zuckerkandl never once considers the possibility of the interaction of the physical and psychological, a "transactional" view of music (and time), as do Reader Response critics in regard to the meaning of a text. Rather, like Eliot (*Knowledge and Experience* 109–11), he maintains there are different orders of experience based on different orders of time; unlike Eliot, he assumes we know which one is real, to which one perception must correspond. Thus, while Zuckerkandl's theory can give us an understanding of music as time (or time as music), as a dynamic system of tonalities, rhythms, and meters, it does not explain how in language these relate to the intuitive aesthetic faculty of speech that Cicero considered basic to eloquence.

15. "The processes of organic life, the processes within an atom, the structures of crystals, the imperceptible shifting of continents on the earth's surface, the revolutions of the celestial bodies, the nebular formations in the depths of the universe—all these, and what not besides, has been called rhythmical. In the animate as well as inanimate, in the microscopic as in the macrocosm, nature has revealed dispositions to which no

concept is better adapted than that of rhythm. Rightly has it been said that rhythm is one manifestation of the law throughout the universe" (Zuckerkandl 158; cf. Barfield 146–47).

16. E.g., Hoover, "Prose Rhythm: A Theory of Proportional Distribution." With the exception of Bollinger, most studies of "the music of language" focus on metrical or linguistic analysis of the sound rather than the experience of the effect, the relation of sound to consciousness. Thus, most analyses of prose rhythm remain mired in problems of meter. But as Croll remarks, the music of language must be studied holistically (431). Like Zuckerkandl, who argues that the essence of music is motion in time, Croll argues that it is in its "time relations" that the phenomenon of the rhythm of language exists (429–30). That is, the meaning of the musical dimension of language exists in the temporal dimension of affect, not the spatial dimension of referential meaning or measured beats.

17. Although this may seem extreme, even a little nonsensical, Zuckerkandl is attempting, against the tide of space, to make a valid point about the temporal nature of musical structure, one that stands in contradistinction to the predominantly spatial notion of structure (even of music), which could apply to the level of language as sound as it counterpoints referential meaning. Certainly there is some truth in the statement that "any turning back of consciousness for the purpose of making past one's present immediately annuls the possibility of musical hearing" (231). If we do not experience music in the present, we do not really experience it, for as sound it only exists in the present. For Zuckerkandl, expectation is not "foreknowledge or forefeeling" (231). In fact, Zuckerkandl states that this kind of expectation in which "one simultaneously imagines the future event which will satisfy the expectation—is foreign to the hearing of melodies and, indeed, is incompatible with it" (231–32). As some listening research suggests (e.g., Rost, "Section I: Attentive Listening"), memory, loosely defined, can interfere with present hearing, as we see in our daydreaming students. But can memory be divorced from listening? Doesn't memory enable comprehension? (see Anderson and Lynch; Rost; Ur). We will take these questions up in the next chapter.

5. Toward a Conclusion of Indeterminacy

1. The fundamental difference between Zuckerkandl and Meyer is where they situate the gestalten of music. For Zuckerkandl, musical gestalten are outside human experience and perception, are created and constituted in the work itself as a dynamic whole. For Meyer, on the other hand, musical gestalten are situated in human experience and perception as patterns on which both the creation and the perception of the work depends. Unlike those Meyer calls "absolutists," for whom the discussion

of emotions is altogether anathema, Meyer seeks "to account for the processes by which perceived sound patterns become experienced as feelings and emotions" (4). It is this relationship between perceived pattern and emotional experience that we probably should try to understand in reading and writing as an oral/aural, temporal performance.

2. For Krashen, acquisition is the natural, unconscious process of learning language through inference; learning is a formal, conscious process of acquiring and using language through analysis, rules, procedures, and so forth (cf. Ochsner 13, who makes a similar point about writing).

3. The correspondence theory of sound was most notably subscribed to by the French symbolist poet Rimbaud, for whom vowels connoted colors (e.g., o = black, e = green, u = blue, i = white, etc.). But for Cassirer, the "meaning of sound" seems not completely universal in language (cf. *Cratylus*) nor wholly subjective in *a* language, but both. For Cassirer, the relation between sound and sensory objects is subjective in the sense that in the origination of language and consciousness (historical and personal) the sounds of language literally imitate the *qualities* of objects—sensory impressions or emotions, not the object itself. "The beginnings of phonetic language seem to be embedded in that sphere of mimetic representation and designation which lies at the base of sign language," Cassirer states; "Here sound seeks to approach the sensory impression and reproduce the diversity as faithfully as possible" (190). Thus, in discussing this relationship between sensuous form and the qualities of physical objects in the world, Cassirer cites the work on the symbolic value of sound of Humboldt, the nineteenth-century philosopher of language, whom he greatly admires: "*st* regularly designates the impression of the enduring and stable, the sound *l* that of the melting and fluid, the sound *v* the impression of uneven, vacillating motion" (192). For Cassirer, the relation between sound and sensory objects is subjective insofar as "the use of certain differences and gradations of vowels to express greater or lesser distance of an object from the speaker is a phenomenon occurring in the most diverse languages and linguistic groups" (193).

Although this sounds plausible, given the sophistic understanding of the power of language to evoke reality through a kind of synesthesia of the senses, one must wonder to what extent these associations of sounds and qualities are cultural connotations acquired through socialization (such as in onomatopoeia), rather than inherent in any specific relationship between word and thing. It would also appear that the relation of sound to sense is also local (and subjective) in that it is partly dependent on meaningful context and partly on the perceptual experience of the reader/listener, as illustrated, for instance, by differences in the meaning of alliteration. The following lines are taken from "Fern Hill" by Dylan Thomas, *Profiles in Courage* by John F. Kennedy, and "The Castle of Indolence" by James Thomson (the second and third examples are found in Corbett,

Classical Rhetoric 436). Read these out loud slowly and enunciate the sound of each word as clearly as possible:

"And the Sabbath rang slowly in the pebbles of the holy streams."

"Already American vessels had been searched, seized, and sunk."

"A sable, silent, solemn forest stood."

In each example, notice the different "sound effect" created by the alliterative *S* sound, depending on context. For me, in the first case, *S* creates the sound of water running through the sentence. In second case, it is not the *S* of holy water that we hear but the hiss of anger and the sound of sinking, burning ships. In the third case, *S* mimics the hiss of silence we might hear in the forest, created by a subtle, steady breeze in the tops of the trees. But the relationship between sound and meaning is not the level of language Cassirer is talking about; rather, Cassirer is interested in *the origins* of language as a sensuous form. For Cassirer, language as a symbolic form gradually moves away from this mimetic imitation in order to express more formal relations. In this new, abstract relationship between sound and the thing imitated, "the word gains its inner freedom by the very fact that in it this connection between the word and the character of "things" is broken off." As "the disembodied element of spoken sound," the word "can no longer immediately reproduce the being of objects" (185).

4. For instance, in arguing for social interaction that leads to the internalization of response and subsequent cognitive growth (decentering), Moffett opposed imitation to the process of social interaction that he advocates as the basis of language learning and writing instruction. Thus, Moffett concludes, "[I]nteraction is a more important learning process than imitation, whatever the age of the learner" (*Universe of Discourse* 71–72). But when reading is taught in terms of secondary orality, there is less of a separation between social interaction and imitation. Reading out loud is an oral response that is internalized. Like Reader Response critics, Moffett does not make the connection between reading out loud and social interaction as processes of imitation. This is understandable, given the powerful epistemology they are trying to refute. But if interaction results in internalization, so does reading out loud, for both are oral and social in nature.

5. The sensuous form of symbols through which the manifestation of inhibitions and drives are constituted in both consciousness and speech begins in social interaction with and response to parents. As Cassirer explains, "[I]n the development of children's speech, the articulated sound breaks away only very gradually from the totality of mimetic move-

ment; even at relatively advanced stages, it remains embedded in this totality. But once the separation is accomplished, language has acquired a new fundamental principle in the new element in which it now moves" (184). Imitation of sound and its internalization in consciousness is inseparable. Thus, according to Cassirer, the early development of language and thought is intimately related to the development of speech organs. But if the articulation of words, and with them the formation of concepts in consciousness, must wait for the further development of the speech organs, the further development of speech organs is also made possible by the simultaneous development of consciousness. "The articulation of sounds now becomes an instrument for the articulation of thoughts, while the latter creates for itself a more and more differentiated and sensitive organ in the elaboration and formation of these sounds" (Cassirer 184).

In Cassirer's philosophy of language we can, then, discern a sort of Piagetian map of the early stages of cognitive development, but one rooted in the physical nature of speech. In fact, for Cassirer, it is the "fluidity" and suppleness of spoken sound that gives speech "an entirely new capacity for configuration, making it capable of expressing not only rigid representative contents but the most subtle vibrations and nuances of the presentative *process*" (184–85). The imitation of sound patterns, and thus of *musical gestalten*, perhaps has much to do with how children learn language. That is, children learn language (both individual words and syntax) by imitating and delighting in sensuality of speech: the tonality and rhythm of sounds, the physical articulation of letters and words, the dynamic, musical patterns of syntax and sentence. Of course, children begin to imitate and learn sound before, as well as subsequent to, the ability to understand the symbolic or semantic or even pragmatic content and import of what they're saying. They do this, as Cicero might say, for the pleasure that is dictated by the ear, as well as trying to influence the minds of their audience—that is, their parents.

6. Although Brown acknowledges that speech is different from music in that speech attaches external referents to sound whereas music does not, he strives to show the relationship between rhythm and pitch; timbre, harmony, and counterpoint; repetition and variation; and balance and contrast; theme and variations in music and literature. He also discusses the various settings of vocal music and the problem presented by opera, literary/poetic forms, and different types of "programmatic" music in a way that supplements my earlier discussion of the shapes of aesthetic response in reading and writing generally.

7. This is especially clear in a chapter in *Feeling and Form* entitled "Poesis," in which Langer considers poetry as a symbolic form. Like the other arts she has considered—painting, music, dance—Langer regards poetry as presentational, nondiscursive. "The poet uses discourse to create an illusion, a pure appearance, which is a non-discursive, symbolic form"

(211). But for Langer, "the poem 'exists' objectively whenever it is presented to us, instead of coming into being only when somebody makes 'certain integrated responses' to what the poet is saying" (211). Thus, like so many literary critics of her time, the differences in a reader's response are not Langer's primary concern (212). She is only concerned with the poet as "maker" of the articulated form and the illusion as an objective *gestalt* itself.

8. "A reading is a performance. The reader must understand what he performs. To avoid the monotone haste . . . the voice must vary pitch, something Americans find hateful to do. Emphasis must be added, tone considered. The reader, that is, must pick up a spirit in which to read. He must choose a relationship with the audience. Sentences must be shaped by the intonation. In long passages, a longer rhythm of thought or argument will emerge, as well as the shorter rhythm of individual sentences. Reading out loud, that is, renders a style, in our sense of the word, opaque. The stylistic surface must be pondered, unavoidably. The sing-song monotone, rhythmical counterpoint to the scientific attitude, does not clarify concepts; it obscures them" (Lanham 100).

Works Cited

Anderson, Anne, and Tony Lynch. *Listening*. Oxford: Oxford UP, 1988.

Anderson, Philip M., and Gregory Rubano. *Enhancing Aesthetic Reading and Response*. Urbana, IL: NCTE, 1991.

Anson, Chris M., ed. *Writing and Response: Theory, Practice, Research*. Urbana, IL: NCTE, 1989.

Aristotle. *Nicomachean Ethics*. Trans. W. D. Ross. *Introduction to Aristotle*. Ed. Richard McKeon. New York: Modern Library, 1947.

———. *The Rhetoric*. Trans. W. Rhys Roberts and I. Bywater. *The Rhetoric and Poetics of Aristotle*. New York: Modern Library, 1954, 1–218.

Austin, Gilbert. *Chironomia; or, A Treatise on Rhetorical Delivery*. Ed. Mary Margaret Robb and Lester Thonssen. Carbondale: Southern Illinois UP, 1966.

Ayer, A. J. *Language, Truth and Logic*. New York: Dover, 1952.

Bacon, Francis. *The Advancement of Learning*. 1605. Vol. 3 of *The Works of Francis Bacon*. Ed. Spedding, Ellis, and Heath. New York: Longman, 1859.

Bacon, Wallace. "The Act of Literature and the Act of Interpretation." Fernandez 1–7.

———. *The Art of Interpretation*. 3rd ed. New York: Holt, 1979.

Baer, Eugene M. "An Evaluation of Integrating Literature in the Composition Class." Paper presented at the Conference on College Composition and Communication. St. Louis, MO, March 17–19, 1988.

Bakhtin Mikhail (V. N. Voloshinov). *Marxism and the Philosophy of Language*. Trans. Ladislav Matejka and I. R. Titunik. New York: Seminar Press.

Bales, Allen. "Oral Interpretation: An Extension of Literary Study." Fernandez 21–27.

Barfield, Owen. *Poetic Diction: A Study in Meaning*. New York: McGraw-Hill, 1964.

Barkas, P. *A Critique of Modern English Prosody (1880–1930)*. Halle: Max Niemeyer Verlag, 1934.

Barrett, William. *The Illusion of Technique*. New York: Doubleday, 1978.

Bazerman, Charles. "Scientific Writing as a Social Act: A Review of the Literature of the Sociology of Science." *New Essays in Scientific and Technical Communication*. Ed. P. Anderson, R. Brochmann, and C. Miller. Farmingdale, NY: Baywood, 1983. 156–84.

Beach, Richard. "The Literary Response Process of College Freshmen." *The English Record* 2 (1973): 98–116.

———. *A Teacher's Introduction to Reader Response Theories*. Urbana, IL: NCTE, 1993.

Beach, Richard, and Susan Hynds. *Research on the Learning and Teaching of Literature: Selected Bibliography*. Albany, NY: Center for the Learning and Teaching of Literature, 1989.

Beloof, Robert, Chester Clayton Long, Seymour Chatman, Thomas O. Sloan, and Mark S. Kyyn. *The Oral Study of Literature*. New York: Random, 1966.

Benson, Thomas W., and Michael H. Prosser. *Readings in Classical Rhetoric*. Bloomington: Indiana UP, 1969.

Berlin, James A. "Rhetoric and Ideology in the Writing Classroom." *College English* 50 (1988): 477–94.

———. "Rhetoric and Poetics in the English Department: Our Nineteenth-Century Inheritance." *College English* 47 (1985): 521–33.

———. "Richard Whately and Current-Traditional Rhetoric." *College English* 42 (1980): 10–17.

Berry, Wendell. *Standing by Words: Essays*. San Francisco: North Point, 1983.

Bertram, Jean DeSales. *The Oral Experience of Literature: Sense, Structure, and Sound*. San Francisco: Chandler, 1967.

Biddle, Arthur W., and Toby Fulwiler, eds. *Reading, Writing, and the Study of Literature*. Manchester, MO: McGraw, 1989.

Bizzell, Patricia. "Arguing about Literacy." *College English* 50 (1988): 141–157.

———. "Beyond Anti-Foundationalism to Rhetorical Authority: Problems Defining 'Cultural Literacy.' " *College English* 52 (1990): 661–75.

———. "Foundationalism and Anti-Foundationalism in Composition Studies." *Pre/Text* 7 (1986): 37–56.

———. Response to Walter J. Ong's "A Comment on 'Arguing About Literacy.' " *College English* 50 (1988): 701–02.

Bizzell, Patricia, and Bruce Herzberg. *The Rhetorical Tradition: Readings from Classical Times to the Present*. Boston: Bedford Books of St. Martin's P, 1990.

Blackmur, R. P. *Form and Value in Modern Poetry.* New York: Doubleday, 1957.

Blake, Robert W., ed. *Reading, Writing, and Interpreting Literature: Pedagogy, Positions, and Research.* New York: State English Council, 1989.

Bleich, David. "Cognitive Stereoscopy and the Study of Language and Literature." *Convergences: Transactions in Reading and Writing.* 99–114.

———. "Discerning Motives in Language Use." *Composition and Literature: Bridging the Gap.* Ed. W. B. Horner. Chicago: U of Chicago P, 1983. 81–95.

———. *The Double Perspective: Language, Literacy, and Social Relations.* New York: Oxford UP, 1988. Urbana: NCTE, 1993.

———. "The Identity of Pedagogy and Research in the Study of Response to Literature." *College English* 42 (1980): 350–66.

———. *Subjective Criticism.* Baltimore: Johns Hopkins UP, 1978.

Bloom, Allan. *The Closing of the American Mind.* Simon, 1987.

Bohr, Niels. *Atomic Physics and Human Reality.* New York: Wiley, 1958.

Bollinger, Dwight. *Intonation and Its Parts: Melody in Spoken English.* Stanford, CA: Stanford UP, 1986.

Booth, Wayne C. *The Company We Keep: An Ethics of Fiction.* Berkeley: U of California P, 1988.

———. *Modern Dogma and the Rhetoric of Assent.* Chicago: U of Chicago P, 1974.

Boulding, Kenneth E. *The Image: Knowledge in Life and Society.* Ann Arbor: U of Michigan P, 1956.

Bowen, Elbert Russell. *Communicative Reading.* New York: Macmillan, 1978.

Bowerstock, G. W. *Greek Sophists in the Roman Empire.* Oxford: Clarendon, 1969.

Boyd, R. "Metaphor and Theory Change: What Is 'Metaphor' a Metaphor For?" Ortony 356–408.

Brand, Alice G. "Defining Our Emotional Life: Valuative System—a Continuum Theory." *Presence of Mind: Writing and the Domain of Cognitive.* Ed. Alice G. Brand and Richard Graves. Portsmouth, NH: Heinemann, 1994.

———. *The Psychology of Writing: The Affective Experience.* New York: Greenwood P, 1989.

Brandt, Deborah. "Social Foundations of Reading and Writing." *Convergences: Transactions in Reading and Writing.* 115–26.

Britton, James. "The Composing Processes and the Functions of Writing." *Research On Composing: Points of Departure.* Ed. Charles R. Cooper and Lee Odell. Urbana, IL: NCTE, 1978. 13–28.

Britton, James, et al. *The Development of Writing Abilities (11–18).* 1975. New York: Macmillan, 1978.

Brock, Werner. Introduction. *Existence and Being*. By Martin Heidegger. 2–231.

Bronowksi, Jacob. *The Origins of Knowledge and Imagination*. New Haven: Yale UP, 1978.

Brooks, Cleanth. *The Well Wrought Urn: Studies in the Structure of Poetry*. New York: Harcourt, 1947.

Brown, Calvin S. *Music and Literature: A Comparison of the Arts*. Athens: U of Georgia P, 1948.

Brown, Richard Harvey. "Reason as Rhetorical: On Relations among Epistemology, Discourse, and Practice." Nelson et al. 184–97.

Brummet, Barry. "Some Implications of 'Process' or 'Intersubjectivity': Postmodern Rhetoric." *Philosophy and Rhetoric* 9 (1976): 21–51.

Buber, Martin. *I and Thou*. Trans. Walter Kaufmann. New York: Scribner's, 1970.

Buchanan, Scott. *Poetry and Mathematics*. 1929. Chicago: U of Chicago P, 1962. Midway rpt. 1975.

Burke, Kenneth. *A Rhetoric of Motives*. New York: Prentice, 1952.

Cain, William. *Crisis in Criticism: Theory, Literature, and Reform in English Studies*. Baltimore: Johns Hopkins UP, 1984.

Capra, Fritjof. *The Tao of Physics*. New York: Bantam, 1975.

Carnap, Rudolf. *Logical Foundations of Probability*. Chicago: U of Chicago P, 1950.

Carter, Michael F. "The Ritual Functions of Epideictic Rhetoric:The Case of Socrates' Funeral Oration." *Rhetorica* 9 (1991): 209–32.

Cassirer, Ernst. *The Philosophy of Symbolic Forms*. Vol. 1. *Language*. Trans. Ralph Manheim. New Haven: Yale UP, 1955. 3 vols.

Chapman, Rev. J. *The Music, or Melody and Rhythmus of Language*. . . . Edinburgh: Anderson, 1818.

Cicero, Marcus Tullius. *Brutus, Orator*. Trans. G. L. Henderson and H. M. Hubbell. Cambridge, MA: Loeb Classical Library, 1939.

———. *De Inventione, De Optimo Genre Oratorum, Topica*. Trans. H. M. Hubbell. Cambridge, MA: Loeb, 1942.

———. *De Oratore*, Books I–II. Trans. E. W. Sutton and H. Rackham. 2 vols. Cambridge, MA: Loeb, 1942.

———. *De Oratore*, Book III. In *De Oratore Book III, De Fato, Paradoxa Stoicorum, Partitiones Oratoriae*. Trans. E. W. Sutton and H. Rackham. Cambridge, MA: Loeb, 1942. 1–185.

Cohen, Edwin. *Oral Interpretation: The Communication of Literature*. Chicago: Science Research Associates, 1977.

Coles, Thomas. *The Origins of Rhetoric in Ancient Greece*. Baltimore: Johns Hopkins UP, 1991.

Conley, Thomas M. *Rhetoric in the European Tradition*. New York: Longman, 1990.

Connolly, John M., and Thomas Keutner. Introduction. *Hermeneutics Ver-*

sus *Science? Three German Views.* Ed. Connolly and Keutner. Notre Dame, IN: U of Notre Dame P, 1988.

Connors, Robert J. "Composition Studies and Science." *College English* 45 (1983): 1–20.

Cooper, Charles R., and Lee Odell. "Considerations of Sound in the Composing Process of Published Writers." *Research in the Teaching of English* 10 (1980): 103–15.

Cooper, Marilyn, and Michael Holzman. "Talking about Protocols." *College Composition and Communication* 34 (1983): 284–93.

Corbett, Edward P. J. *Classical Rhetoric for the Modern Student.* 3rd ed. New York: Oxford UP, 1990.

———. "The Theory and Practice of Imitation in Classical Rhetoric." Graves 303–12.

Corbin, Alain. *The Foul and the Fragrant: Odor and the French Social Imagination.* Cambridge: Harvard UP, 1986.

Cornford, Francis MacDonald. *Plato and Parmenides.* Indianapolis: Bobbs, 1956.

Croll, Morris W. *Style, Rhetoric, and Rhythm.* Ed. J. Max Patrick, Robert O. Evans, with John M. Wallace and R. J. Schoeck. Princeton: Princeton UP, 1966. Rpt. Woodbridge, CT: Ox Bow, 1989.

Culler, Jonathan. *The Pursuit of Signs: Semiotics, Literature, Deconstruction.* Ithaca: Cornell UP, 1981.

Cytowic, Richard E. *The Man Who Tasted Shapes.* New York: Putnam Books, 1993.

Dabney, J. P. *The Musical Basis of Verse.* New York: Longmans, 1901.

De Rivera, Joseph. "Emotional Experience and Qualitative Method." *American Behavioral Scientist* 27 (1984): 677–88.

Derrida, Jacques. *Of Grammatology.* Trans. Gayatri Chakravorty Spivak. Baltimore: Johns Hopkins UP, 1974.

Descartes, René. *Discourse on the Method of Rightly Conducting the Reason.* 1637. Chicago: Encyclopedia Britannica, 1952.

Diels, H., and W. Kranz. *Die Fragmente der Vorsokratiker.* 7th ed. 3 vols. Berlin: Weidmann Verlag, 1951–54.

DiLorenzo, Raymond. "The Critique of Socrates in Cicero's *De Oratore*: *Ornatus* and the Nature of Wisdom." *Philosophy and Rhetoric* 11 (1978): 247–61.

Dobler, Judith M. "Facts, Figures, and Fictions: A Heuristic for Reading and Teaching Figuration." Teaching Guide (052), ERIC Clearing House on Reading and Communication Skills, 1989. ED0301844 CS009425.

Dougherty, Barbey. "Writing Plans as Strategies for Reading, Writing, and Revising." *Convergences: Transactions in Reading and Writing.* 82–96.

Dreyfus, Hubert L. *What Computers Can't Do: The Limits of Artificial Intelligence.* Rev. ed. New York: Harper, 1972.

Eagleton, Terry. *Literary Theory: An Introduction*. Minneapolis: U of Minnesota P, 1983.

Eco, Umberto. *The Limits of Interpretation*. Bloomington: Indiana UP, 1990.

———. *The Role of the Reader: Explorations in the Semiotics of Texts*. Bloomington: Indiana UP, 1979.

Edwards, Paul, ed. *The Encyclopedia of Philosophy*. Vol. 3. New York: MacMillan, 1967. 8 vols.

Einstein, Albert. *Relativity: The Special and the General Theory*. Trans. R. W. Lawson. New York: Crown, 1961.

Elbow, Peter. "The Shifting Relationships Between Speech and Writing." *College Composition and Communication*: 36 (1985): 283–303.

———. *What Is English?* New York: MLA, 1990.

———. *Writing with Power*. New York: Oxford, 1981.

———. *Writing Without Teachers*. New York: Oxford UP, 1973.

Eliot, T. S. "The Frontiers of Criticism." *On Poetry and Poets*. 113–31.

———. "The Function of Criticism." *Selected Essays*. 12–22.

———. "Hamlet and His Problems." *Selected Essays*. 121–26.

———. *Knowledge and Experience in the Philosophy of F. H. Bradley*. New York: Farrar, 1964. Rpt. Columbia UP, 1989.

———. "Literature and Religion." *Selected Essays*. 343–54.

———. "The Music of Poetry." *On Poetry and Poets*. 17–33.

———. *On Poetry and Poets*. New York: Noonday, 1943.

———. "The Perfect Critic." *The Sacred Wood: Essays on Poetry and Criticism*. London: Methuen, 1920. 1–16.

———. *Selected Essays*. New York: Harcourt, 1964.

———. "Tradition and the Individual Talent." *The Sacred Wood*. 1920. 47–59. Rpt. in *Selected Essays*. 3–11.

Ellul, Jacques. *The Technological Society*. Trans. John Wilkinson. New York: Knopf, 1964.

Emig, Janet. "Writing as a Mode of Learning." *College Composition and Communication* 28 (1977): 122–27.

Enos, Richard Leo. "The Composing Process of the Sophist: New Directions (and Cautions) for Composition Research." Paper delivered at the Conference on College Composition. Atlanta, GA, March 19–21, 1987.

———. "The Epistemology of Gorgias' Rhetoric: A Re-Examination." *Southern Speech Communication Journal* 42 (1976): 35–51.

———. *Greek Rhetoric Before Aristotle*. Prospect Heights, IL: Waveland, 1993.

———. *The Literate Mode of Cicero's Legal Rhetoric*. Carbondale: Southern Illinois UP, 1988.

———, ed. *Oral and Written Communication: Historical Approaches*. Newbury Park, CA: Sage, 1990.

———. Rev. of *Rhetorical Traditions and the Teaching of Writing*, by C. H.

Knoblauch and Lil Brannon. *College Composition and Communication* 37 (1986): 502–03.

———. "Rhetorical Theory and Sophistic Composition: A Reconstruction." Report of the 1985 National Endowment for the Humanities Summer Stipend.

Enos, Richard Leo, and Jeanne L. McClaran. "Audience and Image in Ciceronian Rome: Creation and Constraints of the *Vir Bonus* Personality." *Central States Speech Journal* 29 (Summer 1978): 98–106.

Fahnestock, Jeanne. "Accommodating Science: The Rhetorical Life of Scientific Facts." *Written Communication* 3 (1986): 275–96.

Farnan, Nancy. "Critical Reading and Writing Through a Reader Response Approach." *Writing Teacher* 2 (1989): 36–38.

Farnsworth, Rodney. "How the Other Half Sounds: An Historical Survey of Musical Rhetoric During the Baroque and After." *Rhetoric Society Quarterly* 20 (1990): 207–24.

Farrell, Thomas J. Rev. of *Orality and Literacy: The Technologizing of the Word*, by Walter J. Ong. *College Composition and Communication* 36 (1985): 363–65.

Fenstermaker, John J. "Literature in the Composition Classroom." *College Composition and Communication* 28 (1977): 34–37.

Fernandez, Thomas L. *Oral Interpretation and the Teaching of English: A Collection of Readings*. Champaign, IL: NCTE, 1969.

Feyerabend, Paul. *Against Method*. London: Verso, 1978.

———. "Consolations for the Specialist." *Criticism and the Growth of Knowledge*. Ed. Imre Lakatos and Alan Musgrave. Cambridge, England: Cambridge UP, 1970. 197–230.

———. *Farewell to Reason*. London: Verso, 1987.

Fish, Stanley. "Demonstration vs. Persuasion: Two Models of Critical Activity." *Is There a Text in This Class*. 356–71.

———. "How to Do Things with Austin and Searle: Speech Act Theory and Literary Criticism." *Is There a Text in This Class*. 197–245.

———. "Interpreting the *Variorum*." *Is There a Text in This Class*. 147–73.

———. "Introduction, or How I Stopped Worrying and Learned to Love Interpretation." *Is There a Text in This Class*. 1–17.

———. *Is There a Text in This Class: The Authority of Interpretive Communities*. Cambridge: Harvard UP, 1980.

———. "Literature in the Reader: Affective Stylistics." *Is There a Text in This Class*. 21–67.

Fisher, Walter R. *Human Communication as Narration: Toward a Philosophy of Reason, Value, and Action*. Columbia: U of South Carolina P, 1987.

Flower, Linda. "Decision Points: Where Cognition and Attitude Intersect." Paper presented at the Conference on College Composition and Communication. Seattle, WA, March 16–18, 1989.

———. *Problem Solving Strategies for Writing*. New York: Harcourt, 1981.

———. "Writer-Based Prose: A Cognitive Basis for Problems in Writing." *College English* 41 (1979): 19–37.

Flower, Linda, David L. Wallace, Linda Norris, and Rebecca E. Burnett, eds. *Making Thinking Visible: Writing, Collaborative Planning, and Classroom Inquiry.* Urbana, IL: NCTE, 1993.

Foucault, Michel. *The Order of Things: An Archaeology of the Human Sciences.* New York: Random, 1970.

Freeman, Kathleen. *Ancilla to the Presocratic Philosophers: A Complete Translation of the Fragments in Diels, Fragmente der Vorsokratiker.* Cambridge: Harvard UP, 1948.

Frost, Robert. *Poetry and Prose.* Ed. Edward Connery Lathem and Lawrence Thompson. New York: Holt, 1972.

Gadamer, Hans-Georg. *Truth and Method.* New York: Seabury, 1975.

Gallehr, Don. "Writing and Meditation: A Closer Look at Allied Practices." *Life-Studies* 4 (Winter 1988): 24–29.

Geiger, Don. *The Dramatic Impulse in Modern Poetics.* Baton Rouge: Louisiana State UP, 1967.

Gendlin, Eugene T. *Experiencing and the Creation of Meaning: A Philosophical and Psychological Approach to the Subjective.* New York: Free Press of Glencoe, 1962.

———. *Focusing.* New York: Everest House, 1978.

Gibson, Walker. *Tough, Sweet and Stuffy: An Essay on Modern American Prose Styles.* Bloomington: Indiana UP, 1966.

Gilligan, Carol. *In a Different Voice: Psychological Theory and Women's Development.* Cambridge: Harvard UP, 1982.

Gillispie, Charles Coulston. *The Edge of Objectivity: An Essay in the History of Scientific Ideas.* Princeton: Princeton UP, 1960.

Goetz, Ernest T., et al. "Getting a Reading on Reader Response: Relationships Between Ratings, Recall, and Imagery Reports." Paper presented at the Annual Meeting of the Southwest Educational Research Association. Austin, TX, January 25–27, 1990.

———. "The Structure of Emotional Response in Reading: Quantitative and Qualitative Analyses." Paper presented at the Annual Meeting of the Southwest Educational Research Association. Austin, TX, Jan. 25–27, 1990.

Gombrich, E. H. *Art and Illusion: A Study of the Psychology of Pictorial Representation.* Princeton: Princeton UP, 1960.

Gottlieb, Marvin. *Oral Interpretation.* New York: McGraw, 1980.

Graff, Gerald. *Literature Against Itself: Literary Ideas in Modern Society.* Chicago: U of Chicago P, 1979.

Graves, Richard L., ed. *Rhetoric and Composition: A Sourcebook for Teachers.* Rochelle Park, NJ: Hayden, 1976.

Gray, Farnum, and George C. Mager. *Liberating Education: Psychological Learning Through Improvisational Drama.* Berkeley, CA: McCutchan Publishing, 1973.

Greene, Maxine. "Language, Literature, and the Release of Meaning."
College English 41 (1979): 123–34.
Grimaldi, William M. A. *Studies in the Philosophy of Aristotle's Rhetoric.*
Weisbaden: Franz Steiner Verlag GMBH, 1972.
Gross, Alan G. "The Form of the Experimental Paper: A Realization of
the Myth of Induction." *Journal of Technical Writing and Communica-
tion* 15 (1985): 15–26.
Haas, Richard Burton. *The Study of Oral Interpretation: Theory and Com-
ment.* Indianapolis: Bobbs, 1975.
Habermas, Jurgen. "Technology and Science as 'Ideology.' " Trans.
Jeremy Shapiro. *Toward a Rational Society: Student Protest, Science,
and Politics.* Boston: Beacon, 1970. 81–127.
Hagaman, John. Rev. of *Rhetorical Traditions and the Teaching of Writing,*
by C. H. Knoblauch and Lil Brannon. *Rhetoric Society Quarterly* 15
(1985): 39–43.
Halloran, S. Michael. Rev. of *Rhetorical Traditions and the Teaching of Writing,* by C. H. Knoblauch and Lil Brannon. *College Composition and
Communication* 37 (1986): 503–05.
Halloran, S. Michael, and Annette Norris Bradford. "Figures of Speech
in the Rhetoric of Science and Technology." *Essays on Classical Rheto-
ric and Modern Discourse.* Ed. Robert J. Connors, Lisa S. Ede, and
Andrea A. Lunsford. Carbondale: Southern Illinois UP, 1984. 179–92.
Halloran, S. Michael, and Merrill D. Whitburn. "Ciceronian Rhetoric
and the Rise of Science: The Plain Style Reconsidered." *The Rhetorical
Tradition and Modern Writing.* Ed. J. J. Murphy. New York: MLA,
1982. 58–72.
Harding, D. W. "Psychological Processes in the Reading of Fiction." *Brit-
ish Journal of Aesthetics* 2 (1962): 133–41.
———. "The Role of the Onlooker." *Scrutiny* 6 (1937): 247–58.
Harned, Jon. "The Intellectual Background of Alexander Bain's 'Modes
of Discourse.' " *College Composition and Communication* 36 (1985): 42–
50.
Havelock, Eric A. *The Muse Learns to Write: Reflections on Orality and
Literacy from Antiquity to the Present.* New Haven: Yale UP, 1986.
———. "Orality, Literacy, and Star Wars." *Written Communication* 3 (1986):
411–20.
———. *Preface to Plato.* Cambridge: Harvard UP, 1963.
Hawking, Stephen. *A Brief History of Time: From the Big Bang to the
Black Hole.* New York: Bantam, 1988.
Heidegger, Martin. *Existence and Being.* Trans. Stefan Schimanski. South
Bend, IN: Gateway, 1949.
———. *On Being and Time.* Trans. Joan Stambaugh. NY: Harper/Col-
ophon, 1972.
———. *The Question Concerning Technology and Other Essays.* Trans. Wil-
liam Lovitt. New York: Harper, 1977.

Heinig, Ruth Beall, and Lydia Stillwell. *Creative Dramatics for the Classroom Teacher.* Englewood Cliffs, N.J.: Prentice Hall, 1974.

Heisenberg, Werner. *Physics and Philosophy: The Revolution in Modern Science.* New York: Harper, 1958.

Hemingway, Ernest. *A Farewell to Arms.* New York: Scribner's, 1929.

Hernandi, Paul. "Literary Interpretation and the Rhetoric of the Human Sciences." Nelson 263–75.

Herrington, Anne. J. "Classrooms as Disciplinary Forums for Reasoning and Learning." *College Composition and Communication* 35 (1985): 404–13.

Hirsch, E. D., Jr. *The Aims of Interpretation.* Chicago: U of Chicago P, 1976.

———. *The Philosophy of Composition.* Chicago: U of Chicago P, 1977.

Hirsch, E. D., Jr., Joseph Kett, and James Trefil. *Cultural Literacy: What Every American Needs to Know.* Boston: Houghton, 1987.

Hofstadter, Douglas R. *Gödel, Escher, Bach: An Eternal Golden Braid.* New York: Basic Books, 1979.

Holland, Norman N. *The Dynamics of Literary Response.* New York: Oxford UP, 1968.

———. *Five Readers Reading.* New Haven: Yale UP, 1975.

Holton, Gerald. *Thematic Origins of Scientific Thought: Kepler to Einstein.* Cambridge: Harvard UP, 1973.

Hoover, Regina M. "Prose Rhythm: A Theory of Proportional Distribution." *College Composition and Communication* 24 (1973): 366–74.

Horner, Winifred Bryan, ed. *Composition and Literature: Bridging the Gap.* Chicago: U of Chicago P, 1983.

Howell, Wilbur Samuel. *Eighteenth-Century British Logic and Rhetoric.* Princeton: Princeton UP, 1971.

Huizinga, Johan. *Homo Ludens: A Study of the Play Element in Culture.* Boston: Beacon, 1955.

Hunt, Everett Lee. "On the Sophists." *The Province of Rhetoric.* Ed. Joseph Schwartz and John A. Rycenga. New York: Ronald, 1965. 69–84.

Ihde, Don. *Listening and Voice: A Phenomenology of Sound.* Athens: Ohio UP, 1976.

Iser, Wolfgang. *The Act of Reading: A Theory of Aesthetic Response.* Baltimore: Johns Hopkins UP, 1978.

———. "The Reading Process: A Phenomenological Approach." Tompkins 50–69.

Isocrates. *Against the Sophists, Antidosis.* Trans. George Norlin. London: Loeb, 1928.

Jackendoff, Ray. *Semantics and Cognition.* Cambridge: MIT P, 1985.

Jaeger, Werner. "The Rhetoric of Isocrates and Its Cultural Ideal." *Paideia: The Ideals of Greek Culture.* Vol. 3: *The Conflict of Cultural Ideals in the Age of Plato.* Trans. Gilbert Highet. New York: Oxford UP, 1944. 46–70. 4 vols.

Jarratt, Susan C. *Rereading the Sophists: Classical Rhetoric Refigured.* Carbondale: Southern Illinois UP, 1991.

Johnson, George. "Memory: Learning How It Works." *New York Times Magazine* 9 Aug. 1987: 16.

Kant, Immanuel. *Prolegomena to Any Future Metaphysics.* Ed. and trans. Lewis White Beck. Indianapolis: Bobbs, 1950.

Katz, Steven B. "Aristotle's Rhetoric, Hitler's Program, and the Ideological Problem of Praxis, Power, and Professional Discourse." *Journal of Business and Technical Communication* 7 (January 1993): 37–62.

———. "The Epistemic Trend in Rhetorical Theory: A Four-Dimensional Review." *The Technical Writing Teacher* 14 (1977): 355–71.

———. "The Kabbalah as a Theory of Rhetoric: Another Suppressed Epistemology." *Rhetoric, Cultural Studies, and Literacy: Selected Papers from the 1994 Conference of the Rhetoric Society of America.* Hillsdale, NJ: Lawrence Erlbaum Associates. In press.

Kennedy, George. *Classical Rhetoric and Its Christian and Secular Tradition from Ancient to Modern Times.* Chapel Hill: U of North Carolina P, 1980.

———, trans. *On Rhetoric: A Theory of Civic Discourse.* By Aristotle. New York: Oxford UP, 1991.

Kerferd, G. B. *The Sophistic Movement.* Cambridge, England: Cambridge UP, 1981.

Kintgen, Eugene R. "Perceiving Poetic Syntax." *College English* 40 (1978): 17–27.

Knoblauch, C. H., and Lil Brannon. *Rhetorical Traditions and the Teaching of Writing.* Upper Montclair, NJ: Boynton/Cook, 1984.

Krashen, Stephen D. *Second Language Acquisition and Second Language Learning.* New York: Pergamon, 1981.

Kuhn, Thomas S. "Metaphor in Science." Ortony 409–19.

———. *The Structure of Scientific Revolutions.* 2nd ed. Chicago: U of Chicago P, 1970.

Lakatos, Imre. "Falsification and the Methodology of Scientific Research Programmes." *Criticism and the Growth of Knowledge.* Ed. Imre Lakatos and Alan Musgrave. Cambridge, England: Cambridge UP, 1970. 91–195.

Lakoff, George, and Mark Johnson. *Metaphors We Live By.* Chicago: U of Chicago P, 1980.

Langer, Susanne. *Feeling and Form: A Theory of Art.* New York: Scribner, 1953.

———. *Philosophy in a New Key.* Cambridge, MA: Harvard UP, 1942.

Lanham, Richard A. *Style: An Anti-Textbook.* New Haven: Yale UP, 1974.

Lanier, S. *The Science of English Verse.* New York: Schribner's, 1880.

Larson, Richard L. Rev. of *Rhetorical Traditions and the Teaching of Writing,* by C. H. Knoblauch and Lil Brannon. *College Composition and Communication* 37 (1986): 506.

Lasch, Christopher. *The Culture of Narcissism: American Life in an Age of Diminishing Expectations.* New York: Norton, 1978.

Leavis, F. R. *Culture and Environment: The Training of Critical Awareness.* London: Chatto, 1962.

———. *Education and the University: A Sketch for an "English School."* London: Chatto, 1943. Rpt. 1972.

Lecky, J. "The Phonetic Theory of English Prosody." *Transactions of the Philological Society, 1885–7.* Monthly Abstracts of Proceedings, Dec. 19, 1884. ii–vi.

Lee, Dorothy. "Lineal and Nonlineal Codifications of Reality." *Explorations in Communication.* Ed. Edmund Carpenter and Marshall McLuhan. Boston: Beacon, 1960.

Leff, Michael. "Interpretation and the Art of the Rhetorical Critic." *The Western Journal of Speech Communication* 44 (Fall 1980): 337–347.

———. Untitled paper. Presented at the Proceedings of The International Society for the History of Rhetoric. Florence, Italy, 1983.

Lentz, Tony M. *Orality and Literacy in Hellenic Greece.* Carbondale: Southern Illinois UP, 1989.

Levinas, Emmanuel. *The Theory of Intuition and Husserl's Phenomenology.* Trans. André Orianne. Evanston: Northwestern UP, 1973.

Lloyd, G. E. R. *Aristotle: The Growth and Structure of His Thought.* Cambridge, England: Cambridge UP, 1968.

Lodge, David. *Small World: An Academic Romance.* New York: Macmillan, 1984.

Long, Beverly Whitaker. *Group Performance of Literature.* Englewood Cliffs, NJ: Prentice, 1977.

Lord, Albert B. *The Singer of Tales.* Cambridge: Harvard UP, 1960. Rpt. New York: Athenaeum, 1976.

Lundsteen, Sara W. *Listening: Its Impact on Reading and the Other Language Arts.* Urbana, IL: NCTE, n.d.

Luria, Aleksandr R. *The Working Brain: An Introduction to Neuropsychology.* New York: Basic Books, 1973.

MacCormac, Earl R. "Men and Machines: The Computational Metaphor." *Technology in Society* 6 (1984): 207–16.

Machamer, Peter K., and Robert G. Turnbull, eds. *Motion and Time, Space and Matter: Interrelations in the History and Philosophy of Science.* Columbus: Ohio State UP, 1976.

Marrou, Henri I. *A History of Education in Antiquity.* Trans. George Lamb. New York: Sheed and Ward, 1956.

McCormick, Kathleen. "Theory in the Reader: Bleich, Holland, and Beyond." *College English* 47 (1985): 836–50.

McCurdy, Frances L. "Oral Interpretation as an Approach to Literature." Fernandez 9–16.

McLeod, Susan H. "Thinking About Feelings." Paper presented at the

Conference on College Composition and Communication. Seattle, WA, March 16–18, 1989.

Mead, George Herbert. *Mind, Self, Society*. Chicago: U of Chicago P, 1934.

Memering, Dean. "The Reader/Writing Heresy." *College Composition and Communication* 28 (1977): 223–26.

Meyer, L. B. *Emotion and Meaning in Music*. Chicago: U of Chicago P, 1956.

Middleton, Joyce Irene. Rev. of *The Double Perspective: Language, Literacy, and Social Relations*, by David Bleich. *College Composition and Communication* 41 (1990): 231–33.

Miller, Carolyn R. "The Rhetoric of Decision Science, or Herbert A. Simons Says." *The Rhetorical Turn: Invention and Persuasion in the Conduct of Inquiry*. Ed. Herbert W. Simons. U of Chicago P, 1990. 162–84.

———. "Technology as a Form of Consciousness: A Study of Contemporary Ethos." *Central States Speech Journal* 29 (1978): 228–36.

Mitchum, Carl, and Robert Mackey, eds. *Philosophy and Technology: Readings in the Philosophical Problems of Technology*. 2nd ed. New York: Free, 1983.

Moffett, James. *Teaching the Universe of Discourse*. Boston: Houghton, 1968.

Moles, Abraham. *Information Theory and Aesthetic Perception*. Trans. Joel E. Cohen. Urbana, IL: U of Illinois P, 1968.

Moran, Charles. "Teaching Writing/Teaching Literature." *College Composition and Communication* 32 (1981): 21–29.

Morris, Charles W. "Esthetics and the Theory of Signs." *The Journal of Unified Science* VIII.1–3 (131–50).

———. "Foundations for the Theory of Signs." *International Encyclopedia of Unified Sciences*. Vol. 1, no. 2. Chicago, IL: U of Chicago P, 1938.

———. "Science, Art and Technology." *The Kenyon Review* I, 4, 409–23.

Murphy, James J. "Introduction: The Medieval Background." *Three Medieval Rhetorical Arts*. Ed. James J. Murphy. Berkeley and Los Angeles, U of California P, 1971.

———. "Roman Writing Instruction as Described by Quintilian." *A Short History of Writing Instruction: From Ancient Greece to Twentieth Century America*. Ed. James J Murphy. Davis, CA: Hermagoras P, 1990. 19–76.

Murray, Donald M. "Listening to Writing." *Selected Articles on Writing and Teaching*. Ed. Donald Murray. Montclair, NJ: Boynton/Cook, 1982. 53–65.

———. "Teaching the Other Self: The Writer's First Reader." *College Composition and Communication* 33 (1982): 140–47.

Neel, Jasper. *Plato, Derrida, and Writing*. Carbondale: Southern Illinois UP, 1988.

Nelson, John, Allan Megill, and Donald N. McCloskey, eds. *The Rhetoric of the Human Sciences: Language and Argument in Scholarship and Public Affairs.* Madison: U of Wisconsin P, 1987.

Neumann, Erich. *The Great Mother: An Analysis of the Archetype.* Trans. Ralph Manheim. Princeton, NJ: Princeton UP, 1955.

Neville, Margaret M. "Oral Interpretation as an Aid to the Understanding of Literature." Fernandez 17–20.

Ochs, Donovan J. "Cicero's Rhetorical Theory." *A Synoptic History of Classical Rhetoric.* Ed. James J. Murphy. Davis, CA: Hermagoras P, 1983.

Ochsner, Robert S. *Physical Eloquence and the Biology of Writing.* Albany: SUNY P, 1990.

Odell, Lee. "Piaget, Problem-Solving, and Freshman Composition." *College Composition and Communication* 24 (1973): 36–42.

———. "The Process of Writing and the Process of Learning." *College Composition and Communication* 31 (1980): 42–50.

Odell, Lee, and Charles R. Cooper. "Describing Responses to Works of Fiction." *Research in the Teaching of English* 10 (1976): 203–25.

Ong, Walter J. "A Comment on 'Arguing About Literacy.' " *College English* 50 (1988): 700–01.

———. *Orality and Literacy: The Technologizing of the Word.* New York: Methuen, 1982.

———. *The Presence of the Word.* New Haven: Yale UP, 1967.

———. *Ramus, Method, and the Decay of Dialogue.* Cambridge: Harvard UP, 1958.

———. "The Writer's Audience Is Always a Fiction." *PMLA* 90 (1975): 9–21.

Ortony, Andrew, ed. *Metaphor and Thought.* Cambridge, England: Cambridge UP, 1979.

Overington, Michael A. "The Scientific Community as Audience: Toward a Rhetorical Analysis of Science." *Philosophy and Rhetoric* 10 (1977): 143–64.

Pagels, H. R. *Perfect Symmetry: The Search for the Beginning of Time.* New York: Simon, 1985.

Parrish, W. M. "The Concept of Naturalness." *The Study of Oral Interpretation: Theory and Comment.* Ed. Richard Haas and David A. Williams. Indianapolis: Bobbs, 1975.

Parry, Milman. *The Making of Homeric Verse: The Collected Papers of Milman Parry.* Ed. Adam Parry. Oxford: Clarendon, 1971.

Penrose, Roger. *The Emperor's New Mind: Concerning Computers, Minds, and the Laws of Physics.* New York: Oxford UP, 1989.

Perelman, Chaim. *The Realm of Rhetoric.* Trans. William Kluback. Notre Dame: U. of Notre Dame P., 1982.

Perl, Sondra. "Guidelines for Composing." *Writing Beyond the Cognitive Domain: Frontiers in the Teaching and Learning of Writing.*

Think Tank, Conference on College Composition and Communication, Cincinnati, Ohio, March 20, 1992.

———. "Understanding Composing." *College Composition and Communication* 31 (1980): 363–69.

Perrine, Laurence. *Sound and Sense: An Introduction to Poetry.* 7th ed. San Diego: Harcourt, 1987.

Petersen, Bruce T., ed. *Convergences: Transactions in Reading and Writing.* Urbana, IL: NCTE, 1986.

———. "Writing about Responses: A Unified Model of Reading, Interpretation, and Composition." *College English* 40 (1982): 459–68.

Petrosky, Anthony R. "The Effects of Reality Perception and Fantasy on Response to Literature: Two Case Studies." *Research in the Teaching of English* 10 (1976): 239–58.

———. "From Story to Essay: Reading and Writing." *College Composition and Communication* 33 (1982): 19–36.

Piaget, Jean, and B. Inholder. *The Psychology of the Child.* Trans. H. Weaver. London: Routledge, 1969.

Plath, Sylvia. "Mirror." *Crossing the Water: Transitional Poems.* New York: Harper, 1971: 34.

Plato. *Cratylus.* Trans. Benjamin Jowett. *The Dialogues of Plato.* Vol. 1. 3rd. ed. 5 vols. New York: Oxford UP, 1892. Rpt. in The Collected Dialogues of Plato. Ed. Edith Hamilton and Huntington Cairns. New York: Bollingen Foundation-Pantheon, 1961. 421–74.

———. *Gorgias.* Trans. W. C. Helmbold. Indianapolis: Bobbs, 1952.

———. *Phaedrus* Trans. W. C. Helmbold and W. G. Rabinowitz. Indianapolis: Bobbs, 1956.

Plutarch. *The Lives of the Noble Greeks and Romans.* Trans. John Dryden. Revised by Arthur Hugh Clough. New York: Random-Modern Library, n.d.

Polanyi, Michael. *Personal Knowledge.* New York: Harper, 1958.

Polkinghorne, Donald E. *Narrative Knowing and the Human Sciences.* Albany: SUNY P, 1988.

Popper, Karl R. *Conjectures and Refutations: The Growth of Scientific Knowledge.* New York: Basic Books, 1962.

Porush, David. *The Soft Machine: Cybernetics and Fiction.* New York: Methuen, 1985

Poulakos, John. "Toward a Sophistic Definition of Rhetoric." *Philosophy and Rhetoric* 16 (1983): 35–48.

Prigogine, Ilya. *From Being to Becoming: Time and Complexity in the Physical Sciences.* San Francisco: W. H. Freeman, 1980.

Psaty, Bruce M. "Cicero's Literal Metaphor and Propriety." *Central State Speech Journal* 29 (1978): 107–17.

Purves, Alan C. *Elements of Writing about a Literary Work: A Study of Responses to Literature.* Urbana, IL: NCTE, 1968.

———. *How Porcupines Make Love II: Teaching a Response-Centered Literature Curriculum.* Reading, MA: Addison, 1990.

———. "Putting Readers in Their Places: Some Alternatives to Cloning Stanley Fish." *College English* 42 (1980): 228–36.

Pylyshyn, Z. W. "Metaphorical Imprecision and the 'Top Down' Research Strategy." Ortony 420–36.

Quintilian, Marcus Fabius. *Institutio Oratoria.* Trans. H. E. Butler. 4 vols. Cambridge: Harvard UP, 1922.

Rankin, H. D. *Sophists, Socratics and Cynics.* Kent, England: Croom Helm, 1983.

Ransom, John Crowe. "Criticism, Inc." *The World's Body.* 1938. Baton Rouge: Louisiana State UP, 1968.

Reddy, Michael J. "The Conduit Metaphor—A Case of Frame Conflict in our Language About Language." Ortony 284–324.

Reichenbach, Hans. *Experience and Prediction.* Chicago: U of Chicago P, 1938.

Rhetorica ad Herennium. Trans. Harry Caplan. Cambridge: Harvard UP, 1954.

Richards, I. A. *Practical Criticism: A Study of Literary Judgment.* New York: Harcourt, 1929.

———. *Principles of Literary Criticism.* New York: Harcourt, 1925.

———. *Science and Poetry.* New York: Haskell, 1974.

Robertson, Linda. Rev. of *Rhetorical Traditions and the Teaching of Writing,* by C. H. Knoblauch and Lil Brannon. *College Composition and Communication* 37 (1986): 505.

Roe, Rev. R. *The Principles of Rhythm.* Dublin: Grainsberry, 1823.

Rorty, Richard. "Science as Solidarity." Nelson 38–52.

Rosenblatt, Louise M. *Literature as Exploration.* New York: MLA, 1983.

———. *The Reader, the Text, the Poem: The Transactional Theory of the Literary Work.* Carbondale: Southern Illinois UP, 1978.

Roskelly, Hephzibah. "Writing to Read: The Shape of Interpretation." Position Paper (120), 1988.

Rost, Michael. *Listening in Action: Activities for Developing Listening in Language Teaching.* New York: Prentice, 1991.

Rymer, Jone. "Scientific Composing Processes: How Eminent Scientists Write Journal Articles." *Advances in Writing Research.* Vol 2: *Writing in Academic Disciplines.* Ed. David A. Jolliffe. Norwood, NJ: Ablex, 1988. 211–50.

Said, Edward W. *The World, the Text, the Critic.* Cambridge: Harvard UP, 1983.

Saintsbury, George. *A History of English Prose Rhythm.* St. Martin's, 1912. Rpt. Bloomington: Indiana UP, 1965.

Salvatori, Mariolina. "Reading and Writing a Text: Correlations Between Reading and Writing Patterns." *College English* 45 (1983): 657–66.

Schatzberg-Smith, Kathleen. "The Reading-Writing Connection III: Schema Theory and Reading." *Research and Teaching in Developmental Education* 4 (1988): 66–71.

Schiappa, Edward. *Protagoras and Logos: A Study in Greek Philosophy and Rhetoric.* Columbia: U of South Carolina P, 1991.

Schrivner, Louise M. *A Guide to Oral Interpretation.* New York: Odyssey, 1968.

Schrodinger, Erwin. *Science and Humanism: Physics in Our Time.* Cambridge: Cambridge UP, 1952.

Schultz, John. *Writing from Start to Finish: "The Story Workshop" Basic Forms Rhetoric-Reader.* Portsmouth, NH: Boynton/Cook, 1990.

Scriven, Karen. "Writing about Literature: Interpretation Through Exposition." *Teaching English in the Two-Year College* 16 (1989): 280–83.

Serres, Michel. *Hermes: Literature, Science, Philosophy.* Ed. Josué V. Harari and David F. Bell. Baltimore: Johns Hopkins UP, 1982.

Shaughnessy, Mina P. *Errors and Expectations: A Guide for the Teacher of Basic Writing.* New York: Oxford UP, 1977.

Sheridan, Thomas. *A Course of Lectures on Elocution.* NY: B. Blom, 1968.

Shermis, Michael. *Reader Response, Focused Access to Selected Topics (Fast).* Biblio. No. 22. Bloomington, IN: ERIC Clearing House on Reading and Communication Skills. April 1989. ED 307571 CS 009565.

Simon, Herbert A. *The Sciences of the Artificial.* 2nd ed. Cambridge: MIT P, 1982.

Skolimowski, Henryk. "The Structure of Thinking in Technology." *Technology and Culture* 7 (1966): 371–83.

Sloan, Thomas O., ed. *The Oral Study of Literature.* New York: Random, 1966.

Snow, C. P. *The Two Cultures, and A Second Look.* Cambridge: Cambridge UP, 1959.

Sonnenschein, E. A. *What is Rhythm? An Essay by E. A. S. . . .* accompanied by an Appendix on Experimental Syllable-Measurement in which Stephen Jones and Eileen Macleod have co-operated. Oxford: Blackwell, 1925.

Sontag, Susan. "Against Interpretation." *A Susan Sontag Reader.* NY: Farrar, Straus, Giroux, 1982. 95–104.

Spolin, Viola. *Theater Games for the Classroom: A Teacher's Handbook.* Evanston, IL: Northwestern UP, 1986.

Sprague, Rosamond Kent, ed. *The Older Sophists: A Complete Translation by Several Hands of the Fragments in Die Fragmente der Vorsokratiker.* Columbia: U of South Carolina P, 1972. Rpt. 1990.

Sprat, Thomas. *The History of the Royal-Society of London, For the Improving of Natural Knowledge.* London: Royal Society, 1667.

Squire, James R. *The Responses of Adolescents While Reading Four Short Stories.* Urbana, IL: NCTE, 1964.

Stambaugh, Joan. Introduction. *On Time and Being*, by Martin Heidegger. vii–xi.

Stanford, W. B. *The Sound of Greek: Studies in the Greek Theory and Practice of Euphony*. Berkeley: U. of California P, 1967.

Steele, Joshua. *An Essay towards establishing the Melody and Measure of Speech, to be expressed and perpetuated by peculiar symbols*. 2nd ed. London: J Nichols, 1779.

Steinberg, Erwin R. "Protocols, Retrospective Reports, and the Stream of Consciousness." Report No. CDC-TR-8. Carnegie-Mellon University, Communications Design Center, March 1985.

Steiner, George. *In Bluebeard's Castle: Some Notes Toward the Redefinition of Culture*. New Haven: Yale UP, 1971.

Sternglass, Marilyn S. "Writing Based on Reading." *Convergences: Transactions in Reading and Writing*. 151–62.

Stewart, Garrett. *Reading Voices: Literature and the Phonotext*. Berkeley: U of California P, 1990.

Stewig, John W. *Informal Drama in the Elementary Language Arts Program*. New York: Columbia U, 1983.

Stewig, John W., and Carol Buege. *Dramatizing Literature in Whole Language Classrooms*. 2nd ed. New York: Teachers College Press, 1994.

Sticht, Thomas G., Lawrence J. Beck, Robert H. Hauke, Glenn M. Kleiman, and James H. James. *Auding and Reading: A Developmental Model*. Alexandria, VA: Human Resources Research Organization, 1974.

Suhor, Charles. "The Uses of Silence." *Education Week* (January 29, 1992): 2.

Sullivan, Dale. "Attitudes Toward Imitation: Classical Culture and the Modern Temper." *Rhetoric Review* 8 (1989): 5–21.

Sumera, Magdalena. "The Keen Prosodic Ear: A Comparison of Rhythm of Joshua Steele, William Thomson and Morris Croll. Edinburgh: Edinburgh UP, 1981.

Suppe, Frederick, ed. *The Structure of Scientific Theories*. 2nd ed. Urbana: U of Illinois P, 1977.

Sypher, Wylie. *Literature and Technology: The Alien Vision*. New York: Random, 1968.

Taig, T. *Rhythm and Metre*. Cardiff: U of Wales Press Board, 1929.

Tate, Allen. "Literature as Knowledge: Comment and Comparison." *Reason in Madness*. 20–61.

———. "The Present Function of Criticism." *Reason in Madness*. 3–19.

———. *Reason in Madness: Critical Essays*. New York: Putnam, 1941.

———. "Tension in Poetry." *Reason in Madness*. 62–81.

Thelwall, John. *Illustrations of English Rhythmus*. London: McCreery, 1812.

Thomas, Dylan. *The Poems of Dylan Thomas*. New York: New Directions, 1971.

Thompson, David W. *Performance of Literature in Historical Perspective*. Landham, MD: University Press of America, 1983.

Thomson, W. *Illustrations of English Rhythms*. Glasgow: Holmes, 1775.

———. *Rhythm and Scansion*. Edinburgh: Pillans, 1911.

———. *The Rhythms of Speech*. Glasgow: Maclehose, 1923.

Tierney, Robert J., et al. *Reading Strategies and Practices. A Compendium*. Old Tappan, NJ: Allyn, 1985.

Tompkins, Jane P. Introduction. *Reader Response Criticism*. ix–xxvi.

———. "The Reader in History: The Changing Shape of Literary Response." *Reader Response Criticism*. 201–32.

———, ed. *Reader Response Criticism: From Formalism to Post-Structuralism*. Baltimore: Johns Hopkins UP, 1980.

Toulmin, Stephen, and June Goodfield. *The Architecture of Matter*. New York: Harper, 1962. Rpt. Chicago: U of Chicago P, 1962.

Turbayne, Colin Murray. *The Myth of Metaphor*. Columbia: U of South Carolina P, 1962.

Turing, A. M. "Computing Machinery and Human Intelligence." *Mind* 59 (1950): 433–60.

Tyrwhitt, Jacqueline. "The Moving Eye." *Explorations in Communication: An Anthology*. Ed. Edmund Carpenter and Marshall McLuhan. Boston: Beacon, 1960. 90–95.

Untersteiner, Mario. *The Sophists*. Trans. Kathleen Freeman. Oxford: Basil Blackwell, 1954.

Ur, Penny. *Teaching Listening Comprehension*. Cambridge: Cambridge UP, 1984.

VanDeWeghe, Richard. "Making and Remaking Meaning: Developing Literary Responses Through Purposeful, Informal Writing." *English Quarterly* 20 (1987): 38–51.

Veilleux, Jene Shanor. *Oral Interpretation: The Recreation of Literature; a Text-Anthology for Oral Interpretation*. New York: Harper, 1967.

Vincent, Stephen, and Ellen Zweig. *The Poetry Performance: A Contemporary Compendium on Language and Performance*. San Francisco: Momo's, 1981.

Vine, Harold A., and Mark A. Faust. *Situating Readers: Students Making Meaning of Literature*. Urbana, IL: NCTE, 1993.

Weiskrantz, I., ed. *Thought Without Language*. New York: Oxford UP, 1988.

Weizenbaum, Joseph. *Computer Power and Human Reason*. San Francisco: Freeman, 1976.

Welch, Kathleen E. "Writing Instruction in Ancient Athens After 450 BC." *A Short History of Writing Instruction: From Ancient Greece to*

Twentieth Century America. Ed. James J Murphy. Davis, CA: Hermagoras P, 1990. 1–17.

Wellek, Rene, and Austin Warren. *Theory of Literature*. New York: Harcourt, 1942.

Welty, Eudora. *One Writer's Beginnings*. New York: Warner, 1983.

Whorf, Benjamin. *Language, Thought and Reality*. Ed. John B. Carroll. Cambridge: MIT P, 1956.

Wiener, Norbert. *Cybernetics: Or Control and Communication in the Animal and the Machine*. 2nd ed. Cambridge: MIT P, 1948 and 1961.

Williams, Miller. *Patterns of Poetry: An Encyclopedia of Forms*. Baton Rouge: Louisiana State UP, 1986.

Wilson, James. *Responses of College Freshmen to Three Novels*. Urbana, IL: NCTE, 1966.

Wimsatt, William K., and Monroe C. Beardsley. *The Verbal Icon: Studies in the Meaning of Poetry*. Lexington: U of Kentucky, 1954.

Wimsatt, William K., and Cleanth Brooks. *Literary Criticism: A Short History*. New York: Random, 1957.

Winner, Langdon. *Autonomous Technology: Technics-out-of-Control as a Theme in Political Thought*. Cambridge: MIT P, 1977.

Witkin, Robert W. *The Intelligence of Feeling*. London: Heinemann, 1974.

Wittgenstein, Ludwig. *Philosophical Investigations*. 3rd ed. Trans. G. E. M. Anscombe. New York: Macmillan, 1953.

Yates, Frances A. *The Art of Memory*. Chicago: U of Chicago P, 1966.

Young, Richard E., A. L. Becker, and K. L. Pike. *Rhetoric: Discovery and Change*. New York: Harcourt, 1970.

Young, W. "An Essay on Rhythmical Measures." *Transactions of the Royal Society of Edinburgh*, vol. II, part II, section II. 1790: 55–110.

Zuckerkandl, Victor. *Sound and Symbol: Music and the External World*. New York: Pantheon, 1956.

Zukav, Gary. *The Dancing Wu Li Masters: An Overview of the New Physics*. New York: Marrow, 1979.

Index

Formalism, epistemology defined, 17
Frost, Robert, 139–41, 308n. 4

Gendlin, Eugene, 60, 144–45, 225
Gestalten: aural in music, 168, 172–
73, 178, 181–82, 186, 190, 195;
models in science, 33, 57; temporal in consciousness, 199,
204, 205; visual in Reader Response Criticism, 42, 155. See
also Anticipation and resolution
or retrospection; Schemata
Gillispie, Charles Coulston, 24, 27,
37, 279n. 5
Gorgias: and Isocrates, style of, 96,
105, 302n. 15; relativism and
epistemic style, 89–93, 236,
253, 254, 296n. 5; and science,
251; style and memory 181
Gymnastic: and rhetoric, 99–100, 125

Habermas, Jurgen: technological reasoning, 19, 73, 278n. 3, 293n.
33
Halloran, Michael, and Merrill
Whitburn, 233, 299–300n. 11
Harmony: in Cicero, of style and
thought, 120, 125, 128; and dissonance in music, 167, 176; and
dissonance in reading, 146,
147, 150; as epistemic metaphor, 155; intuitive practice
reflects, 129, 134; and Principles of Pattern Perception, 186;
temporal form, 204, 205; of the
universe, 118, 119. See also Dissonance and disequilibrium;
Eloquence
Havelock, Eric: orality, 83, 86–87,
88, 97, 135; orality vs. abstraction, 231–32, 305–6n. 1
Hearing incompleteness, 171–74,
194. See also Principles of Pattern Perception: "completion
and closure," principle of
Heidegger, Martin, 74, 163, 271–72,
274–75, 293n. 32
Heisenberg, Werner, 33–36, 38, 54,
282n. 11
Heraclitus, 249, 253
Heuristics: aural, for invention and
imitation, 140, 196, 218 (see also
Principles of Pattern Percep-

tion); rational, in Aristotle, 82,
84; rejected by sophists, Cicero,
88, 109, 120, 132; spatial, of response, 53, 57–68, 128, 185; for
writing, using response, 3, 50–
57. See also Gestalten; Schemata
Holland, Norman, 51, 52
Holton, Gerald: "Hypothetico-induc-
tive, or deductive method," 24–
25, 279n. 6; thematic hypotheses in science, 6, 29–30, 67

Ideal Forms: a priori categories as,
37; Aristotle moves, 294n. 2;
Cicero rejects, 120–21, 133,
304n. 19; Isocrates rejects, 101,
103; Platonic, 81, 250, 254
Ideal orator, 115, 120, 132
Ideal reader, 53, 72
"Imaginary" vs. "real hearing," 208–9
Imitation: aural, 129, 131–32, 145,
256–67; of emotion in delivery,
122; internalization of musical
style, 26, 179, 181; in language
acquisition, 203, 218, 319–20n.
3, 320–21n. 5; in science, 21,
36; sensuous form and consciousness, 196–97, 200–202,
320n. 4; somatic for sophists,
87, 103
"Impotency proposition," 67, 164,
290n. 23. See also Thematic hypothesis
Indeterminacy: and affect, 61–68;
and consciousness, 16, 204;
defined, 19; in interpretation,
71–72; limits of, 10, 41, 67–68,
164; of method, 102–3, 114,
116–21, 235–36; musical principle of, 194–95; in New Physics, "principle of uncertainty,
or," 33, 34, 284n. 14; at Newtonian level, 40; probability
function in, 33, 54, 58, 289–
90n. 22; in Reader Response
Criticism and writing, principle of, 50–56; the shape of indeterminacy (see also Principles of
Pattern Perception) and sound,
146; strong principle of, 38, 57,
236; and time, 163, 185, 195;
weak principle of, 40

Ong, Walter J. (continued)
sponse, theory of, 158, 159–60,
175; sound, nature of, 93–94,
155–58, 159, 161; spatiality of
logic, 73
Oral interpretation, 81, 107, 117,
121, 125, 126, 129–30, 221, 222
Orality: and literacy dichotomy, 10,
12, 85, 87; ontology of, 93–95;
112–14, 119–21, 134, 156–58,
159, 250; reasoning, as mode
of, 2, 96 (see also Sophists);
ubiquity of, 12–13, 93, 153; and
writing, 83–88, 93, 105–6,
129–34, 135–45 (see also Isocrates). See also Literacy
Oral techniques, ancient and modern, 130, 131
Oratorical prose style, 15, 105, 299–
300n. 12, 300–301n. 13.
Ornatus as kosmos, 121, 127, 246,
252, 255, 303n. 18
"Outer" vs. "inner" environment,
58, 78, 290n. 24, 291n. 25

Parmenides, 250, 254
Penrose, Roger: on indeterminacy,
38, 67, 234, 290n. 23; quantum
physics and consciousness, 53,
54, 55–56, 61–64, 164; time,
163, 164, 268, 273
Performance: Cicero's three stylistic
registers based on, 110; as imitation of sensuous form, 203–4,
208–19; vs. interpretation in sophistic rhetoric, 81, 93; musical
style, rooted in (for Cicero),
106–8, 120–22; physical (for
Isocrates), 99–100, 102; response as rhetoric of musical,
178, 186, 195, 196, 223–25,
322n. 8 (see also Principles of
Pattern Perception); and
resymbolization, 124–26, 128–
33; sophistic and contemporary
pedagogy, 131–34, 138, 159,
222, 228–31, 233–234, 301n. 14
Perl, Sondra, 144–45, 147, 225
Petersen, Bruce, 66, 288n. 19, 291n.
27
Petrosky, Anthony, 49, 53, 291n. 27
Physical eloquence, 136, 138, 232
Pitch: and affect in speech, 87, 137,
140; judgment, intuitive basis of,

109; music, compared to, 169,
311n. 7; in prose (for Cicero),
109; tone not a difference of,
167–68
Plain style, in reading and speaking,
215. See also Attic, plain style;
Cicero: style, three registers of;
Scientific plain style
Plato: and Cicero, 117–18, 119–121;
formalism, rationalism rooted
in, 23, 37, 90, 254; and Isocrates,
95–96, 97, 100, 102; and sophists, 81–82, 83, 84, 85, 89, 90–
91, 250
Polanyi, Michael, 61, 76, 290n. 25
Poulakos, John, 98
"Presence," 127
"Presentational" patterns vs. discursive patterns, 204–8
Principles of Pattern Perception,
186–95; "completion and closure," principle of, 190, 193;
Good Continuation, the Law
of, 173, 186–94; recurrence,
188, 189, 190; reiteration, 188,
190; repetition, 187, 189, 190,
191; "return, the law of," 187;
reversal, 186–87; "weakening
of shape, the," 187, 190, 191,
192. See also Rhythm
Propriety: cannot be taught abstractly, 125, 133; and eloquence, 111–12, 301–2n. 15;
and emotion in delivery, 121;
and invisibility of style, 113
Protagoras, 90, 91, 92, 248–49, 250,
254, 296n. 5
Protocol analysis, 55, 225
Psaty, Bruce M., 112, 302–3n. 17
"Psychological maturity," 128
Purves, Alan, 51, 52–53, 289n. 21
Pythagoras, 120, 121, 247, 254,
304n. 19

"Quantum formalism," 40
Quantum mechanics: and consciousness, 53, 55–56, 61–64; Copenhagen school of, 33, 37, 38, 45,
63; disputes in, 38–39; indeterminacy principle of, 33–36; and
Reader Response Criticism, 41–
68, 71–72, 76–79
"Quantum parallelism," 53
Quintilian, 258–60, 264, 265, 266

Steven B. Katz is an associate professor of English at North Carolina State University, where he teaches rhetorical theory, scientific and technical communication, and poetry writing. He earned his Ph.D. in communication and rhetoric from Rensselaer Polytechnic Institute in 1988. His *College English* article, "The Ethic of Expediency: Classical Rhetoric, Technology, and the Holocaust," received the 1993 NCTE Award for Excellence in Technical and Scientific Communication in the category of Best Article on Philosophy or Theory. He also has published poetry in a variety of journals, including *Southern Poetry Review*, *Postmodern Culture*, and *Isaac Asimov's Science Fiction Magazine*. He lives in Raleigh, North Carolina, with his wife and son and is a perpetual student of classical guitar.